ENGLISH

COMMUNICATION SKILLS IN THE NEW MILLENNIUM

LEVEL 1

LANGUAGE HANDBOOK

J.A. Senn
Carol Ann Skinner

PERFECTION LEARNING® CORPORATION

PROJECT MANAGER
Sandra Stucker Blevins

EDITORIAL DIRECTOR
Sandra Mangurian

EDITORIAL STAFF
Marianne Murphy
Kim Choi
Marlene Greil
Donna Laughlin
Susan Sandoval
Vicki Tyler
Catherine Foy
Michelle Quijano
Elizabeth Wenning
Cheryl Duksta
Margaret Rickard

PRODUCTION DIRECTORS
Gene Allen
Pun Nio

PHOTO RESEARCH AND
PERMISSIONS
Laurie O'Meara

ART AND DESIGN
Pun Nio
Leslie Kell
Rhonda Warwick

PRODUCTION
Bethany Powell
Isabel Garza
Rhonda Warwick

COVER
Leslie Kell Designs
Pun Nio
Images © Photodiscs, Inc.

EDITORIAL AND PRODUCTION
SERVICES
Book Builders, Inc.
Gryphon Graphics
Inkwell Publishing
  Solutions, Inc.
NETS

For information, contact Perfection Learning®
1000 North Second Avenue, P.O. Box 500
Logan, Iowa 51546-0500.
Phone: 1-800-831-4190 • Fax: 1-800-543-2745
perfectionlearning.com

ISBN-13: 978-1-58079-399-5   5 6 7 8 9 10 RRD 18 17 16 15 14 13
ISBN-10: 1-58079-399-1

SENIOR CONSULTANTS

Tommy Boley, Ph.D.
Director of English Education
The University of Texas at El Paso
El Paso, TX

Deborah Cooper, M.Ed.
Coordinating Director of PK-12
    Curriculum
Charlotte-Mecklenburg Public Schools
Charlotte, NC

Susan Marie Harrington, Ph.D.
Associate Professor of English,
    Director of Writing, Director of
    Placement and Assessment, and
    Adjunct Assistant Professor
    of Women's Studies
Indiana University-Purdue University,
    Indianapolis
Indianapolis, IN

Carol Pope, Ed.D.
Associate Professor of Curriculum
    and Instruction
North Carolina State University
Raleigh, NC

Rebecca Rickly, Ph.D.
Department of English
Texas Tech University
Lubbock, TX

John Simmons, Ph.D.
Professor of English Education and
    Reading
Florida State University
Tallahassee, FL

John Trimble, Ph.D.
University Distinguished Teaching
    Professor of English
The University of Texas
Austin, TX

CONTRIBUTING WRITERS

Jeannie Ball

Grace Bultman

Richard Cohen

Elizabeth Egan-Rivera

Laurie Hopkins Etzel

Bobbi Fagone

Lesli Favor

Nancy-Jo Hereford

Susan Maxey

Linda Mazumdar

Elizabeth McGuire

Shannon Murphy

Carole Osterink

Michael Raymond

Duncan Searl

Jocelyn Sigue

Lorraine Sintetos

James Strickler

Diane Zahler

Kathy Zahler

CRITICAL READERS

Alan Altimont
St. Edwards University,
Austin, TX

Larry Arnhold
Deer Park High School,
Houston, TX

Kerry Benson
Santa Fe Public School,
Santa Fe, NM

Elaine Blanco
Gaither High School,
Lutz, FL

Peter Bond
Randolph School,
Huntsville, AL

**Christina M.
Brandenburg**
Rancho Cotate
High School,
Rohnert Park, CA

Paulette Cwidak
John Adams High
School, South Bend, IN

Jean Ann Davis
Miami Trace High
School, Washington
Courthouse, OH

Terri Dobbins
Churchill High School,
San Antonio, TX

Susan Drury
Springwood High
School, Houston, TX

David Dunbar
Masters School,
Dobbs Ferry, NY

Chuck Fanara
Brebeuf Preparatory,
Indianapolis, IN

Jason Farr
Anderson High School,
Austin, TX

Marilyn Gail
Judson High School,
San Antonio, TX

Gary Gorsuch
Berea High School,
Berea, OH

Monica Gorsuch
MidPark Sr. High School,
Cleveland, OH

Donna Harrington
Churchill High School,
San Antonio, TX

Janis Hoffman
John Adams High
School, South Bend, IN

Norma Hoffman
John Adams High
School, South Bend, IN

David Kidd
Norfolk Academy,
Norfolk, VA

Kate Knopp
Masters School,
Dobbs Ferry, NY

Suzanne Kuehl
Lewis-Palmer High
School, Monument, CO

Michelle Lindner
Milken Community High
School, Los Angeles, CA

Stephanie Lipkowitzs
Albuquerque Academy,
Albuquerque, NM

Sarah Mfon
Hubbard High School,
Chicago, IL

Linda Martin
Valley Torah,
North Hollywood, CA

Lisa Meyer
Lincoln High School,
Tallahassee, FL

Karla Miller
Durango High School,
Durango, CO

Stacy Miller
Santa Fe High School,
Santa Fe, NM

Eddie Norton
Oviedo High School,
Oviedo, FL

Diana Perrin
Johnson High School,
Huntsville, AL

William Petroff
R. Nelson Snider High
School, Ft. Wayne, IN

Linda Polk
Deer Park High School,
Houston, TX

Lila Rissman
Suwanne Middle School,
Live Oak, FL

Carmen Stallard
Twin Springs High
School, Nickelsville, VA

Jeanette Taylor
Rye Cove High School,
Duffield, VA

Eric Temple
Crystal Springs Uplands
School, Hillsborough, CA

Sherry Weatherly
Denton High School,
Denton, TX

Grammar

CHAPTER 3   Verbs

CHAPTER 4   Adjectives and Adverbs

CHAPTER 5   Other Parts of Speech

CHAPTER 6   Complements

CHAPTER 7 Phrases

Usage

CHAPTER 12 — Subject and Verb Agreement

CHAPTER 15 · End Marks and Commas

CHAPTER 16 Italics and Quotation Marks

CHAPTER 17 Other Punctuation

Spelling

CHAPTER 18 Spelling

Study and Test-Taking Skills Resource

LANGUAGE

e firs
nd almo
oped for so
hless. The ho
miraculo
9 fe

CHAPTER 1

The Sentence

Directions
Write the letter of the term that correctly identifies the underlined word or words in each sentence.

EXAMPLE
1. <u>Many species of plants</u> are used for medicinal purposes.
   1 A simple subject
   B complete subject
   C simple predicate
   D complete predicate

ANSWER   **1 B**

1. Last summer my aunt <u>invited</u> me to her farm in New Mexico.
2. One morning I <u>cooked</u> some toast and <u>made</u> some orange juice.
3. I <u>shoved a rack with sliced bread into the oven and burned my finger</u>.
4. <u>Aunt May</u> broke off a piece of a spiny plant on her windowsill.
5. She <u>squeezed</u> a gooey substance from the plant and <u>rubbed</u> it on my burn.
6. In no time my <u>finger</u> felt as good as new.
7. <u>Learned the name of this miraculous plant—aloe</u>.
8. Aloe <u>looks somewhat like a cactus but belongs to the lily family</u>.
9. <u>Many gardeners in the southern and southwestern parts of the United States</u>.
10. <u>Have you ever seen the leaves of an aloe plant</u>?

1 **A** simple subject
   B complete subject
   C simple predicate
   D complete predicate

2 **A** complete subject
   B complete predicate
   C compound subject
   D compound verb

3 **A** simple subject
   B complete subject
   C complete predicate
   D simple predicate

4 **A** complete predicate
   B complete subject
   C compound subject
   D compound verb

5 **A** complete subject
   B complete predicate
   C compound subject
   D compound verb

6 **A** simple subject
   B complete subject
   C simple predicate
   D complete predicate

7 **A** sentence fragment
   B inverted order
   C simple predicate
   D compound subject

8 **A** complete subject
   B complete predicate
   C compound subject
   D simple predicate

9 **A** sentence fragment
   B inverted order
   C simple predicate
   D compound subject

10 **A** sentence fragment
   B inverted order
   C simple predicate
   D compound subject

Jaune Quick-to-See Smith.
Family Tree, 1986.
Pastel on paper, 30 by 22 inches.
Collection of Bernice and Harold
Steinbaum. Courtesy of Bernice
Steinbaum Gallery, Miami, FL.

Describe What images do you recognize in this drawing? Is one image more striking than the others?

Analyze What ideas do you think the artist wanted to convey? How do the artist's name and the title of the drawing support this message?

Interpret How could a writer express in words the same ideas that Jaune Quick-to-See Smith expresses in images?

Judge Do you think this pastel drawing or the written word would make the more powerful statement about these ideas? Why do you think so?

At the end of this chapter, you will use the artwork to stimulate ideas for writing.

Recognizing Sentences

A **sentence** is a group of words that expresses a complete thought.

In conversation, people sometimes express their ideas incompletely.

> KIM: Do you want to play a game of football?
> ALLEN: In this weather? No way!

Kim easily understood Allen's reply, even though he used only parts of a sentence to answer her. However, in standard written English, you need to use complete sentences to be sure your message is clear and your reader understands it accurately.

CONNECT TO SPEAKING AND WRITING

When you speak, you convey your ideas not only with your words but also with your facial expression, body language, and tone of voice. When you write, your words alone convey your thoughts and feelings.

The following groups of words are incomplete thoughts:

> The player in the torn jersey.   Blocking the defense.
> Made a touchdown.   When the game ended.

A group of words that expresses an incomplete thought is a **sentence fragment.**

To change these fragments into sentences, you need to add the missing information.

> The player in the torn jersey **is the team's best player.**
> **The running back** made a touchdown.
> Blocking the defense **allowed the running back to score.**
> When the game ended, **the team celebrated.**

You can learn more about fragments on pages 257–266.

PRACTICE YOUR SKILLS

● Check Your Understanding
Recognizing Sentences and Fragments

Contemporary
Life
Label each group of words *S* if it is a sentence or *F* if it is a fragment.

1. The fans at the football game cheered wildly.
2. Because the weather turned cold.
3. Brought a blanket to the game.
4. The quarterback for the winning team.
5. My family watched the game from the fifty-yard line.
6. Buying hot chocolate from the concession stand.
7. Since we know the coach of the team.
8. Practices for four hours each day.

● Connect to the Writing Process: Revising
Writing Complete Sentences from Fragments

9.–14. Add information to expand each fragment above into a sentence. When you write your sentences, remember to begin each sentence with a capital letter and end it with a punctuation mark.

Communicate Your Ideas

APPLY TO WRITING

Friendly Letter: *Complete Sentences*

Write a letter to your school coach asking to attend a summer sports camp. Decide on the type of sports camp you would like to attend. List the reasons you want to attend. Include the following sentence fragments, written correctly as sentences.

- Is important to me.
- Instruction at camp.
- Practicing for next season.
- My favorite sport.

Subjects and Predicates

A sentence has two main parts: a subject and a predicate.

The **subject** names the person, place, thing, or idea that the sentence is about.

The **predicate** tells something about the subject.

	SUBJECT	PREDICATE
PERSON	Albert Einstein	was a very famous scientist.
PLACE	The United States	became his home.
THING	Many inventions	came from his ideas.
IDEA	His intelligence	made him a celebrity.

▶ Complete and Simple Subjects

A **complete subject** includes all the words used to identify the person, place, thing, or idea that the sentence is about.

To find a complete subject, ask yourself *Whom?* or *What?* the sentence is about.

The tour guide at the science museum told us about atoms.

(Whom is this sentence about? Who told us about atoms? *The tour guide at the science museum* is the complete subject.)

Microscopes with powerful lenses magnify the atoms.

(What is this sentence telling about? What magnifies the atoms? *Microscopes with powerful lenses* is the complete subject.)

PRACTICE YOUR SKILLS

● Check Your Understanding
Finding Complete Subjects

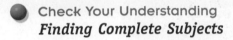 Science Topic **Write the complete subject in each sentence.**

1. Young Albert Einstein showed an interest in math and science.

2. His grades in other subjects were poor.

3. The future scientist finished high school and technical college in Switzerland.

4. The Swiss patent office hired Einstein in 1902.

5. Scholarly journals gave Einstein a forum for his ideas.

6. A German physics journal published some of his articles.

7. These articles discussed radical theories about the nature of matter.

8. Publication of these articles changed scientists' view of the universe.

9. The theory of relativity was Einstein's most important contribution.

10. The Nobel Prize in physics was awarded to Einstein in 1921.

Simple Subjects

A **simple subject** is the main word in the complete subject.

The simple subject is the one word that directly answers the question *Who?* or *What?*

Many immigrants arrived at Ellis Island in the early part of the twentieth century.

Officials at the station processed more than twelve million immigrants.

Sometimes a complete subject and a simple subject are the same.

Albert Einstein came to the United States in 1933.
He became a United States citizen seven years later.

Throughout the rest of this book, the word subject *refers to the simple subject.*

PRACTICE YOUR SKILLS

● Check Your Understanding
Finding Complete and Simple Subjects

Social Studies Topic **Write the complete subject in each sentence. Then underline each simple subject.**

1. New York Harbor is home to the Statue of Liberty.

2. This figure of a woman with a torch stands at the entrance to the harbor.

3. She holds a tablet in her left hand.

4. Seven rays surround her head.

5. Broken chains lie at her feet.

6. The statue weighs 225 tons.

7. The people of France gave the statue to the United States.

8. A formal presentation occurred in 1886.

9. Major repairs were made to the statue in the 1980s.

10. Tourists from around the world visit this famous lady.

● Connect to the Writing Process: Drafting
Writing Complete Subjects

Add a complete subject to each of the following sentences.

11. ▦ work very hard at their jobs.

12. ▦ climb the tall tower.

13. ▦ could be considered dangerous.

14. ▦ may mean hours of extra work.

15. ■ makes the effort worthwhile.

16. ■ is not finished.

17. ■ will complete the assignment soon.

18. ■ will be admired by many people.

19. ■ should do well in the Olympics.

20. ■ finished the school yearbook.

Communicate Your Ideas

APPLY TO WRITING

Writer's Craft: *Analyzing the Use of Subjects*

Writers often choose words and phrases to create an effect on their audience. In this paragraph from "The Washwoman," Isaac Bashevis Singer writes about an old woman who does laundry for his family. Read the paragraph and then follow the instructions below.

> She would bring the laundry back about two weeks later. My mother had never been so pleased with any washwoman. Every piece of linen sparkled like polished silver. Every piece was neatly ironed. Yet she charged no more than the others. She was a real find. Mother always had her money ready ....
>
> —*Isaac Bashevis Singer,* "The Washwoman"

- Write the complete subject of each sentence and then underline the simple subject.

- Referring to your list of subjects, explain who or what seems to be most important in this paragraph.

- What is the total effect of Singer's choice of subjects on the reader?

Complete and Simple Predicates

A **complete predicate** includes all the words that tell what the subject is doing or that tell something about the subject.

To find a complete predicate, first find the subject. Then ask, *What is the subject doing?* or *What is being said about the subject?*

Wild horses roamed across the prairie.

(The subject is *horses*. What did the horses do? *Roamed across the prairie* is the complete predicate.)

PRACTICE YOUR SKILLS

Check Your Understanding
Finding Complete Predicates

History Topic **Write the complete predicate in each sentence.**

1. Prehistoric humans hunted horses for food.
2. Humans later recognized the value of live horses.
3. The knights of the Middle Ages rode strong horses into battle.
4. The horses wore armor for protection.
5. The Spanish conquistadors brought horses to the New World.
6. Native Americans captured wild horses.
7. They became expert riders.
8. The settlers traveled west in covered wagons.
9. Horses pulled the wagons from Missouri to Oregon.
10. The horse is no longer a principal means of transportation.

Simple Predicates

> A **simple predicate,** or **verb,** is the main word or phrase in the complete predicate.

In the following examples, the simple predicate, or verb, is underlined:

> Everyone in the park <u>enjoyed</u> **the fireworks.**
>
> The Roman candle <u>burned</u> **beautifully in the night sky.**

Sometimes verbs are hard to find because they do not show action; instead, they tell something about a subject. The following common verb forms are used to make a statement about a subject:

> am   is   are   was   were   be   being   been

Verbs that make a statement are also called linking verbs.

You can learn more about linking verbs on pages L75–L78.

CONNECT TO SPEAKING AND WRITING

When you speak or write, vivid verbs can make your ideas more interesting. Because the predicate conveys action in a sentence, choosing strong verbs can help your audience visualize what is happening. Notice the difference between the verbs in the following sentences.

> The noise of the fireworks **affected** the baby.
> The noise of the fireworks **frightened** the baby.

PRACTICE YOUR SKILLS

● Check Your Understanding
Finding Complete and Simple Predicates

General Interest   **Write the complete predicate in each sentence. Then underline the verb.**

1. Millions of Americans watch displays of fireworks on the Fourth of July.

2. Pyrotechnics is another name for fireworks.

3. Fireworks are not a recent invention.

4. The Chinese invented fireworks centuries ago.

5. They used them for celebrations.

6. Fireworks existed before the invention of guns and gunpowder.

7. The Italians manufactured fireworks during the 1500s.

8. Gases propel the fireworks into the air.

9. The fireworks explode in an array of colors.

10. The bright colors of fireworks come from different metallic salts.

Connect to the Writing Process: Revising
Using Vivid Verbs

Write each sentence, replacing each verb with a more vivid verb.

11. The fireworks went into the night sky.

12. The colors of the rockets showed against the dark sky.

13. My sister ran to the edge of the water.

14. The colors appeared on the surface of the lake.

15. The firecrackers popped loudly.

Communicate Your Ideas

APPLY TO WRITING

Description: *Predicates*

A new student from another country has never been to a Fourth of July celebration. Write a description, telling him about a celebration and fireworks display that you have seen. Include details about the sights, sounds, and smells, using vivid verbs to make your writing come alive.

History Topic **Write the subject and verb in each sentence.**

1. In 1848, a settler discovered gold in northern California's mountains.

2. That discovery transformed San Francisco from a frontier town into a busy city.

3. People on the East Coast heard of the discovery of gold.

4. Thousands of gold prospectors invaded the city on their way to the mountains.

5. Two steamship companies brought an endless stream of people to San Francisco.

6. Other people arrived by stagecoach.

7. The Pony Express brought mail to the population.

8. Soon, telegraph lines provided additional communication to the city.

9. Few prospectors found gold in San Francisco.

10. However, many of them settled there.

Verb Phrases

A **verb phrase** includes the main verb plus any helping, or auxiliary, verbs.

The helping verb or verbs are underlined in the following examples:

Kerry **is choosing** plants for the garden.

Those seeds **can be planted** next month.

The tulip bulbs **should have been planted** in the fall.

As you can see from the examples above, a verb phrase may include as many as three helping verbs. The following verbs are often used as helping verbs.

COMMON HELPING VERBS	
be	am, is, are, was, were, be, being, been
have	has, have, had
do	do, does, did
OTHERS	may, might, must, can, could, shall, should, will, would

PRACTICE YOUR SKILLS

● Check Your Understanding
Finding Verb Phrases

Science Topic   **Write the verb phrase in each sentence.**

1. Trees are known as the largest of all plants.
2. They have been identified as the oldest living things.
3. Some giant sequoia trees have lived for thousands of years.
4. The fruit of the coconut palm can be eaten.
5. You might bake a tasty pie from the fruit of apple trees.
6. Pine trees will remain green all year long.
7. Broadleaf trees do not lose their leaves in winter.
8. Trees can prevent the loss of topsoil.
9. For a very long time, people have used trees for wood.
10. Malaria is treated with quinine from the bark of the cinchona tree.

Sometimes a verb phrase is *interrupted* by other words.

A bloodhound **can** easily **follow** a day-old scent.
Most household pets **have** never **hunted** for food.

In a question the subject may come in the middle of a verb phrase.

Is Toto **scratching** at the door?

The word *not* and its contraction, *n't,* often interrupt verb phrases. Neither is part of the verb.

Health laws **do** not **allow** dogs in grocery stores.
The pet store in the mall **isn't selling** fish.

When you are doing a piece of formal writing, you should spell out the word *not*. You should use the contraction *n't* only in speaking and informal writing situations.

Throughout the rest of this book, the word verb *also refers to the verb phrase.*

PRACTICE YOUR SKILLS

● Check Your Understanding
Finding Verbs

General Interest **Write the verb in each sentence. Remember that words that interrupt a verb phrase are not part of the verb.**

1. German shepherds are often trained as guide dogs.

2. Guide dogs are always allowed in public places with their owners.

3. The guide dog must quickly adjust to the leather harness and stiff handle.

4. The dog doesn't obey all commands from its owner.

5. A command could sometimes place an owner in a dangerous situation.

6. A dog will not lead its owner into the middle of a busy street.

7. Labrador retrievers and golden retrievers are also used as guide dogs.

8. Golden retrievers have often been recommended as the best dog for a family.

9. Dogs do not usually live longer than twelve to fifteen years.

10. Have you ever had a dog for a pet?

● Connect to the Writing Process: Revising
Using Verb Interrupters

11.–15. Verb interrupters change the meaning of sentences. Add verb interrupters to the following sentence and write five new sentences, each with a different meaning.

Cats have threatened dogs.

Communicate Your Ideas

APPLY TO WRITING

Informal Speech: *Verbs*

Your guidance counselor has written you a note telling you that the local veterinarian is looking for an assistant. She believes that you would be perfect for the job. She wants to meet with you before the end of the day so that you can tell her why the job is one you want or do not want. Write a short speech that you will present to the guidance counselor to explain how you feel about the possibility of working in a veterinarian's office. Use the following verbs, with or without interrupters, in your speech.

- have enjoyed
- am suited for
- is challenging
- would be interested
- was happy

Compound Subjects

A **compound subject** is two or more subjects in one sentence that have the same verb and are joined by a conjunction.

The conjunctions that usually join compound subjects are *and, or,* or *nor.* Pairs of conjunctions, such as *either/or, neither/nor, not only/but also,* and *both/and* may also be used. In the following examples, each subject is underlined once, and the verb is underlined twice. Notice that the conjunction is not part of a compound subject.

> Janice spent the hot day at the beach.
>
> Janice and Kate spent the hot day at the beach.
>
> Janice, Kate, and Sue spent the hot day at the beach.
>
> Either Kate or Sue had brought the food.
>
> Neither Janice nor Kate ate much dessert.
>
> Not only Kate but also Janice went swimming.

CONNECT TO SPEAKING AND WRITING

To make your writing smoother and less repetitious, you can combine two or more sentences that have the same verb but different subjects.

> **Jon** has a surfboard.
> **Rick** has a surfboard.
> **Tammy** has a surfboard.
> **Jon, Rick,** and **Tammy** have surfboards.

Sometimes, when you are speaking, you might not want to combine subjects. For example, if you are trying to persuade your parents to let you have a surfboard, you might want to repeat the entire sentence each time.

PRACTICE YOUR SKILLS

● Check Your Understanding
Finding Compound Subjects

Contemporary Life | **Write the subject in each sentence.**

1. Rick and Tammy brought their surfboards to the beach.
2. Both the wind and the waves were impressive.
3. Jamie and Rob rented jet skis.
4. Their beach towels and sandals were almost swallowed up by the tide.
5. Two baby crabs and a starfish washed up on shore.
6. The sandwiches and fruit in the lunches were a target for the seagulls.
7. Neither Tammy nor Rick stayed up on a surfboard for very long.
8. Thunder and lightning signaled a storm in the distance.
9. The beach patrol and the lifeguards ordered everyone out of the water.
10. Jamie, Rob, Tammy, and Rick quickly gathered up their belongings and headed for the car.

● Connect to the Writing Process: Revising
Combining Sentences

Combine each pair of sentences into one sentence with a compound subject. Use *and* or *or* to connect your sentences.

11. Cod feed along the ocean bottom. Flounder feed along the ocean bottom.
12. Clams live on the sea floor. Lobsters live there, too.
13. Manatees stay in the ocean for their entire lives. Whales also stay in the ocean for their entire lives.
14. Sea lions spend time on land. Walruses spend time on land.
15. Winds cause ocean waves. Earthquakes cause ocean waves.

Compound Verbs

A **compound verb** is formed when two or more verbs in one sentence have the same subject and are joined by a conjunction.

Just as some sentences have compound subjects, some sentences may have compound verbs. Conjunctions such as *and, or, nor,* and *but* are used to connect the verbs. In the following examples, each subject is underlined once, and each verb is underlined twice.

Jeff pours the juice into his glass.

Jeff pours the juice into his glass and rinses the bottle.

Jeff pours the juice into his glass, rinses the bottle, and places it in the recycling bin.

Some sentences have both a compound subject and a compound verb.

Nancy and Pete save their newspapers and bring them to the collection center.

PRACTICE YOUR SKILLS

 Check Your Understanding
Finding Compound Verbs

 Contemporary Life **Write the verbs in the following sentences.**

1. Many people drink the last sip of soda and throw the can away.

2. You should save your cans and deliver them to a recycling center.

3. An employee will take the cans and give you some money.

4. Trucks collect the old cans and unload them at a recycling plant.

5. Machines at the plant flatten the cans and dump them onto conveyor belts.

6. The cans are then shredded and cleaned.

7. Next, workers load the pieces into a hot furnace and soften them.

8. The soft metal is made into long sheets and cooled.

9. Beverage companies buy the sheets and make new cans out of them.

10. With these new cans, the beverage companies have prevented extra waste and thereby have saved everyone money.

Connect to the Writing Process: Revising
Combining Sentences

Combine each pair of sentences into one sentence with a compound verb. Use *and, or, nor,* or *but* to connect your sentences.

11. Our county has a mandatory recycling program. Our county provides each household with special bins.

12. You can put your cans and bottles in the green bin. You can save your newspapers in the orange bin.

13. The county collects plastic drink containers. The county refuses all other plastic containers.

14. Yard waste is also picked up. Yard waste must be in plastic bags.

15. Tree limbs must be cut up. The limbs must be bundled together with rope or heavy twine.

16. Hazardous materials should not be thrown out with the trash. They should be taken to special collection centers.

17. Batteries are considered hazardous materials. Batteries must never be placed with ordinary trash.

APPLY TO WRITING

Writer's Craft: *Combining Sentences*

Writers often combine sentence parts to make their writing less wordy and avoid repetition. Occasionally a writer chooses not to combine sentences. Read the first stanza of this poem by Lilian Moore and then follow the instructions below.

> Three poets see a star.
>   One says *how cold.*
>   One thinks *how bright.*
>   One sighs *how far.*
>
> *—Lilian Moore, "Each in a Different Voice"*

- Write the three sentences that have the same subject. Then combine the sentences into one sentence with a compound verb.

- Read the new sentence. Compare it with the original sentences. Why do you think the writer chose not to combine the sentences? Try to give at least two reasons.

Position of Subjects

When the subject in a sentence comes before the verb, the sentence is in **natural order.**

When the verb or part of a verb phrase comes before the subject, the sentence is in **inverted order.**

To find the subject and verb in a sentence that is in inverted order, put the sentence in its natural order. To do this, first find the verb. Then ask who or what is doing the action. In the following examples, each subject is underlined once, and each verb is underlined twice.

Into the dungeon marched the prisoners.
The prisoners marched into the dungeon.

Questions are often in inverted order. To find the subject in a question, turn the question around so that it makes a statement.

Do you like mystery stories?
You do like mystery stories.

Sentences that begin with *here* or *there* are often in inverted order. To find the subject of this kind of sentence, drop the word *here* or *there*. Then put the rest of the words in their natural order. Remember that *here* or *there* can never be the subject.

Here comes the librarian with my favorite book.
The librarian comes with my favorite book.

There are several mysteries in the book.
Several mysteries are in the book.

CONNECT TO WRITER'S CRAFT

Professional writers use sentences in both natural and inverted order. Changing the normal subject-verb order creates sentence variety and adds interest. Notice the position of the subjects and verbs in Poe's description of some rooms.

The panes here were scarlet—a deep blood color. Now in no one of the seven apartments was there any lamp or candelabrum, amid the profusion of golden ornaments that lay scattered to and fro or depended from the roof. There was no light of any kind emanating from lamp or candle within the suite of chambers.

—*Edgar Allan Poe*, "The Masque of the Red Death"

You can learn more about sentences in inverted order on pages L392–L393.

PRACTICE YOUR SKILLS

● Check Your Understanding
Finding Subjects in Sentences in Inverted Order

Write the subject and verb in each sentence.

1. Do you enjoy Edgar Allan Poe's short stories?
2. From "The Cask of Amontillado" comes a scary scene.
3. There is no happy ending for Fortunato.
4. Behind a wall of Montresor's house lie Fortunato's bones.
5. How did the bones get behind the wall?
6. From the brain of a madman came the plot.
7. There were many wrongs done to Montresor.
8. Had Montresor really been the victim of slights by Fortunato?
9. Did Fortunato deserve his fate?
10. There exists scant evidence against Fortunato.
11. Have you ever read "The Pit and the Pendulum"?
12. In that story are some very macabre events.
13. There is a pendulum with a sharp scythe.
14. For the squeamish reader, there are even some rats.

● Connect to the Writing Process: Revising
Varying Sentence Beginnings

15.–19. Add interest to this paragraph by varying five sentence beginnings.

The band marched onto the football field. Two helicopters flew directly overhead. The helicopters hovered over the crowd. The noise from the helicopters was loud. The band could not be heard. The helicopters finally rose higher into the sky. They flew away. The crowd cheered in grateful response.

APPLY TO WRITING

News Article: *Position of Subjects*

Edouard Manet, *The Exposition Universelle in Paris,* 1867.
Oil on canvas, 42¹/₈ by 76¹/₁₆ inches. National Gallery, Oslo, Norway.

The year is 1867, and you are a newspaper reporter from the United States. You have just arrived in Paris to cover the World's Fair. This painting shows the scene before you. You decide to write an article about your first impressions for your readers back home. In your article be sure to vary the position of the subjects of your sentences so your readers will not be bored.

Understood Subjects

When the subject of a sentence is not stated, the subject is an **understood *you***.

The subject of a command or a request is an understood *you.*

> (You) Meet me in the cafeteria at lunchtime.
> (You) Please wait for me.

In the following example, *you* is still the understood subject.

> Danielle, (you) please be there also.

Practice Your Skills

 Check Your Understanding
Finding Subjects

Contemporary Life **Write the subject and verb in each sentence. If the subject is an understood *you*, write (you).**

1. The lunch line is always long.
2. Hand me a tray, please.
3. Save a place for me at your table.
4. May I have a slice of pizza?
5. Ken, have your money ready.
6. Please pass me some milk.
7. Do the potatoes need some salt?
8. Pile the empty trays by the kitchen window.
9. Take this ticket for your lunch.
10. Maria, try some of this strawberry applesauce.

Connect to the Writing Process: Revising
Using Understood You

Instructions are usually easier to follow when an understood *you* is the subject. Revise these instructions for washing a car, using the understood *you*.

11. First, you should have a bucket with soap and hot water.
12. Then, you wet the car with a hose.
13. You put the sponge in the bucket and soap it well.
14. Next, you wash the car with the sponge.
15. The hose is used to rinse away the soap.
16. Last, you dry the car with a soft cloth.

APPLY TO WRITING

Directions: *Understood* You

Do you know how to change a flat tire? Do you know how to make a tasty pizza? Perhaps you know how to make a great-looking holiday decoration. Share what you know with your classmates by writing directions for what you can do well. Use sentences with an understood *you* so that your directions are easy to follow.

QuickCheck Mixed Practice

General Interest **Write the subject and verb in each sentence. If the subject is an understood *you*, write (you).**

1. Have you ever been to an automobile museum?
2. Visit one soon.
3. There are cars from every era on display.
4. Do not sit in any of the cars, though.
5. By each car is usually found an information card.
6. Read the card for interesting facts.
7. There was an old Rolls-Royce in the center of the floor.
8. To the right of it was a Model T Ford.
9. Does the crank on that car turn?
10. Please crank it for me.

Diagraming Subjects and Verbs

A **sentence diagram** is a picture made up of lines and words. It can help you clearly see the different parts of a sentence. These parts make up the structure of your sentences. By varying your sentence structure, you can make your writing more interesting.

Subjects and Verbs   All sentence diagrams begin with a baseline. A straight, vertical line then separates the subject (or subjects) on the left from the verb (or verbs) on the right. Notice in the following diagram that the capital letter in the sentence is included, but not the punctuation. Also notice that the whole verb phrase is included on the baseline.

She has remembered.

She	has remembered

Inverted Order   A sentence in inverted order, such as a question, is diagramed like a sentence in natural order.

Were you talking?

you	Were talking

Understood Subjects   When the subject of a sentence is an understood *you,* put parentheses around it in the subject position. When a name is included with the understood subject, place it on a horizontal line above the understood subject.

Ted, listen.

Ted

(you)	listen

Compound Subjects and Verbs Place compound subjects and verbs on parallel lines. Put the conjunction connecting them on a broken line between them. Notice in the following example that two conjunctions are placed on either side of the broken line.

Both cameras and computers were displayed.

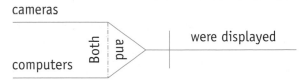

Jan has gone but will return.

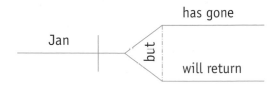

Balloons, hats, and horns were bought but have been lost.

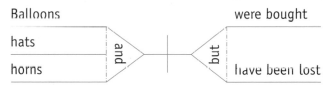

PRACTICE YOUR SKILLS

Diagraming Subjects and Verbs

Diagram the following sentences or copy them. If you copy them, draw one line under each subject and two lines under each verb. If the subject is an understood *you*, write *you* in parentheses.

1. Pigeons are landing.
2. Look!
3. Both males and females are eating.
4. Are you looking?
5. Birds leave but return.
6. Ben and Zach have come and are watching.
7. Zach, listen.
8. Birds are cooing.
9. Do pigeons migrate?
10. They might stay or leave.

Finding Subjects and Verbs

Write the subjects and verbs in the following sentences. Label each word *S* for subject or *V* for verb.

1. Often volcanoes will remain inactive for centuries.
2. Then they will erupt and blow tops of mountains completely off!
3. Some eruptions have killed tens of thousands of people.
4. A few really powerful volcanoes have buried cities and covered mountains.
5. Here is an incredible fact.
6. The force of a few volcanoes has even changed the world's weather for years!
7. Despite the dangers of molten or hot rock, many people live near volcanoes.
8. Can you guess the reason why?
9. Several kinds of crops and plants grow extremely well in volcanic soil.
10. Many valuable ores and metals are also found in volcanic soil.
11. In A.D. 79, the eruption of Mount Vesuvius buried the Roman city of Pompeii and left a time capsule of Roman life.
12. Centuries later archaeologists found houses and bodies under ten feet of hard ash.
13. Today many scientists and tourists visit this site in Italy each year.
14. Have you ever visited this famous city?
15. There is no other place on Earth like it.

Finding Subjects and Verbs

Write the subjects and verbs in the following sentences. If the subject is an understood *you*, write the word *you* in parentheses.

1. Do you know anything about elephants?
2. Look at this book about elephants.
3. Here are many very interesting facts.
4. Elephants, for example, are the largest land animals in the world.
5. An elephant can run at a rate of twenty-four miles per hour!
6. The trunk of an elephant is longer than the nose of any other animal.
7. There are forty thousand muscles and tendons in the elephant's trunk.
8. With its trunk, an elephant can pick a single flower or carry a huge log.
9. For centuries the elephant has been a good friend to people throughout the world.
10. Read more about elephants on your own.

Writing Sentences

Write five sentences that follow the directions below. (The sentences may come in any order.) Write about one of the following topics or a topic of your choice: an animal in the natural world or an event in nature.

1. Write a sentence with a compound subject.
2. Write a sentence with a compound verb.
3. Write a sentence that starts with the word *there*.
4. Write a question.
5. Write a sentence with an understood *you* as the subject.

Underline each subject once and each verb twice. Remember to add capital letters and end punctuation.

Language and *Self-Expression*

American Indian artist Jaune Quick-to-See Smith uses her art to help others understand her heritage. For example, her great-great-grandmother, great-grandmother, and grandmother were all involved in trading. Her father, who was raised by these women, then became a horse trader. How does the artist show this in *Family Tree*?

Imagine the stories that Jaune Quick-to-See Smith may have heard during her childhood. What stories have you heard about your relatives or ancestors? Which of these have become a part of your family's lore? Write the story in a few paragraphs, using the third person (*Mother, he, she*). Form sentences that express your ideas clearly. Vary your writing by using compound subjects and verbs. Then tape your story and play it for your family members.

Prewriting You may want to create a cluster diagram showing your subject's most interesting characteristics. Then make a Sequence of Events chart detailing the main events in the story.

Drafting Use the Sequence of Events chart to tell the story and the cluster diagram to bring your subject to life. Your first sentence should capture the tone of the story or set the scene. Your concluding sentence should summarize the story or state its main point.

Revising Read aloud your first and last sentences to a classmate. Ask him or her how they relate to each other. Then have your partner read and give you feedback on your story. Make sure that each sentence expresses a complete thought.

Editing Check your story for errors in spelling and punctuation. Be sure that you have capitalized people's names and the names of places.

Publishing Prepare a final copy and use an audiocassette recorder to tape it. If possible, play it for your family.

Another Look

Recognizing Sentences

A **sentence** is a group of words that expresses a complete thought.

A **sentence fragment** is a group of words that expresses an incomplete thought.

Subjects and Predicates

The **subject** names the person, place, thing, or idea that the sentence is about. *(page L7)*

A **complete subject** includes all the words used to identify the person, place, thing, or idea that the sentence is about. *(page L7)*

A **simple subject** is the main word in the complete subject. *(pages L8–L9)*

A **compound subject** is two or more subjects in one sentence that have the same verb and are joined by a conjunction. *(page L18)*

The **predicate** tells something about the subject. *(page L7)*

A **complete predicate** includes all the words that tell what the subject is doing or that tell something about the subject. *(page L11)*

A **simple predicate,** or **verb,** is the main word or phrase in the complete predicate. *(page L12)*

A **verb phrase** includes the main verb plus any helping, or auxiliary, verbs. *(pages L14–L15)*

A **compound verb** is two or more verbs in one sentence that have the same subject and are joined by a conjunction. *(page L20)*

Position of Subjects

When the subject in a sentence comes before the verb, the sentence is in **natural order.** *(page L22)*

When the verb or part of a verb phrase comes before the subject, the sentence is in **inverted order.** *(pages L22–L23)*

When the subject of a sentence is not stated, the subject is an **understood you.** *(pages L25–L26)*

 **Posttest**

Directions

Write the letter of the term that correctly identifies the underlined word or words in each sentence.

EXAMPLE   **1.** Scientists <u>have developed new ways to keep food fresh</u>.

    1 **A** simple subject
       B complete subject
       C simple predicate
       D complete predicate

ANSWER   **1** **D**

1. <u>Fruits</u> and <u>vegetables</u> can spoil if they become too ripe.

2. Many <u>foods</u> need to refrigerated so they will be safe for eating.

3. <u>A candy maker in France</u> developed the method of canning in the 1790s.

4. <u>Made it possible for fruits and vegetables to be stored for a long time</u>.

5. He <u>cooked</u> the foods and <u>poured</u> them into clean glass bottles.

6. <u>He</u> sealed and sterilized the bottles by heating them in boiling water.

7. <u>High temperatures</u> will destroy organisms in food.

8. <u>Charles Birdseye</u>, a scientist, developed a way to keep foods fresh.

9. <u>Did he freeze the foods</u>?

10. <u>Today routinely freeze the foods</u>.

1	A	complete subject	6	A	simple subject
	B	complete predicate		B	compound subject
	C	compound subject		C	simple predicate
	D	compound verb		D	complete predicate

2	A	simple subject	7	A	sentence fragment
	B	complete subject		B	inverted order
	C	simple predicate		C	simple predicate
	D	complete predicate		D	complete subject

3	A	simple subject	8	A	simple subject
	B	complete subject		B	complete predicate
	C	simple predicate		C	compound subject
	D	complete predicate		D	compound verb

4	A	sentence fragment	9	A	sentence fragment
	B	inverted order		B	inverted order
	C	simple predicate		C	simple predicate
	D	compound subject		D	compound subject

5	A	complete subject	10	A	sentence fragment
	B	complete predicate		B	inverted order
	C	compound subject		C	simple predicate
	D	compound verb		D	compound subject

CHAPTER 2

Nouns and Pronouns

 **Pretest**

Directions

Write the letter of the term that correctly identifies the underlined word or words in each sentence.

EXAMPLE   **1.** Many people learn to cook at the <u>Culinary Institute of America</u>.

   1 **A** abstract noun

       B common noun

       C proper noun

       D collective noun

ANSWER   **1** **C**

1. At the CIA, <u>chefs</u> teach the classes.
2. Each <u>class</u> learns a different kind of cooking.
3. The <u>classrooms</u> are equipped with stoves and refrigerators.
4. The students are responsible for cleaning <u>their</u> workstations.
5. <u>Each</u> must pass an intensive cooking examination to graduate.
6. The students get great <u>satisfaction</u> from learning cooking skills.
7. <u>Those</u> are the skills they will use all their lives.
8. <u>Who</u> will go on to cook professionally?
9. They <u>themselves</u> do not know the answer until after graduation.
10. They must prepare <u>themselves</u> for a difficult job search.

1	**A**	common noun	**6**	**A**	compound noun
	B	collective noun		**B**	proper noun
	C	abstract noun		**C**	abstract noun
	D	proper noun		**D**	collective noun

2	**A**	proper noun	**7**	**A**	interrogative pronoun
	B	abstract noun		**B**	indefinite pronoun
	C	compound noun		**C**	reflexive pronoun
	D	collective noun		**D**	demonstrative pronoun

3	**A**	abstract noun	**8**	**A**	demonstrative pronoun
	B	collective noun		**B**	intensive pronoun
	C	compound noun		**C**	interrogative pronoun
	D	proper noun		**D**	personal pronoun

4	**A**	personal pronoun	**9**	**A**	intensive pronoun
	B	reflexive pronoun		**B**	interrogative pronoun
	C	intensive pronoun		**C**	indefinite pronoun
	D	indefinite pronoun		**D**	reflexive pronoun

5	**A**	intensive pronoun	**10**	**A**	indefinite pronoun
	B	indefinite pronoun		**B**	reflexive pronoun
	C	personal pronoun		**C**	demonstrative pronoun
	D	reflexive pronoun		**D**	intensive pronoun

Marc Chagall. *I and the Village*, 1911.
Oil on canvas, 75⅝ inches by 59⅝ inches. The Museum of Modern Art, New York.

Describe   What figures do you see in the painting? What do you think they represent?

Analyze   What is the center of interest in the painting? How does the painter draw the eye to it?

Interpret   What do you think the artist is trying to express about his village? Explain.

Judge   How well do you think Chagall's use of color and image conveys a sense of memory? Explain.

At the end of the chapter, you will use this artwork to stimulate ideas for writing.

Nouns

A dictionary lists thousands of words. All these words can be divided into eight groups called the parts of speech. A word's part of speech is determined by the job it does in a sentence.

THE EIGHT PARTS OF SPEECH	
noun (names)	**adverb** (describes, limits)
pronoun (replaces)	**preposition** (relates)
verb (states action or being)	**conjunction** (connects)
adjective (describes, limits)	**interjection** (expresses strong feeling)

In English, there are more nouns than any other part of speech.

A **noun** is the name of a person, place, thing, or idea.

Concrete and Abstract Nouns

Nouns can be divided into **concrete nouns** and **abstract nouns.** You can easily identify concrete nouns because they name people, places, and things you can usually see or touch. Abstract nouns are harder to identify because they name ideas and qualities.

CONCRETE NOUNS	
PEOPLE	sailor, brother, Mrs. Wong, singers, Heather
PLACES	forest, mountains, amusement park, Texas, beach, Empire State Building, rooms, Germany
THINGS	rug, flower, explosion, flu, chipmunk, colors, guitar, slogan, lists

ABSTRACT NOUNS	
IDEAS AND QUALITIES	freedom, fun, love, inflation, bravery, anger, honesty, sickness, faith, democracy, thought, honor, belief, hunger

CONNECT TO SPEAKING AND WRITING

When you speak or write, the words you use create certain pictures in the minds of your audience. The nouns you choose can make these pictures dull and fuzzy or clear and exact. Vague, general nouns should almost always be replaced with specific nouns to bring your word pictures into sharper focus. Notice the difference between the two sentences that follow.

The **bugs** crawled over the **flower.**

The **ants** crawled over the **daisy.**

You can learn more about forming plurals of nouns on pages L627–L634. You can learn more about possessive nouns on pages L575–L577.

PRACTICE YOUR SKILLS

● Check Your Understanding
Finding Nouns

Science Topic   **Write the nouns in each sentence.**

1. During springtime, flowers bloom.
2. The fragrance of the buds fills the air.
3. Bees are attracted to the perfume of flowers.
4. These insects see color, pattern, and movement.
5. Bees taste blooms with their front legs and antennae.
6. These creatures have short bodies covered with hair.
7. Pollen clings to the hair on the body of the insect.
8. Bees make honey from the nectar of flowers.
9. Humans have harvested honey for many centuries.
10. Our appreciation of this golden liquid continues today.

● Connect to the Writing Process: Revising
Using Specific Nouns

Rewrite the following sentences, changing the underlined general noun to a specific noun that creates a clearer picture.

11. The tree was covered with insects.

12. Fruit hung from its branches.

13. A bird circled above the building.

14. A cool wind blew across the land.

Communicate Your Ideas

APPLY TO WRITING

Writer's Craft: *Analyzing the Use of Nouns*

Writers often choose nouns to create a specific picture in the minds of their readers. In this paragraph from "In the Heart of the Heart of the Country," William H. Gass writes about two fruit trees that remind him of his childhood. Read the paragraph, and then follow the instructions below.

> I knew nothing about apples. Why should I? My country came in my childhood, and I dreamed of sitting among the blooms like the bees. I failed to spray the pear tree too. I doubled up under them at first, admiring the sturdy low branches I should have pruned, and later I acclaimed the blossoms. Shortly after the fruit formed there were . . . apples the size of goodish stones which made me wobble on my ankles when I walked about the yard. Sometimes a piece crushed by a heel would cling on the shoe to track the house. . . .
>
> —*William H. Gass*, "In the Heart of the Heart of the Country"

- List the nouns in the passage.
- Underline the nouns that are specific nouns.
- What is the effect of the author's use of specific nouns?

Common and Proper Nouns

A **common noun** names any person, place, or thing.

A **proper noun** names a particular person, place, or thing.

All nouns are either common nouns or proper nouns. Every proper noun begins with a capital letter.

COMMON NOUNS	PROPER NOUNS
woman	Maria Chavez
city	Paris
building	World Trade Center
team	Houston Astros
day	Sunday

A proper noun sometimes includes more than one word. For example, even though *World Trade Center* is three words, it is considered one noun. It is the name of *one* place.

You can learn more about the capitalization of proper nouns on pages L464–L467.

PRACTICE YOUR SKILLS

 Check Your Understanding
Finding Common and Proper Nouns

General Interest **Make two columns on your paper. Label the first column *Common Nouns* and the second column *Proper Nouns.* Then, in the appropriate column, write the nouns from the following sentences.**

1. In Colombia, ants are sold as snacks by vendors on the street.

2. Fried worms are eaten in Mexico.

3. People in Uganda crush flies and shape them into pancakes.

4. In other parts of Africa, termites are munched like pretzels.

5. Certain spiders are roasted in New Guinea.

6. Some insects taste like nuts.

7. Restaurants in New York City serve ants dipped in chocolate.

8. In recent years the North American Bait Farms have held a cooking contest using worms.

9. In some cookbooks you can find a recipe for peppers stuffed with earthworms.

10. Actually, insects give people necessary protein and vitamins.

● Connect to the Writing Process: Editing
Capitalizing Proper Nouns

The following postcard message contains many proper nouns, but the writer forgot to begin them with capital letters. Rewrite the message, capitalizing all the proper nouns.

Dear sandy,

My vacation in europe has been great! I have been eating my way across the continent. After touring the louvre in paris, I dined on escargots. A few days later, I enjoyed spaghetti near the coliseum in rome. Today, I ate feta cheese in greece. Tomorrow I will try borscht after seeing the hermitage in st. petersburg.

On wednesday, I will fly home to denver and begin a diet. See you soon!

Your friend,

josie

APPLY TO WRITING

E-Mail Message: *Proper Nouns*

You have invited a friend to come for dinner. Send her an E-mail message giving her details about the meal. Be sure to include the day and time when the dinner will be held. You should also give her directions to your house. Take special care to capitalize the proper nouns in the message.

Compound and Collective Nouns

A noun that includes more than one word is called a **compound noun.**

Some nouns include more than one word. *Post* is one noun, *office* is one noun, but *post office* is also one noun. *Post office* is an example of a compound noun. It is not always easy to know how to write a particular compound noun. The best way to find out is to check in a dictionary. Compound nouns can take one of three forms.

COMPOUND NOUNS	
SEPARATE WORDS	living room, home run, peanut butter, ice cream
HYPHENATED	break-in, attorney-at-law, bird-watcher, great-grandmother
COMBINED	birdhouse, headband, flashlight, crosswalk, brainpower

You can learn more about punctuation of compound nouns on page L603.

A **collective noun** names a group of people or things.

COMMON COLLECTIVE NOUNS			
band	crew	flock	nation
committee	crowd	herd	orchestra
colony	family	league	swarm

PRACTICE YOUR SKILLS

● Check Your Understanding
Finding Compound and Collective Nouns

Contemporary Life **Make two columns on your paper. Label the first column *Compound Nouns* and the second column *Collective Nouns*. Then, in the appropriate column, write each noun.**

1. My classmates and I listened to presentations by members of an environmental group.

2. One speaker discussed water pollution and how it affects a species of wild ducks.

3. Another pair of presenters warned of the decline in the population of the grasshopper.

4. According to the organization, a number of animals have recently been declared endangered.

5. Because the group was so interesting, the entire faculty of the high school came to hear them.

● Connect to the Writing Process: Editing
Writing Nouns Correctly

Edit the following advertisement copy to eliminate errors in capitalization of proper nouns and misspellings of compound nouns. Write the corrected paragraph.

Let ollie's outdoor expeditions take you to visit

mothernature for the day! Join our group as we travel to

the st. francis river, where we will spend the day discussing the flora and fauna, as well as the wild-life of the area. Birdwatchers will enjoy viewing the flock of geese that live in the area, while animallovers will appreciate the herd of deer that often come to drink at the river. Children will enjoy building bird houses while their parents become fossilhunters for the day. Stop by ollie's outdoor expeditions at 211 sunnyvale street for more details.

✔ QuickCheck   Mixed Practice

General Interest   **Write the nouns in each sentence.** (There are 33 nouns.)

1. How did Houdini escape from jails, straitjackets, and strange containers?
2. Sometimes he kept keys in his throat.
3. He used the same method sword-swallowers use.
4. Once, when escaping from a jail in New York, he hid a piece of metal in a callus in the heel of one foot.
5. He attached it to a wire that he had hidden in his hair to make a key.
6. He also designed trick cabinets with locks and hinges in secret places.
7. This magician also had great strength and agility.
8. Like a professional athlete, he kept his body and mind in top shape.
9. Moreover, he could dislocate his joints.
10. His skill mystified audiences throughout the world.

Pronouns

A **pronoun** is a word that takes the place of one or more nouns.

Speaking and writing would be very repetitious if there were no words to take the place of nouns. Pronouns do this job. The second example below reads more smoothly and is easier to understand when pronouns are substituted for two of the nouns.

> Holly took Holly's sweater with Holly on the class trip.
> Holly took **her** sweater with **her** on the class trip.

Pronoun Antecedents

The noun a pronoun refers to or replaces is called its **antecedent.**

In the following examples, an arrow has been drawn from the pronoun to its antecedent. Notice that the antecedent usually comes before the pronoun.

> **Dion** said that **he** couldn't go to the zoo.
>
> **Lynn** asked **Sandy**, "Did **we** miss the dolphin show?"

You can learn more about pronouns and antecedents on pages L355–L356.

PRACTICE YOUR SKILLS

● Check Your Understanding
Finding Antecedents

Contemporary Life **Write the antecedent for each underlined pronoun.**

1. Juanita brought <u>her</u> camera on the trip to the zoo.

2. Steve asked Juanita to take a picture of <u>him</u>.

3. Linda said, "<u>I</u> enjoy the reptiles."

4. Gretchen and Margo said <u>they</u> were looking for the penguins.

5. Ms. Jackson told Henry that <u>she</u> liked to watch the monkeys.

6. The monkey cage had a tire swing in <u>it</u>.

7. Jeff asked Ms. Jackson, "Did <u>you</u> bring the monkeys a banana?"

8. Chris and Jesse asked the teacher, "Are <u>we</u> leaving now?"

9. Juanita said that <u>she</u> wanted one more picture of the peacocks.

10. Ms. Jackson's students enjoyed <u>their</u> trip to the zoo.

Connect to the Writing Process: Revising
Replacing Nouns with Pronouns

Rewrite the paragraph, replacing nouns with pronouns where they are needed.

Investigations into the intelligence of gorillas show that gorillas are much smarter than people once thought gorillas were. Gorillas will stack boxes to help gorillas reach bananas that are too high to pick. Gorillas will use sticks as tools to pull food into gorillas' cages. One scientist, Dr. James White, trained a female gorilla named Congo to perform various actions. When the scientist returned some years later, Congo remembered the scientist. Congo also repeated some of the actions the scientist had taught Congo. Congo's behavior in these instances helped convince scientists of gorillas' intelligence.

APPLY TO WRITING

Journal Entry: *Pronouns*

Rosa Bonheur. *The King of the Desert,* 19th century. Oil on canvas, 39⅜ by 37⅝ inches.

The year is 1850, and you are an explorer who has come to Africa. Today, while on safari for the first time, you came face-to-face with a magnificent lion. This painting of "the king of the desert" shows your memory of that moment. It is evening now. As you sit in your tent reflecting calmly on the experience, write a description of the big cat for your travel journal. In your journal entry, be sure to describe the lion's appearance, as well as any sounds you may have heard or feelings you may have had. Use pronouns to prevent your writing from becoming repetitious.

▶ Personal Pronouns

Personal pronouns are the most common type of pronoun. These pronouns can be divided into the following three groups.

PERSONAL PRONOUNS	
FIRST PERSON	(the person speaking)
SINGULAR	I, me, my, mine
PLURAL	we, us, our, ours
SECOND PERSON	(the person spoken to)
SINGULAR	you, your, yours
PLURAL	you, your, yours
THIRD PERSON	(the person or thing spoken about)
SINGULAR	he, him, his, she, her, hers, it, its
PLURAL	they, them, their, theirs

The following sentences use personal pronouns.

FIRST-PERSON PRONOUNS	**I** want to take **my** notebook with **me** to the convention.
	We think **our** plan of political action is best for **us.**
SECOND-PERSON PRONOUNS	Did **you** bring **your** list of questions for the candidate?
	Are these pamphlets **yours** or do they belong to Mary?
THIRD-PERSON PRONOUNS	The reporter took **his** camera and film with **him.**
	They enjoyed **their** new leader's speech to the delegates.

PRACTICE YOUR SKILLS

 Check Your Understanding
Finding Personal Pronouns

History Topic **Write the personal pronouns in each sentence.**

1. In the United States, Elizabeth Cady Stanton and Susan B. Anthony devoted their lives to women's suffrage.

2. If you are a woman in the United States, you owe many of your legal and political rights to these courageous suffragists.

3. At the time when Anthony began her work, women had few legal rights.

4. When African American men were given the right to vote in 1869, she began a movement to secure the same rights for women.

5. In 1869, the territory of Wyoming was the first area in the U.S. to allow its female citizens to vote.

6. Anthony was president of the American Woman Suffrage Association until she was eighty.

7. Anthony voted in the election of 1872, but she was fined $100 for breaking the law.

8. She refused to pay it.

9. We can see that few people are as devoted to a cause as she.

10. American women did not gain their right to vote until 1920.

11. Elizabeth Cady Stanton studied law in her father's office when he was a Supreme Court justice.

12. In 1848, she helped lead the first convention that demanded women's suffrage.

13. Stanton also wrote articles for a newspaper that she and Anthony ran together.

Reflexive and Intensive Pronouns

Reflexive pronouns and **intensive pronouns** refer to or emphasize another noun or pronoun.

These pronouns are formed by adding *–self* or *–selves* to certain personal pronouns.

REFLEXIVE AND INTENSIVE PRONOUNS	
SINGULAR	myself, yourself, himself, herself, itself
PLURAL	ourselves, yourselves, themselves

Although the reflexive and intensive pronouns are the same words, their function in a sentence differs. A reflexive pronoun reflects back to a noun or a pronoun mentioned earlier in the sentence. An intensive pronoun is used directly after its antecedent to intensify, or emphasize, a statement. A reflexive pronoun is necessary to the meaning of the sentence, but an intensive pronoun is not.

> REFLEXIVE   Pioneers organized **themselves** into wagon trains before their long journey.
>
> INTENSIVE   I **myself** could not have survived the hardships of the westward trek.

PRACTICE YOUR SKILLS

Check Your Understanding
Finding Pronouns

History Topic   **Write the personal, reflexive, and intensive pronouns in each sentence and label them *P* for personal, *R* for reflexive, and *I* for intensive.**

1. In the early 1840s, adventurous settlers readied themselves for the overland trip to the West.

2. Life in the Oregon country held new promise for them.

3. The settlers themselves could never have anticipated all the hardships they encountered on the two-thousand-mile Oregon Trail.

4. When it was loaded, a covered wagon often weighed thousands of pounds.

5. It was pulled across various types of terrain by teams of horses, mules, or oxen.

6. The wagons were uncomfortable for the passengers themselves.

7. On many occasions, settlers might walk beside them rather than ride.

8. The journey was hard for the travelers, but many nights they sang by their campfires.

9. The route was mapped in 1804 by Lewis and Clark themselves.

10. Today, we can drive our cars along modern roads beside the historic trail.

● Connect to the Writing Process: Revising
Using Intensive Pronouns

Add intensive pronouns to the following sentences to make the statements stronger.

11. On many days, a woman rode alone in the covered wagon.

12. She often drove the long miles and cared for her children at the same time.

13. Sometimes on the trail, disputes arose among the settlers.

14. The wagon master often served as the mediator of these disputes.

15. He knew how dangerous fights among the settlers could be.

APPLY TO WRITING

Persuasive Letter: *Pronouns*

Imagine that you are a settler traveling to Oregon in a covered wagon. Write a letter to a friend back home in the East, encouraging or discouraging him or her to take the same trip. Give at least three reasons to explain your viewpoint. As you write, use pronouns to keep your writing from being repetitive.

Other Kinds of Pronouns

Three other kinds of pronouns are indefinite pronouns, demonstrative pronouns, and interrogative pronouns.

Indefinite Pronouns

Indefinite pronouns refer to unnamed people, places, things, or ideas.

Indefinite pronouns often do not have definite antecedents as personal pronouns do.

> **Several** have qualified for the contest.
> **Many** collected the newspapers.
> I've gathered **everything** now.

	COMMON INDEFINITE PRONOUNS
SINGULAR	another, anybody, anyone, anything, each, either, everybody, everyone, everything, much, neither, nobody, no one, one, somebody, someone, something
PLURAL	both, few, many, others, several
SINGULAR/PLURAL	all, any, most, none, some

The ten indefinite pronouns in color on the preceding chart may be singular or plural. The other indefinite pronouns are always singular. When you speak or write, remember that a pronoun must agree with its antecedent. If singular indefinite pronouns serve as antecedents to other pronouns, both pronouns must be singular.

Everything was in **its** place.

Everyone at the gym has **his** or **her** own locker.

Each of the girls ate **her** lunch.

Several brought **their** lunches.

You can learn more about indefinite pronouns as antecedents on pages L357–L358.

PRACTICE YOUR SKILLS

● Check Your Understanding
Finding Indefinite Pronouns

Contemporary Life **Write the indefinite pronouns in each sentence.**

1. Many feel they cannot help the environment.
2. Some say the problem is too large.
3. However, anyone can recycle.
4. Almost everything has more than one use.
5. Everybody can conserve natural resources.
6. A small action is better than none.
7. We should encourage others in this pursuit.
8. Nothing is wrong with thanking citizens who recycle their trash.
9. Anyone can join the effort.
10. No one should forget to recycle.
11. Each can make a difference.
12. Everyone can learn how to recycle.

13. We should do anything to reduce waste.

14. All have a right to a cleaner environment.

15. Most have access to recycling bins nowadays.

● Connect to the Writing Process: Revising
Making Pronouns and Their Antecedents Agree

Change the underlined pronouns in the following sentences so that they agree with their antecedents. Write the new sentences.

16. Either of the girls could have reused their paper scraps in art projects.

17. Both of the boys recycled his cans.

18. Does everyone know where their recycling bin is?

19. Some of the men left his cans on the table.

20. Each of the girls cleaned up their area.

21. Few forget to recycle her newspapers.

22. Neither recycles their glass.

23. Several remembered to label his recycling bins.

24. Many keep her recycling bins handy.

25. Everyone takes their recycling seriously.

Demonstrative Pronouns

Demonstrative pronouns point out a specific person, place, thing, or idea.

DEMONSTRATIVE PRONOUNS			
this	that	these	those

This is Mary's coat on the hanger.
Are **these** John's glasses?

Interrogative Pronouns

Interrogative pronouns are used to ask questions.

INTERROGATIVE PRONOUNS				
what	which	who	whom	whose

What is known about the case?
Who is coming to the party?

You can learn about another type of pronoun, the relative pronoun, on pages L229–L234.

PRACTICE YOUR SKILLS

 Check Your Understanding
Finding Demonstrative and Interrogative Pronouns

Contemporary Life **Write the demonstrative pronouns and the interrogative pronouns. Use the label *D* for demonstrative and *I* for interrogative.**

1. Who is going to the dance on Saturday?

2. That is the most important question on our minds.

3. This is my outfit for the dance.

4. Of all my shoes, these will match my dress best.

5. What is the first song going to be?

6. Those are great tunes for dancing.

7. Which is your favorite?

8. That is a good example of rap.

9. Are those the latest style?

10. Whom did you meet at the last school dance you attended?

Using Pronouns

Add pronouns to complete the following sentences. Choose personal, indefinite, demonstrative, or interrogative pronouns.

11. The little girl found ■ all alone in the department store.

12. ■ began to cry.

13. ■ in the store turned to look at ■.

14. Suddenly, ■ felt a hand on ■ small shoulder.

15. ■ had found her?

16. ■ mother smiled down at her.

17. "■ was a scary feeling," she told her mother.

18. ■ is why little girls should not wander from ■ mothers.

19. "Well, ■ are safe now," said the mother.

20. "May ■ get two ice cream cones for ■?"asked the little girl.

21. "Should ■ eat lunch first?" asked her mother.

22. "■ should we eat for lunch?" she also asked the girl.

23. "■ good," the girl decided.

Communicate Your Ideas

APPLY TO WRITING

Personal Narrative: *Nouns and Pronouns*

Write a narrative for your classmates about your first day in ninth grade. Did you feel lost or right at home? Did you know most of the people or did you have to make new friends? Use a variety of nouns and pronouns to make your narrative interesting.

Contemporary Life

Write the pronouns in the following sentences. Label each *P* for personal, *Ind* for indefinite, *D* for demonstrative, or *Int* for interrogative.

1. That was the year we built the tree house in our backyard.

2. Whose was it?

3. Who actually helped build it for your younger brothers and sisters?

4. This was the block where we used to live when all of us were in grade school.

5. These are the streets where we played ball with others.

6. Which is the school you and the rest of your family attended?

7. What are the subjects you studied with my older brother?

8. Whom among all of your mathematics teachers did you like the best?

9. Those were the days when no one realized how quickly our lives would change.

10. That used to be fun when we played ball on summer evenings.

Identifying Nouns and Pronouns

Write each noun and pronoun in the following sentences. Then label each one *N* for noun or *P* for pronoun. Note: A date, such as 1533, is a noun.

1. Born in 1533, Elizabeth I was one of the most famous rulers of England.

2. Her court was well known for its artists and playwrights.

3. When she was a young girl, Elizabeth was locked up in the Tower of London by her half-sister Mary.

4. When Mary died, Elizabeth came to the throne of England and ruled for forty-five years.

5. Born in 1769, Napoleon was a famous ruler of France.

6. He conquered large parts of Europe and made himself emperor over them.

7. He was born on the island of Corsica.

8. Eventually he became the most powerful man in the French army and won many victories throughout Europe.

9. He reorganized France and improved the law, banks, trade, and education.

10. When his enemies in Europe invaded France, Napoleon was exiled to an island off the coast of Italy.

11. He eventually returned to France with his soldiers, but he was finally defeated at the Battle of Waterloo.

12. Whom do you remember from centuries ago?

13. Only a few stand out in our history books for their bravery, great deeds, or incredible lives.

14. In the modern world, however, people instantly become famous because of television, movies, and newspapers.

15. Of course, few of these instant celebrities will be remembered next month.

Recognizing Pronouns and Their Antecedents

Write each personal pronoun and its antecedent in the following sentences.

1. Because Jamie was absent, he missed the field trip.
2. When the twins dress alike, they look identical.
3. An anteater can extend its tongue about two feet.
4. Lisa told Tim, "If you bring your racket, we can play a game."
5. Ken took his raincoat with him to the baseball game.
6. Mr. Ash told Nancy, "You should give your report now."
7. Bill and Ron rode their bicycles to school today.
8. "I didn't see you at the mall," Pam told Terry.
9. Linda said she is making her own dinner tonight.
10. "My friends asked me to visit them," Daniel told his dad.

Using Nouns and Pronouns

Write ten sentences that follow the directions below. (The sentences may include other nouns and pronouns besides those listed, and they may come in any order.) Write about one of the following topics or a topic of your own choice: a famous leader, sports figure, or musician. Write *N* above each noun and *P* above each pronoun.

Write a sentence that . . .

1. includes nouns that name a person, a place, and a thing.
2. includes a noun that names an idea.
3. includes a common noun and a proper noun.
4. includes a collective noun.
5. includes a compound noun.
6. includes several personal pronouns.
7. includes a reflexive pronoun.
8. includes one or two indefinite pronouns.
9. includes a demonstrative pronoun.
10. includes an interrogative pronoun.

Language and *Self-Expression*

Marc Chagall (1887–1985) grew up in Vitebsk, Russia. He left home to study art in St. Petersburg and then moved to Paris. Many of his paintings show people and animals floating across the canvas in a dreamlike state, and others include scenes of his childhood home, Vitebsk.

Think of a scene from your own childhood that stirs fond memories. It can be an actual event or something as simple as the memory of a dinner table, spread with food and surrounded by familiar faces. Write a description of that event or scene. Include as many different kinds of nouns and pronouns as you can.

Prewriting You may wish to make a cluster diagram of your memory of the scene. Include people, places, things, and ideas in your diagram.

Drafting Use the cluster diagram to organize your description as you begin drafting. Tell what people and things are part of your memory and explain how the memory makes you feel.

Revising Read your description to a partner. Ask your partner if you have conveyed the feelings the memory brings you. Make sure all your pronouns have clear antecedents.

Editing Check your description for errors in spelling and punctuation. Be sure you have capitalized all proper names.

Publishing Prepare a final copy. If possible, find a photograph to accompany your description. Place it in a class book of memories.

Another Look

A **noun** is the name of a person, place, thing, or idea.

Classification of Nouns
A **concrete noun** names people, places, or things you can see or touch. *(page L39)*
An **abstract noun** names ideas or qualities. *(pages L39–L40)*
A **common noun** names any person, place, or thing. *(page L42)*
A **proper noun** names a particular person, place, or thing. *(page L42)*
A **compound noun** includes more than one word. *(page L44)*
A **collective noun** names a group of people or things. *(page L45)*

A **pronoun** is a word that takes the place of one or more nouns.

The noun that a pronoun refers to or replaces is called its **antecedent.**

Kinds of Pronouns
Personal pronouns can be divided into several groups. *(page L50)*
Reflexive pronouns and **intensive pronouns** refer back to or emphasize another noun or pronoun. *(page L52)*
Indefinite pronouns refer to unnamed people, places, things, or ideas. *(pages L54–L55)*
Demonstrative pronouns point out specific persons, places, things, or ideas. *(page L56)*
Interrogative pronouns are used to ask questions. *(page L57)*

Directions
Write the letter of the term that correctly identifies the underlined word or words in each sentence.

EXAMPLE

1. For ten <u>months</u> during 1997 and 1998, fires burned in Indonesia.

   1 A proper noun
     B abstract noun
     C collective noun
     D common noun

ANSWER

   1 D

1. <u>Indonesia</u> had been in the grip of a long drought throughout the year.

2. The <u>rain forests</u> were drier than we remembered them ever being before.

3. <u>They</u> burned with a hot intensity day and night for months.

4. <u>This</u> produced a severe smog over much of the country and surrounding areas.

5. <u>What</u> were the results of this disaster?

6. <u>Everything</u> in the country came to a halt.

7. Farm <u>families</u> were left without livelihoods.

8. <u>Sickness</u> and hunger were rampant.

9. If they stayed outdoors, people found <u>themselves</u> wheezing and fainting.

10. Indonesia <u>itself</u> lost over a billion dollars in farm and other products.

1	A	abstract noun	6	A	reflexive pronoun
	B	proper noun		B	demonstrative pronoun
	C	common noun		C	intensive pronoun
	D	collective noun		D	indefinite pronoun

2	A	compound noun	7	A	compound noun
	B	proper noun		B	collective noun
	C	collective noun		C	abstract noun
	D	abstract noun		D	proper noun

3	A	reflexive pronoun	8	A	abstract noun
	B	intensive pronoun		B	compound noun
	C	personal pronoun		C	proper noun
	D	demonstrative pronoun		D	collective noun

4	A	personal pronoun	9	A	intensive pronoun
	B	demonstrative pronoun		B	indefinite pronoun
	C	intensive pronoun		C	reflexive pronoun
	D	indefinite pronoun		D	interrogative pronoun

5	A	intensive pronoun	10	A	indefinite pronoun
	B	indefinite pronoun		B	reflexive pronoun
	C	interrogative pronoun		C	intensive pronoun
	D	demonstrative pronoun		D	demonstrative pronoun

Verbs

**Write the letter of the term that correctly identifies the
underlined word or words in each sentence.**

EXAMPLE
1. The class <u>has selected</u> a play.

1   **A**   transitive verb

B   intransitive verb

C   helping verb

D   linking verb

ANSWER
1   **A**

1. The students <u>chose</u> William Shakespeare's *Julius Caesar*
    for their class play.

2. William very much <u>wanted</u> the part of Caesar in the
    school production.

3. He <u>would have been</u> a great Caesar.

4. Instead, the rest of the class <u>chose</u> Nick for the part of
    the famous Roman leader.

5. Nick <u>was</u> good in rehearsals.

6. No one <u>could have worked</u> harder.

7. Julia <u>designed</u> the sets for the play.

8. She <u>painted</u> after school every day.

9. Raul and Sally <u>were</u> the costume designers as well as
    the make-up artists.

10. They must <u>have</u> sewn more than a dozen togas for the
    actors.

1   **A**   transitive verb
    B   intransitive verb
    C   linking verb
    D   helping verb

6   **A**   helping verb
    B   linking verb
    C   transitive verb
    D   intransitive verb

2   **A**   linking verb
    B   transitive verb
    C   helping verb
    D   intransitive verb

7   **A**   intransitive verb
    B   helping verb
    C   linking verb
    D   transitive verb

3   **A**   helping verb
    B   linking verb
    C   transitive verb
    D   intransitive verb

8   **A**   helping verb
    B   intransitive verb
    C   transitive verb
    D   linking verb

4   **A**   linking verb
    B   intransitive verb
    C   helping verb
    D   transitive verb

9   **A**   intransitive verb
    B   transitive verb
    C   linking verb
    D   helping verb

5   **A**   intransitive verb
    B   helping verb
    C   linking verb
    D   transitive verb

10   **A**   transitive verb
    B   helping verb
    C   intransitive verb
    D   linking verb

Joan Mitchell. *George Went Swimming at Barnes Hole, But It Got Too Cold,* 1957. Oil on canvas, 85¼ by 78¼ inches. Albright-Knox Art Gallery, Buffalo, New York. Gift of Seymour H. Knox, 1958. © Estate of Joan Mitchell.

Describe What colors and patterns do you see in this painting?

Analyze How do the light and dark areas work in the painting? What effect do they have?

Interpret The artist stated that the painting reflected "the memory of a feeling." What feeling do you think she was remembering as she painted?

Judge How do the bold strokes and colors of the painting affect you? Do you feel the artist clearly expresses her ideas in her style? Explain.

At the end of this chapter, you will use the artwork to stimulate ideas for writing.

Action Verbs

An essential part of every sentence is the verb because a verb breathes life into a sentence.

A **verb** is a word that expresses action or a state of being.

One kind of verb, an action verb, gives a subject action and movement.

An **action verb** tells what action a subject is performing.

Most action verbs show physical action.

> Marine biologists **observe** the creatures of the sea.
>
> Many fish **swim** in the world's oceans.

Some action verbs show mental action. Others show ownership or possession.

> Our class **studied** water mammals.
>
> The teacher **has** a photograph of a killer whale.

You may recall that helping verbs are often used with an action verb to form a verb phrase.

A **verb phrase** includes a main verb plus any helping, or auxiliary, verbs.

The verb phrase may contain more than one helping verb. It may also be interrupted by other words.

> The whales **will have migrated** by October.
>
> The students **could** certainly **learn** more about the sea.
>
> **Should** our class **visit** the ocean?
>
> I **have** never **seen** a killer whale.

Here is a list of the most common helping verbs.

COMMON HELPING VERBS	
be	am, is, are, was, were, am, be, being, been
have	has, have, had
do	do, does, did
OTHERS	may, might, must, can, could, shall, should, will, would

You can learn about regular and irregular verbs on pages L279–L288.

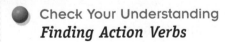

CONNECT TO SPEAKING AND WRITING

When you speak or write, the verbs you use show action in the sentence. You can use these words to make your audience see what is happening. When you choose your verbs carefully, you can also help your audience hear the action in the sentence.

The motorboat **cut** through the water.

The motorboat **whirred** through the water.

Verbs have the power to appeal to all five senses. You can make your writing more interesting by choosing the action words in your sentences carefully.

PRACTICE YOUR SKILLS

● Check Your Understanding
Finding Action Verbs

Science Topic **Write the verb or verb phrase in the following sentences. Remember, words that interrupt a verb phrase are not part of the verb.**

1. Dr. Lilly, a scientist from California, has been experimenting with dolphins for many years.

2. He has made some curious claims about them.

3. Dolphins have larger brains than humans.

4. Their language contains at least fifty thousand words.

5. Their brains can handle four different conversations at one time.

6. They can also judge between right and wrong.

7. Dolphins can remember sounds and series of sounds.

8. They can even communicate among themselves.

9. They use a series of clicks, buzzes, and whistles.

10. Dolphins have discharged some of these sounds at the rate of seven hundred times a second.

● Check Your Understanding
Finding Verb Phrases

Science Topic **Write the verb or verb phrase in the following sentences.**

11. Humans have been fascinated by the whale for centuries.

12. Whales can be divided into two basic types.

13. They are classified by scientists as either baleen or toothed whales.

14. Some small whales must surface for air several times each hour.

15. The larger creatures can remain underwater for an hour or more.

16. One species of baleen whale, the blue whale, can weigh up to fifteen hundred tons.

17. This species of whale was almost hunted to extinction in the early 1900s.

18. Didn't early whale hunters see their beauty and grace?

19. Some of them may not have realized the consequences of their actions.

20. Today, many wildlife organizations protect whales from hunters.

Replacing Verbs

Change the underlined verbs in the following sentences to help the reader "hear" rather than "see" the action.

21. The waterfall <u>ran</u> over the rocks.

22. Children <u>have been playing</u> in the water throughout the morning.

23. The tugboat <u>moved</u> through the water.

24. The waves <u>rushed</u> against the rocks.

25. The whale <u>blew</u> water from its spout.

Communicate Your Ideas

APPLY TO WRITING

Postcard: *Action Verbs*

You are vacationing at the seashore. Your younger brother has never been to the beach. Write a postcard to him describing your first day on the beach. Remember to include vivid action verbs to make your writing interesting.

Transitive and Intransitive Verbs

A **transitive verb** is an action verb that passes the action from a doer to a receiver.

An **intransitive verb** expresses action or states something about the subject but does not pass the action from a doer to a receiver.

All action verbs fall within two general classes: transitive or intransitive. You can determine whether a verb is transitive or intransitive by identifying the subject and the verb. Then ask,

What? or *Whom?* A word that answers either question is called an object. An action verb that has an object is transitive. An action verb that does not have an object is intransitive.

TRANSITIVE Many birds **eat** insects.

(Birds eat what? *Insects* is the object. Therefore, *eat* is a transitive verb.)

INTRANSITIVE Most geese **travel** in flocks.

(Geese travel what? Geese travel whom? Since there is no object, *travel* is an intransitive verb.)

The same verb may be transitive in one sentence and intransitive in another.

TRANSITIVE We **hung** birdhouses in the trees.

(We hung what? *Birdhouses* is the object.)

INTRANSITIVE The birdhouse **hung** from a rope in the oak tree.

(Birdhouse hung what? There is no object.)

You can learn about object complements, which follow transitive verbs, on pages L149–L150.

PRACTICE YOUR SKILLS

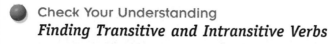

Check Your Understanding

Finding Transitive and Intransitive Verbs

Science Topic **Write the action verb in each sentence. Then label each one *T* for transitive or *I* for intransitive.**

1. Birds live in trees, on the ground, and in the sides of cliffs.

2. Many different birds nest near the seashore.

3. Some owls build their nests in burrows.

4. Eagles keep the same nest throughout their lives.

5. Hummingbirds sometimes fly backward.

6. Snow buntings lose their brown feathers in winter.

7. Lice live on some birds and mammals.

8. Ibises often steal material for their nests from other birds.

9. Robins migrate in winter.

10. Due to population growth, humans pose the greatest danger to the bird population.

Connect to the Writing Process: Editing
Using Action Verbs

Supply an action verb for each of the following sentences. Label each one *T* for transitive or *I* for intransitive.

11. Scientists ▨ the migration patterns of birds.

12. During autumn many birds ▨ from the north to the south.

13. Most adult birds ▨ their young from dangers.

14. In forests you ▨ birds' songs all around you.

15. Two cardinals ▨ across the wooded path.

16. Falcons ▨ down on their prey at speeds of more than 200 miles per hour.

17. Penguins ▨ their wings like flippers in the water.

18. Most birds ▨ the nest when they are a few months old.

19. A bobwhite can ▨ up to 15,000 seeds a day.

20. Many people around the world ▨ birds as pets.

Linking Verbs

A **linking verb** links the subject with another word in the sentence. The other word either renames or describes the subject.

The farm **is** my home.

(*Is* links *home* with *farm*. *Home* renames the subject.)

Have you **been** sad lately?

(Turn a question into a statement: *You have been sad lately.* Then you can easily see that *have been* links *sad* and the subject *you*. *Sad* describes the subject.)

Here is a list of common linking verbs. They are all forms of the verb *be*. Any verb phrase ending in *be* or *been* is a form of *be* and can be used as a linking verb.

COMMON FORMS OF *BE*		
be	shall be	have been
is	will be	has been
am	can be	had been
are	could be	could have been
was	should be	should have been
were	would be	may have been
	may be	might have been
	might be	must have been

The forms of *be* are not always linking verbs. To be a linking verb, a verb must link the subject with another word that renames or describes it. The word that renames or describes the subject is known as the subject complement. In the examples on the next page, the verbs simply make statements and are not linking verbs.

Our farm **is** over that hill.
The cows **will be** in the barn.

You can learn more about subject complements on pages L154–L155.

Practice Your Skills

Check Your Understanding
Finding Linking Verbs

General Interest **Write the linking verb in each sentence. Then write the two words that the verb links.**

1. My childhood on the farm was great.

2. Childhood memories should be happy for everyone.

3. My mother had been a city girl.

4. My father could have been a doctor.

5. Instead, he was a farmer.

6. Wheat can be a difficult crop.

7. Dad was always lucky with our harvests.

8. In summer our fields were golden.

9. Because of this, gold will always be my favorite color.

10. I could never be happy anywhere else.

Additional Linking Verbs

A few other verbs besides *be* can be linking verbs.

ADDITIONAL LINKING VERBS			
appear	grow	seem	stay
become	look	smell	taste
feel	remain	sound	turn

These verbs also link the subject with a word that describes or renames it.

The air **feels** humid today.
(*Humid* describes the *air*.)

The tornado **remains** a destructive force of nature.
(*Force* renames *tornado*.)

PRACTICE YOUR SKILLS

● Check Your Understanding
Finding Linking Verbs

General
Interest
Write the linking verb in each sentence. Then write the two words that the verb links.

1. The weather suddenly turned colder.
2. The sky looks dark today.
3. The clouds have grown thicker.
4. The gentle breeze became a strong wind.
5. The raindrops felt cold against my skin.
6. The dog appeared quite upset.
7. The thunder sounded very loud.
8. Does the weather seem scary to you?
9. I remained calm throughout the storm.
10. Afterward, the air smelled fresh.

● Connect to the Writing Process: Revising
Changing Questions into Statements

Change the following questions into statements. Underline the linking verb in each of your sentences.

11. Does the rain seem heavier?
12. Are you afraid of storms?
13. Are the windows in your bedroom shut?

14. Do I look pale?

15. Was that the worst storm ever in your town?

Communicate Your Ideas

APPLY TO WRITING

Descriptive Paragraph: *Linking Verbs*

Your town has just experienced a devastating tornado. You are standing in a neighborhood looking at the damage. A radio reporter walks up to you and asks you to describe how the neighborhood looked before the storm. Write a paragraph describing how the neighborhood looked. Underline the linking verbs you use in your description.

Linking Verb or Action Verb?

Most linking verbs can also be action verbs.

LINKING VERB   The darkness **felt** oppressive to us.

(*Oppressive* describes the subject.)

ACTION VERB   In the darkness my little sister **felt** for my hand.

(*Felt* shows action. It tells what *sister* did.)

You can decide whether a verb is a linking verb or an action verb by asking two questions: *Does the verb link the subject with a word that renames or describes the subject? Does the verb show action?*

LINKING VERB   My little sister **looked** afraid.

ACTION VERB   My mother **looked** for the candles.

PRACTICE YOUR SKILLS

● Check Your Understanding
Distinguishing Between Linking Verbs and Action Verbs

Contemporary Life **Write the verb in each sentence. Then label each one A for action or L for linking.**

1. Suddenly the room grew dark.
2. Did you turn off the light?
3. I looked for the light switch.
4. The night turned darker.
5. The phone rang suddenly.
6. My sister grew afraid in the dark.
7. Tall vines grew outside the window.
8. In the moonlight, they become a prowler.
9. The clock sounded loud in the darkness.
10. We felt better with the lights on.

● Connect to the Writing Process: Drafting
Writing Sentences

Write a sentence using each verb as a linking verb. Then use the verb as an action verb. Label each one A for action or L for linking.

11. taste
12. look
13. smell
14. appear
15. grow
16. sound
17. turn
18. become
19. remain
20. feel

APPLY TO WRITING

Personal Narrative: *Action and Linking Verbs*

Have you ever experienced a storm like the one pictured above? Might that be a tornado forming between the streaks of lightning?

Think back to a time when you experienced a bad storm. What happened? Were you caught outside without shelter, or did you watch from the relative safety of a basement window? How did you feel? Write a brief narrative account of the occurrence to share with your classmates. As you write, remember to vary your use of action and linking verbs. Be prepared to identify the verbs in your narrative and to tell whether they are transitive or intransitive.

Science
Topic

Write the verb or verb phrase in each sentence. Then label the verb *A* for action verb or *L* for linking verb. If the verb is an action verb, label it *T* for transitive or *I* for intransitive.

1. Cryogenics is the study of cold.

2. At very cold temperatures, your breath will turn into a liquid.

3. At colder temperatures, it actually freezes into a solid.

4. Cold steel becomes very soft.

5. A frozen banana can serve as a hammer.

6. Shivers can raise the body temperature seven degrees.

7. People with a low body temperature feel lazy.

8. One should wear layers of clothing for protection from cold.

9. Chipmunks have found a good solution to the cold.

10. They hibernate all winter long!

11. Other animals also appear lifeless during the cold winter months.

12. The heavy coats of bears protect them from the cold during hibernation.

Identifying Verbs and Verb Phrases

Write each verb or verb phrase in the following sentences. Then label each one *action verb* or *linking verb*.

1. The world is filled with incredible creatures.
2. Facts about these creatures will be equally incredible.
3. A dragonfly is extremely small.
4. Dragonflies, however, have been clocked at fifty miles per hour.
5. The largest animal in the world actually swims in the ocean.
6. The blue whale can weigh more than thirty elephants.
7. Your pet goldfish might live as long as thirty or forty years!
8. Does a goldfish ever look old?
9. The fastest land animal probably would be given a ticket on a highway.
10. The cheetah can actually run faster than sixty miles per hour.
11. Cockroaches are the oldest species on earth.
12. They looked similar more than 320 million years ago.
13. Do baby cockroaches appear beautiful to their mothers?
14. A skunk can hit something twelve feet away with its smell.
15. Have you ever smelled a skunk's scent?
16. The spray of a skunk smells absolutely horrible!
17. The ostrich egg is by far the biggest egg.
18. Some have actually weighed almost four pounds.
19. An ostrich egg must cook for at least two hours.
20. Have you read about any other incredible creatures?

Understanding Transitive and Intransitive Verbs

Write the verb or verb phrase in each sentence. Then label each verb or verb phrase _T_ for transitive or _I_ for intransitive.

1. Most of the apples fell from the tree during the storm.
2. Spiders have transparent blood.
3. Dad is reading on the porch.
4. Most American car horns beep in the key of F.
5. I usually answer the phone on the second ring.
6. Did you read this book for your book report?
7. Cut the grass tomorrow.
8. The robot will always answer politely.
9. Thomas Jefferson invented the calendar clock.
10. The fire engine rushed through the red light.

Using Verbs

Write ten sentences that follow the directions below. (The sentences may come in any order.) Write about one of the following topics or a topic of your own choice: a pet you have had, a pet you would like to have, a wild animal, or an endangered animal. You also could write about what animal you would like to be and why.

Write a sentence that . . .

1. includes an action verb.
2. includes a linking verb.
3. includes a verb phrase.
4. includes an interrupted verb phrase.
5. includes _taste_ as an action verb.
6. includes _taste_ as a linking verb.
7. includes _look_ as an action verb.
8. includes _look_ as a linking verb.
9. includes _appear_ as an action verb.
10. includes _appear_ as a linking verb.

Underline each verb or verb phrase.

Language and *Self-Expression*

Joan Mitchell paints in a style known as Abstract Expressionism. In this type of painting, techniques such as slashing and sweeping with the brush and dripping, spattering, and pouring paint help artists express their feelings about life.

Think back to a swimming experience you have had that reminds you in some way of the painting. If you prefer, you can imagine such an experience, using the painting as an inspiration. Write a few paragraphs that explain what happened in your experience. Use different kinds of verbs to make the action in your story interesting.

Prewriting Brainstorm some ideas for your story. After you have chosen one of your ideas, you may wish to make a chart showing the sequence of events in your story. Include words such as *first, next, then,* and *finally* to indicate the order of events.

Drafting Use your chart to organize your writing as you draft your story. Choose your verbs carefully to help your readers see, hear, and feel what happens.

Revising Read your story aloud to a classmate. Have your partner tell you if your action verbs are vivid and give life to your work. Replace dull, ordinary verbs with vivid, precise ones.

Editing Check your story for errors in spelling and punctuation. Make any corrections that are necessary. Be sure you spell irregular verbs correctly.

Publishing Make a final copy of your story. Collect it in a volume with classmates' stories. Take the time to read your classmates' stories and think about how the artwork inspired you in different directions.

Another Look

A **verb** is a word used to express an action or a state of being.

Classification of Verbs

An **action verb** tells what action a subject is performing. *(page L69)*

A **helping verb** is used with an action verb or linking verb to form a verb phrase. *(pages L69–L70)*

A **verb phrase** includes a main verb plus any helping verbs. *(page L69)*

COMMON HELPING VERBS	
be	am, is, are, was, were, am, be, being, been
have	has, have, had
do	do, does, did
OTHERS	may, might, must, can, could, shall, should, will, would

A **transitive verb** is an action verb that passes the action from a doer to a receiver. *(pages L72–L73)*

An **intransitive verb** expresses action or states something about the subject, but does not pass the action from a doer to a receiver. *(pages L72–L73)*

A **linking verb** links the subject with another word in the sentence. The other word either renames or describes the subject. Most linking verbs are forms of the verb *be*. *(pages L75–L78)*

Common forms of the verb *be* can be used as linking verbs. *(page L75)*

Other verbs besides *be* can be linking verbs. *(pages L76–L77)*

Most **linking verbs** can also be **action verbs.** *(page L78)*

 **Posttest**

Directions

Write the letter of the term that correctly identifies the underlined word or words in each sentence.

EXAMPLE

1. Jesse's family <u>has</u> visited the same cabin in Maine each summer for eight years.

   1 A transitive verb

      B intransitive verb

      C helping verb

      D linking verb

ANSWER

   1 C

1. Jesse and his father <u>fish</u> for their dinner each day after Jesse comes home from school.

2. They <u>have caught</u> some enormous bass and pickerel that Jesse's father cooks on the grill.

3. Ducks and loons <u>swim</u> on the lake in the pleasant summer evenings.

4. The loon's call <u>sounds</u> eerie.

5. Sometimes the family <u>will hear</u> the loon calls for hours into the night.

6. The water <u>is</u> great for swimming, boating, and skipping stones, too.

7. Jesse's mother <u>can</u> swim for miles.

8. The whole family <u>canoes</u> around the lake in a sturdy craft built by Jesse's grandfather.

9. Sometimes they <u>will paddle</u> the canoe to the small island in the center.

10. There, a huge raven <u>has</u> made a nest.

1	A	transitive verb	6	A	linking verb
	B	intransitive verb		B	transitive verb
	C	helping verb		C	intransitive verb
	D	linking verb		D	helping verb
2	A	helping verb	7	A	transitive verb
	B	intransitive verb		B	helping verb
	C	transitive verb		C	linking verb
	D	linking verb		D	intransitive verb
3	A	linking verb	8	A	intransitive verb
	B	helping verb		B	linking verb
	C	transitive verb		C	transitive verb
	D	intransitive verb		D	helping verb
4	A	transitive verb	9	A	linking verb
	B	helping verb		B	transitive verb
	C	linking verb		C	helping verb
	D	intransitive verb		D	intransitive verb
5	A	intransitive verb	10	A	linking verb
	B	linking verb		B	transitive verb
	C	transitive verb		C	intransitive verb
	D	helping verb		D	helping verb

CHAPTER 4

Adjectives and Adverbs

Pretest

Directions
Write the letter of the term that correctly identifies the underlined word in each sentence.

EXAMPLE   **1.** The <u>county</u> fair is always fun.

    1 **A** adjective
        B proper adjective
        C adverb
        D pronoun

ANSWER   **1** **A**

1. There are <u>wild</u> rides in the carnival section.

2. Sometimes young children become <u>nervous</u> or frightened.

3. The food section <u>always</u> features exotic treats from around the world.

4. The <u>deep-dish</u> pizza is a real favorite among the carnivalgoers.

5. Many people enjoy the <u>Greek</u> salads topped with feta cheese.

6. In long barns the <u>farm</u> animals are judged on appearance and merit.

7. The cows and horses behave <u>well</u>.

8. Last year <u>several</u> of the sheep got loose from their pens.

9. The sheep led their owners on a <u>merry</u> chase around the fair.

10. Needless to say, <u>those</u> sheep did not win prizes.

1	A	adjective	6	A	article
	B	adverb		B	adjective
	C	pronoun		C	adverb
	D	compound adjective		D	noun

2	A	adjective	7	A	adverb
	B	adverb		B	adjective
	C	pronoun		C	article
	D	article		D	pronoun

3	A	adjective	8	A	adverb
	B	proper adjective		B	pronoun
	C	adverb		C	proper adjective
	D	article		D	article

4	A	article	9	A	article
	B	proper adjective		B	compound adjective
	C	adverb		C	adjective
	D	compound adjective		D	pronoun

5	A	adverb	10	A	pronoun
	B	compound adjective		B	adverb
	C	proper adjective		C	article
	D	article		D	adjective

Clara Maria
Nauen-von Malachowski.
Little Girl in a Blue Apron,
ca. 1938.
Oil on board, 27 by 19 inches.
Stadtische Museum,
Monchengladbach.

Describe   What colors stand out in the painting? Why do you think the artist used such vivid colors?

Analyze   What is unusual about the little girl? What do you think this reveals about her?

Interpret   What do you think the artist reveals about herself in this painting?

Judge   What sort of person do you think the child in the painting might be? Do you feel the artist has captured her personality in the portrait? Explain your answer.

At the end of the chapter, you will use this artwork to stimulate ideas for writing.

Your sentences would be very short and dull with only nouns and pronouns.

> The girls watched movies.

However, you can use adjectives and adverbs to give color and sharper meaning to a sentence.

> The **teenage** girls **avidly** watched the **classic** movies **yesterday.**

Adjectives modify, or make more precise, the meanings of nouns and pronouns. For example, what is your favorite movie like? Is it *long, short, happy, interesting,* or *scary?* All these possible answers are adjectives because they all make the meaning of the word *movie* more precise.

An **adjective** is a word that modifies a noun or a pronoun.

To find an adjective, first find each noun and pronoun in a sentence. Then ask yourself, *What kind? Which one(s)? How many?* or *How much?* about each one. The answers will be adjectives.

WHAT KIND?	The **silent** crowd watched the film.
	Do you like **scary** movies?
WHICH ONE(S)?	**That** role was written for the actress.
	I like the **funny** parts.
HOW MANY?	**Thirty** people stood in line to buy a ticket.
	I have seen the movie **many** times.
HOW MUCH?	He deserves **much** praise for his performance.
	Few seats in the theater were empty.

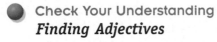

When you speak and write, adjectives should help your listeners or readers picture what you are describing. Some adjectives, however, are used so often that they lose their meaning. When you are revising something you have written, you can look for fresh adjectives in a thesaurus.

OVERUSED ADJECTIVE   I just watched a **great** movie.

FRESH ADJECTIVE   I just watched an **extraordinary** movie.

PRACTICE YOUR SKILLS

● Check Your Understanding
Finding Adjectives

History Topic   **Write the adjectives from the following sentences.**

1. For more than 100 years, people have been entertained in dark theaters.

2. Movies have a rich and interesting history.

3. Thomas Edison and a helpful assistant were among the first people to use celluloid film.

4. Early movies amazed most audiences.

5. Because of a sunny climate, California became the home of modern movies.

6. After many years the first permanent studio was built in Los Angeles in 1911.

7. Because early films did not have sound, a pianist would play musical pieces to accompany the action of the silent film.

8. One of the first filmmakers to shoot different angles with a camera was D. W. Griffith.

9. The lavish costumes and elaborate settings of early films cost a lot of money.

10. Even so, most people went to early movies not to see beautiful costumes but to see popular stars of the era.

Connect to the Writing Process: Drafting
Supplying Adjectives

Write an adjective to complete each sentence.

11. The ■ movie will be opening soon.

12. Do you want a ■ seat or one at the back of the room?

13. It was hard to find my friend in the ■ theater.

14. If we are late, there will be ■ seats available.

15. I love to eat the ■ popcorn from the concession stand.

Connect to the Writing Process: Revising
Using Vivid Adjectives

Write each sentence, replacing the underlined adjective with a more vivid one.

16. Training animals to star in movies is a <u>hard</u> job.

17. How do trainers get <u>cute</u> dogs to bark on cue?

18. <u>Big</u> bears are trained to wrestle with actors without hurting them.

19. Chimpanzees make <u>funny</u> faces at the camera.

20. The <u>good</u> trainers are paid well for their services.

Communicate Your Ideas

APPLY TO WRITING

Movie Review: *Adjectives*

You have been asked to write a review of your favorite movie for the school newspaper. Be sure to include the stars' names. Remember to write about the plot, setting, and costumes. Use descriptive details, including vivid adjectives that will compel others to see the movie. Underline all the adjectives you use in your review.

Different Positions of Adjectives

Adjectives can modify different nouns or pronouns, or they can modify the same noun or pronoun.

DIFFERENT NOUNS	Mandy wore a **red** vest with a **white** shirt.
THE SAME NOUN	The vest had **big blue** buttons.

PUNCTUATION WITH TWO ADJECTIVES

Sometimes you will write two adjectives before the noun they describe. If the adjectives are not connected by a conjunction—such as *and* or *or*—you might need to put a comma between them.

To decide whether a comma belongs, read the adjectives and add the word *and* between them.

- If the adjectives make sense, put a comma in to replace the *and*.
- If the adjectives do not make sense with the word *and* between them, do not add a comma.

COMMA NEEDED	The **soft, furry** vest is on the hanger.
NO COMMA NEEDED	The **red corduroy** vest is in the drawer.

You can learn more about placing commas between multiple adjectives that come before nouns on page L508.

Usually an adjective comes before the noun or pronoun it modifies. However, an adjective can also follow a noun or pronoun, or it can follow a linking verb.

BEFORE A NOUN	She wore the **latest** fashion.
AFTER A NOUN	His shirt, **big** and **baggy,** hung down to his knees.
AFTER A LINKING VERB	Ron looks quite **handsome** today.

You can learn more about adjectives that follow linking verbs on pages L75–L78.

Professional writers use a variety of positions for adjectives, placing some of them before the nouns they modify and others after the nouns they modify. This is one of the ways that writers add variety to their descriptions and make their writing more interesting. Notice the position of the underlined adjectives in Bradbury's description of a Martian spaceship. What does Bradbury do with his adjectives that adds to the effect of his description?

> In the blowing moonlight, like <u>metal</u> petals of some <u>ancient</u> flower, like <u>blue</u> plumes, like <u>cobalt</u> butterflies <u>immense</u> and <u>quiet</u>, the <u>old</u> ships turned and moved over the shifting sands, the masks beaming and glittering, until the <u>last</u> shine, the <u>last blue</u> color, was lost among the hills.

> —*Ray Bradbury*, The Martian Chronicles

PRACTICE YOUR SKILLS

● Check Your Understanding
Finding Adjectives

History Topic **Write the adjectives in each sentence. Then beside each adjective, write the word it modifies.**

1. For several centuries men dressed with more color and greater style than women.

2. During the 1600s, men wore lacy collars and fancy jackets with shiny buttons.

3. Their curly long hair reached their shoulders.

4. Men even carried small purses on huge belts.

5. After all, there were no pockets in the warm, colorful tights they wore.

6. By 1850, men's clothing had become drab and conservative.

7. Gone were the elegant white silk shirts, purple vests, lacy cuffs, and stylish black boots.

8. Men's clothing stayed colorless and dreary until the Beatles came along in the 1960s.

9. Their clothes, bright and informal, created a new style for men.

10. Today, people don't follow one style; everyone dresses to suit personal taste.

11. Still, we are all influenced by current trends.

12. Who knows what strange and wonderful clothes we will be wearing in 2050?

Proper Adjectives

You have learned that a proper noun is the name of a particular person, place, or thing—*Mexico* or *Northeast,* for example. A **proper adjective** is an adjective formed from a proper noun—*Mexican* food and *Northeastern* states, for example. Like a proper noun, a proper adjective begins with a capital letter.

PROPER NOUNS	PROPER ADJECTIVES
Greece	**Greek** salad
France	**French** bread
Mexico	**Mexican** fiesta

Some proper adjectives keep the same form as the proper noun.

PROPER NOUNS	PROPER ADJECTIVES
New York	**New York** restaurant
Monday	**Monday** dinner
Thanksgiving	**Thanksgiving** holiday

You can learn more about capitalizing proper adjectives on pages L479–L480.

 **Compound Adjectives**

You have also learned that compound nouns are nouns made up of two or more words. **Compound adjectives** are adjectives that are made up of two or more words.

COMPOUND ADJECTIVES	
rooftop café	**household** word
faraway lands	**record-breaking** sprint

 Articles

A, an, and *the* form a special group of adjectives called **articles.** *A* comes before words that begin with consonant sounds and *an* before words that begin with vowel sounds.

> **A** new theater showed **an** old movie.

You will not be asked to list the articles in the exercises in this book.

PRACTICE YOUR SKILLS

● Check Your Understanding
Finding Proper and Compound Adjectives

Contemporary Life · **Write the proper adjectives and the compound adjectives in each sentence below. Then beside each adjective, write the word it modifies.**

1. That seafront restaurant offered a variety of dishes from faraway lands.

2. The straightforward waitress described the European delicacies in simple language.

3. While Caribbean music played, diners enjoyed Russian caviar served with Italian bread.

4. One couple ate a Caesar salad with Greek olives.

5. Some Japanese tourists ate Indian food and drank Turkish coffee.

6. The restaurant recently received a five-star rating in an American travel magazine.

7. Our after-dinner treat was some Hawaiian pineapple.

8. The tuxedo-clad waiter brought a Chinese fortune cookie with our check.

9. When they visit, our Canadian friends and I will probably dine at the award-winning restaurant.

10. Of course, I usually prefer a hamburger with Swiss cheese from a fast-food restaurant.

Connect to the Writing Process: Editing
Capitalizing Proper Adjectives

Find the proper adjective in each sentence and rewrite it with a capital letter.

11. Our european vacation took us to some historic places.

12. The london subway system was quite a marvel.

13. Our english hotel was once a famous poet's home.

14. My favorite activity was visiting ancient roman ruins.

15. We even had the opportunity to ski in the swiss Alps.

Communicate Your Ideas

APPLY TO WRITING
Description: *Adjectives*

You have just returned from a visit to a beautiful place. Write a description of the place for your class. Be sure to include details about where and with whom you went. Write about what you did while you were there. Use at least three proper adjectives and three compound adjectives in your description.

Adjective or Noun?

The same word can be an adjective in one sentence and a noun in another sentence.

ADJECTIVE   I hope to finish my **school** assignment before dinner. (*School* tells what kind of work.)

NOUN   I left my English book at **school.** (*School* is the name of a place.)

ADJECTIVE   While setting the table, I broke a **dinner** plate.

NOUN   My father often cooks **dinner.**

PRACTICE YOUR SKILLS

● Check Your Understanding
Distinguishing Between Adjectives and Nouns

Contemporary Life   **Write the underlined word in each sentence. Then label each word *A* for adjective or *N* for noun.**

1. Dad put our dinner in the <u>oven</u>.
2. We sat down to watch a <u>television</u> show.
3. We watched our favorite <u>news</u> program.
4. The reception on our set was bad, so the <u>picture</u> was fuzzy.
5. I put on <u>oven</u> mitts to take the casserole out of the stove.
6. As I brought out the casserole, I dropped the <u>glass</u> dish.
7. My brother and I cleaned up the <u>glass</u>.
8. My mom turned off the <u>television</u>.
9. The <u>news</u> was over.
10. Instead of casserole, we ate sandwiches as we looked out the <u>picture</u> window.

Writing Sentences Using Adjectives and Nouns

Write two sentences for each of the following words. In the first sentence, use the word as an adjective. In the second sentence, use the word as a noun. Label the use of each one.

11. birthday

12. rose

13. bicycle

14. top

15. paper

16. movie

17. snow

18. road

19. lemon

20. school

Adjective or Pronoun?

The following words can be used as adjectives or pronouns.

WORDS USED AS ADJECTIVES OR PRONOUNS			
Demonstrative	**Interrogative**	**Indefinite**	
this	what	all	many
these	which	another	more
that	whose	any	most
those		both	neither
		each	other
		either	several
		few	some

All these words are adjectives if they come before a noun and if they modify a noun. They are pronouns when they stand alone.

ADJECTIVE	I have been to **this** camp before.
PRONOUN	Do you like **this?**
ADJECTIVE	**What** time is it?
PRONOUN	**What** is planned for today?
ADJECTIVE	I called you **several** times before we left.
PRONOUN	**Several** of the campers got poison ivy.

Sometimes the possessive pronouns *my, your, his, her, its, our,* and *their* are called adjectives because they answer the question *Which one?* Throughout this book, however, these words will be considered pronouns.

PRACTICE YOUR SKILLS

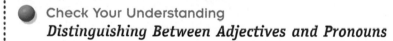

● Check Your Understanding
Distinguishing Between Adjectives and Pronouns

Contemporary Life **Write the underlined word in each sentence. Then label each word *A* for adjective or *P* for pronoun.**

1. <u>Both</u> of my brothers came to camp with me last summer.
2. <u>Some</u> friends came along as well.
3. I prefer <u>this</u> camp to the one I attended two years ago.
4. <u>These</u> mosquitoes will not stop biting me!
5. <u>Which</u> of the canoes do you want?
6. I dropped <u>both</u> paddles into the water.
7. <u>These</u> are designed to float.
8. After <u>this</u>, let's go horseback riding.
9. <u>Which</u> horse is the most gentle?
10. <u>Some</u> of them are very well trained.

Writing Sentences Using Adjectives and Pronouns

Write two sentences for each of the following words. In the first sentence, use the word as an adjective. In the second sentence, use the word as a pronoun. Label the use of each one.

11. many

12. each

13. what

14. several

15. that

16. some

17. both

18. which

19. few

20. neither

Communicate Your Ideas

APPLY TO WRITING

Advertisement: *Adjectives*

You have been hired by an advertising agency to write an ad for a summer camp for teenagers. Decide first what kind of camp you will advertise. Is it a camp in the country, a sports camp, a space camp, or another type of camp? Remember to make the camp appealing to someone like you, but also try to describe a summer experience for which parents would gladly pay. Describe activities, meals, and other aspects of the camp that are enticing. Underline all the adjectives you use in your description.

History Topic **Write each adjective and the word it modifies.**

Nikolai, a Russian athlete, helped the American team win the Olympic ice hockey championship in 1960. The Americans had beaten the Canadian team and the Russian team. Now all they had to do was defeat the Czechs in the final game. After two periods, the Americans were losing. The thin air in the California mountains was slowing them down. Between the second period and the third period, Nikolai visited the weary Americans. Unfortunately he didn't speak any English. Through many gestures, however, he told them to inhale some oxygen. The team immediately felt lively and energetic. For the first time, an American team won the title.

Adverbs

An **adverb** is a word that modifies a verb, an adjective, or another adverb.

Just as adjectives add more information about nouns and pronouns, adverbs make verbs, adjectives, and other adverbs more precise. You probably know that many adverbs end in *-ly*.

> **Recently** my family voted **unanimously** for a vacation in the national forest.
>
> We strolled **casually** through the woods.

Following is a list of common adverbs that do not end in *-ly*.

COMMON ADVERBS			
afterward	far	not (n't)	soon
again	fast	now	still
almost	hard	nowhere	straight
alone	here	often	then
already	just	outside	there
also	late	perhaps	today
always	long	quite	tomorrow
away	low	rather	too
before	more	seldom	very
down	near	so	well
even	never	sometimes	yesterday
ever	next	somewhat	yet

You probably use many contractions in casual conversation. *Not* and its contraction *n't* are always adverbs.

> We could **not** find our binoculars.
> **Don't** disturb the other campers.

Adverbs That Modify Verbs

Most adverbs modify verbs. To find these adverbs, first find the verb. Then ask yourself, *Where? When? How?* or *To what extent?* about the verb. The answers to these questions will be adverbs. The adverbs in the following examples are in bold type. An arrow points to the verb each adverb modifies.

WHERE?	Look **everywhere** for wildlife.
	Wild animals are **there.**
WHEN?	We **frequently** camp in the forest.
	I **sometimes** sleep in a tent.
HOW?	I **carefully** approached the deer.
	The animal **swiftly** and **surely** jumped over the boulder.
TO WHAT EXTENT?	My sister **completely** enjoys the experience.
	We have **almost** arrived at the waterfall.

An adverb can come before or after the verb or in the middle of a verb phrase.

CONNECT TO SPEAKING AND WRITING

Sentence variety is important in effective writing. You can give your writing added variety by beginning some sentences with an adverb.

The group of hikers **wearily** trudged into camp.
Wearily the group of hikers trudged into camp.

They saw mosquitoes **everywhere.**
Everywhere they saw mosquitoes.

PRACTICE YOUR SKILLS

Finding Adverbs That Modify Verbs

Science Topic | **Write the adverbs in each sentence. Then beside each adverb, write the verb it modifies.**

1. Porcupines never shoot their quills.
2. Usually the quills catch on something.
3. Then they fall out.
4. Porcupines always use their quills for protection.
5. Occasionally another animal will greatly disturb a porcupine.
6. The porcupine's quills will immediately stand upright.
7. Often the porcupine will bump the other animal.
8. The quills do not miss.
9. They stick swiftly and securely in the animal's skin.
10. An animal rarely bothers a porcupine twice.

Connect to the Writing Process: Drafting
Using Adverbs for Sentence Variety

Use each of the following adverbs at the beginning of a sentence about a forest.

11. suddenly
12. twice
13. happily
14. soon
15. clumsily
16. surprisingly
17. always
18. narrowly
19. tomorrow
20. totally

APPLY TO WRITING

Writer's Craft: *Analyzing the Use of Adverbs*

Writers often use the placement of words to create an effect on their audiences. In this passage from *The Great Gatsby,* F. Scott Fitzgerald describes a tense encounter between two of the main characters. Read the passage and then follow the instructions below.

> The telephone rang inside, startlingly, and as Daisy shook her head decisively at Tom the subject of the stables, in fact all subjects, vanished into air. Among the broken fragments of the last five minutes at table I remember the candles being lit again, pointlessly.
>
> —*F. Scott Fitzgerald*, The Great Gatsby

- Write all of the adverbs in the passage. (You should find five adverbs.)
- What do you notice about Fitzgerald's placement of adverbs?
- What is the total effect of this placement?

Adverbs That Modify Adjectives and Other Adverbs

A few adverbs modify adjectives and other adverbs.

MODIFYING AN ADJECTIVE	Visiting national parks is **always** fun.
MODIFYING AN ADVERB	You should approach wild animals **very** cautiously.

To find adverbs that modify adjectives or other adverbs, first find the adjectives and the adverbs in a sentence. Then ask yourself *To what extent?* about each one. Notice in the preceding examples that the adverbs that modify adjectives or other adverbs usually come before the word they modify.

PRACTICE YOUR SKILLS

● Check Your Understanding
Finding Adverbs that Modify Adjectives and Other Adverbs

General
Interest
Write each adverb that modifies an adjective or another adverb. Then beside each adverb, write the word it modifies.

1. Yellowstone National Park is an exceptionally beautiful place.
2. The drive through the park can be rather long.
3. As they drive, tourists go very slowly as they attempt to see wildlife.
4. Bison and moose are quite abundant in the park.
5. Bears are almost never seen from the roadways.
6. Geysers are surprisingly common attractions in the park.
7. Old Faithful, a large geyser, is the most famous one in the park.
8. The benches around Old Faithful are extremely full of tourists.
9. Due to minerals in the water, a sulfur smell is very strong throughout the park.
10. If you decide to go, plan your vacation very early in the summer.
11. The park is unusually busy in July.
12. May is most assuredly the best month to visit the park.

Rewrite the following sentences, adding an adverb to modify the underlined adjective or adverb.

13. My trip to Yellowstone this past summer was <u>interesting</u>.

14. I met <u>active</u> people.

15. They were <u>friendly</u>.

16. The park is full of <u>attractive</u> sites.

17. I liked the <u>famous</u> geyser.

18. I camped <u>comfortably</u> in my tent.

19. <u>Often</u> I went fishing for trout and salmon in a <u>rushing</u> stream.

20. The water I stood in was <u>cold</u>.

21. I caught a trout that was <u>lively</u>.

22. I also climbed a <u>nearby</u> rock face.

23. It was a <u>steep</u> climb to the top.

24. I saw that the water in the Morning Glory Pool is <u>clear</u>.

25. The time flew by <u>quickly</u> during that week.

26. Although I enjoyed the trip, I was <u>glad</u> to return to my home.

27. I had missed my <u>familiar</u> friends.

28. It felt <u>good</u> to sleep in a bed again.

29. I missed the <u>wonderful</u> sights and sounds of the natural world, however.

30. I can almost hear the <u>noisy</u> crickets.

31. I still dream of the <u>beautiful</u> trees.

32. I did not miss bumping into other campers at <u>every</u> turn.

Adverb or Adjective?

As you have seen in the previous section, many adverbs end in -*ly*. You should, however, be aware that some adjectives end in -*ly*. In addition, many words can be used as either adverbs or adjectives. Always check to see how a word is used in a sentence before you decide what part of speech it is.

ADVERB	We visit my Aunt Sylvia **yearly.**
ADJECTIVE	Our **yearly** visits to Aunt Sylvia are filled with fun.
ADVERB	My cousin hit the baseball quite **hard.**
ADJECTIVE	The **hard** ball broke Aunt Sylvia's window.

You can learn about the comparison of adverbs and adjectives on pages L413–L421.

PRACTICE YOUR SKILLS

Check Your Understanding
Distinguishing Between Adjectives and Adverbs

Contemporary Life   **Write the underlined word in each sentence. Then label each one as *adverb* or *adjective*.**

1. My <u>early</u> memories are filled with visits to Aunt Sylvia's house in the country.
2. She had a warm smile and <u>lively</u> eyes.
3. I <u>especially</u> loved her delicious apple pies.
4. Her house was <u>high</u> on a hill overlooking an open field of wildflowers.
5. My cousins and I <u>joyfully</u> roamed the countryside near her home.
6. <u>Sometimes</u> we would swim in the lake.
7. We knew the area very <u>well</u>.
8. We <u>always</u> had a good time.

9. All of Aunt Sylvia's neighbors were <u>friendly</u> to us.
10. We would run <u>loudly</u> through her house.
11. Aunt Sylvia was <u>extremely</u> patient.
12. My cousins would climb to <u>high</u> perches in Aunt Sylvia's trees.
13. After a big supper on the porch, we went to bed <u>early</u>.
14. It was <u>easy</u> for us to fall asleep.
15. We were feeling <u>well</u> the next morning.
16. The <u>rich</u> smell of hot pancakes greeted us.
17. We <u>happily</u> raced to the table.
18. We ate <u>slowly</u> so we could savor the maple syrup she had warmed for us.
19. Those pancakes were the <u>best</u> I have tasted.
20. The sausage Aunt Sylvia served with them was <u>excellent</u>.

● Connect to the Writing Process: Drafting
Writing Sentences

Write two sentences for each word. In the first, use the word as an adverb and in the second as an adjective.

21. monthly
22. low
23. closer
24. just
25. kindly
26. late
27. higher
28. farthest
29. daily
30. hard

APPLY TO WRITING
Description: *Adverbs*

Carmen Lomas Garza. *Sandía/Watermelon,* 1986. Gouache painting, 20 by 28 inches. Collection of Dudley D. Brooks and Tomas Ybarra-Frausto, New York. ©1986 Carmen Lomas Garza.

Look carefully at Carmen Lomas Garza's painting *Sandía/ Watermelon*. Pretend that you are the boy sitting on the steps. Describe the scene from his point of view, as if he were talking to a friend. What is happening? Remember to include details such as what time of day it is and who the other people are. Use adverbs in your description to make the picture come alive. Underline each adverb you use in your writing.

QuickCheck Mixed Practice

General Interest **Write the adverbs in the following paragraphs. Then beside each adverb, write the word or words it modifies.**

The first pair of roller skates appeared in 1760. They were unsuccessfully worn by Joseph Merlin. Merlin had unexpectedly received an invitation to a very large party. Quite excitedly, he planned a grand entrance. The night finally arrived. Merlin rolled unsteadily into the ballroom on skates as he played a violin. Unfortunately, he couldn't stop. Merlin crashed into an extremely large mirror. The mirror broke into a million pieces. Merlin also smashed his violin and hurt himself severely

Roller skates were never used again until 1823. Robert Tyers eventually made another attempt. His skates had a single row of five very small wheels. In 1863, James Plimpton finally patented the first pair of four-wheel skates. With these skates, people could keep their balance easily. They could even make very sharp turns. In-line skates would not be reinvented for many years.

Diagraming Adjectives and Adverbs

Adjectives and adverbs are diagramed on slanted lines below the words they modify.

My small brother swam.

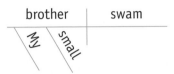

He swam skillfully.

He | swam

skillfully

My small but strong brother swam fast and skillfully.

An adverb that modifies an adjective or another adverb is written on a line parallel to the word it modifies.

The extremely smart child won.

child | won

The   *smart*

extremely

She ate too quickly.

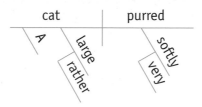

A rather large cat purred very softly.

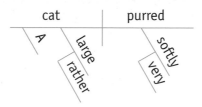

PRACTICE YOUR SKILLS

Diagraming Adjectives and Adverbs

Diagram the following sentences or copy them. If you copy them, draw one line under each subject and two lines under each verb. Then label each modifier *adj.* for adjective or *adv.* for adverb.

1. A large octopus appeared.

2. It paused briefly.

3. Octopuses can move very quickly.

4. They also swim forward and backward.

5. The extremely large arms stretched out.

6. Suddenly an inky fluid squirted out.

7. Some small fish were blinded.

8. Others were even poisoned.

9. Then this large but flexible creature turned.

10. Suddenly it swam away forever.

Identifying Adjectives and Adverbs

For each sentence below, draw a line under each modifier and label each one *adj.* for adjective or *adv.* for adverb. Do not include articles (*a, an,* and *the*).

1. Recently thirty students and several teachers took a bus trip from South Carolina to the Everglades National Park in the southern part of Florida.

2. This national park uniquely combines prairies, swamps, saltwater marshes, and freshwater lakes.

3. The Everglades is actually a river, a very unusual river.

4. It flows from Lake Okeechobee southward to the Gulf of Mexico.

5. Everyone carefully got into canoes for a tour of the Everglades.

6. Initially the landscape seemed somewhat monotonous to these first-time visitors.

7. Then they looked closely and saw hundreds of unusual things.

8. The park is the home to a large variety of animals.

9. Alligators are the most famous occupants of the park.

10. The ranger pointed to the tall, dense grasses.

11. Students immediately and excitedly saw two huge alligators in the grass.

12. Suddenly everyone looked up into the cloudless blue sky.

13. A roseate spoonbill, large and graceful, landed nearby on a park pond. (*Roseate spoonbill* is the whole name of the bird.)

14. The pink color of the bird comes from the many shrimp it eats.

15. Every South Carolina student also saw many different birds, fish, turtles, and snakes.

Distinguishing Among Different Parts of Speech

Write the underlined words in each sentence. Then label each one *N* for noun, *P* for pronoun, *adj.* for adjective, or *adv.* for adverb.

1. Your <u>apple</u> pie tastes much better than <u>this</u>.
2. <u>Both</u> of my brothers went to the <u>play</u> rehearsal.
3. <u>Most</u> drivers couldn't see the <u>street</u> sign.
4. <u>Some</u> of the fawns stood <u>close</u> to their mothers.
5. I have waited a long time to see <u>this</u> <u>play</u>.
6. The <u>car</u> roared down the <u>street</u>.
7. The <u>kindly</u> gentleman offered <u>some</u> good advice.
8. <u>Most</u> of the <u>car</u> dealers are holding sales.
9. <u>Apples</u> were given to <u>both</u> children.
10. She spoke <u>kindly</u> of her <u>close</u> friend.

Using Adjectives and Adverbs

Write ten sentences that follow the directions below. (The sentences may come in any order.) Write about one of the following topics or a topic of your own choice: a place you have visited or a place you would like to visit.

Write a sentence that. . .

1. includes two adjectives before a noun.
2. includes an adjective after a linking verb.
3. includes two adjectives after a noun.
4. includes a proper adjective.
5. includes a compound adjective.
6. includes *that* as an adjective.
7. includes an adverb at the beginning of a sentence.
8. includes the adverb *very*.
9. includes *daily* as an adjective.
10. includes *daily* as an adverb.

Language and *Self-Expression*

Clara Maria Nauen-von Malachowski was a German painter who worked in the style known as German Expressionism. Expressionists used simple designs and brilliant colors to express feelings, thoughts, and moods. How do you think the artist uses color and design to express a mood in the portrait?

A portrait can tell us a great deal about a person. You can paint a portrait in words, too. Think of someone you know who would make a good subject for a portrait in words. What is special, unusual, or memorable about the person? Write a description of the person, using vivid adjectives and adverbs to paint an effective word portrait.

Prewriting Create a Character-Traits Chart for your subject. In it, briefly describe his or her physical characteristics and personality traits.

Drafting Use the Character-Traits Chart to organize your description. Your sentences should include adjectives and adverbs that tell why your subject is special.

Revising Reread your description. Have you introduced your subject in a way that will grab a reader's attention? Is your word portrait vivid enough? Substitute interesting adjectives and adverbs for less vivid words.

Editing Check your description for errors in spelling and punctuation. Place your adjectives and adverbs in a variety of positions in your sentences. If you use more than one adjective to describe a noun or pronoun, separate the adjectives with a comma if necessary. Capitalize proper adjectives.

Publishing Make a final copy of your description and show it to your subject.

Another Look

> An **adjective** is a word that modifies a noun or a pronoun.

Kinds of Adjectives

A **proper adjective** is an adjective that is formed from a proper noun and begins with a capital letter. *(page L96)*

A **compound adjective** is an adjective that is made up of two or more words. *(page L97)*

A, an, and *the* form a special group of adjectives called **articles.** *A* comes before words that begin with consonant sounds and *an* before words that begin with vowel sounds. *(page L97)*

> An **adverb** is a word that modifies a verb, an adjective, or another adverb.

To find adverbs that modify verbs, find the verb. Then ask *Where? When, How?* or *To what extent?* about the verb. The answers to these questions will be adverbs. *(page L105)*

To find adverbs that modify adjectives and other adverbs, find the adjectives and adverbs in a sentence. Then ask *To what extent?* about each one. The answers to this question will be adverbs. *(pages L107–L108)*

Many adverbs end in -ly. *(page L104)*

Not and its contraction *n't* are always adverbs. *(page L104)*

Other Information About Adjectives and Adverbs

Using punctuation with two adjectives *(page L94)*
Distinguishing between adjectives and nouns *(page L99)*
Distinguishing between adjectives and pronouns *(pages L100–L101)*
Distinguishing between adverbs and adjectives *(page L110)*

Posttest

Directions

Read the passage. Write the letter of the answer each underlined adjective or adverb modifies.

EXAMPLE   Flying squirrels <u>actually</u> glide rather than fly
                                    (1)

through the air.

  1 **A** Flying squirrels

      B glide

      C fly

      D air

ANSWER   **1** **B**

The wooly flying squirrel is very <u>rare</u>. It is found only in <u>the</u>
                                    (1)   (2)

Himalayan Mountains of northern Pakistan. It is <u>much</u> larger than
                                                   (3)

other flying squirrels and may be the largest squirrel in the world.

It sails <u>gracefully</u> off cliff ledges and glides to the trees <u>below</u>.
            (4)   (5)

Skin membranes between its wrists and hind legs allow it to glide

<u>long</u> distances. It uses its <u>flat</u> tail to guide its flight. For <u>many</u>
  (6)   (7)   (8)

years, scientists thought the wooly flying squirrel was extinct.

Scientists <u>recently</u> rediscovered it, and its <u>high-altitude</u> habitat is
              (9)   (10)

now being preserved.

1	A	the	6	A	allow
	B	flying squirrel		B	it
	C	is		C	distances
	D	wooly		D	wrists
2	A	Himalayan Mountains	7	A	uses
	B	it		B	tail
	C	Pakistan		C	guide
	D	only		D	flight
3	A	flying	8	A	scientists
	B	other		B	years
	C	larger		C	squirrel
	D	squirrels		D	extinct
4	A	cliff	9	A	rediscovered
	B	sails		B	scientists
	C	it		C	it
	D	glides		D	habitat
5	A	glides	10	A	its
	B	cliff		B	scientists
	C	sails		C	preserved
	D	ledges		D	habitat

CHAPTER 5

Other Parts of Speech

· ·

✓ Pretest

Directions
Write the letter of the term that correctly identifies the underlined word in each sentence.

EXAMPLE   **1.** Danielle decided to give a dinner party <u>during</u> spring vacation.

    1 A interjection
       B preposition
       C adverb
       D coordinating conjunction

ANSWER   **1 B**

1. Danielle had never cooked a whole dinner before, <u>but</u> she was eager to try.
2. Danielle began <u>at</u> noon.
3. <u>First</u> she baked an apple pie.
4. <u>Not only</u> did she put too much flour in the crust, <u>but</u> she <u>also</u> forgot the sugar.
5. She then placed a large rump roast on a tray <u>in</u> the oven.
6. First she forgot to turn on the oven, <u>and</u> then she turned it on too high.
7. <u>Oh, no!</u> The smoke alarm went off!
8. At the same time, two pots on the stove boiled <u>over</u>.
9. <u>In spite of</u> these disasters, Danielle remained cool and collected.
10. Before the guests could figure out what had happened, Danielle whisked them off <u>to</u> a pizza parlor.

1.
   A coordinating conjunction
   B preposition
   C correlative conjunction
   D adverb

2.
   A coordinating conjunction
   B correlative conjunction
   C interjection
   D preposition

3.
   A preposition
   B interjection
   C adverb
   D adjective

4.
   A coordinating conjunctions
   B correlative conjunctions
   C prepositions
   D adverbs

5.
   A interjection
   B coordinating conjunction
   C preposition
   D adverb

6.
   A adverb
   B coordinating conjunction
   C correlative conjunction
   D preposition

7.
   A interjection
   B preposition
   C adverb
   D adjective

8.
   A interjection
   B adjective
   C adverb
   D preposition

9.
   A coordinating conjunction
   B preposition
   C correlative conjunction
   D interjection

10.
   A adjective
   B correlative conjunction
   C coordinating conjunction
   D preposition

Artist unknown. *Hall of Bulls and Horses,* date unknown.
Montignac, France.

Describe What colors did the artist use? What images do you recognize?

Analyze What do you think the artist intended to represent? What story was he or she telling?

Interpret What information can you infer about the artist from the images in the painting? What might some of his or her hopes and fears have been?

Judge Do you think cave paintings such as this one are important to our understanding of Ice Age peoples? How might they supplement discoveries of tools or other artifacts? Explain.

At the end of the chapter, you will use this artwork to stimulate ideas for writing.

Prepositions

A **preposition** is a word that shows the relationship between a noun or a pronoun and another word in the sentence.

The three words in **bold** print in the following sentences are prepositions. Each of these prepositions shows a different relationship between Lori and the letter. As a result, changing only the preposition will alter the meaning of the whole sentence.

> The letter **to** Lori was lost.
>
> The letter **from** Lori was lost.
>
> The letter **about** Lori was lost.

Following is a list of the most common prepositions.

COMMON PREPOSITIONS				
aboard	before	down	off	till
about	behind	during	on	to
above	below	except	onto	toward
across	beneath	for	opposite	under
after	beside	from	out	underneath
against	besides	in	outside	until
along	between	inside	over	up
among	beyond	into	past	upon
around	but (except)	like	since	with
as	by	near	through	within
at	despite	of	throughout	without

A preposition that is made up of two or more words is called a **compound preposition.**

COMMON COMPOUND PREPOSITIONS		
according to	by means of	instead of
ahead of	in addition to	in view of
apart from	in back of	next to
as of	in front of	on account of
aside from	in place of	out of
because of	in spite of	prior to

PRACTICE YOUR SKILLS

 Check Your Understanding

Finding Prepositions

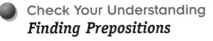 History Topic **Write the prepositions from the following sentences.**

1. The legendary Pony Express rode its way into American history.

2. The riders' trail began at Joseph, Missouri.

3. A weary rider would often reach California in ten days.

4. Wild Bill Cody was one of the riders for this early mail system.

5. In spite of its popularity, the Pony Express lasted only eighteen months.

6. Because of its expense, the Pony Express cost its owners $200,000.

7. Later, dromedary camels were imported from the Middle East.

8. However, the camels were not used for regular mail service.

9. These dromedaries delivered salt between several western towns.

10. Today, the United States mail is transported by airplanes and trucks.

Supplying Prepositions

Write each sentence twice, using a different preposition to fill each blank.

11. The mail plane flew ▨ the storm clouds.

12. The package ▨ the chair is mine.

13. Caleb should go ▨ the post office.

14. A letter came ▨ Christopher.

15. Get the mail ▨ the mailbox.

16. ▨ that package you will find the tape dispenser.

17. Will you open the box ▨ me?

Prepositional Phrases

A **prepositional phrase** begins with a preposition and ends with a noun or a pronoun.

A preposition is always part of a group of words called a prepositional phrase. The noun or pronoun that ends the prepositional phrase is called the **object of the preposition.** Any number of modifiers can come between a preposition and its object.

> England is the setting *of* **this suspenseful mystery.**
>
> The detective chases the criminal *through* **London's streets.**

A sentence can have several prepositional phrases, and the phrases can come anywhere in the sentence.

> *Without* **a moment's hesitation,** the detective leaped *into* **the criminal's path.**
>
> *Before* **the end** *of* **books** *by* **Agatha Christie,** I usually can identify the criminal.

You can create sentence variety by starting some sentences with prepositional phrases.

The true villain is always discovered *by the book's end.*
By the book's end, the true villain is always discovered.

I like mysteries *because of the suspense.*
Because of the suspense, I like mysteries.

PRACTICE YOUR SKILLS

● Check Your Understanding
Finding Prepositional Phrases

General Interest **Write the prepositional phrases in the following sentences.**

1. A nurse at a London hospital had a young girl in her ward.

2. None of the doctors could find a cure for her.

3. Before work the nurse read a chapter in a mystery by Agatha Christie.

4. After several pages she put the book into her bag and hurried to the hospital.

5. According to the book, someone had taken a rare poison called thallium.

6. The description of the victim's symptoms matched the symptoms of the young girl.

7. The nurse placed the book in front of the doctors.

8. She told them about her suspicions.

9. Within minutes the doctors prescribed a new series of treatments for the girl.

10. Because of a mystery by Agatha Christie, a young girl's life was saved.

Use each preposition below in a sentence. Then rewrite the sentence, changing the position of the prepositional phrase to create a variation on the original sentence.

11. next to   **13.** because of   **15.** in back of

12. through   **14.** beyond   **16.** around

Communicate Your Ideas

APPLY TO WRITING

Setting: *Prepositional Phrases*

You are working for a famous movie producer who is look-ing for a location for a film based on a mystery novel. You come across this building and determine it would be per-fect. After realizing your camera is not working, you decide to write a description of the setting. Remember that prepositional phrases will help your producer picture the setting. Underline the prepositional phrases you use.

Preposition or Adverb?

The same word can be used as a preposition in one sentence and an adverb in another sentence. Just remember that a preposition is always part of a prepositional phrase. An adverb stands alone.

PREPOSITION	**Below the stairs** is the storage area for our new sleds.
ADVERB	The snow fell from the roof to the ground **below.**
PREPOSITION	We raced **up the hill**
ADVERB	Pull your sled **up** onto the porch.

You can learn more about prepositional phrases on pages L173–L182.

PRACTICE YOUR SKILLS

● Check Your Understanding
Distinguishing Between Prepositions and Adverbs

Contemporary Life **Write the underlined word in each sentence. Then label it *P* for preposition or *A* for adverb.**

1. Last week a blizzard raged <u>outside</u> our warm house.
2. Snow accumulated <u>around</u> the town.
3. The flakes drifted <u>off</u> our roof.
4. Today, the weather <u>outside</u> is perfect for sledding.
5. My friends and I looked <u>around</u> for our sleds.
6. I went <u>down</u> the hill before Jaime.
7. <u>Down</u> the hill I raced on my sled.
8. I fell <u>off</u> near the bottom of the hill.
9. Jaime had never been sledding <u>before</u>.
10. He squealed as his sled raced <u>down</u>.
11. It was hard pulling our sleds back <u>up</u> the hill.
12. <u>Behind</u> me Jamie complained loudly.

Writing Sentences

Write two sentences using each of the words below. In the first sentence, use the word as a preposition. In the second sentence, use it as an adverb.

13. near
14. across
15. out
16. aboard
17. within
18. beneath

19. outside
20. before
21. on
22. over
23. around
24. beyond

QuickCheck Mixed Practice

General Interest **Write the prepositional phrases from the following paragraph.**

In the Beartooth Mountains of Montana, there is a most unusual glacier. Within the ice of the glacier are frozen millions of grasshoppers. According to scientists, an immense swarm of grasshoppers made a forced landing on the glacier two centuries ago! They were then quickly frozen by a snowstorm. Today the grasshoppers are still well preserved. During the warm weather, birds and animals throughout the region flock to the glacier for an addition to their normal sources of food. When the ice melts, the grasshoppers provide them with a most unusual meal.

Conjunctions

A **conjunction** connects words or groups of words. One kind of conjunction is the **coordinating conjunction,** a single connecting word.

COORDINATING CONJUNCTIONS						
and	but	for	nor	or	so	yet

SINGLE WORDS

An astronomer observes **stars *and* planets.** (nouns)

He *or* she watches the night sky. (pronouns)

They **watch** asteroids ***and* chart** their courses. (verbs)

The astronomer's job is **difficult *but* interesting.** (adjectives)

Now *and* then, they discover a new comet. (adverbs)

GROUPS OF WORDS

He looked **through the telescope *and* into space.** (prepositional phrases)

Earth has one moon, *but* Neptune has eight satellites. (sentences)

Correlative conjunctions are pairs of connecting words.

CORRELATIVE CONJUNCTIONS		
both/and	either/or	neither/nor
not only/but also		whether/or

Both **Gretta** *and* **Emmaline** own telescopes.

You should study *either* **comets** *or* **asteroids**.

You can learn about the third type of conjunction, a subordinating conjunction, on pages 225–226.

CONNECT TO WRITER'S CRAFT

When you revise your writing, you can often use conjunctions to make your writing more interesting. You can combine sentences or elements of sentences to make your writing less repetitive.

The moon is bright tonight. We can see only see a few stars.
The moon is bright tonight, **so** we can see only a few stars.

Our group can study the moon. We can study the planets.
Our group can study **either** the moon **or** the planets.

PRACTICE YOUR SKILLS

● Check Your Understanding
Finding Conjunctions

Science Topic **Write the coordinating or correlative conjunctions in each sentence.**

1. Neither Mercury nor Venus has its own natural satellite.

2. After Mars and before Jupiter, there lies an asteroid belt.

3. Earth rotates on its axis and revolves around the sun.

4. Pluto is the most distant planet, so it was not discovered until 1930.

5. Each planet is classified as either an inner or an outer planet.

6. Ceres is a large asteroid, but most asteroids are relatively small.

7. Both beautiful and mysterious, Saturn's rings can be observed from Earth through binoculars.

8. Slowly but surely, the planets make their way around the sun.

9. A meteor is a rock or a metal fragment that enters Earth's atmosphere.

10. Humans have studied the heavens for centuries, yet many mysteries remain.

Connect to the Writing Process: Revising
Using Conjunctions to Combine Sentences

Combine each pair of sentences into one sentence using coordinating or correlative conjunctions.

11. Carmen wrote a report about black holes. Maria wrote a report about black holes.

12. You can read a book about quasars. You can see a video about quasars.

13. My dad knows nothing about space. My mom took astronomy in college.

14. Tell Jesse about meteors. Tell Jesse about comets.

15. Mercury is my favorite planet. I wrote a play about Mercury.

Communicate Your Ideas

APPLY TO WRITING

Directions: *Conjunctions*

You are writing directions to your house for a new friend. Write directions that begin at your school and explain the best way to reach your home. Remember to be specific and make the directions easy to follow. Use at least two coordinating conjunctions and one correlative conjunction. After completing your directions, underline the conjunctions you used in your writing.

Interjections

An **interjection** is a word that expresses strong feeling or emotion.

Interjections express feelings such as joy or anger. They usually come at the beginning of a sentence. Since they are not related to the rest of the sentence, they are separated from it by a comma or an exclamation point.

Hurrah! Our team won.

Well, they have worked hard.

Yeah, now they compete for the championship.

Wow! I can't believe it.

PRACTICE YOUR SKILLS

 Check Your Understanding
Finding Interjections

Contemporary Life **Write the interjections from the following sentences.**

1. Oh, did you see that pass?
2. Whew! I can't believe Jim caught it.
3. Hurrah, he's running down the field!
4. Great, he made a touchdown!
5. Gee, what a great play that was!
6. Hey, wait for me!
7. Goodness, what a heavy suitcase this is.
8. No! What more can go wrong?
9. Ugh! This is awful.
10. Yeah, I'm on my way.

Using the following interjections, write sentences about the hockey game in the picture. Remember to separate the interjection from the rest of the sentence with a comma or an exclamation point.

11. aha

12. ouch

13. well

14. oops

15. wow

16. yes

17. no

18. terrific

19. oh

20. surprise

How a word is used in a sentence determines its part of speech. For example, the word *near* can be used as four different parts of speech.

VERB	The plant will **near** its full growth soon.
ADJECTIVE	I will plant my flower garden in the **near** future.
ADVERB	The best planting time is drawing **near.**
PREPOSITION	Plant the flowers ***near*** *the house.*

To find out what part of speech a word is, ask yourself, *What is each word doing in this sentence?*

NOUN	Is the word naming a person, place, thing, or idea?
	Nathaniel bought **plants** at the **nursery.**
PRONOUN	Is the word taking the place of a noun?
	This is **my** favorite flower.
VERB	Is the word showing action?
	Kiki **planted** the rose bush.
	Does the word link two words in the sentence?
	The daisy **is** a simple flower.
ADJECTIVE	Is the word modifying a noun or a pronoun? Does it answer *What kind? Which one(s)? How many?* or *How much?*
	Three yellow tulips bloomed today.
ADVERB	Is the word modifying an adverb, an adjective, or another adverb? Does it answer the question *How? When? Where?* or *To what extent?*
	The seedling grew **very quickly** in the **extremely** rich soil.

PREPOSITION	Is the word showing a relationship between a noun or pronoun and another word in the sentence?
	***Because of* the sunlight,** the plant grew well *on* **the windowsill.**
CONJUNCTION	Is the word connecting words or groups of words?
	Kiki and I grow **neither** fruits **nor** vegetables.
	I planted marigolds, **but** they didn't grow.
INTERJECTION	Is the word expressing strong feelings?
	Wow! The petunias in the window box are blooming.

PRACTICE YOUR SKILLS

● Check Your Understanding
Determining Parts of Speech

General
Interest
Write the underlined words. (There are 25 words.) Then beside each word, write its part of speech, using the following abbreviations:

noun = *n.*
pronoun = *pron.*
verb = *v.*
adverb = *adv.*

adjective = *adj.*
preposition = *prep.*
conjunction = *conj.*
interjection = *interj.*

Caution! Music may wilt your leaves. In 1969, Dorothy Retallack ran some experiments with plants and music. She proved that music affects the growth of plants. In one test, loud rock greatly stunted the growth of corn, squash, and several flowers. In another test, several of the plants grew tall, but their leaves were extremely small. Also, they needed water, and their roots were very short. Within several weeks all the marigolds in one experiment died. Identical healthy flowers, however, bloomed nearby. These flowers had been listening to classical music!

● Connect to the Writing Process: Drafting
Writing Sentences

Write two sentences using the underlined word as directed.

26. Use light as a verb and a noun.

27. Use that as a pronoun and an adjective.

28. Use below as a preposition and an adverb.

29. Use these as a pronoun and an adjective.

30. Use secret as an adjective and a noun.

Communicate Your Ideas

APPLY TO WRITING

Informative Writing: *Parts of Speech*

You are a creature from another planet who has been sent to Earth by your government to report on the lives of human beings. Your ship lands near a high school gymnasium. Unseen, you enter the gym and watch a basketball game. Since you have no idea what is going on, you decide that you must write a report to the people of your planet describing this bizarre Earth ritual. Be sure to include details of the things you see around you. Describe them from the point of view of someone who is totally foreign to this world. In your report use each of the parts of speech at least once. Be prepared to point out one or more nouns, pronouns, verbs, adjectives, adverbs, prepositions, conjunctions, and interjections.

Identifying Prepositions, Conjunctions, Interjections, and Prepositional Phrases

Write each sentence. Then label each of the following parts of speech *preposition, conjunction,* **and** *interjection.* **Finally, underline each prepositional phrase.**

1. Wow! You have a really big test ahead of you on Friday.
2. Never wait until the last minute.
3. Start two nights before any test.
4. Review both your material and your notes from class.
5. Yes! Study with a friend or classmate.
6. Not only review old tests throughout your notebook, but also look for certain kinds of familiar questions.
7. During the night before the test, review the most important points and the main topics.
8. Neither study late nor stay up late.
9. According to many studies, your brain will need proper food and rest for the best results.
10. Avoid sweets like doughnuts around the time of the test.

Determining Parts of Speech

Write the underlined words. Then beside each word, write its part of speech using the following abbreviations.

noun = *n.*   pronoun = *pron.*   verb = *v.*
adjective = *adj.*   adverb = *adv.*   preposition = *prep.*
conjunction = *conj.* interjection = *interj.*

In 1928, a farmer was planting <u>horseradishes</u> in a field <u>in</u> <u>West Virginia</u>. He noticed a greasy, <u>shiny</u> stone. He picked it <u>up</u> and took <u>it</u> home. <u>Ten</u> years later he made a startling discovery. The stone was a thirty-two-carat diamond. Wow!

Diamonds, however, are not necessarily rare in the United States. The Eagle diamond was found in Wisconsin. Other large stones have also been discovered in Ohio, Illinois, and Indiana.

Determining Parts of Speech

Write the underlined words. Then beside each word, write its part of speech using the following abbreviations.

noun = *n.*   pronoun = *pron.*   verb = *v.*
adjective = *adj.*   adverb = *adv.*   preposition = *prep.*
conjunction = *conj.*   interjection = *interj.*

1. Steel workers were laid off because demand for steel dropped.
2. Did those horses really eat those?
3. Turn left because a left turn will take you to the park.
4. Will you water the plants with the water in this can?
5. Everyone drew near and sat near the fire.

Completing Sentence Skeletons

Make up ten sentences matching the ten skeletons below. You can use an article (*a, an,* or *the*) for an adjective. Use the following abbreviations: noun (*n.*), pronoun (*pron.*), verb (*v.*), adjective (*adj.*), adverb (*adv.*), preposition (*prep.*), conjunction (*conj.*), or interjection (*interj.*).

EXAMPLE   *adj.   n.   prep.   adj.   n.   v.   adj.*
POSSIBLE ANSWER   **The winner of the contest was happy.**

1. n.   v.   adj.   adj.   n.
2. pron.   v.   adv.
3. adj.   adj.   n.   prep.   adj.   n.   v.   adj.
4. n.   conj.   n.   v.   adv.
5. n.   v.   adj.   prep.   adj.   n.

Language and *Self-Expression*

This painting was found in a cave in Lascaux, France, by four boys who were looking for a lost dog. It was done by Cro-Magnon people sometime between 15,000 and 10,000 B.C. The artist or artists used ground-up rocks mixed with animal fat to create the colors in the painting.

Imagine what the four boys experienced when they found this ancient painting. Write the scene in a few paragraphs. Use prepositions, conjunctions, and interjections to add variety. Then read your scene aloud to the class.

Prewriting You may wish to create a plot diagram for your scene. Include information about the characters, setting, rising action, climax, falling action, and resolution in your diagram.

Drafting Use your plot diagram to tell the story of the boys' discovery. Include interjections to show the boys' reactions to what they have found.

Revising Reread your scene carefully. Vary your sentences by placing prepositional phrases in different parts of the sentences. To make your writing less repetitive, combine sentences or elements of sentences with conjunctions.

Editing Check your scene for errors in spelling and punctuation. Be sure you have separated each interjection from the rest of the sentence with a comma or exclamation point.

Publishing Read your scene aloud to the class. When everyone has had a chance to read, discuss how the stories differ. Talk about which ones work best and why.

Another Look

A **preposition** is a word that shows the relationship between a noun or a pronoun and another word in the sentence.

A **prepositional phrase** begins with a preposition and ends with a noun or a pronoun.

A **conjunction** connects words or groups of words.

A **coordinating conjunction** is a single connecting word.

Correlative conjunctions are pairs of connecting words.

An **interjection** is a word that expresses strong feeling or emotion.

Parts of Speech Review

To find out what part of speech a word is, ask yourself these questions:

Is the word naming a person, place, thing, or idea? It is a **noun.** *(page L137)*

Is the word taking the place of a noun? It is a **pronoun.** *(page L137)*

Is the word showing action or linking two words in the sentence? It is a **verb.** *(page L137)*

Is the word modifying a noun or a pronoun? It is an **adjective.** *(page L137)*

Is the word modifying a verb, an adjective, or another adverb? It is an **adverb.** *(page L137)*

Is the word showing a relationship between a noun or pronoun and another word in the sentence? It is a **preposition.** *(page L138)*

Is the word connecting words or groups of words? It is a **conjunction.** *(page L138)*

Is the word expressing strong feelings? It is an **interjection.** *(page L138)*

Posttest

Directions

Read the passage. Write the letter of the term that correctly identifies the underlined word or words in each sentence.

EXAMPLE   English <u>royalty</u> has a troubled
                          (1)
                  history.

        1 **A** noun
        2 **B** verb
        3 **C** adjective
        4 **D** adverb

ANSWER   **1 A**

For hundreds of years, historians have wondered what

happened to the two sons <u>of</u> the <u>English</u> king, Edward IV. When
                        (1)   **(2)**

Edward IV died, his eldest son <u>should have become</u> king. However,
                                  (3)

Edward's brother Richard took the throne <u>and</u> put his nephews in
                                  (4)

the Tower of London. <u>After</u> July of 1483, no one ever saw the boys
                   (5)

again. <u>Either</u> they were killed on Richard's orders, <u>or</u> they were
       (6)   **(6)**

sent away in exile. Richard III's supporters <u>claimed</u> that someone
                                 (7)

else killed the princes. <u>Well</u>, that may be true, <u>but</u> there is no way
                    (8)   **(9)**

to prove it. No one but Richard himself will <u>ever</u> know the truth.
                                    (10)

1 **A** adverb
B preposition
C verb
D interjection

6 **A** prepositions
B adverbs
C correlative conjunctions
D interjections

2 **A** proper adjective
B compound adjective
C preposition
D adverb

7 **A** verb
B preposition
C adjective
D correlative conjunction

3 **A** action verb
B adverb
C linking verb
D adjective

8 **A** adverb
B article
C interjection
D preposition

4 **A** interjection
B correlative conjunction
C preposition
D coordinating conjunction

9 **A** correlative conjunction
B coordinating conjunction
C article
D interjection

5 **A** verb
B adverb
C preposition
D adjective

10 **A** adjective
B preposition
C coordinating conjunction
D adverb

CHAPTER 6

Complements

Pretest

Directions
Write the letter of the term that correctly identifies the underlined word in each sentence.

EXAMPLE 1. The whole Northeast faced a <u>drought</u> that year.
1 **A** predicate adjective
B indirect object
C direct object
D predicate nominative

ANSWER 1 **C**

1. It was the worst <u>drought</u> in decades.
2. Lawns turned <u>brown</u> and died.
3. Town governments sent <u>citizens</u> warnings about the need to conserve water.
4. People could not even wash their <u>cars</u>.
5. They were <u>unhappy</u> but resigned.
6. Some watered their <u>gardens</u> after dark because they were not allowed to do so between certain hours of the day.
7. Police could give <u>them</u> a ticket if they were caught.
8. The weather remained <u>dry</u> for weeks.
9. Radio announcers gave <u>listeners</u> the same report every day.
10. "It will be <u>sunny</u> and in the eighties, with no chance of rain."

1	**A**	direct object	**6**	**A**	indirect object
	B	predicate adjective		**B**	direct object
	C	indirect object		**C**	predicate adjective
	D	predicate nominative		**D**	predicate nominative
2	**A**	predicate adjective	**7**	**A**	predicate adjective
	B	direct object		**B**	predicate nominative
	C	predicate nominative		**C**	direct object
	D	indirect object		**D**	indirect object
3	**A**	direct object	**8**	**A**	predicate nominative
	B	indirect object		**B**	predicate adjective
	C	predicate adjective		**C**	indirect object
	D	predicate nominative		**D**	direct object
4	**A**	indirect object	**9**	**A**	indirect object
	B	predicate nominative		**B**	predicate nominative
	C	direct object		**C**	direct object
	D	predicate adjective		**D**	predicate adjective
5	**A**	predicate adjective	**10**	**A**	direct object
	B	predicate nominative		**B**	indirect object
	C	indirect object		**C**	predicate adjective
	D	direct object		**D**	predicate nominative

Clara McDonald Williamson. *The Old Chisholm Trail,* 1952.
Oil on panel, 24 by 36½ inches. The Roland P. Murdock Collection, Wichita Art Museum, Wichita, Kansas.

Describe What event does this painting depict? What kind of people does it show? When does it take place?

Analyze What details in the painting tell you about the job of moving cattle?

Interpret How do you think the artist uses perspective to give viewers a sense of the cattle drive?

Judge Do you think the painting gives an effective sense of a real cattle drive? What might be different on a more modern drive? Explain.

At the end of this chapter, you will use the artwork to stimulate ideas for writing.

Kinds of Complements

Sometimes a complete thought can be expressed with just a subject and a verb. At other times a subject and a verb need another word to complete the meaning of the sentence.

> Greg likes.   Ruth seems.

To complete the meaning of these subjects and verbs, a completer, or complement, must be added.

> Greg likes **snakes.**   Ruth seems **wary.**

There are four common kinds of complements: direct objects, indirect objects, predicate nominatives, and predicate adjectives. Together, a subject, a verb, and a complement are called the sentence base.

Direct Objects

A **direct object** is a noun or pronoun that receives the action of the verb.

Direct objects complete the meaning of action verbs. To find a direct object, first find the subject and the action verb in a sentence. Then ask yourself, *What?* or *Whom?* after the verb. The answer to either question will be a direct object. In the following sentences, subjects are underlined once, and verbs are underlined twice.

> ┌d.o.┐
> Dylan saw a **snake** in the river.
>
> (Dylan saw what? He saw a snake. *Snake* is the direct object.)
>
> ┌d.o.┐
> He called **Nicole** over to the water.
>
> (He called whom? *Nicole* is the direct object.)

Verbs that show ownership are action verbs and take direct objects.

>   ┌ d.o. ┐
> Anna owns a **python.**

Sometimes two or more direct objects, called a **compound direct object**, will follow a single verb. On the other hand, each part of a compound verb may have its own direct object. The verbs are underlined in the sentences below.

>   ┌ d.o. ┐   ┌ d.o. ┐
> Did you see a **cobra** or a **viper** at the zoo?
>
>   ┌— d.o. —┐   ┌d.o.┐
> I took **pictures** at the zoo and developed the **film** later.

A direct object can never be part of a prepositional phrase.

>   ┌d.o.┐
> At the petting zoo, Caroline touched **one** of the snakes.
> (*One* is the direct object. *Snakes* is part of the prepositional phrase *of the snakes.*)
>
> Our class walked around the zoo.
> (*Zoo* is part of the prepositional phrase *around the zoo.* Even though this sentence has an action verb, it has no direct object.)

You can learn more about transitive verbs, or verbs that take direct objects, on pages L72–L73.

Practice Your Skills

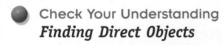

   Check Your Understanding
   Finding Direct Objects

> General Interest   **Write each direct object. If a sentence does not have a direct object, write *none*.**
>
> **1.** Many people fear snakes because of their slimy appearance and slithery movements.

2. Thousands of people die from venomous snakebites each year.

3. Humans kill many of them each year.

4. However, some snakes serve a useful purpose.

5. Snakes eat rats and other small mammals.

6. Some people buy nonvenomous reptiles and keep them as pets.

7. Snakes are found throughout the world.

8. Boa constrictors suffocate their prey.

9. Rattlesnakes periodically shed their fangs.

10. The rattlesnake gets its name from the noisemaking rattles on its tail.

● Connect to the Writing Process: Drafting
Writing Sentences with Direct Objects

Write sentences using each of the words below as a direct object. Remember that a sentence must contain an action verb to have a direct object.

11. cobra		**16.** tail	
12. mouse		**17.** venom	
13. teeth		**18.** cage	
14. teacher		**19.** food	
15. zoo		**20.** prey	

● Indirect Objects

An **indirect object** answers the questions *To* or *For whom?* or *To* or *For what?* after an action verb.

If a sentence has a direct object, it also can have another complement, called an indirect object. To find indirect objects, first find the direct object. Then ask yourself, *To whom? For whom? To what?* or *For what?* about each direct object. The answers to these questions will be an indirect object. An indirect object always comes before a direct object in a sentence.

      ┌─ i.o. ─┐ ┌──d.o. ──┐
Daniel sent his **friends** invitations to his birthday party.

(*Invitations* is the direct object. Daniel sent invitations to whom? *Friends* is the indirect object.)

      ┌i.o.┐ ┌d.o.┐
Daniel gave his **pets** a bath before the party.

(*Bath* is the direct object. Daniel gave a bath to what? *Pets* is the indirect object.)

A verb in a sentence can have two or more indirect objects called a **compound indirect object**.

      ┌─ i.o. ─┐   ┌─ i.o. ─┐ ┌d.o.┐
Daniel's aunt read **Daniel** and his **friends** a poem about birthdays.

            ┌i.o.┐   ┌i.o.┐┌d.o.┐
Daniel should not have given his **dog** and **cat** cake.

Keep in mind that an indirect object is never part of a prepositional phrase.

           ┌i.o.┐   ┌─d.o. ─┐
Daniel's dad showed **us** a baby picture of Daniel.

(*Us* is the indirect object. It comes between the verb and the direct object, and it is not a part of a prepositional phrase.)

               ┌d.o.┐
Daniel's dad showed a baby picture of Daniel to us.

(*Us* is not an indirect object. It does not come between the verb and the direct object. It follows the direct object and is part of the prepositional phrase *to us*.)

You cannot have an indirect object without a direct object in a sentence.

PRACTICE YOUR SKILLS

● Check Your Understanding
Finding Indirect Objects

Contemporary Life

Write the indirect objects from the sentences below. If a sentence does not have an indirect object, write _none_.

1. The whole class came to the party.
2. Daniel gave all his friends party favors.
3. Show his mother those beautiful pictures of our recent class trip.
4. I already gave the pictures to his sister.
5. Daniel's mom showed us some home movies.
6. We told his aunt and uncle a story about Daniel and his dog.
7. I handed him my present first.
8. I gave Daniel a collar for his dog.
9. My sister sent him a card.
10. We will visit his family again.

● Connect to the Writing Process: Revising
Adding Indirect Objects to Sentences

Add indirect objects to the following sentences by changing each underlined prepositional phrase into an indirect object.

11. Daniel also sent an invitation to our homeroom teacher.
12. Mrs. Jenkins brought some delicious lemon cookies for Daniel.
13. Cindi and Josh taught some great new tricks to Daniel's dog.
14. Will you show the presents to me?
15. We will send a note of thanks to his parents.
16. Have you made a present for Aunt Liz yet?
17. I will mail the present to her.

APPLY TO WRITING

Description: *Direct and Indirect Objects*

Your family is planning a birthday party for you. They are trying to decide what the party's theme should be. They also need to decide what food should be served and who should be invited. For your family, write a description of what you consider to be the perfect birthday party. Whom would you invite? Where would the party take place? What presents would you receive? Be sure to include plenty of detail. Underline three direct objects and two indirect objects that you use in your description.

Predicate Nominatives

A **predicate nominative** is a noun or a pronoun that follows a linking verb and identifies, renames, or explains the subject.

Direct objects and indirect objects follow action verbs. Two other kinds of complements follow linking verbs. They are called **subject complements** because they either rename or describe the subject. One subject complement is a predicate nominative.

To find a predicate nominative, first find the subject and the verb. Check to see if the verb is a linking verb. Then find the noun or the pronoun that identifies, renames, or explains the subject. This word will be a predicate nominative. Notice in the second example that a predicate nominative can be a compound.

> ⌐p.n.¬
> The cat has become America's favorite **pet.**
> (pet = cat)
>
> ⌐p.n.¬ ⌐p.n.¬
> Two common house cats are the **manx** and the **Burmese.**
> (manx = cats, Burmese = cats)

Following is a list of common linking verbs.

COMMON LINKING VERBS	
BE VERBS	is, am, are, was, were, be, being, been, shall be, will be, can be, should be, would be, may be, might be, has been, have been, had been
OTHERS	appear, become, feel, grow, look, remain, seem, smell, sound, stay, taste, turn

Like a direct object and an indirect object, a predicate nominative cannot be part of a prepositional phrase.

The Siamese is **one** of the most exotic breeds.
(*One* is the predicate nominative. *Breeds* is part of the prepositional phrase *of the most exotic breeds.*)

You can learn more about linking verbs on pages L75–L78.

PRACTICE YOUR SKILLS

● Check Your Understanding
Finding Predicate Nominatives

General Interest **Write the predicate nominatives from the sentences below.**

1. The cat can be an excellent companion.

2. The two classifications of cats are the long-haired Persian cat and the short-haired domestic feline.

3. Cats were sacred creatures to the ancient Egyptians.

4. Until recently, the most popular pet in America was the dog.

5. Some house cats can be rather large animals.

6. The cat's most effective weapon might be its claws.

7. Its claws are excellent tools for defense.

8. Its whiskers can be sense organs of touch.

9. The Siberian tiger is the largest member of the cat family.

10. Is the cheetah the fastest land animal?

Connect to the Writing Process: Drafting
Writing Sentences with Predicate Nominatives

Write a sentence using the words below as predicate nominatives. Remember that a sentence must contain a linking verb to have a predicate nominative.

11. pet

12. fur

13. friends

14. cat

15. lion

Predicate Adjectives

A **predicate adjective** is an adjective that follows a linking verb and modifies the subject.

The second kind of subject complement is a predicate adjective. Notice the difference between a predicate nominative and a predicate adjective in the following examples.

p.n.
The test was a long **one.**

(A predicate nominative renames the subject.)

p.a.
The test was **long.**

(A predicate adjective modifies or describes the subject.)

To find a predicate adjective, first find the subject and the verb. Check to see if the verb is a linking verb. Then find an adjective that follows the verb and describes the subject. This word will be a predicate adjective. Notice in the second example that there is a compound predicate adjective.

> Does our assignment for history seem **easy** to you?
> ⌐p.a.⌐
>
> (*Easy* describes the assignment.)
>
> The project for science was **fun** and **interesting.**
> ⌐p.a.⌐   ⌐———p.a.———⌐
>
> (*Fun* and *interesting* describe the project.)

Do not confuse a regular adjective with a predicate adjective. Remember that a predicate adjective must follow a linking verb and describe the subject of a sentence.

> REGULAR ADJECTIVE   Some dinosaurs were **great** hunters.
>
> PREDICATE ADJECTIVE   The dinosaurs were **great** as hunters.

You can learn more about adjectives on pages L91–L103.

PRACTICE YOUR SKILLS

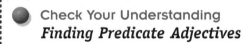

● Check Your Understanding
Finding Predicate Adjectives

Contemporary Life **Write each predicate adjective. If the sentence does not have a predicate adjective, write *none*.**

1. Today was the first day of school.
2. This year most of my classes will be difficult.
3. I was very nervous.
4. The hallways at my new high school are long and narrow.
5. Most classrooms appeared large.
6. In my science class, the lab tables are high off the floor.
7. For some reason the seniors in the auditorium seemed very tall.

8. The locker room in the gym smelled bad.
9. The cafeteria food tastes delicious.
10. After the first day, I felt better.

● Connect to the Writing Process: Drafting
Adding Predicate Adjectives to Sentences

Write the sentences, adding a predicate adjective to each sentence.

11. On the first day of school, my stomach always feels ■.
12. Of all my classes, English has become my ■.
13. The weekends are ■.
14. Our art teacher should be ■.
15. Most of the time, school is ■.
16. Last year's rock concert was ■.
17. Unfortunately, the lead singer was ■.
18. This year's concert will be ■.

Communicate Your Ideas

APPLY TO WRITING

Friendly Letter: *Subject Complements*

A new girl has just come to your school from another country. Write a friendly letter to this new student welcoming her to your school. Then, in order to make her feel more comfortable, describe what a day is like at your campus. Use your own experience as a basis for your description. What do you do in school? What are your classes? Where do you eat lunch? You may even wish to give her advice about what classes to take or which clubs to join. Be prepared to point out the predicate adjectives and the predicate nominatives in your letter.

General Interest **Write each complement. Then label each one *direct object, indirect object, predicate nominative,* or *predicate adjective*. If there is no complement, write *none*.**

1. The 1960s were an interesting decade for entertainment.
2. In 1960, Chubby Checker started a new dance craze.
3. Dancers loved the twist.
4. The Beach Boys were also popular.
5. Their songs filled the heads of young people with dreams of California sun and surf.
6. The most popular rock group was the Beatles.
7. At that time the Beatles' hair was fairly short.
8. By the end of the decade, this band was legendary.
9. Americans watched more and more television.
10. *American Bandstand* was popular with the teenagers of the day.
11. *Sesame Street* taught young children letters and numbers.
12. Other popular television programs were *Captain Video* and *Captain Midnight.*
13. Elephant jokes were the rage in the early 1960s.
14. For example, why do elephants wear green sneakers?
15. Their blue ones are dirty.
16. The miniskirt became the fashion rage.
17. Christiaan Barnard transplanted a human heart.
18. Olympic officials gave Peggy Fleming a gold medal for figure skating.
19. President Kennedy had wanted an astronaut on the moon by the end of the decade.
20. In 1969, humans landed on the moon.

Sentence Patterns

Using Sentence Patterns

The boy ran.
The four-year-old boy ran frantically down the street.

These two sentences are exactly alike in one respect. They both follow the same subject-verb sentence pattern. Even though there are an endless number of sentences that can be written, there are only a few basic sentence patterns.

Pattern 1:   S-V (subject-verb)

        S   V   S   V

Everyone cheered.   Everyone at the game cheered wildly.

Pattern 2:   S-V-O (subject-verb-direct object)

      S   V   O   S   V   O

Birds eat insects.   Many birds eat harmful insects.

Pattern 3:   S-V-I-O (subject-verb-indirect object-direct object)

         S   V   I   O

Grandfather sends me coins.

           S   V   I   O

My grandfather from Ohio always sends me coins from foreign countries.

Pattern 4:   S-V-N (subject-verb-predicate nominative)

        S   V   N

The chair is an antique.

                   S   V   N

The blue velvet chair is an antique from the 1800s.

Pattern 5:   S-V-A (subject-verb-predicate adjective)

        S   V   A

The siren sounds scary.

        S   V   A

The siren on the fire truck always sounds very scary.

PRACTICE YOUR SKILLS

Check Your Understanding

Write the sentence pattern that each sentence follows.

EXAMPLE   The jacket with the hood is the one for me.

ANSWER   S–V–N

1. The Japanese have developed a half-inch camera.
2. The action in a hockey game is fast and furious.
3. My radio alarm doesn't work anymore.
4. A guppy is a small tropical fish.
5. At the student assembly, the principal gave the athlete a trophy.
6. The holiday catalog was large and colorful.
7. The scholarship award was a check for five hundred dollars.
8. My grandparents from Iowa travel extensively throughout the United States.
9. Pure radium resembles ordinary table salt.
10. The computer gave us the answer to the question.

Writing a Short Story

If you had to become a piece of food, what would you be—a bunch of grapes, a piece of cheese, a turkey leg? Make a list of your favorite foods and choose one. Then imagine what it would be like to be that piece of food for a day. Write freely for several minutes. Write a story about one day, or one incident, in your life as a piece of food. Write the story from the first-person point of view using the pronouns *I, me,* and *my.*

When you have finished, read over your story. Make sure that your sentences have followed a variety of different sentence patterns. Check your ending. Is it as interesting or unexpected as it could be? Revise your story until it is the best it can be. If you have included any dialogue, edit it for correct punctuation. Then edit the rest of your story for any other errors. Finally, write a clean copy.

Diagraming Complements

Together, a subject, a verb, and a complement are called the **sentence base.** Since complements are part of the sentence base, they are diagramed on or below the baseline.

Direct Objects A direct object is placed on the baseline after the verb. It is separated from the verb by a vertical line that stops at the baseline.

Some sharks have no natural enemies.

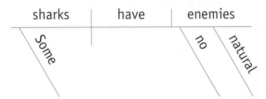

Indirect Objects An indirect object is diagramed on a horizontal line that is connected to the verb.

Phil prepared his friends a big dinner.

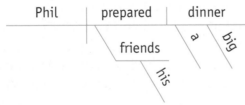

Subject Complements Both subject complements are diagramed in the same way. They are placed on the baseline after the verb. They are separated from the verb by a slanted line that points back toward the subject.

This tree is an oak.   The painting is very old.

The winners are two freshmen and one senior.

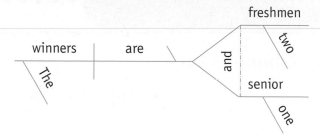

PRACTICE YOUR SKILLS

Diagraming Complements

Diagram the following sentences or copy them. If you copy them, draw one line under each subject and two lines under each verb. Then label each complement *d.o.* for direct object, *i.o.* for indirect object, *p.n.* for predicate nominative, or *p.a.* for predicate adjective.

1. My soft sculpture won first prize.
2. Don gave me a new notebook.
3. The director is a wonderful man.
4. I have visited pretty gardens and parks.
5. That flower looks very delicate.
6. Will you show Jan and me your coin collection?
7. Haven't you given him your answer yet?
8. The books were very old and dusty.
9. Sing us another song. (You)
10. My favorite sports are basketball and baseball.

Identifying Complements

Write each complement. Then label each one, using the following abbreviations.

direct object = *d.o.*	predicate nominative = *p.n.*
indirect object = *i.o.*	predicate adjective = *p.a.*

1. In an average lifetime, a person will walk seventy thousand miles.
2. One out of every twenty people is left-handed.
3. Matt gave me some help with my homework.
4. The loud crash of thunder frightened our dog and cat.
5. The moon looked hazy behind the thick clouds.
6. Bananas are the most popular fruit in the world.
7. The receptionist greeted Matthew and me at the door.
8. Your brain is 80 percent water.
9. Hand me the scissors.
10. Ricardo is president of the Honor Society.
11. Fish have no eyelids.
12. Eric is only one of the contestants in the show.
13. The crowd at City Hall grew loud and angry.
14. Americans eat approximately two billion pounds of cookies a year.
15. Send your grandparents a card for their anniversary.
16. The two most popular items in a grocery store are cereals and sodas.
17. I offered Ben a slice of pizza.
18. An ocean sunfish can lay 300 million eggs in one year.
19. Before the big game, the sky looked cloudy and dark.
20. The benefit concert was a huge success.

Identifying Complements

Write each complement. Then label each one, using the following abbreviations.

direct object = *d.o.*	predicate nominative = *p.n.*
indirect object = *i.o.*	predicate adjective = *p.a.*

1. I will tell you an unusual story.
2. During World War I, a Canadian pilot was flying a small military plane over Germany.
3. Of course, in those days, military planes were open.
4. Captain J. H. Hedley was the other person in the plane.
5. Suddenly an enemy plane attacked their plane.
6. The pilot took the plane into a nearly vertical dive, and Hedley shot out of his seat and into the air.
7. Several hundred feet lower the plane was finally level again.
8. Then, incredibly, Hedley grabbed the tail of the plane.
9. Apparently the extremely powerful suction of the steep dive had pulled Hedley back to the plane.
10. With tremendous relief, he eventually reached his seat on the plane.

Using Complements

Write five sentences that follow the directions below. (The sentences may come in any order.) Write about one of the following topics or a topic of your choice: the funniest present you ever gave or the funniest present you ever received.

Write a sentence that . . .

1. includes a direct object.
2. includes an indirect object and a direct object.
3. includes a predicate nominative.
4. includes a predicate adjective.
5. includes a compound predicate adjective.

Underline and label each complement.

Language and *Self-Expression*

Clara McDonald Williamson (1875–1976) was from Texas and often painted Texan subjects. The Old Chisholm Trail extended from Texas to Kansas, and cattle were often driven along it to market or to new pastures.

Young boys were sometimes taken on cattle drives to learn cowboy ways. Imagine that you are one of those boys, and that you are keeping a journal of your days on the trail. Write an entry for your journal about one day of your trip. Create variety in your sentences by including direct objects, indirect objects, predicate nominatives, and predicate adjectives.

Prewriting You might wish to create a cluster diagram showing what you would see, hear, smell, taste, and feel on the trail. Include events as well as sense impressions in your diagram.

Drafting Use your cluster diagram to write your journal entry. After you date the entry, describe your experiences on that particular day.

Revising Reread your entry carefully. Be sure your sentences include direct objects, indirect objects, predicate nominatives, and predicate adjectives.

Editing Check your entry for errors in spelling and punctuation. Capitalize all proper nouns and proper adjectives.

Publishing Make a final copy of your journal entry. Then collect it with classmates' entries to make a complete journal of the cattle drive.

Another Look

A **complement** is a word or group of words that completes the meaning of subjects and verbs.

Kinds of Complements

A **direct object** is a noun or pronoun that receives the action of the verb. *(pages L149–L150)*

An **indirect object** answers the question *To* or *for whom?* or *To* or *for what?* after an action verb. *(pages L151–L152)*

A **predicate nominative** is a noun or pronoun that follows a linking verb and identifies, renames, or explains the subject. *(pages L154–L155)*

COMMON LINKING VERBS	
BE VERBS	is, am, are, was, were, be, being, been, shall be, will be, can be, should be, would be, may be, might be, has been, have been, had been
OTHERS	appear, become, feel, grow, look, remain, seem, smell, sound, stay, taste, turn

A **predicate adjective** is an adjective that follows a linking verb and modifies the subject. *(pages L156–L157)*

Directions

Write the letter of the term that correctly identifies the underlined word in each sentence.

EXAMPLE   **1.** Honeybees use special <u>dances</u> to find new homes.

    1 A direct object
    B indirect object
    C predicate adjective
    D predicate nominative

ANSWER   **1 A**

1. In spring, queen bees send worker <u>bees</u> signals to vacate the hive.

2. Half the hive becomes <u>eager</u> to leave.

3. Scout bees search the <u>area</u> for new nest sites.

4. When a scout finds a nest site, it gives the other <u>bees</u> a dance signal.

5. The bees are amazing <u>dancers</u>.

6. The dances tell the <u>bees</u> the location of the new nesting place.

7. The bees investigate many different <u>sites</u> as possible nesting places.

8. They are very picky <u>insects</u>.

9. All the bees must be <u>happy</u> with the site in order to begin the move.

10. Then the worker bees give the <u>swarm</u> directions to the new nest.

1   **A**   predicate adjective
    B   indirect object
    C   direct object
    D   predicate nominative

6   **A**   direct object
    B   indirect object
    C   predicate adjective
    D   predicate nominative

2   **A**   indirect object
    B   direct object
    C   predicate nominative
    D   predicate adjective

7   **A**   indirect object
    B   predicate nominative
    C   predicate adjective
    D   direct object

3   **A**   direct object
    B   indirect object
    C   predicate adjective
    D   predicate nominative

8   **A**   predicate adjective
    B   predicate nominative
    C   direct object
    D   indirect object

4   **A**   predicate nominative
    B   predicate adjective
    C   direct object
    D   indirect object

9   **A**   direct object
    B   indirect object
    C   predicate adjective
    D   predicate nominative

5   **A**   predicate adjective
    B   direct object
    C   predicate nominative
    D   indirect object

10   **A**   predicate adjective
    B   predicate nominative
    C   direct object
    D   indirect object

CHAPTER 7

Phrases

Directions

Write the letter of the term that correctly identifies the underlined phrase in each sentence.

EXAMPLE
1. <u>In the West</u> coyotes have been considered pests for decades.

1 **A** participial
B infinitive
C appositive
D prepositional

ANSWER
1 D

1. These animals, <u>the subject of many Native American legends</u>, have spread eastward.
2. There were no coyotes in the East <u>until the twentieth century</u>.
3. Coyotes have managed <u>to spread quickly</u>.
4. Hunters <u>with permits</u> kill hundreds each year.
5. Coyotes have been known <u>to eat cats and small dogs</u>.
6. <u>Yipping loudly</u> is the way the coyote announces its presence.
7. <u>Adapting easily to harsh conditions</u>, the coyote is a survivor.
8. Coyotes could not flourish when there were wolves <u>to compete with them</u>.
9. The wolf, <u>a relative of the coyote</u>, is a better predator.
10. <u>With its fierce instincts</u>, a wolf could kill a coyote.

1 A gerund
   B appositive
   C participial
   D prepositional

2 A gerund
   B participial
   C appositive
   D prepositional

3 A participial
   B gerund
   C infinitive
   D prepositional

4 A participial
   B prepositional
   C appositive
   D infinitive

5 A infinitive
   B prepositional
   C appositive
   D participial

6 A gerund
   B infinitive
   C participial
   D prepositional

7 A infinitive
   B prepositional
   C participial
   D gerund

8 A prepositional
   B gerund
   C participial
   D infinitive

9 A appositive
   B gerund
   C prepositional
   D participial

10 A gerund
   B appositive
   C prepositional
   D participial

Fernando Botero. *Dancing in Colombia*, 1980.
Oil on canvas, 74 by 91 inches. The Metropolitan Museum of Art. ©Fernando Botero, courtesy Marlborough Gallery, N.Y.

Describe What instruments are the people playing in this painting? What else are they doing?

Analyze Which figures are the focal point of the painting? Why do you think the artist made them the focal point?

Interpret How do you think the size of the figures affects the meaning of the painting?

Judge Do you think the artist has effectively created an atmosphere of joyous movement? Explain.

At the end of this chapter, you will use the artwork to stimulate ideas for writing.

Prepositional Phrases

A **phrase** is a group of related words that function as a single part of speech. A phrase does not have a subject and a verb.

You know that a prepositional phrase begins with a preposition and ends with a noun or pronoun called the object of the preposition.

> Why don't you go **with Jennifer?**
>
> The man **beneath the tightrope** was a famous person **in New York.**
>
> **On Monday** we will ride **around the stadium** when we get **out of school.**

Following is a list of common prepositions.

COMMON PREPOSITIONS			
about	beneath	inside	over
above	beside	instead of	past
across	between	into	since
after	beyond	near	through
against	by	next to	throughout
ahead of	down	of	to
along	during	off	toward
among	except	on	under
around	for	on account of	until
at	from	onto	up
before	in	out	with
behind	in addition to	out of	within
below	in back of	outside	without

You can learn more about prepositions and prepositional phrases on pages L125–L130.

Check Your Understanding
Finding Prepositional Phrases

General
Interest **Write the prepositional phrases in this paragraph.**

In 1859, Charles Blondin walked across Niagara Falls on a tightrope. He was high above the water. Later he crossed with a blindfold over his eyes. Then he crossed on stilts. Finally, he really amazed everyone. Halfway across the falls, he stopped for breakfast. He cooked some eggs, ate them, and continued to the other side!

Adjective Phrases

An **adjective phrase** is a prepositional phrase that is used to modify a noun or a pronoun.

Like a single adjective, an adjective phrase answers the question *Which one(s)?* or *What kind?* about a noun or pronoun.

WHICH ONE(S)   The dog **with the short legs** is a dachshund.

WHAT KIND?   Please give me that bag **of dog food.**

An adjective phrase usually modifies the noun or the pronoun directly in front of it. Occasionally, an adjective phrase will modify a noun or a pronoun in another phrase.

The story *about* the dog *with* a broken leg was sad.

Two adjective phrases can also modify the same noun or pronoun.

That spaniel *with* the red collar *on* the porch is mine.

To avoid short, choppy sentences in your writing, you can combine sentences by using adjective phrases.

Have you seen that movie? It's about two dogs and a cat.
Have you seen that movie **about two dogs and a cat?**

Combining sentences makes your writing smoother.

PRACTICE YOUR SKILLS

● Check Your Understanding
Recognizing Adjective Phrases as Modifiers

Contemporary Life **Write each adjective phrase. Then beside each phrase, write the word it modifies.** Some sentences have more than one adjective phrase.

1. Dogs can be great friends to humans.

2. There are many breeds of dogs.

3. The smallest type of canine is the Chihuahua.

4. One of the largest breeds in the American Kennel Club is the Irish wolfhound.

5. Some of these dogs are taller than their owners!

6. The news stories about dogs without homes make me sad.

7. A friend of mine adopted a tiny puppy with little brown spots.

8. The puppy from the shelter was a mix of many different breeds.

9. The size of that tiny puppy changed rapidly.

10. Now the tiny puppy is a huge dog with big, brown spots.

11. My friend is writing a short story about her dog.

12. Another friend across the street just got a Persian kitten.

Connect to the Writing Process: Revising

Using Adjective Phrases to Combine Sentences

Combine each pair of sentences, putting some information into an adjective phrase.

13. Have you read this book? It is about dog training.

14. That dog protects their home. He has a scary bark.

15. A beautiful dog is the collie. The collie has long fur.

16. My cousin lives on a farm. He has many dogs.

17. I took a picture. The photo showed dogs at the shelter.

18. My cousin wrote me a letter. He described his vacation.

19. He helped an elderly couple. He did the farmwork.

20. The barn was new. It sat on the hilltop.

Communicate Your Ideas

APPLY TO WRITING

Persuasive Letter: *Adjective Phrases*

You wish to adopt a puppy from the local shelter. Make a list of some possible objections a parent might have to your owning a dog. Then make a list of positive things about having a dog that might answer your parent's concerns. After that, write a letter to your parent in which you attempt to persuade him or her to let you adopt a dog. Underline four adjective phrases you used in your letter.

Adverb Phrases

An **adverb phrase** is a prepositional phrase that is used to modify a verb, an adjective, or an adverb.

The following examples show how adverb phrases may be used to modify verbs.

SINGLE ADVERB	A mosquito buzzed **by.**
ADVERB PHRASE	A mosquito buzzed **by my ear.**
SINGLE ADVERB	Everyone came **here.**
ADVERB PHRASE	Everyone came **to the picnic.**

Like a single adverb, an adverb phrase answers the question *Where? When? How? To what extent?* or *To what degree?* Most adverb phrases modify the verb. Notice that an adverb phrase modifies the whole verb phrase, just as a single adverb does.

WHERE?	We should meet **at the park.**
WHEN?	We will meet **by noon.**
HOW?	We planned the picnic **with excitement.**

Adverb phrases also modify adjectives and adverbs.

MODIFYING AN ADJECTIVE	Liz was happy **with her new kite.**
	The picnic blanket was soft **against my skin.**
MODIFYING AN ADVERB	The picnic continued late **into the evening.**
	Liz's kite soared high **into the sky.**

An adverb phrase does not necessarily come next to the word it modifies. Also, several adverb phrases can modify the same word.

On Saturday meet us *by* noon *at* the park entrance.

During our vacation we will go **to the zoo on Monday afternoon.**

PUNCTUATION WITH ADVERB PHRASES

If a short adverb phrase comes at the beginning of a sentence, usually no comma is needed. You should, however, place a comma after an introductory phrase of four or more words or after several introductory adverb phrases.

No Comma	**At noon** we met at the park.
Comma	**Because of the heavy traffic,** Dee was late.
	In the shade under the tree, we ate our picnic lunch.

PRACTICE YOUR SKILLS

● Check Your Understanding
Recognizing Adverb Phrases as Modifiers

Contemporary Life **Write each adverb phrase. Then beside each phrase, write the word it modifies.** Some sentences have more than one adverb phrase.

1. Since Monday we have been planning a picnic.
2. On Saturday I awakened with happy anticipation.
3. My brother drove me across town to the park.
4. I brought sandwiches and cold drinks in a large blue ice chest.
5. Before noon my friends had arrived at the park.
6. We put a blanket on the ground over the rocks.
7. Near our picnic blanket, Amanda tossed a baseball to her little brother.
8. For a while we watched the many joggers.
9. After that Luke and Brittany flew their kites into the wind.
10. After a long day, we put our trash into the garbage cans and left the park.

Punctuating Adverb Phrases

Rewrite the following sentences, placing commas after the introductory phrases, if needed. If a comma is not necessary, write *C* for correct.

11. Because of our love for the outdoors my friends and I helped clean the park.

12. For years the park has been the heart of our city.

13. Within two or three hours we had removed most of the trash from the area.

14. In a recent election the citizens of our city voted for park improvements.

15. During the spring the city will plant more trees.

Communicate Your Ideas

APPLY TO WRITING

Compare and Contrast: *Adverb Phrases*

Susan Merritt. *Picnic Scene,* ca. 1853.
Watercolor and collage on paper, 26 by 36 ½ inches. The Art Institute of Chicago.

Alma Gunter. *Dinner on Grounds,* 1979–80.
Acrylic on canvas, 24 by 18 inches. African American Museum, Dallas, Texas.

Many painters use everyday scenes of life as subjects for their art. Susan Merritt's *Picnic Scene* on the preceding page and Alma Gunter's *Dinner on Grounds* above both show people at a picnic. While the works have a few similarities, the style of these two paintings is different. Write a paper for your teacher, pointing out two similarities and two differences in these paintings. Underline at least four adverb phrases in your writing. Remember, use commas with introductory phrases as needed.

▶ Misplaced Modifiers

Because a prepositional phrase is used as a modifier, it should be placed as close as possible to the word it describes. If a phrase is too far away from the word it modifies, the result may be a **misplaced modifier.** Misplaced modifiers create confusion and misunderstanding for readers.

MISPLACED	On the stage the audience applauded for the performers.
CORRECT	The audience applauded for the performers **on the stage.**
MISPLACED	The actor told us about his career in his dressing room.
CORRECT	**In his dressing room**, the actor told us about his career.

PRACTICE YOUR SKILLS

Check Your Understanding

Identifying Misplaced Modifiers

Contemporary Life

Write *MM* for misplaced modifier if the underlined prepositional phrase is too far away from the word it modifies. Write *C* for correct if the underlined prepositional phrase is correctly placed.

1. From the script the actor practiced his lines.
2. Tonight the audience will see the actor's first performance in the play.
3. The cast waited for the start of the play behind the curtain.
4. The character actor heard a strange noise from the back row.
5. The actors bowed to the appreciative audience in their costumes.
6. We looked in the program for the names of the talented cast.
7. From a blue glass, the villain took a long drink.
8. The stage manager directed the entrances of the cast.
9. With a scream the actor fell to the floor.
10. We read about the play in the newspaper.

✔ QuickCheck   Mixed Practice

History Topic   **Write each prepositional phrase. Then label each one *adjective* or *adverb*.**

1. The Braille family lived in a village near Paris, France.

2. As a boy, Louis Braille played in his father's shop.

3. On one fateful afternoon, young Louis was playing with an awl.

4. His father made holes in leather with the sharp tool.

5. Without any warning the awl accidentally went into Louis's left eye.

6. After several days an infection in this injured eye spread to his good eye.

7. Because of the accident, Louis became totally blind.

8. Louis later entered the school in his neighborhood.

9. He could hear his teachers, but he couldn't learn from books.

10. At ten he entered a school for the blind in Paris.

11. Children at that school were reading from special books.

12. Letters of the alphabet were pressed into thick paper.

13. This pressing created raised outlines on the paper.

14. The students would feel the outlines with their fingers.

15. The books were heavy because of the huge letters.

16. One day a retired captain came to the school with a code.

17. His system of dots and dashes proved too difficult.

18. By the age of fifteen, Braille had developed a new system of only dots.

Appositives and Appositive Phrases

An **appositive** is a noun or a pronoun that identifies or explains another noun or pronoun in the sentence.

Sometimes a noun or a pronoun is followed immediately by another noun or pronoun that identifies or explains it. This identifying noun or pronoun is called an appositive.

> My brother **Pat** returned from his trip.
>
> On vacation he visited his favorite city, **Washington, D.C.**

Most of the time, an appositive is used with modifiers to form an **appositive phrase.**

> The president, **the nation's leader,** lives in the White House.
>
> The nation's capital is named for George Washington, **the first president.**

Notice that a prepositional phrase can be part of an appositive phrase.

> Washington's nickname, **the Father of Our Country,** is familiar to all Americans.

PUNCTUATION WITH APPOSITIVES AND APPOSITIVE PHRASES

If the information in an appositive is essential to the meaning of a sentence, no commas are needed. The information is usually essential if it names a specific person, place, or thing.

A comma is needed before and after an appositive or an appositive phrase if the information is not essential to the meaning of the sentence.

ESSENTIAL	Last year in American history, we read Lincoln's speech "The Gettysburg Address."
NONESSENTIAL	"The Gettysburg Address," a speech by Abraham Lincoln, is read by many students of history.

PRACTICE YOUR SKILLS

 Check Your Understanding

Finding Appositives and Appositive Phrases

History Topic **Write the appositive or appositive phrase in each sentence. Then, beside each one, write the word or words it identifies or explains.**

1. We know many interesting details about the men of America's highest office, the presidency.

2. Our president Grover Cleveland entered the White House as a bachelor.

3. While in office he married Frances Graves, a beautiful young woman.

4. Thomas Jefferson, the author of the *Declaration of Independence,* was an architect, a writer, and a politician.

5. William Henry Harrison, our ninth president, died after only one month in office.

6. His vice president, John Tyler, succeeded him as president.

7. Woodrow Wilson, a great intellectual, led America through World War I.

8. President Bill Clinton plays the saxophone, a woodwind instrument.

9. Ronald Reagan, a former actor, was elected president in 1980.

10. Theodore Roosevelt, a sickly child, grew up to become a war hero.

Punctuating Appositive Phrases

Rewrite the following sentences placing commas before and after the appositive or appositive phrase if needed. If commas are not necessary, write *C* for correct.

11. Only one American president Richard Nixon resigned from office.

12. From 1953 to 1961, Nixon served as vice president during the terms of Dwight Eisenhower the thirty-fourth president.

13. Nixon was defeated by a narrow margin in the 1960 presidential election by the young senator from Massachusetts John F. Kennedy.

14. In 1968, Nixon was elected to the nation's highest office the presidency.

15. In 1974, he resigned because of Watergate a political scandal.

16. Nixon's vice president Gerald R. Ford was sworn in as the nation's thirty-eighth president.

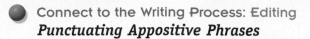

Communicate Your Ideas

APPLY TO WRITING

Editorial: *Appositives*

You are a newspaper reporter who has been asked to write an opinion piece about leadership. Consider the qualities that are important in a leader. What does one need to be effective in that role? Describe three characteristics of a good leader. In your editorial, use specific examples of people from history or people you have known who have been effective leaders. Use at least three appositives or appositive phrases in your editorial.

Verbals and Verbal Phrases

You are already familiar with some of the information you will cover in this section. For example, you already know that the words *exhausted* and *cheering* in the following sentence are used as adjectives.

> The **exhausted** singers bowed before the **cheering** fans.

What you may not know is that they belong to a special group of words called verbals. A **verbal** is a verb form that is used as some other part of speech. In the example above, for instance, *exhausted* and *cheering* look like verbs but are actually used as adjectives.

There are three kinds of verbals: participles, gerunds, and infinitives. All of these verbals are important writing tools. They add variety when placed at the beginning of a sentence, and they add conciseness when they are used to combine two simple sentences.

▶ Participles

A **participle** is a verb form that is used as an adjective.

The words *exhausted* and *cheering* in the example above are participles. To find a participle, ask the adjective questions *Which one?* or *What kind?* about each noun or pronoun. If a verb form answers one of these questions, it is a participle. The participles in the following examples are in **bold** type. An arrow points to the noun or pronoun each participle modifies.

> The **screaming** fans surrounded the **delighted** vocalists.
>
> Their manager, **surprised** and **frightened,** pulled them
>
> away from the **adoring** crowd.

There are two kinds of participles. **Present participles** end in
–ing. **Past participles** usually end in –ed, but some have irregular
endings such as –n, –t, or –en.

PARTICIPLES	
PRESENT PARTICIPLE	adoring, screaming, cheering
PAST PARTICIPLE	surprised, frightened, torn, bent, fallen

Everyone enjoyed the sound of the **singing** group.

Their voices filled the **hushed** stadium.

PRACTICE YOUR SKILLS

● Check Your Understanding
Recognizing Participles as Modifiers

Contemporary
Life

**Write each participle that is used as an adjective.
Then, beside each one, write the word it modifies.**

1. The rock band stepped into the blinding spotlights.
2. Their fans, standing and applauding, welcomed their
   entrance.
3. One musician struck a loud, ringing chord on his guitar.
4. The drummer and the bass player joined the screaming
   melody.
5. After the first song, the dancing crowd yelled for more.
6. The obliging band played another great song.
7. The pleased crowd sang along with the band.
8. After the concert many fans stayed to meet the
   exhausted band.
9. These loyal fans held up crumpled pieces of paper to
   the performers.
10. The band members signed the papers and handed them
    back to the thrilled fans.

Participle or Verb?

Because a participle is a verb form, you must be careful not to confuse it with the verb in a verb phrase. When a participle is used in a verb phrase, it is part of the verb, not an adjective.

PARTICIPLE   The **burning** forest poses a threat to nearby homes.

VERB   The fire **is burning** out of control.

PARTICIPLE   Many **injured** animals escaped the blaze.

VERB   No campers **were injured** by the fire.

Also be careful not to confuse a participle with the main verb. Sometimes the participle form is the same as the past tense verb form.

PARTICIPLE   The **charred** trees were black against the blue sky.

VERB   The fire **charred** many acres of forest.

PRACTICE YOUR SKILLS

● Check Your Understanding
Distinguishing Between Participles and Verbs

Contemporary Life   **Write the underlined word in each sentence. Then label it *P* for participle or *V* for verb.**

1. The firefighter is <u>caring</u> for an injured deer.
2. <u>Caring</u> campers thoroughly douse their campfires.
3. The <u>questioning</u> reporter inquired about the cause of the fire.
4. The police officer was <u>questioning</u> several nearby residents.
5. The paramedic <u>discarded</u> her dirty gloves.
6. A <u>discarded</u> cigarette started the blaze.

7. The man's <u>camping</u> gear was destroyed in the fire.

8. That couple had been <u>camping</u> near the man.

9. A man was <u>talking</u> to the couple in a quiet voice.

10. The <u>talking</u> man was a park ranger.

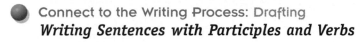

Connect to the Writing Process: Drafting
Writing Sentences with Participles and Verbs

Use each of the following words in two sentences. In the first sentence, use the word as a participle. In the second sentence, use it as part of a verb phrase.

11. ringing

12. rusted

13. barking

14. organized

15. swinging

16. swimming

▶ Participial Phrases

A **participial phrase** is a participle with its modifiers and complements—all working together as an adjective.

Because a participle is a verb form, it can have modifiers or a complement. A participle plus any modifiers or complements forms a participial phrase. The following examples show three variations of a participial phrase. Notice that a participial phrase can come at the beginning, the middle, or the end of a sentence.

PARTICIPLE WITH AN ADVERB	**Flying low**, the plane circled the airport.
PARTICIPLE WITH A PREPOSITIONAL PHRASE	The crowd **standing on the ground** watched the airplane.
PARTICIPLE WITH A COMPLEMENT	A cheer went up for the woman **piloting the small craft**.

PUNCTUATION WITH PARTICIPIAL PHRASES

A participial phrase that comes at the beginning of a sentence is always followed by a comma.

Slowly turning the plane, Amelia Earhart flew away.

Participial phrases that come in the middle or at the end of a sentence may or may not need commas. If the information in the phrase is essential, no commas are needed. Information is essential if it identifies a person, place, or thing in the sentence.

If the information is nonessential, commas are needed to separate it from the rest of the sentence. A participial phrase is nonessential if it can be removed without changing the meaning of the sentence.

ESSENTIAL	The photograph **hanging on the wall** is of Amelia Earhart.
NONESSENTIAL	The picture, **given to me as a gift**, was taken in 1937.

PRACTICE YOUR SKILLS

Check Your Understanding
Finding Participial Phrases

History Topic — **Write the participial phrase in each sentence. Then underline the participle.**

1. Gaining fame in 1928, Amelia Earhart was the first woman to fly across the Atlantic.

2. She was not the pilot but a passenger riding in that plane.

3. Flying solo, Earhart first soared across the Atlantic Ocean in 1932.

4. Greatly interested in commercial aviation, Earhart worked for an early airline service.

5. Amelia Earhart, flying with navigator Fred Noonan, left Miami, Florida, in June of 1937.

6. Attempting an around-the-world flight, Amelia Earhart flew a twin-engine plane.

7. The mystery surrounding her disappearance is still debated today.

8. Vanishing near Howland Island, the plane was never found.

9. Some historians, suspecting foul play, believe that Earhart and Noonan were forced down and killed by the Japanese.

10. Others, believing a different story, claim that she and Noonan crashed on a Pacific island.

● Check Your Understanding
Recognizing Participial Phrases as Modifiers

History Topic **Write the participial phrase in each sentence. Then beside each one, write the word it modifies.**

11. Charles Lindbergh, born in 1902, was raised in Minnesota.

12. Known by the nickname "Lucky Lindy," Lindbergh was a pioneer of aviation.

13. In 1927, he flew solo across the Atlantic in a plane called *Spirit of St. Louis*.

14. Departing from Long Island, the plane flew into a stormy sky.

15. Awaiting Lindbergh in Paris, the crowd grew extremely anxious.

16. Two Frenchmen, attempting the same feat, had recently lost their lives.

17. The enthusiastic crowd cheered the plane landing on the strip.

18. Emerging a hero, Lindbergh waved to the crowd.

19. Marrying Anne Morrow in 1929, Charles Lindbergh gained more than a wife.

20. Flying with Lindbergh, Anne Morrow Lindbergh served as his copilot and navigator on later flights.

Using Participial Phrases in Sentences

Write a sentence for each of the following participial phrases. Use commas where needed.

21. lost in the Pacific Ocean

22. flying a small airplane

23. stored in the attic

24. using a compass

25. buying a ticket

Communicate Your Ideas

APPLY TO WRITING

The Writer's Craft: *Analyzing the Use of Participles*

Writers use participles and participial phrases to describe nouns and pronouns throughout their works. Read the following paragraphs by Isaac Asimov from *Science Past— Science Future* and follow the directions at the top of the next page.

On December 17, 1903, the American gliding enthusiasts Wilber and Orville Wright placed an engine on a glider and successfully flew 120 feet, remaining in the air for 12 seconds. That was the first powered flight of a heavier-than-air machine.

Other "airplanes" were built. In 1905, one of the Wright brothers stayed in the air half an hour and flew 24 miles. In 1909, the French aeronaut Louis Blériot flew from France to England, across the English Channel, in a home-built plane—the first international flight.

As late as 1914, though, airplanes were still little more than engines mounted on gliders, with daredevil stuntmen riding them.

—*Isaac Asimov*, Science Past–Science Future

- Write each participle or participial phrase from the paragraphs. Beside each one, write the word it modifies.

- Could Asimov have placed any of the participial phrases in a different place in the sentence? Why do you think he chose the placement that he did?

- How do participles affect Asimov's description?

Gerunds

A **gerund** is a verb form that is used as a noun.

Both the gerund and the present participle end in *–ing*. A gerund, however, is used as a noun, not as an adjective. A gerund is used in all the ways in which a noun is used.

SUBJECT	**Swimming** is my favorite activity.
DIRECT OBJECT	Do you enjoy **skiing?**
INDIRECT OBJECT	I gave **diving** my full attention.
OBJECT OF THE PREPOSITION	The lifeguard saved her from **drowning.**
PREDICATE NOMINATIVE	My sister's favorite pastime is **boating.**
APPOSITIVE	I have a new hobby, **sailing.**

PRACTICE YOUR SKILLS

Check Your Understanding
Finding Gerunds

Contemporary Life

Write the gerund in each sentence. Then label it *subject, direct object, indirect object, object of the preposition, predicate nominative, or appositive.*

1. In the summer swimming is a great way to stay cool.

2. I just finished a book about sailing.

3. Another enjoyable activity at the lake is water skiing.

4. The hardest part of skiing is balance.

5. Kim has always enjoyed boating.

6. My new exercise, rowing, keeps me fit.

7. The little child gave swimming a try.

8. At first, the sound of laughing came from the water's edge.

9. Suddenly, I heard yelling from that direction.

10. By running, the lifeguard was able to reach the child first.

Gerund or Participle?

It is easy to confuse a gerund and a present participle because they both end in –ing. Just remember that a gerund is used as a noun. A participle is used as an adjective.

GERUND	My best friend earns extra money by **sewing.**
	(*Sewing* is the object of the preposition.)
PARTICIPLE	I might take a **sewing** class.
	(*Sewing* modifies *class.*)

PRACTICE YOUR SKILLS

● Check Your Understanding
Distinguishing Between Gerunds and Participles

Contemporary Life **Write the underlined word in each sentence. Then label it *G* for gerund or *P* for participle.**

1. Many teenagers start <u>working</u> to make extra money.

2. Others become <u>working</u> people to help out their families.

3. Cooking is another good way to earn some extra money.

4. Meg took a cooking class to improve her culinary skills.

5. Jason's singing helps bring in some cash.

6. People pay him to hear his beautiful singing voice.

7. Can you get paid for reading?

8. There are some reading services for the visually impaired.

9. If you're good at swimming, you could be a lifeguard at the beach.

10. My cousin teaches swimming classes.

Connect to the Writing Process: Drafting
Using Gerunds and Participles in Sentences

Write two sentences for each word. In the first sentence, use the word as a gerund. In the second, use the word as a participle.

11. falling

12. singing

13. laughing

14. talking

15. screaming

16. running

Gerund Phrases

A **gerund phrase** is a gerund with its modifiers and complements—all working together as a noun.

Like a participle, a gerund can be combined with modifiers or a complement to form a **gerund phrase.** At the top of the following page are four variations of a gerund phrase.

GERUND WITH AN ADJECTIVE	**His heavy breathing** was due to an intense workout.
GERUND WITH AN ADVERB	**Exercising daily** is important for everyone.
GERUND WITH A PREPOSITIONAL PHRASE	**Jogging in the park** is a pleasant form of exercise.
GERUND WITH A COMPLEMENT	**Walking a mile** every day will help keep you healthy.

Be sure to use the possessive form of a noun or pronoun before a gerund. A possessive form before a gerund is considered part of the gerund phrase.

We were not surprised by **Keisha's** winning the marathon.
The family has always encouraged **her** running.

PRACTICE YOUR SKILLS

Check Your Understanding
Finding Gerund Phrases

Contemporary Life
Write the gerund phrase in each sentence. Then underline the gerund.

1. At the mall many people choose riding the escalator.
2. You can stay fit by walking up the stairs.
3. Exercising regularly is not just good for your body.
4. Doing a little workout each day helps fight depression.
5. Most athletes do not go for a day without working their bodies.
6. Lifting weights is a good way to build muscles.
7. Another way is rowing a boat.
8. Many people work out by aerobic dancing.
9. Playing basketball daily helps many people stay fit.
10. Making a daily workout goal will focus your mind on fitness.

Understanding the Uses of Gerund Phrases

General Interest **Write the gerund phrase in each sentence. Then label the use of each one, using the following abbreviations.**

subject = *subj.*   direct object = *d.o.*
indirect object = *i.o.*   object of a preposition = *o.p.*
appositive = *appos.*   predicate nominitive = *p.n.*

11. Every four years the world enjoys watching the Summer Olympics.

12. Breaking records is the goal of many Olympic athletes.

13. One event, long-distance running, captures a great deal of attention.

14. Another exciting event is the jumping of the hurdles.

15. Successful hurdlers win by barely skimming the barrier.

16. Running fast between hurdles also helps a competitor win the race.

17. Throwing the discus takes a very strong arm.

18. An especially difficult event is competing in the two-day decathlon.

19. Data tables are used in this event for comparing the athletes' performances.

20. Competing in the Olympics is the dream of many athletes.

● Connect to the Writing Process: Drafting
Using Gerunds in Sentences

Write a sentence for each of the following gerund phrases.

21. driving a car

22. swimming ten laps

23. reading a book

24. writing a story

25. completing my homework

APPLY TO WRITING

Informative Article: *Gerunds*

The editor of your school newspaper has asked you to write an informative article about fitness. Interview three classmates, asking them what they do to stay in shape. Write a brief description of each person's method of achieving fitness and why it is important. Underline the gerunds or gerund phrases in your article.

▶ Infinitives

An **infinitive** is a verb form that usually begins with *to.* It is used as a noun, an adjective, or an adverb.

A third kind of verbal is called the infinitive. It looks different from a participle or a gerund because it usually begins with the word *to.* An infinitive is used in almost all the ways in which a noun is used. It can also be used as an adjective or an adverb.

NOUN	**To succeed** was his only goal in life.
	(subject)
	He wanted **to win** more than anything else.
	(direct object)
ADJECTIVE	That is a difficult goal **to accomplish.**
	(*To accomplish* modifies the noun *goal.*)
	His desire **to win** was very strong.
	(*To win* modifies the noun *desire.*)

ADVERB   He was eager **to triumph.**

(*To triumph* modifies the adjective *eager.*)

He worked hard **to succeed.**

(*To succeed* modifies the verb *worked.*)

PRACTICE YOUR SKILLS

● Check Your Understanding
Finding Infinitives

General Interest **Write the infinitive in each sentence. Then label it** *noun, adjective,* **or** *adverb.*

1. In the 1960s and 1970s, Muhammad Ali was the boxer to see.
2. His life is interesting to research.
3. He had one goal, to win.
4. As a young child, he learned to box.
5. For his opponents his punches were too fast to avoid.
6. For several years he was not allowed to compete.
7. When he was drafted by the army, he refused to go.
8. He refused on religious grounds to fight.
9. In 1979, Muhammad Ali decided to retire.
10. Later he came out of retirement to fight again.

Infinitive or Prepositional Phrase?

Because an infinitive usually begins with the word *to,* it is sometimes confused with a prepositional phrase. Just remember that an infinitive is *to* plus a verb form. A prepositional phrase is *to* plus a noun or a pronoun.

INFINITIVE	I am learning **to drive.**
	(ends with the verb form *drive*)
PREPOSITIONAL PHRASE	My mom drove me **to school.**
	(ends with the noun *school*)

PRACTICE YOUR SKILLS

● Check Your Understanding
Distinguishing Between Infinitives and Prepositional Phrases

Contemporary Life — **Write the underlined words in each sentence. Then label them *I* for infinitive or *PP* for prepositional phrase.**

1. We need some time to rest.

2. What do you want to do?

3. Now I would like to go.

4. Should I take my bag with me to gym?

5. That bag is too heavy to carry.

6. Give your bag to Dylan.

7. Take my bag to class with you.

8. Let's go to band.

9. I think the drums are the most fun to play.

10. Let's walk to lunch together.

● Connect to the Writing Process: Drafting
Using Infinitives in Sentences

Use the following infinitives in complete sentences. Use at least one as a noun, one as an adjective, and one as an adverb.

11. to glow

12. to spin

13. to shriek

14. to see

15. to ride

 Infinitive Phrases

An **infinitive phrase** is an infinitive with its modifiers and complements—all working together as a noun, an adjective, or an adverb.

The following examples show three variations of an infinitive phrase.

INFINITIVE WITH AN ADVERB	My friends have learned **to read quickly.**
INFINITIVE WITH A PREPOSITIONAL PHRASE	Alexandra and I plan **to go to the library.**
INFINITIVE WITH A COMPLEMENT	Haley went to the library **to get a book.**

Sometimes *to* is omitted when an infinitive follows such verbs as *dare, feel, hear, help, let, need, see,* and *watch.*

Will you and Jesse help me **find** the library's reference section?
(to find)

No one dared **talk** in the quiet reading room.
(to talk)

Molly helped her little sister **read** an illustrated children's book.
(to read)

Will the librarian let you **check out** five books?
(to check out)

A **split infinitive** occurs when modifiers are placed between *to* and the verb. Until recently, a split infinitive was considered grammatically incorrect. Although split infinitives are usually acceptable nowadays, you should still avoid them in formal speaking and writing situations.

SPLIT INFINITIVE — The librarian asked us **to quickly move** at the sound of the bell.

BETTER — The librarian asked us **to move quickly** at the sound of the bell.

PRACTICE YOUR SKILLS

Check Your Understanding

Finding Infinitive Phrases

Contemporary Life

Write the infinitive phrase in each sentence. Then underline the infinitive. Remember that sometimes the word *to* is omitted.

1. I like to spend time at the public library.

2. Sometimes I go to choose a book.

3. To research a topic, I use the reference section.

4. Those reference books help me understand several complex topics.

5. Many go to the library to find rare magazines and academic journals.

6. On Thursday mornings my mom takes my little sister to hear a storyteller.

7. The friendly staff will help us locate specific books.

8. To determine a book's call number, use the computer system or card catalog.

9. Libraries offer books on tape to serve the visually impaired.

10. A quiet library is a great place to study for a test.

Recognizing Infinitive Phrases as Modifiers

Literature Topic **Write the infinitive phrase in each sentence. Then label it *noun, adjective,* or *adverb.***

11. In English classes many students are asked to read the novels of John Steinbeck.

12. After high school Steinbeck left Salinas to attend Stanford University.

13. He did not stay to earn his degree.

14. To support himself, Steinbeck worked as a laborer.

15. He began to publish novels in 1929.

16. In 1935 with *Tortilla Flat*, he managed to gain critical acclaim.

17. Critics consider his greatest work to be *The Grapes of Wrath*.

18. Steinbeck traveled to North Africa to serve as a war correspondent.

19. Throughout his life he continued to write novels and short stories.

20. In 1962, Steinbeck was honored to win the Nobel Prize for literature.

● Connect to the Writing Process: Revising
Correcting Split Infinitives

Rewrite each sentence to avoid using split infinitives.

21. While he was a laborer, Steinbeck continued to diligently write.

22. He managed to daily meet interesting people.

23. Some of his novels, like *Tortilla Flat,* attempt to humorously portray the workers' struggle.

24. Others, like *The Grapes of Wrath,* show characters trying to bravely overcome their circumstances.

25. Modern critics continue to greatly praise his body of work.

APPLY TO WRITING

Writer's Craft: *Analyzing the Use of Infinitives*

Writers often use infinitives in their works. In this passage from *Cannery Row,* John Steinbeck uses infinitives to explain Doc's motivation for walking. Read the passage and then answer the questions that follow.

> Because he loved true things he tried to explain. He said he was nervous and besides he wanted to see the country, smell the ground and look at grass and birds and trees, to savor the country, and there was no other way to do it save on foot. And people didn't like him for telling the truth.
>
> —*John Steinbeck,* Cannery Row

- List the infinitives in the passage.

- In the lengthy second sentence, Steinbeck uses *and* to string together a compound infinitive phrase. How many infinitives does he use? How does this construction affect the reader?

- Why do you think Steinbeck places commas around the infinitive phrase *to savor the country?* What effect is he trying to achieve?

Misplaced and Dangling Modifiers

Participial phrases and infinitive phrases can be used as modifiers. Therefore, they should be placed as close as possible to the word they modify. When they are placed too far from the word they modify, they become **misplaced modifiers.**

MISPLACED	We saw an elk hiking along with our cameras.
CORRECT	**Hiking along with our cameras,** we saw an elk.
	(The participial phrase modifies *we.*)

Notice that to correct a misplaced modifier, you simply move the verbal phrase closer to the word it modifies.

At other times verbal phrases that should be functioning as modifiers have nothing to describe. These phrases are called **dangling modifiers.**

DANGLING	To go on the camping trip, a permission slip must be signed.
CORRECT	**To go on the camping trip,** you must bring a signed permission slip.
	(The infinitive phrase modifies *you.*)

Notice that to correct a dangling modifier, you must add words or change the sentence around so that the verbal phrase has a noun or pronoun to modify.

PRACTICE YOUR SKILLS

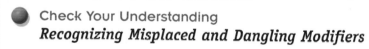

● Check Your Understanding
Recognizing Misplaced and Dangling Modifiers

Contemporary Life

Label the underlined verbal phrases in the following sentences *MM* for misplaced modifier or *DM* for dangling modifier. If there is no mistake in the placement of the verbal, write *C* for correct.

1. To avoid last-minute problems, our teacher made plans for the field trip well in advance.

2. We saw a deer riding along on the bus.

3. Studying the plants and wildlife around us, we collected data for a report.

4. We admired the autumn leaves gliding along in our canoe.

5. Weighed down by our packs, the trail seemed endless.

6. Jack noticed two woodpeckers hiking through the woods.

7. Lost on the trail, my compass was a big help.

8. We ate our lunches sitting on the ground.

9. Having hiked for hours, weariness overcame us.

10. Returning from the field trip, we all fell asleep.

 Connect to the Writing Process: Revising
Correcting Misplaced and Dangling Participles

11.–17. Rewrite the incorrect sentences above so that the modifiers are used correctly.

 **QuickCheck** Mixed Practice

General Interest

Write each verbal or verbal phrase from the following sentences. Then label it _P_ for participle, _G_ for gerund, or _I_ for infinitive.

1. Weighing over three hundred pounds, Louis Cyr may have been the strongest man in recorded history.

2. Lifting a full barrel of cement with one arm was an easy task for him.

3. One story, known to everyone in Quebec, tells about his pushing a heavy freight car up an incline.

4. To entertain townspeople, Cyr also would lift 588 pounds off the floor by using only one finger!

5. Pitting himself against four horses in 1891 was, however, his greatest feat.

6. Standing before a huge crowd, Cyr was fitted with a special harness.

7. The horses, lined up two on each side, were attached to the harness.

8. Planting his feet wide apart, Cyr stood with his arms on his chest.

9. The signal was given, and the horses began to pull.

10. Moving either arm from his chest would disqualify him.

11. The horses strained hard to dislodge him.

12. The grooms urged the slipping horses to pull harder.

13. Not budging an inch, Louis held on.

14. After minutes of tugging, the winner of the contest was announced.

15. Louis Cyr bowed before the cheering crowd.

16. Another amazing perfomer was Harry Houdini.

17. Known not for his strength but for his escapes, Houdini held the attention of large crowds.

18. His most daring feat was escaping from an airtight tank.

19. The airtight tank, filled with water, could easily have caused the death of Houdini.

20. However, Houdini quickly freed himself from the doom of suffocating or drowning.

Diagraming Phrases

In a diagram a prepositional phrase is connected to the word it modifies. The preposition is placed on a connecting slanted line. The object of a preposition is placed on a horizontal line that is attached to the slanted line.

Adjective Phrase An adjective phrase is connected to the noun or pronoun it modifies. Notice that sometimes a phrase modifies the object of a preposition of another phrase.

The squirrel with the fluffy tail gathered acorns from the ground under the oak tree.

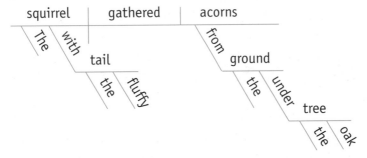

Adverb Phrase An adverb phrase is connected to the verb, adjective, or adverb it modifies.

We drove to the park on Sunday.

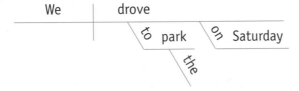

Notice in the next example that an adverb phrase that modifies an adjective or an adverb needs an additional line.

The score was tied early in the inning.

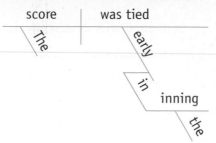

Appositive and Appositive Phrase
An appositive is diagramed in parentheses next to the word it identifies or explains.

I bought a new calendar, one with pictures of horses.

PRACTICE YOUR SKILLS

Diagraming Phrases

Diagram the following sentences or copy them. If you copy them, draw one line under each subject and two lines under each verb. Then put parentheses around each phrase and label each one *adj.* for adjective, *adv.* for adverb, or *appos.* for appositive.

1. Many children can swim at an early age.
2. I just bought a new radio, a small portable one.
3. The posters for the dance are beautiful.
4. I went to Mexico with my sisters.
5. My friend Bert collects stamps from foreign countries.
6. The tips of the daffodils showed through the snow.
7. Meg left the store with the groceries.
8. Wendy, my best friend, went to the horse show.
9. At the signal every swimmer dived into the water.
10. The summit of Mount McKinley is always covered with snow.

Diagraming Verbal Phrases

How a verbal phrase is used in a sentence will determine how it is diagramed.

Participial Phrases   Because a participial phrase is always used as an adjective, it is diagramed under the word it modifies. The participle, however, is written in a curve.

Hiking through the mountains, we used the trails marked by the rangers.

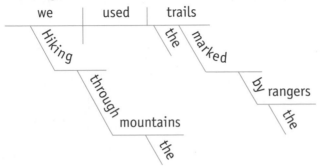

Gerund Phrases   Because a gerund phrase is used as a noun, it can be diagramed in any noun position. In the following example, a gerund phrase is used as a direct object. Notice that the complement *plants* and a prepositional phrase are part of the gerund phrase.

José enjoys growing plants in his room.

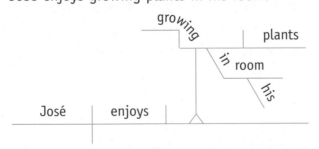

Infinitive Phrases   Because an infinitive phrase may be used as an adjective, an adverb, or a noun, it is diagramed in several ways. The following example shows how an infinitive phrase used as an adjective is diagramed.

This is the best place to stop for lunch.

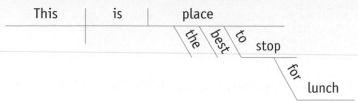

An infinitive phrase used as a noun can be diagramed in any noun position. In the following example, an infinitive phrase is used as the subject of the sentence.

To arrive on time is important.

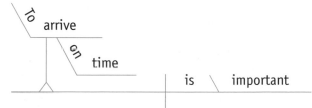

PRACTICE YOUR SKILLS

Diagraming Verbal Phrases

Diagram the following sentences or copy them. If you copy them, draw one line under each subject and two lines under each verb. Then put parentheses around each verbal phrase and label each one *part.* for participial, *ger.* for gerund, or *inf.* for infinitive.

1. Sitting on the doorstep, the dog waited for its owner.
2. Spilled by accident, the milk dripped from the counter.
3. No one noticed Sally tiptoeing down the stairs.
4. I enjoy speaking before an audience.
5. The team practiced kicking the football between the goalposts.
6. Eating food in the halls is not permitted.
7. This is the best shovel to use for that job.
8. To rush into a decision is a mistake.
9. The uniform to wear to the banquet is the blue one.
10. We want to watch this movie.

Identifying Prepositional and Appositive Phrases

Write each prepositional phrase and each appositive phrase. Then label each one *adj.* for adjective, *adv.* for adverb, or *appos.* for appositive.

1. The "Zip" in *Zip Code* stands for *zone improvement plan.*
2. The Abyssinian, a beautiful short-haired feline, developed entirely from the African wildcat.
3. The largest of the python family of snakes grows to a length of twenty-five feet.
4. The center of the earth, a ball of solid iron and nickel, has a temperature of 9,000°F.
5. Lungfish of Africa sleep out of water for an entire summer.
6. A famous art museum in New York City has a collection of 200,000 baseball cards.
7. A completely blind chameleon will still change to the color of its environment.
8. A year is eighty-eight days on Mercury, the planet closest to the sun.
9. A grasshopper's sense of hearing is centered in its front knees.
10. James Naismith, the inventor of basketball, was a YMCA instructor in Massachusetts.

Identifying Verbal Phrases

Write each verbal phrase. Then label each one *participial, gerund,* or *infinitive.*

1. Steam is water expanded sixteen hundred times.
2. The first apples to reach America arrived from England in 1629.

3. A house cat can be expected to live from eight to twenty years.

4. Ancient Egyptian boats were constructed by binding together bundles of papyrus stems.

5. One out of every four human beings living in the world today is Chinese.

6. Pumping blood steadily through our bodies, our hearts never take a rest.

7. Eating honey from a beehive has provided nourishment for lost hikers.

8. It takes approximately ten seconds to slice six cucumbers in a food processor.

9. Long ago doctors used leeches for sucking blood from patients.

10. Polo is the oldest game played with a stick and ball.

Using Phrases

Write five sentences that follow the directions below. (The sentences may come in any order.) Write about one of the following topics or a topic of your own choice: a singer at a concert, a score at a hockey game, or the final lap of a car race.

Write a sentence that . . .

1. includes at least two prepositional phrases.
2. includes an appositive phrase.
3. includes an introductory participial phrase.
4. includes a gerund phrase.
5. includes an infinitive phrase.

Underline and label each phrase. Then check for correct punctuation in each sentence.

Language and *Self-Expression*

Fernando Botero began painting at the age of fourteen. Even then, he used large figures in his work. These figures became rounder and fuller, and Botero called their appearance *plasticity.* In what ways do the figures appear plastic in *Dancing in Colombia?*

Imagine you are a news reporter whose assignment is to write a news story about the social event shown in the painting. Write the article in a few paragraphs. To create sentence variety, include as many different kinds of phrases as you can.

Prewriting You may wish to create an outline using a news reporter's five questions: *Who? When? What? Where?* and *Why?* Jot down answers to your questions.

Drafting Use the outline you have created to write your news story. Include descriptions of the people and their actions in the story. Make your word pictures as vivid as the artist's images.

Revising Reread your news story. Be sure you have answered all the reporter's questions. Correct any misplaced or dangling modifiers and split infinitives.

Editing Check your story for errors in spelling and punctuation. Add commas after long adverb phrases or several phrases in a row. Also add a comma after participial phrases that begin sentences. Set off nonessential appositive phrases with commas.

Publishing Make a final copy of your article. Read it into a tape recorder as if you were a television news reporter. Then play the tape for the class.

Another Look

A **phrase** is a group of related words that function as a single part of speech. A phrase does not have a subject and a verb.

Classification of Phrases

A **prepositional phrase** begins with a preposition and ends with a noun or pronoun called the object of the preposition. *(page L173)*

An **adjective phrase** is a prepositional phrase that is used to modify a noun or a pronoun. *(page L174)*

An **adverb phrase** is a prepositional phrase that is used to modify a verb, an adjective, or an adverb. *(pages L176–L177)*

An **appositive** is a noun or a pronoun that identifies or explains another noun or pronoun in the sentence. An appositive used with modifiers forms an **appositive phrase.**

Verbals and Verb Phrases

A **participle** is a verb form that is used as an adjective. *(pages L186–L187)*

A **participial phrase** is a participle with its modifiers and complements— all working together as an adjective. *(pages L189–L190)*

A **gerund** is a verb form that is used as a noun. *(page L193)*

A **gerund phrase** is a gerund with its modifiers and complements—all working together as a noun. *(pages L195–L196)*

An **infinitive** is a verb form that usually begins with *to*. It is used as a noun, an adjective, or an adverb. *(pages L198–L199)*

An **infinitive phrase** is an infinitive with its modifiers and complements— all working together as a noun, an adjective, or an adverb. *(page L201)*

Other Information About Phrases

Punctuating adverb phrases *(page L178)*

Punctuating appositives and appositive phrases *(pages L525–L526)*

Punctuating participial phrases *(page L513)*

Avoiding misplaced and dangling modifiers *(pages L204–L205)*

Directions

Write the letter of the term that correctly identifies the underlined phrase in each sentence.

EXAMPLE   **1.** Some dogs are trained specifically <u>to help disabled people</u>.

 1 **A** gerund
        B participial
        C infinitive
        D adjective

ANSWER   **1 C**

1. Service dogs are trained <u>to aid people with problems of mobility, strength, or coordination</u>.

2. They help people in many ways <u>in their homes</u>.

3. Dogs help people <u>to get to the bathroom</u>.

4. <u>Using a dog for support</u>, a disabled person can keep his or her balance.

5. Dogs help deaf people <u>recognize important sounds</u>.

6. They alert their owners to <u>the ringing of a phone</u>.

7. <u>Noticing a dog with a person in a wheelchair</u>, people are more likely to be friendly.

8. A well-trained assistant, <u>a service dog</u>, can allow a disabled person to interact with others more fully.

9. Service dogs usually work <u>for eight years</u> before they are replaced.

10. <u>Overlapping with a new dog</u>, the old service dog can help the young one.

1 A prepositional
   B gerund
   C appositive
   D infinitive

2 A infinitive
   B prepositional
   C participial
   D gerund

3 A participial
   B infinitive
   C gerund
   D prepositional

4 A gerund
   B participial
   C prepositional
   D infinitive

5 A prepositional
   B participial
   C infinitive
   D gerund

6 A adjective
   B adverb
   C participial
   D gerund

7 A prepositional
   B participial
   C appositive
   D gerund

8 A adjective
   B adverb
   C appositive
   D prepositional

9 A gerund
   B infinitive
   C prepositional
   D participial

10 A participial
    B prepositional
    C appositive
    D gerund

CHAPTER 8

Clauses

Directions
Write the letter of the term that correctly identifies each sentence or underlined part of a sentence.

EXAMPLE

1 Because I have neat handwriting, Maisie asked me to design the card.

1 A simple sentence

B compound sentence

C complex sentence

D compound-complex sentence

ANSWER **1 C**

1. I used my calligraphy pen and blue ink.

2. Before I made a final version, I practiced on a separate sheet of paper.

3. The card was for a teacher who was leaving in June.

4. She had been there twenty years, and everyone would miss her.

5. Because she was so well-liked, we expected a big turnout, and we were not disappointed.

6. Mrs. Strout was the person <u>who taught me calligraphy</u>.

7. <u>When I first met her</u>, I was just starting middle school.

8. Her art class was harder <u>than I had expected</u>.

9. <u>That I'd had art in the past</u> did not prepare me for Mrs. Strout's class.

10. Her talents, <u>which were many</u>, inspired me.

1	**A**	simple sentence	**6**	**A**	independent clause
	B	compound sentence		**B**	adverb clause
	C	complex sentence		**C**	adjective clause
	D	compound-complex sentence		**D**	noun clause
2	**A**	simple sentence	**7**	**A**	independent clause
	B	compound sentence		**B**	adverb clause
	C	complex sentence		**C**	adjective clause
	D	compound-complex sentence		**D**	noun clause
3	**A**	simple sentence	**8**	**A**	independent clause
	B	compound sentence		**B**	adverb clause
	C	complex sentence		**C**	adjective clause
	D	compound-complex sentence		**D**	noun clause
4	**A**	simple sentence	**9**	**A**	independent clause
	B	compound sentence		**B**	adverb clause
	C	complex sentence		**C**	adjective clause
	D	compound-complex sentence		**D**	noun clause
5	**A**	simple sentence	**10**	**A**	independent clause
	B	compound sentence		**B**	adverb clause
	C	complex sentence		**C**	adjective clause
	D	compound-complex sentence		**D**	noun clause

Jacob Lawrence. "In a free government, the security of civil rights must be the same as that for religious rights. It consists in the one case in the multiplicity of interest, and in the other, in the multiplicity of sects." (the words of James Madison), 1976.
Opaque watercolor and pencil on paper, mounted on fiberboard 30 X 22⅛ inches. National Museum of American Art, Smithsonian Institution, Washington, D.C.

Describe Who is portrayed in this painting? Where do they seem to be?

Analyze What symbols does the artist use in this painting? Based on the title of the painting, why do you think he included these symbols?

Interpret How might the same quotation inspire a writer of fiction? How might it inspire a writer of nonfiction?

Judge Would you rather look at a political painting or read a political story or essay? Why?

At the end of the chapter, you will use this artwork to stimulate ideas for writing.

Independent and Subordinate Clauses

In the preceding chapter, you learned about a group of words called a phrase that can be used as a noun, an adjective, or an adverb. In this chapter you will learn about another group of words called a clause, which can also be used as a noun, an adjective, or an adverb.

A clause is a group of words that has a subject and a verb.

From the definition of a clause, you can easily see the difference between a clause and a phrase. A clause has a subject and a verb, but a phrase does not.

PHRASE   I wrote a letter **after dinner.**

After dinner is a prepositional phrase that modifies the verb *wrote*.

CLAUSE   I wrote a letter **after dinner was finished.**

(*Dinner* is the subject of the clause; *was finished* is the verb.)

There are two kinds of clauses. One kind is called an independent clause or a main clause.

An independent (main) clause can stand alone as a sentence because it expresses a complete thought.

An independent clause is called a sentence when it stands by itself. However, it is called a clause when it appears in a sentence with another clause.

In the following example, each subject is underlined once, and each verb is underlined twice.

I will write a few sentences, and you can analyze my handwriting.

The sentence at the bottom of the preceding page has two independent clauses. Each clause could be a sentence by itself.

> I will write a few sentences. You can analyze my handwriting.

The second kind of clause is called a subordinate clause or a dependent clause.

A **subordinate (dependent clause)** cannot stand alone as a sentence because it does not express a complete thought.

The subordinate clause in each of the following examples does not express a complete thought—even though it has a subject and a verb.

> ┌─subordinate clause ┐ ┌───────independent clause────────┐
> If you are interested, you can read about handwriting analysis.

> ┌─independent clause─┐┌─────subordinate clause──────┐
> My friends read a book that was about graphology.

CONNECT TO WRITER'S CRAFT

When writers want to persuade an audience to adopt a particular viewpoint, they can acknowledge the opposing point of view by presenting it in a subordinate clause rather than in an independent clause.

> **Although some argue that art and music classes take valuable time and budget resources away from basic academic subjects,** new findings indicate that art and music instruction adds to a student's overall intelligence.

By beginning the statement with a subordinate clause, the writer lets the audience know he or she understands the arguments against retaining art and music in the curriculum but believes these subjects benefit learning in all areas. Putting each viewpoint in its own independent clause would, by contrast, give each position equal weight.

PRACTICE YOUR SKILLS

● Check Your Understanding
Distinguishing Between Kinds of Clauses

General Interest **Write each underlined clause. Then label each one I for independent or S for subordinate.**

1. Graphology, which is the study of handwriting, has existed for many years.
2. Many people think that handwriting can reveal personality traits.
3. Because some businesses accept this theory, they analyze job applicants' handwriting.
4. When you apply for a job, watch your handwriting.
5. You can always go back to your old ways after you have been hired.
6. If your writing slants to the right, you are probably friendly and open.
7. If your writing slants to the left, you might very well be a nonconformist.
8. Writing uphill indicates an optimist, and writing downhill suggests a reliable person.
9. Capital letters that are inserted in the middle of a word reveal a creative person.
10. An *i* dotted with a circle shows an artistic nature, and a correctly dotted *i* indicates a careful person.
11. When an *i* is dotted high above the letter, the writer is thought to be a serious thinker.
12. None of this should be taken too seriously, however, since graphology is not a technical science.

Uses of Subordinate Clauses

A subordinate clause can be used in several ways. It can function as an adverb, an adjective, or a noun.

● Adverb Clauses

An **adverb clause** is a subordinate clause that is used like an adverb to modify a verb, an adjective, or an adverb.

A subordinate clause can be used like a single adverb or like an adverb phrase. When it functions in one of those ways it is called an adverb clause.

> SINGLE ADVERB   Our plane left **early.**
>
> ADVERB PHRASE   Our plane left **at dawn.**
>
> ADVERB CLAUSE   Our plane left **as the sun came up over the horizon.**

An adverb clause answers the adverb question *How? When? Where? How much?* or *To what extent?* An adverb clause also answers the question *Under what condition?* or *Why?*

> WHEN?   We will travel **until we have seen all of England.**
>
> UNDER WHAT CONDITION?   **If our flight is late,** the tour guide will wait for us.
>
> WHY?   We took an early flight **because it was less expensive.**

The adverb clauses in the preceding examples all modify verbs. Notice that they modify the whole verb phrase. Adverb clauses also modify adjectives and adverbs.

MODIFYING AN ADJECTIVE

I am happy **whenever I am traveling.**

MODIFYING AN ADVERB

The flight lasted longer **than I had expected.**

Subordinating Conjunctions

All adverb clauses begin with a **subordinating conjunction**. Keep in mind that *after, as, before, since,* and *until* can also be prepositions.

COMMON SUBORDINATING CONJUNCTIONS

after	as soon as	in order that	until
although	as though	since	when
as	because	so that	whenever
as far as	before	than	where
as if	even though	though	wherever
as long as	if	unless	while

Unless you hear from me, I will return at six o'clock.

The flight has not changed **as far as I know.**

PUNCTUATION WITH ADVERB CLAUSES

Always place a comma after an adverb clause that comes at the beginning of a sentence.

Before we visited Ireland, we saw the sights of London.

Sometimes an adverb clause will interrupt an independent clause. If it does, place a comma before and after the adverb clause.

Our schedule, **as far as I can tell**, seems reasonable.

When an adverb clause follows an independent clause, no comma is needed.

We will drive **so that we can see the countryside.**

PRACTICE YOUR SKILLS

● Check Your Understanding
Finding Subordinating Conjunctions

Contemporary Life **Write the adverb clause in each sentence. Then underline the subordinating conjunction.**

1. Because we flew into London, we toured England first.

2. My mother toured a castle while my sister and I watched the changing of the guard.

3. I will remember that trip as long as I live.

4. Although we were interested, we did not see Shakespeare's birthplace.

5. Unless we hurry, we will miss our flight.

6. Tourism in Europe increases when summer comes.

7. We rented a car after we left London.

8. As Mother drove, my sister studied the road map.

9. If we had arranged for a longer vacation, we would have traveled to Scotland as well.

10. We visited Wales even though we were in a hurry.

● Check Your Understanding
Recognizing Adverb Clauses as Modifiers

Social Studies **Write the adverb clause in each sentence. Then beside it, write the verb, adjective, or adverb that it modifies.**

11. After Theodore Roosevelt visited Yellowstone, he established the country's first national park.

12. In order that the United States would have public lands, the government has created many more national parks.

13. These lands are protected so that all Americans can see the beauty of nature.

14. Campers are happy whenever they sleep under the stars of California's Yosemite National Park.

15. The drive through Glacier National Park takes longer than most tourists realize.

16. The Grand Canyon in Arizona stretches farther than the eye can see.

17. Because it is unusually beautiful, many tourists visit Arches National Park in Utah.

18. When people visit Big Bend National Park in Texas, they are surprised by the Chisos Mountains.

19. If you like mountains, you will love Rocky Mountain National Park in Estes Park, Colorado.

20. Because they belong to all of us, Americans should visit these magnificent places.

● Connect to the Writing Process: Editing
Punctuating Adverb Clauses

Rewrite the following sentences adding commas if needed. If no punctuation is necessary, write C for correct.

21. All national parks as far as I know charge an entrance fee.

22. You should still go since the fee is more reasonable than other vacation costs.

23. Because most national parks have a museum you can learn a great deal about the area.

24. Whenever you are ready to camp you should look for a park ranger.

25. They will tell you where you can set up a tent for the night.

Writing Sentences Using Adverb Clauses

Write sentences about taking a trip that follow the directions below. Then underline each adverb clause. Include commas where needed in your sentences.

26. Include an adverb clause that begins with *than*.

27. Include an adverb clause that begins with *even though*.

28. At the beginning of the sentence, include an adverb clause that begins with *because*.

29. Include an adverb clause that begins with *unless* and interrupts an independent clause.

30. At the beginning of the sentence, include an adverb clause that begins with *whenever*.

Communicate Your Ideas

APPLY TO WRITING

Persuasive Letter: *Adverb Clauses*

Your local newspaper is having a contest. The newspaper will send the winner of the contest on a trip anywhere in the world. To enter, contestants must write a letter of one hundred words or less stating what place in the world they would like to visit and what they would like to do there. The newspaper will give the grand prize to the person who writes the most persuasive letter.

- Write a letter for the contest. Remember that your letter must be no more than one hundred words and it must be very persuasive.

- Underline at least three adverb clauses that you use in your letter. Check that you have used commas correctly with all of your adverb clauses.

▶ Adjective Clauses

An adjective clause is a subordinate clause that is used like an adjective to modify a noun or a pronoun.

A subordinate clause can be used like a single adjective or an adjective phrase. It is then called an adjective clause.

SINGLE ADJECTIVE	My great-uncle witnessed a **famous** disaster.
ADJECTIVE PHRASE	My great-uncle witnessed a disaster **of air travel.**
ADJECTIVE CLAUSE	My great-uncle witnessed a disaster **that is still remembered today.**

An adjective clause answers the adjective question *Which one?* or *What kind?*

WHICH ONE?	He saw one man **who jumped to the ground.**
WHAT KIND?	The airship, **which was a zeppelin,** came down in flames.

Relative Pronouns

Most adjective clauses begin with a relative pronoun. A **relative pronoun** relates an adjective clause to its antecedent—the noun or pronoun it modifies.

RELATIVE PRONOUNS				
who	whom	whose	which	that

The crash, **which occurred in 1937,** destroyed the *Hindenburg.*

The zeppelin carried a fuel **that was highly flammable.**

Sometimes a word such as *where* or *when* can also introduce an adjective clause.

Frankfurt, Germany, is the place **where the *Hindenburg's* flight originated.**

This was an era **when commercial air travel was just beginning.**

PRACTICE YOUR SKILLS

● Check Your Understanding
Finding Relative Pronouns

 History Topic **Write the adjective clause in each sentence. Then underline the relative pronoun.**

1. The *Hindenburg,* which was a magnificent zeppelin, left Frankfurt, Germany, for a two-day flight to the United States.
2. The passengers who made the journey enjoyed great comfort on the airship.
3. The world was interested in the flight of the *Hindenburg,* which was the largest human-made object ever to fly.
4. The passengers had a glorious view from the windows that lined the zeppelin.
5. In the United States, the people who gathered at the naval airstation awaited the *Hindenburg's* arrival.
6. The *Hindenburg* was over Lakehurst, New Jersey, which was its destination, when a spark ignited the airship.

7. Some spectators who had family members on board began to scream in horror.

8. The zeppelin was filled with hydrogen, which is a very combustible gas.

9. Another cause for the blaze may have been the flammable material that covered the outside of the airship.

10. About one third of the people who were on board the *Hindenburg* died in the disastrous accident.

● Check Your Understanding
Recognizing Adjective Phrases as Modifiers

History Topic **Write the adjective clause in each sentence. Then, beside it, write the noun or pronoun it modifies.**

11. In 1912, the *Titanic* was crossing the North Atlantic, where icebergs were a constant threat.

12. The passengers, who felt secure on this great ship, were enjoying themselves.

13. Several iceberg warnings, which should have been heeded, were ignored by the crew.

14. An iceberg, whose size was tremendous, suddenly appeared in front of the ship.

15. A slight impact, which scarcely disturbed the passengers, had actually struck the ship a fatal blow.

16. At first the passengers, who were unaware of their danger, chatted casually about the accident.

17. The lifeboats that were on board could carry only a fraction of the passengers.

18. Lifeboats that were launched in haste were not filled completely.

19. The panic that overcame the passengers at the end might have been avoided.

20. The disaster, which resulted in the loss of 1,513 lives, will never be forgotten.

Functions of a Relative Pronoun

In addition to introducing an adjective clause, a relative pronoun has another function. It can serve as a subject, a direct object, or an object of a preposition within the adjective clause. It can also show possession.

SUBJECT

The Great Depression, **which began in 1929,** was a bleak time in American history.

(*Which* is the subject of *began.*)

DIRECT OBJECT

The economic confidence **that most Americans enjoyed** was shattered.

(*That* is the direct object of *enjoyed.*)

OBJECT OF A PREPOSITION

The time period **about which I am writing** lasted for eleven years.

(*Which* is the object of the preposition *about.*)

POSSESSION

Few were the Americans **whose lives were unaffected.**

(*Whose* shows possession of *lives.*)

Sometimes the relative pronoun *that* is omitted from an adjective clause. Nevertheless, it still has its function within the clause.

The *Grapes of Wrath* is a novel **John Steinbeck wrote about the Depression.**

(*That John Steinbeck wrote about the Depression* is the adjective clause. *That* [understood] is the direct object within the adjective clause.)

PUNCTUATION WITH ADJECTIVE CLAUSES

If an adjective clause contains information that is essential to identifying a person, place, or thing in the sentence, do not set it off with commas from the rest of the sentence.

If a clause is nonessential, do set it off with commas. A clause is nonessential if it can be removed without changing the basic meaning of the sentence.

ESSENTIAL	Dorothea Lange's photograph **that shows a tired-looking mother with her children** is on display.
	(No commas are used because the clause is essential to identify which photograph is on display.)
NONESSENTIAL	The photograph, **which was taken in 1936,** is striking.
	(Commas are needed because the clause could be removed from the sentence without changing its meaning.)

It is customary to use the relative pronoun *that* in an essential clause and *which* in a nonessential clause.

The photograph, **which** was taken in 1936, shows an image **that** is striking.

PRACTICE YOUR SKILLS

 Check Your Understanding
Determining the Function of a Relative Pronoun

History Topic **Write each adjective clause and underline the relative pronoun. Label its use in the adjective clause as *subject, direct object, object of the preposition*, or *possessive*. If *that* is omitted from the clause, write *that* in parentheses.**

1. "Black Tuesday" refers to the stock market crash that occurred on Tuesday, October 24, 1929.

2. The Great Depression devastated America's farmers, who were contending with a terrible drought.

3. Many farmers left their homes in states like Oklahoma and Kansas, which were especially hard hit.

4. These states were located in the Great Plains region, which became known as the "Dust Bowl."

5. Farmers headed west to California, which offered many job opportunities.

6. In large cities soup kitchens that fed hungry people had long lines at every meal.

7. Woody Guthrie was an American folksinger who sang about the Depression.

8. One song he wrote is still familiar to almost every American.

9. "This Land Is Your Land" is a song whose words still resonate with Americans.

10. Herbert Hoover, on whom the blame for the economic disaster was placed, was not reelected in 1932.

11. Franklin Roosevelt, whose 1932 election brought him to the presidency, enacted programs to put Americans back to work.

12. Most Americans, for whom finding work was impossible, welcomed Roosevelt's programs.

● Connect to the Writing Process: Drafting
Writing Sentences Using Relative Pronouns

Write a sentence using each adjective clause. Use commas where needed.

13. who is a hero

14. whom we know

15. whose style is charismatic

16. which is important to me

17. that I found most enjoyable

18. to whom we owe a debt

19. for which we need an example

20. whose character is above reproach

APPLY TO WRITING
Friendly Letter: *Adjective Clauses*

Dorothea Lange. *Migrant Mother, Nipomo, California,* 1936. Black-and-white photograph. The Oakland Museum of California.

Look closely at this photograph. The year is 1936, and you are the woman in this photograph. Two days ago, you and your family left your home in Kansas. You are bound for California, where you have heard that jobs are available. Write a letter to your mother, describing your feelings. What are your hopes and desires? What are your concerns? Are you optimistic or pessimistic about your prospects? As you write, remember to include adjective clauses in your letter.

Misplaced Modifiers

Remember to place an adjective clause as near as possible to the word it modifies. A clause that is too far away from the word it modifies is called a **misplaced modifier.**

MISPLACED	Mark plays the guitar **who lives down the street.**
CORRECT	Mark, **who lives down the street,** plays the guitar.

PRACTICE YOUR SKILLS

● Check Your Understanding
Identifying Misplaced Modifiers

Contemporary Life **Each sentence below contains an adjective clause. If the clause is correctly placed, write C for correct.** If the clause is too far away from the noun or pronoun it modifies, write **MM** for misplaced modifier.

1. Some kids started a rock band who live in my neighborhood.

2. Heather's garage is very small where they practice each evening.

3. I can hear them from my house, which is way down the street.

4. Shelby plays the bass guitar who is my age.

5. Heather's father works at a factory that makes amplifiers.

6. The neighbors call Heather's unconcerned parents who hate the noise.

7. The songs were written by Mark that their rock band plays.

8. Mark's guitar screams across the neighborhood which is electric.

9. We will have a big party on my sixteenth birthday, which is in June.

10. The band will play at my party, which will really be fun.

● Connect to the Writing Process: Editing
Correcting Misplaced Modifiers

> **11.–16. Correctly rewrite the sentences on the preceding page that contain misplaced modifiers. Remember to use commas where they are needed.**

▶ Noun Clauses

A **noun clause** is a subordinate clause that is used like a noun.

A subordinate clause can also be used like a single noun. It is then called a noun clause.

Single Noun	I just learned an interesting **fact.**
Noun Clause	I just learned **that Russia was once ruled by tsars.**

A noun clause can be used in all the ways in which a single noun can be used.

Subject	**Whatever you read** is fine with our English teacher.
Direct Object	Does anybody know **when Leo Tolstoy was born?**
Indirect Object	Give **whoever comes to class** a copy of the reading list.
Object of a Preposition	I was intrigued by **what our teacher said.**
Predicate Nominative	The literature of Russia is **what interests me most.**

A list of words that often begin noun clauses appears on the following page.

Uses of Subordinate Clauses **L237**

how	whatever	which	whomever
if	when	who	whose
that	where	whoever	why
what	whether	whom	

Keep in mind that the words *who, whom, whose, which,* and *that* may also begin an adjective clause. Therefore, do not rely on the introductory words themselves to identify a clause. Instead, decide how a clause is used in a sentence.

NOUN CLAUSE	**That Leo Tolstoy is a great Russian writer** is common knowledge.
	(used as a subject)
ADJECTIVE CLAUSE	The short story **that I like best** is "The Death of Ivan Ilych."
	(used to modify *story*)

PRACTICE YOUR SKILLS

● Check Your Understanding
Finding Noun Clauses

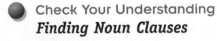 **Write the noun clause from each sentence.**

Literature Topic

1. That Leo Tolstoy is revered today is a testament to his genius.
2. Many critics believe that *War and Peace* is Tolstoy's greatest novel.
3. The contention of others is that *Anna Karenina* is his greatest work.
4. His works bring great pleasure to whoever reads them.
5. That Tolstoy was a member of the Russian upper class is obvious in his novels.

6. He did, however, write about what the peasants' lives were like.

7. His novels and short stories give whoever reads them a taste of Russian life.

8. Why *Anna Karenina* is known as a psychological novel is easy to explain.

9. The reason for this label is that Tolstoy reveals the thoughts of all the characters in the book.

10. What makes Tolstoy's novels so realistic is their mixture of tragedy and happiness.

11. Most critics agree that Fyodor Dostoyevsky is second only to Tolstoy as Russia's greatest writer.

12. That Dostoyevsky spent four years in a prison in Siberia affected his life profoundly.

13. His early novel *Poor Folks* gives whoever reads it a look at the first Russian social novel.

14. The truth is that Dostoyevsky's great novels are clever murder mysteries on the surface.

15. On a deeper level, they show that humanity is in a constant struggle between good and evil.

● Check Your Understanding
Determining the Uses of Noun Clauses

16.–30. Label each noun clause in the preceding sentences as *subject, direct object, indirect object, object of a preposition,* or *predicate nominative*.

● Connect to the Writing Process: Drafting
Writing Sentences with Subordinate Clauses

Finish the subordinate clauses and write complete sentences. Then underline the subordinate clause and label it *adverb, adjective,* or *noun*.

31. What ■ amazed all of the readers.

32. Since ■, we were all late for English.

33. Those are the books that ■.

34. The book review mentioned that ■.

35. The writer who ▇ made a speech in our town.

36. Did you know that ▇?

37. Because ▇, we never finished the book.

38. That some books ▇ is certainly true.

39. We were not disappointed even though ▇.

40. The character who ▇ really made me think.

Communicate Your Ideas

APPLY TO WRITING

The Writer's Craft: *Analyzing the Use of Subordinate Clauses*

Writers use subordinate clauses to fill their sentences with interesting details. Read the following passage from "Family Happiness" by Leo Tolstoy and follow the directions below.

> It was three days since Sergey Mikhaylych had been to see us; we were expecting him, all the more because our bailiff reported that he had promised to visit the harvest-field. At two o'clock we saw him ride on to the rye-field. With a smile and a glance at me, Katya ordered peaches and cherries, of which he was very fond, to be brought; then she lay down on the bench and began to doze. I tore off a crooked flat lime-tree branch, which made my hand wet with its juicy leaves and juicy bark.
>
> —*Leo Tolstoy*, "Family Happiness"

- Write the subordinate clauses in the passage. Label each one *noun, adjective,* or *adverb.*

- Find the sentence that begins with the words "With a smile." Rewrite the sentence, making the subordinate clause into an independent clause. What happens to the flow of the sentence?

- Why do you think an author might choose to include information in a subordinate clause rather than writing two separate sentences?

 **QuickCheck** Mixed Practice

History Topic **Write each subordinate clause in the following paragraphs and label each one *adverb, adjective,* or *noun.* (There are 14 subordinate clauses.)**

The Panama Canal, which connects two oceans, is the greatest constructed waterway in the world. Because it was completed more than eighty-five years ago, few people can remember the tragic problems that occurred during its construction. In 1881, a French firm that was headed by Ferdinand de Lesseps began to dig the canal. Although the work was hard, it was possible. What wasn't possible was finding a way to overcome the mosquitoes that infested the whole area. Within eight years, nearly twenty thousand men had died of malaria as they worked on the canal. The French company that had first built the Suez Canal finally went bankrupt after it had lost $325 million.

After eighteen years, some Americans tried their luck. They first found a plan that wiped out the mosquitoes. Their work then proceeded without the hazard that had doomed the French. The construction, which began at both ends, moved inland through the dense jungle. Finally, after ten billion tons of earth had been removed, the canal was opened in 1914.

Kinds of Sentence Structure

Once you know the difference between independent and subordinate clauses, you can understand the four kinds of sentence structure: simple, compound, complex, and compound-complex.

A simple sentence consists of one independent clause.

The subject and the verb in a simple sentence, however, can be compound. In the following examples, each subject is underlined once and each verb is underlined twice.

> The blueberry pie cooled on the windowsill.
> Tyrone and Lili prepared and baked the blueberry pie.

A compound sentence consists of two or more independent clauses.

> ┌──────independent clause──────┐ ┌──independent clause──┐
> Dad just baked an angel food cake, and I can't wait to taste it.

> ┌────independent clause────┐ ┌──independent clause──┐
> Mom and Tyrone set the table; Lili poured the milk and
>
> served the food.

CONNECT TO WRITER'S CRAFT

When you write compound sentences, be sure the ideas in each clause are closely related. If two ideas are not related, they should be placed in different sentences. Notice that the clauses in the following sentences are not closely related, so a compound sentence is not a good choice.

> My favorite dish is spaghetti, but the plates are in the cabinet.
>
> My favorite dish is **spaghetti. The** plates are in the cabinet.

PUNCTUATION WITH COMPOUND SENTENCES

You can join independent clauses in a compound sentence with a comma and a conjunction.

The pie had baked for a while, **but** it still was not done.

You can also join independent clauses with a semicolon and no conjunction.

A hot cake is impossible to ice; you must wait for it to cool.

A **complex sentence** consists of one independent clause and one or more subordinate clauses.

┌─────subordinate clause─────┐ ┌────────independent clause────────┐
Since I learned to cook, I have made dinner each Friday.

┌─────subordinate clause─────┐ ┌────independent clause────┐ ┌──subordinate
After the game is over, we can go to my house where we

clause────────┐
can eat dinner.

A **compound-complex sentence** consists of two or more independent clauses and one or more subordinate clauses.

┌────────independent clause────────┐ ┌────independent clause────┐
Baking a cake is easy for me, so I baked three of them

┌─────subordinate clause─────┐ ┌────subordinate clause────┐
so that we could sell them when we had our bake sale.

To punctuate compound-complex sentences, follow the rules for both compound and complex sentences.

CONNECT TO WRITER'S CRAFT

You can often tell an author's intended audience by the complexity of the sentence structure in his or her work. When authors write for children, they generally use simple or compound sentences. Notice the structure of the sentences in the following passage from a book for children.

Spring slipped away and it was summer again. The children helped Father and Robert cut and store the wild hay. Then the three adventurers took their buckets and went out into the woods to harvest the summer berries for their mother.

—*Carol Ryrie Brink*, Caddie Woodlawn

When they write for more mature readers, authors tend to use longer, more complex sentences with more phrases and clauses. Notice the difference in the sentence structure in this passage from a novel written for adults.

The dinner, the dining-room, the dinner-service, the waiting at table, the wine, and the food were not only in keeping with the general air of up-to-date luxury throughout the house, but were, if anything, even more sumptuous and modern. Dolly observed all this luxury, which was novel to her, and, being herself the mistress of a house, she instinctively noted every detail (though she had no hope of introducing anything she saw to her own household—such luxury was far above her means and manner of life), and wondered how it was all done and by whom.

—*Leo Tolstoy*, Anna Karenina

PRACTICE YOUR SKILLS

 Check Your Understanding
Classifying Sentences

General Interest **Label each sentence *simple, compound, complex,* or *compound-complex.***

1. The hamburger came from Hamburg, Germany, and the hot dog came from Frankfurt.

2. The idea of placing meat on a bun, however, came from the United States.

3. When the hamburger first arrived in the United States, it was eaten raw.

4. The French still prefer their meat rare, but the Germans eat raw hamburger meat.

5. Hamburgers first became popular among German immigrants who lived in Cincinnati.

6. Hamburger meat wasn't placed on a bun until the twentieth century.

7. Officially, the first hamburger sandwich appeared in 1904 in St. Louis, Missouri, which is also the birthplace of the ice-cream cone.

8. Today the hot dog is not as popular, but the hamburger is on the rise.

9. Chopped meat now accounts for about thirty percent of all meat sales.

10. Because people have become more health conscious, they are eating less meat, so many stores now sell hamburger patties made from soybeans.

● Connect to the Writing Process: Drafting
Writing Different Types of Sentences

Write four sentences about food. Make the first a simple sentence, the second a compound sentence, the third a complex sentence, and the fourth a compound-complex sentence. Remember to punctuate the sentences properly.

Communicate Your Ideas

APPLY TO WRITING

Commercial: *Sentence Structure*

Write a commercial about your favorite food. Give all the reasons why it is better than any other food. As you write your commercial, use variety in your sentence structure. Write at least one simple, one compound, one complex, and one compound-complex sentence. Be prepared to point out these different sentence types.

Diagraming Clauses

The simple sentences that you diagramed earlier in this book had only one baseline. In the diagrams for compound, complex, and compound-complex sentences, each clause has its own baseline.

Compound Sentences   These sentences are diagramed like two simple sentences, except that they are joined by a broken line on which the conjunction is placed. The broken line connects the verbs.

Mysteries are interesting, but I prefer biographies.

Complex Sentences   In a complex sentence, an adverb clause is diagramed beneath the independent clause. The subordinating conjunction goes on a broken line that connects the verb in the adverb clause to the word the clause modifies.

I read my report after I typed it.

An adjective clause is also diagramed beneath the independent clause. The relative pronoun is connected by a broken line to the noun or pronoun the clause modifies.

This song is one that I will never forget.

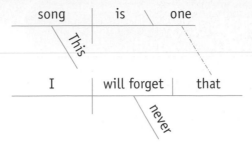

A noun clause is diagramed on a pedestal in the same place a single noun with the same function would be placed. The noun clause in the following diagram is used as the subject.

What the teacher said pleased Jane.

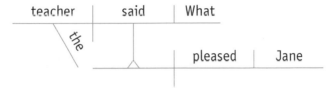

Compound-Complex Sentences   To diagram this kind of sentence, apply what you just learned about diagraming compound and complex sentences.

PRACTICE YOUR SKILLS

Diagraming Clauses

Diagram the following sentences or copy them. If you copy them, draw one line under each subject and two lines under each verb. Put parentheses around each subordinate clause. Label each clause *adverb, adjective,* or *noun*.

1. *Skylab* orbited the earth in the 1970s, and from *Skylab* astronauts studied the sun.
2. A million planets that are the size of the earth could be squashed inside the sun.
3. If the sun were dark for a few days, most life-forms on Earth would die.
4. Some scientists believe that the sun will grow hotter.
5. Never look at the sun because the light could blind you.

Identifying Subordinate Clauses

Write the subordinate clause in each sentence. Then label each one *adverb, adjective,* or *noun.*

1. Do you know what metal is used to make most cans?
2. If you can crush a can, it probably was made from aluminum.
3. Aluminum, which makes up nearly eight percent of the earth's crust, is the most common metal in the world.
4. Although aluminum is so abundant, it has been used for only about one hundred years.
5. The problem is that aluminum is found only in combination with other substances in the rocks.
6. In 1886, it was Charles Hall who finally separated the aluminum from these other substances.
7. What he accomplished changed the canning industry forever.
8. Today you see aluminum products wherever you look.
9. Aluminum is useful because it is strong and lightweight.
10. Some aluminum products that you have heard of are pots and pans and parts for airplane and automobile engines.
11. Aluminum is also useful in wiring because it is a good conductor of heat and electricity.
12. Pure aluminum is soft and lacks strength although its alloys have many useful properties.
13. Another good thing about aluminum is that you can recycle it.
14. You should save empty soda cans until you can take them to a recycling center.
15. Did you know that you can earn money by recycling aluminum cans?

Classifying Sentences

Label each sentence *simple, compound, complex,* or *compound-complex.*

1. Does color affect you in any way?
2. Color experts say that different colors make a big difference in people's lives.
3. For example, people won't buy ice cream in a red carton because they associate red with meat.
4. Pink calms people, and yellow makes them nervous.
5. As a result, you should never paint your bedroom yellow.
6. People will eat less from blue plates, but they will eat more from red plates.
7. People who like candy prefer it in pink boxes.
8. Younger children go mainly for colors that are bright, but as teenagers they prefer softer colors.
9. Do you know what is the most popular color?
10. Most Americans pick blue as their favorite color, and red comes next.

Using Sentence Structure

Write five sentences that follow the directions below. (Clauses may come in any order.) Write about one of the following topics or a topic of your choice: your favorite color, your favorite game, or your favorite food.

1. Write a simple sentence.
2. Write a complex sentence with an introductory adverb clause.
3. Write a complex sentence with an adjective clause.
4. Write a compound sentence.
5. Write a complex sentence with a noun clause.

Label each sentence and check its punctuation.

Language and *Self-Expression*

Jacob Lawrence is known for his narrative images of African Americans. This painting is part of the *Great Idea Series.* In the series, Lawrence explores American history as the source of his imagery. The words of James Madison are his inspiration for this painting.

Famous people can inspire writers as well as artists. Choose one of the quotations below, and explain in an essay what you think the speaker meant. Vary your sentences by combining clauses.

"If a nation expects to be ignorant and free, in a state of civilization, it expects what never was and never will be."
—*Thomas Jefferson*

"If a free society cannot help the many who are poor, it cannot save the few who are rich."
—*John F. Kennedy*

"Power in defense of freedom is greater than power in behalf of tyranny and oppression."
—*Malcolm X*

Prewriting Choose one quotation and brainstorm a list of ideas about it. Number them in order of their importance.

Drafting Use your numbered ideas to draft your essay. Include a topic sentence, then follow with details that explain the quotation. Conclude with a sentence summarizing your ideas.

Revising Read your essay critically, looking for ideas that do not flow. Cut and add material as needed.

Editing Correct any errors in grammar, capitalization, punctuation, and spelling.

Publishing Prepare a final copy of your essay. You might publish it by sharing it with your class.

Another Look

A **clause** is a group of words that has a subject and a verb.

Kinds of Clauses
An **independent (or main) clause** can stand alone as a sentence because it expresses a complete thought. *(pages L221–L222)*

A **subordinate (or dependent) clause** cannot stand alone as a sentence because it does not express a complete thought. *(page L222)*

Uses of Subordinate Clauses
An **adverb clause** is a subordinate clause that is used like an adverb to modify a verb, an adjective, or an adverb. *(pages L224–L225)*

All adverb clauses begin with a **subordinating conjunction.** *(page L225)*

An **adjective clause** is a subordinate clause that is used like an adjective to modify a noun or pronoun. *(page L229)*

Most adjective clauses begin with a **relative pronoun.** *(pages L229–L230)*

A **noun clause** is a subordinate clause that is used like a noun.
(pages L237–L238)

Kinds of Sentence Structure
A **simple sentence** consists of one independent clause. *(page L242)*

A **compound sentence** consists of two or more independent clauses.
(page L242)

A **complex sentence** consists of one independent clause and one or more subordinate clauses. *(page L243)*

A **compound-complex sentence** consists of two or more independent clauses and one or more subordinate clauses. *(page L243)*

Other Information About Clauses
Recognizing misplaced modifiers *(pages L235–L236)*
Punctuating adverb clauses *(pages L225–L226)*
Determining the function of a relative pronoun *(page L232)*
Punctuating adjective clauses *(pages L232–L233)*

Posttest

Directions
Write the letter of the term that correctly identifies each sentence or underlined part of a sentence.

EXAMPLE
1. The boat left the dock as the clock struck eight.

  1 A simple sentence

    B compound sentence

    C complex sentence

    D compound-complex sentence

ANSWER
  1 C

1. The evening dinner cruise was considerably more fun than I had expected.

2. We traveled up the west shore of Seneca Lake.

3. After we had been aboard for half an hour, dinner finally was served.

4. The food was unexciting, but the exotic atmosphere was truly delightful.

5. When dinner was over, we all went downstairs, and a band serenaded us.

6. The man <u>who led the band</u> was really a showman.

7. <u>How he danced around</u> made everyone laugh.

8. <u>As the band took a break</u>, I watched a nearby sailboat.

9. I asked the two women next to me <u>whether they enjoyed sailing</u>.

10. As it turned out, <u>one of them was a sailing instructor</u>.

1	A	simple sentence	6	A	independent clause
	B	compound sentence		B	adverb clause
	C	complex sentence		C	adjective clause
	D	compound-complex sentence		D	noun clause

2	A	simple sentence	7	A	independent clause
	B	compound sentence		B	adverb clause
	C	complex sentence		C	adjective clause
	D	compound-complex sentence		D	noun clause

3	A	simple sentence	8	A	independent clause
	B	compound sentence		B	adverb clause
	C	complex sentence		C	adjective clause
	D	compound-complex sentence		D	noun clause

4	A	simple sentence	9	A	independent clause
	B	compound sentence		B	adverb clause
	C	complex sentence		C	adjective clause
	D	compound-complex sentence		D	noun clause

5	A	simple sentence	10	A	independent clause
	B	compound sentence		B	adverb clause
	C	complex sentence		C	adjective clause
	D	compound-complex sentence		D	noun clause

CHAPTER 9

Sentence Fragments and Run-ons

Pretest

Directions

Read the passage. Write the letter of the best way to write each underlined section. If the underlined section contains no error, write D.

EXAMPLE
Ancient Greece was a <u>civilization. That</u>
(1)
produced important thinkers.

   1 **A** civilization, and that

        B civilization that

        C civilization; that

        D No error

ANSWER
   1 **B**

Pythagoras was a Greek <u>philosopher. Lived</u> in the sixth
(1)
century B.C. The Pythagoreans, his followers, were skilled

mathematicians. They were the first to <u>teach. That the</u> earth
(2)
rotates daily on its axis. Pythagoras is famous for a

<u>theorem. We</u> studied this year. It involves <u>triangles geometry</u>
(3)   (4)
depends on it. According to the <u>theorem, the</u> square of the
(5)
length of the hypotenuse of a right triangle equals the sum of

the squares of the lengths of the other two sides.

1   **A**   philosopher. Who lived
    B   philosopher he lived
    C   philosopher who lived
    D   No error

2   **A**   teach that the
    B   teach that. The
    C   teach, and the
    D   No error

3   **A**   theorem. Which we
    B   theorem we
    C   theorem, we
    D   No error

4   **A**   triangles. And geometry
    B   triangles, and geometry
    C   triangles, geometry
    D   No error

5   **A**   theorem. The
    B   theorem; the
    C   theorem the
    D   No error

Charles Willson Peale.
The Artist in His Museum, 1822.
Oil on canvas, 103¾ by 79⅞ inches. Courtesy of the Museum of American Art of the Pennsylvania Academy of the Fine Arts, Philadelphia. Gift of Mrs. Sarah Harrison (The Joseph Harrison Jr., Collection).

Describe Who is the focus of this painting? Where is he located? What is in the foreground? What is in the background?

Analyze Considering that the person portrayed is the artist himself, what message does he seem to be sending to the viewer? How does his stance help to convey that message?

Interpret Imagine that Peale chose to write a brochure inviting people to his museum. What words might he use on the cover to convey the same message that he is sending in his painting?

Judge Would a brochure be a better means of inviting people to visit the museum? Why or why not?

At the end of this chapter, you will use the artwork as a visual aid for writing.

Sentence Fragments

A **sentence fragment** is a group of words that does not express a complete thought.

Writers sometimes express an incomplete thought as a sentence. These incomplete thoughts are called sentence fragments. Some sentence fragments are missing either a subject or a verb. These are fragments due to incomplete thoughts.

No Subject	Was running and catching snowflakes on her tongue.
	Skate at the ice rink.
No Verb	Gretchen and her two little sisters.
	The snow shovel next to the snowblower in the garage.

Some sentence fragments are due to incorrect punctuation.

Part of a Compound Verb	Will you wait for us? **Or come back to get us?**
	We rushed to the ice. **And started to skate.**
Items in a Series	We will have to take warm clothes with us. **Coats, wool scarves, and gloves.**
	Rachel brought snacks for us. **Pretzels, chips, and hot chocolate.**

▶ Ways to Correct Sentence Fragments

When you edit your writing, always check specifically for any missing subjects or missing verbs. You can fix these kinds of fragments by adding a subject or verb.

FRAGMENT	Was running and catching snowflakes on her tongue.
SENTENCE	**My little sister** was running and catching snowflakes on her tongue. (A complete subject, *my little sister,* was added.)

FRAGMENT	The snow shovel next to the snowblower in the garage.
SENTENCE	The snow shovel **is** next to the snowblower in the garage. (The verb *is* was added.)

Another way to correct a sentence fragment is to attach it to a related group of words near it. Sometimes you can simply include the information from the fragment into another sentence. Other times you can write two separate sentences.

SENTENCE AND FRAGMENT	Will you wait for the two of us? **Or come back to get us?**
ATTACHED	Will you wait for the two of us **or come back to get us?**
SEPARATE SENTENCES	Will you wait for the two of us? Will you come back to get us?

SENTENCE AND FRAGMENT	Rachel brought snacks for us. **Pretzels, chips, and hot chocolate.**
ATTACHED	Rachel brought pretzels, chips, and hot chocolate for us.
SEPARATE SENTENCES	Rachel brought snacks for us. She brought pretzels, chips, and hot chocolate for us.

You can learn more about complete sentences on page L5.

PRACTICE YOUR SKILLS

● Check Your Understanding
Recognizing Fragments

Contemporary
Life

Label each group of words *sentence* or *fragment*.

(1) Skating is my favorite winter activity. I usually go with friends from my neighborhood. **(2)** We hurry to the ice. **(3)** And skate as fast as possible. **(4)** Try to catch each other. **(5)** Sometimes I fall down. **(6)** And go sliding across the ice. **(7)** Since we all own them, usually bring our own skates. **(8)** Yesterday, however, Katie had to rent skates. **(9)** Her feet had grown since last winter. **(10)** Her old skates too small.

● Connect to the Writing Process: Revising
Correcting Sentence Fragments

11.–15. Rewrite each fragment from the previous exercise as a complete sentence. You may add words or attach the fragment to another sentence.

Communicate Your Ideas

APPLY TO WRITING

E-mail Message: *Complete Sentences*

Write an E-mail message to two friends. Invite them to join you as you do your favorite winter activity. Decide what you will invite them to do. Then write your message. Tell them the day, time, and place of the activity. Use the following fragments written correctly as sentences in your message.

- Coming with me.
- And drop you off at home.
- You need to bring.
- Hope you can come!

Other Kinds of Sentence Fragments

There are other kinds of sentence fragments. Each one of them is missing one or more essential elements to make it a complete sentence.

 Phrase Fragments

Since a phrase does not have a subject and a verb, it can never stand alone as a sentence. When phrases are written alone, they are called **phrase fragments.** Following are examples of different phrase fragments in **bold** type. Notice that they are capitalized and punctuated as if they were sentences.

PREPOSITIONAL PHRASES	Mandy and Grant Saunders vacationed in Africa. **During the winter just after Christmas.**
	Before their trip to Zimbabwe and South Africa. Grant read about the continent.
APPOSITIVE PHRASES	Mandy was fascinated by the African elephant. **The largest land mammal.**
	Have you seen Grant's books? **The ones about Africa.**
PARTICIPIAL PHRASES	**Traveling by canoe on a wild river.** They saw a crocodile.
	Their canoe glided through a river. **Teeming with dangerous animals.**
INFINITIVE PHRASES	Grant and Mandy bought a new camera. **To bring along on the trip.**
	They went to their doctor for vaccinations. **To prevent illness.**

Ways to Correct Phrase Fragments

When you edit your written work, always look for phrase fragments. If you find any, correct them in one of two ways: (1) add words to turn the phrase into a sentence; or (2) attach the phrase to a related group of words that has a subject and a verb.

SENTENCE AND PHRASE FRAGMENT	Mandy and Grant Saunders vacationed in Africa. **During the winter just after Christmas.**
SEPARATE SENTENCES	Mandy and Grant Saunders vacationed in Africa. **Their vacation was during the winter just after Christmas.**
ATTACHED	Mandy and Grant Saunders vacationed in Africa **during the winter just after Christmas.**
SENTENCE AND PHRASE FRAGMENT	Mandy was fascinated by the African elephant. **The largest land mammal.**
SEPARATE SENTENCES	Mandy was fascinated by the African elephant. **The African elephant is the largest land mammal.**
ATTACHED	Mandy was fascinated by the African elephant, **the largest land mammal.**
SENTENCE AND PHRASE FRAGMENT	Their canoe glided through a river. **Teeming with dangerous animals.**
SEPARATE SENTENCES	Their canoe glided through a river. **It was teeming with dangerous animals.**
ATTACHED	Their canoe glided through a river **teeming with dangerous animals.**
SENTENCE AND PHRASE FRAGMENT	They went to their doctor for vaccinations. **To prevent illness.**
SEPARATE SENTENCES	They went to their doctor for vaccinations. **The shots prevent illness.**
ATTACHED	They went to their doctor for vaccinations **to prevent illness.**

● Check Your Understanding
Recognizing Phrase Fragments

Science Topic **Label each group of words *S* for sentence or *PF* for phrase fragment.**

1. To learn more about wild animals.
2. Living in bushes and forest areas.
3. Gorillas are herbivores.
4. Scavengers like jackals and hyenas.
5. Lionesses raise their cubs together.
6. Found in Africa on game reserves.
7. One interesting animal in Africa is the zebra.
8. The lemur is found only in Madagascar.
9. On a photographic safari with an African guide.
10. Seeing animals in their natural habitats.
11. The aardvark has short and stumpy legs.
12. To scare away predators.

● Connect to the Writing Process: Revising
Correcting Phrase Fragments

13.–19. Rewrite each phrase fragment from the previous exercise as a complete sentence. You may add words or attach the fragment to another sentence.

Communicate Your Ideas

APPLY TO WRITING

Writer's Craft: *Analyzing the Use of Phrase Fragments*

Rather than use complete sentences, writers often intentionally use phrase fragments to express themselves. Read the following excerpt from *The Woman Warrior* by Maxine Hong Kingston and then follow the directions.

To shut the door at the end of the workday, which does not spill into evening. To throw away books after reading them so they don't have to be dusted. To go through boxes on New Year's Eve and throw out half of what's inside. Sometimes for extravagance to pick a bunch of flowers for the one table. Other women besides me must have this daydream about a carefree life.

—*Maxine Hong Kingston*, The Woman Warrior

- Write the one complete sentence from the excerpt.
- What kind of phrase fragment does Kingston use again and again in this passage?
- Rewrite two of the phrase fragments to form a complete sentence. Compare your work to Kingston's original. Which do you prefer? Why?
- In the final sentence, Kingston points out that the previous phrases describe daydreams. Why do you think she chose to describe these daydreams in fragments rather than in complete sentences?

Clause Fragments

All clauses have a subject and a verb, but only an independent clause can stand alone as a sentence. As you know, a subordinate clause does not express a complete thought. When a subordinate clause stands alone, it is known as a **clause fragment.**

Following are examples of clause fragments in **bold** type. Notice they are punctuated and capitalized as if they were complete sentences.

ADVERB CLAUSE FRAGMENT	You will miss the exhibit. **If you don't purchase advance tickets.**
ADJECTIVE CLAUSE FRAGMENT	This is a masterpiece. **That Pablo Picasso painted.**

Ways to Correct Clause Fragments

Looking for fragments should always be a part of your editing process. If you find a clause fragment, you can correct it in one of two ways. First, you can add words to make it into a separate sentence. Second, you can attach it to the sentence next to it.

SENTENCE AND CLAUSE FRAGMENT	You will miss the exhibit. **If you don't purchase advance tickets.**
SEPARATE SENTENCES	You will miss the exhibit. **You should purchase advance tickets.**
ATTACHED	You will miss the exhibit **if you don't purchase advance tickets.**

SENTENCE AND CLAUSE FRAGMENT	This is a masterpiece. **That Pablo Picasso painted.**
SEPARATE SENTENCES	This is a masterpiece. **Pablo Picasso painted it.**
ATTACHED	This is a masterpiece **that Pablo Picasso painted.**

PRACTICE YOUR SKILLS

● Check Your Understanding
Recognizing Clause Fragments

Art Topic **Label each group of words *S* for sentence or *CF* for clause fragment.**

(1) Pablo Picasso who was born in 1881. (2) He led the artistic movement against naturalism. (3) Which is realism in art. (4) His father was an art teacher. (5) Who realized very early his son's great talent.

(6) His painting evolved throughout his life. **(7)** When he was a young man. **(8)** He painted more realistic works. **(9)** As he matured, he experimented with line, form, and color. **(10)** Which allowed him to create amazing pieces of art.

● **Connect to the Writing Process: Revising**
Correcting Clause Fragments

11.-15. Rewrite each clause fragment from the previous exercise as a complete sentence. You may add words or attach the fragment to another sentence.

Communicate Your Ideas

APPLY TO WRITING

Narrative: *Complete Sentences*

Pablo Picasso. *The Tragedy,* 1903. Wood, 41½ by 27⅛ inches. National Gallery of Art, Washington, D.C.

Imagine that you are the child in this painting by Pablo Picasso. Write a narrative account for your teacher of what has happened to create the scene before you. How do you feel? How has what happened affected these adults? What will happen next? Use the following clause fragments written correctly as sentences in your narrative.

- As we stood barefoot on the sand.
- That they had heard the story.
- Who is such a kind person.

 QuickCheck Mixed Practice

History Topic

Rewrite the following paragraphs, correcting all sentence fragments. Add capital letters and punctuation marks where needed.

When Jesse Owens graduated from East Technical High School in Cleveland, Ohio. He had established three national high school records in track. At Ohio State University, Jesse broke a few more world records. Then in the 1936 Olympic Games at Berlin. He acquired world fame by winning four gold medals!

Owens's performance on May 25, 1935, at the Big Ten Conference championships, however, will always be remembered. Getting up from a sickbed. He ran the 100-yard dash in 9.4 seconds. To tie the world record. Ten minutes later in the broad jump. He leaped 26 feet 8.25 inches on his first try. To beat a world record. When the 220-yard dash was over. Owens had smashed another world record. He then negotiated the hurdles in 22.6 seconds. And shattered another record. Within three quarters of an hour. Jesse Owens had established world records in four events.

Run-on Sentences

A mistake some writers make is to combine several thoughts and write them as one sentence. This results in a run-on sentence.

A **run-on sentence** is two or more sentences that are written together and are separated by a comma or no mark of punctuation at all.

Generally, run-on sentences are written in either of two ways.

WITH A COMMA	The class trip was in April, **we went to Washington D.C.**
WITH NO PUNCTUATION	On the trip we visited four museums **the Smithsonian was the best.**

Ways to Correct Run-on Sentences

To correct a run-on sentence, you can turn it into (1) separate sentences; (2) a compound sentence; or (3) a complex sentence.

RUN-ON SENTENCE	I walked all over the city my feet were very tired at the end of the day.
SEPARATE SENTENCES	I walked all over the city. My feet were very tired at the end of the day. (separated with a period and a capital letter)
COMPOUND SENTENCES	I walked all over the city, so my feet were very tired at the end of the day. (clauses combined with a comma and a conjunction)
	I walked all over the city; my feet were very tired at the end of the day. (clauses combined with a semicolon)
COMPLEX SENTENCE	Because I walked all over the city, my feet were very tired at the end of the day. (clauses combined by changing one of them into a subordinate clause)

Another way to edit for sentence errors is to use two different colored highlighting markers. Highlight your first sentence in one color; highlight your second sentence in another color. Continue alternating. Then you can easily see the length of each sentence. If a group of words looks short, read it carefully to be sure it's a complete sentence. If a sentence looks long, read closely to be sure it is not a run-on.

PRACTICE YOUR SKILLS

● Check Your Understanding
Recognizing Run-on Sentences

History Topic **Label each group of words S for sentence or RO for run-on.**

(1) George Washington was the first president he was not the first to live in the White House. (2) The second president, John Adams, was the first head of state to live in the White House. (3) In 1800, John and Abigail Adams moved in the builders had completed only six rooms. (4) Still, Abigail Adams was impressed by the place she was glad to live in such a beautiful mansion.

(5) The White House wasn't always white, it started out gray. (6) During the War of 1812, British troops invaded Washington they burned the structure on August 24, 1814. (7) Only a shell was left standing. (8) Under the direction of the original architect, the building was restored. (9) The work was completed in 1817. (10) "The White House" did not become its official name until 1902, Theodore Roosevelt adopted it.

● Connect to the Writing Process: Revising
Correcting Run-on Sentences

11.–16. Correct each run-on sentence from the previous exercise. Add capital letters and punctuation marks where needed.

APPLY TO WRITING

Description: *Complete Sentences*

Your parents have just told you that you can redesign your room. Write a description for your parents of what you consider to be the perfect bedroom. Don't forget to include all the details you've always desired in your living space! After writing your description, read it aloud to a classmate. As you read, listen for any sentence errors that you may have made. Correct any fragments and run-ons.

QuickCheck · Mixed Practice

General Interest **Rewrite the following paragraphs, correcting all sentence fragments and run-on sentences. Add capital letters and punctuation marks where needed.**

If you owned *Marvel Comics #1* You would be a rich person. In 1939, it cost a dime today it is worth fifteen thousand dollars! No one knows exactly which comic books to save. There are, however, a few things. To look for when you're buying them. Buy the first issue of any comic book. And hold onto it. Origin issues are also valuable, they are the issues in which a character is born or comes into being.

Do you have any old comic books? Lying around the house. You can find out how much they are worth by looking in a book it's called *The Comic Book Price Guide* by Robert Overstreet. It can be found in most public libraries.

Correcting Sentence Fragments and Run-on Sentences

Write the following sentences, correcting each sentence fragment or run-on sentence. Use capital letters and punctuation marks where needed.

1. A large tree had fallen. At the end of the road leading to the lake.

2. We have three kinds of trees growing in our yard. Oak, maple, and spruce.

3. "Smith" is a very common name. Appearing in over forty languages.

4. In 1946, there were 10,000 television sets in the United States, there were twelve million five years later.

5. Of all the ore dug in a diamond mine. Only one carat in every three tons proves to be a diamond.

6. Yesterday I mowed the lawn. And trimmed the bushes and hedges.

7. If the moon were placed on the surface of the United States. It would extend from California to Ohio.

8. The hardiest of all the world's insects is the mosquito, it can be found in all parts of the world.

9. South American Indians introduced tapioca to the world it comes from the root of a poisonous plant.

10. We must have loaned the snowblower to Uncle Pete I can't find it.

Correcting Sentence Fragments and Run-on Sentences

Rewrite the following paragraph, correcting all sentence fragments and run-on sentences. Be sure to correct the errors in a variety of ways. Add capital letters and punctuation where needed.

According to a common superstition. The groundhog is supposed to come out of its underground home on February 2. National Groundhog Day. If the animal sees its shadow. It hurries back to its snug bed. For another six weeks. This means that there will be six more weeks of winter, people should not put their winter coats away. Of course, if the little critter stays out of its burrow, spring will soon begin. Should you believe this superstition? The National Geographic Service says that the groundhog. Has been right only 28 percent of the time that's not a very good record. Still, next February 2, hundreds of reporters will be waiting. To see if the groundhog will see its shadow.

Writing Sentences

Write five sentences that follow the directions below. Beware of sentence fragments and run-ons. Write about your favorite holiday or about a topic of your choice.

1. Write a sentence that contains only a subject and a verb.

2. Write a sentence that consists of a simple sentence with an attached phrase.

3. Write a sentence that consists of a simple sentence with an attached dependent clause.

4. Write a compound sentence containing the word *and*.

5. Write a compound sentence with a semicolon.

Language and *Self-Expression*

Charles Willson Peale is known for his portraits of colonial Americans, including a very famous portrait of George Washington. Peale also founded a natural history museum. This self-portrait shows the artist inviting the viewer into his museum.

A descriptive paragraph in spatial order is a paragraph that is organized—not step-by-step over time—but step-by-step from one place to another. Use the painting by Charles Willson Peale as a visual aid to imagine that you are standing in the artist's place in the foreground of the painting. Now imagine that you walk slowly along the corridor to the end. What do you see? Tell a visitor to the museum about it in spatial order, moving from the foreground to the background of the painting. Use your imagination to picture what is on the shelves of the natural history museum.

Prewriting Make a list of the objects you might see in Peale's museum. Number these in the order a visitor might see them as he or she walks down the corridor.

Drafting Begin with a sentence that states the main idea of your paragraph. Use your notes and the painting to add details in the order in which a visitor would see them.

Revising Reread your paragraph and add descriptive words that give specific details. If you find any sentence fragments or run-ons, correct them. Make sure that your paragraph uses spatial order.

Editing Review your paragraph, looking for errors in grammar, capitalization, punctuation, and spelling. Make any corrections that are necessary.

Publishing Prepare a final copy of your paragraph. Share your paragraph with a classmate to see how you differed in your imaginative descriptions of Peale's museum.

 **Another Look**

A **sentence fragment** is a group of words that does not express a complete thought.

Kinds of Fragments

Because a phrase does not have a subject and verb, it cannot stand alone. If it does, it is called a **phrase fragment.** *(page L260)*

KINDS OF PHRASE FRAGMENTS	
PREPOSITIONAL PHRASE	After the storm.
APPOSITIVE PHRASE	The worst storm of all.
PARTICIPIAL PHRASE	Blowing up a storm.
INFINITIVE PHRASE	To clean up the storm's debris.

All clauses have a subject and verb, but only an independent clause can stand alone. If a subordinate clause stands alone, it is called a **clause fragment.** *(page L263)*

KINDS OF CLAUSE FRAGMENTS	
ADVERB CLAUSE	If you don't watch out.
ADJECTIVE CLAUSE	That I ever saw.
NOUN CLAUSE	Whatever happened to the survivors.

A **run-on sentence** is two or more sentences that are written as one sentence and are separated by a comma or no mark of punctuation at all.

Other Information About Fragments and Run-ons

Correcting phrase fragments *(page L261)*
Correcting clause fragments *(page L264)*
Correcting run-on sentences *(page L267)*

Posttest

Directions

Read the passage. Write the letter of the best way to write each underlined section. If the underlined section contains no error, write D.

EXAMPLE   I just finished a very interesting book. About
                                                          (1)
               a mountain climbing expedition.

    1 **A** book about

        B book, about

        C book its about

        D No error

ANSWER   **1** **A**

At its peak the Incan empire controlled the entire Andean
  (1)
mountain region. Despite the rough terrain, the Incas were able to

grow crops. They did this by terracing the ground. And they
                                                (2)
irrigated extensively. The Incas raised llamas and alpacas. With
(3)
their heavy coats. These unusual animals are well suited to the
        (4)
mountain climate. The Incan civilization was quite advanced. The

Incas built extraordinary structures and their artwork is still
                          (5)
admired today.

1 **A** At, its peak the
   B At its peak. The
   C At its peak of the
   D No error

2 **A** ground and they
          irrigated
   B ground and irrigating
   C ground and, they
          irrigated
   D No error

3 **A** alpacas, with their
   B alpacas with their
   C alpacas and with their
   D No error

4 **A** coats, these unusual
   B coats these, unusual
   C coats and these
          unusual
   D No error

5 **A** structures. And their
          artwork
   B structures, and their
          artwork
   C structures and, their
          artwork
   D No error

CHAPTER 10

Using Verbs

· ·

Pretest

Directions

Read the passage and choose the word or group of words that belongs in each underlined space. Write the letter of the correct answer.

EXAMPLE Every July and August many people __(1)__ to new homes.

    1 A move
     B had been moving
     C will move
     D had moved

ANSWER   **1 A**

  Moving day __(1)__ at last! Yesterday I __(2)__ all my belongings into boxes. Later, when my friend Jason arrives, I __(3)__ them into the back of a rental truck. He __(4)__ his help. I __(5)__ him at the door now. Jason __(6)__ used to moving because he moves to a new apartment every other year. He __(7)__ some old blankets for us to use today. Before Jason arrived, I __(8)__ to protect my furniture with towels. He __(9)__ some blankets over the piano, and we are ready to go. I feel a little sad to leave because I __(10)__ in this apartment a long time.

1	A	will have been coming	6	A	will be
	B	had been coming		B	will have been
	C	has been coming		C	is being
	D	has come		D	is

2	A	packed	7	A	has been bringing
	B	pack		B	has brought
	C	will pack		C	will have brought
	D	am packing		D	had been bringing

3	A	had loaded	8	A	will try
	B	loaded		B	try
	C	will load		C	had been trying
	D	have loaded		D	will have tried

4	A	will have offered	9	A	lays
	B	has offered		B	will lay
	C	will have been offering		C	had laid
	D	offers		D	will have laid

5	A	will hear	10	A	live
	B	hear		B	will live
	C	had heard		C	have lived
	D	will have heard		D	will have lived

Ant Farm (Charles L. Lord, Hudson Marquez, Doug Michels).
Cadillac Ranch, 1974. © Ant Farm (Lord, Marquez, and Michels).

Describe   How would you describe this sculpture to someone who hasn't seen it?

Analyze   What does the artwork make you think of? What, in the artwork, causes you to make that connection?

Interpret   What techniques do you think a writer of a short story could use to evoke similar thoughts?

Judge   Would you rather view a sculpture or read a short story about this subject? Explain why you feel as you do.

At the end of this chapter, you will use the artwork to stimulate ideas for writing.

The Principal Parts of a Verb

This chapter begins the section of the book on usage. You will learn how to use the various elements of grammar covered in Chapters 1–9.

In this chapter you will look more closely at verbs. Because verbs have so many forms, people often make mistakes when they use them in writing and in speaking. Even though verbs can be the most informative—and most powerful—words in the English language, they can also be difficult to master. This chapter will help you learn more about the various forms of the verbs you use every day. The chapter will also show you how the tense of a verb is used to express time when you are writing a story. The different tenses of a verb are based on its four basic forms, called principal parts.

> The **principal parts of a verb** are the present, the present participle, the past, and the past participle.

The principal parts of the verb *jog* are used in the following examples. Notice that the present participle and the past participle must have a helping verb when they are used as verbs.

PRESENT	I **jog** two miles every day.
PRESENT PARTICIPLE	I *am* **jogging** to the lake and back.
PAST	Today I **jogged** with Ashley.
PAST PARTICIPLE	I *have* **jogged** every day for a year.

 Regular Verbs

> A **regular verb** forms its past and past participle by adding *–ed* or *–d* to the present.

The following chart shows the principal parts of the regular verbs *paint, share, stop,* and *trim.* Notice that the present participle is formed by adding *–ing* to the present form and the past participle is formed by adding *–ed* or *–d* to the present form.

REGULAR VERBS			
PRESENT	**PRESENT PARTICIPLE**	**PAST**	**PAST PARTICIPLE**
paint	(is) painting	painted	(have) painted
share	(is) sharing	shared	(have) shared
stop	(is) stopping	stopped	(have) stopped
trim	(is) trimming	trimmed	(have) trimmed

Notice that when endings such as *–ing* and *–ed* are added to some verbs, such as *share, stop,* and *trim,* the spelling changes. If you are unsure of the spelling of a verb form, look it up in the dictionary.

PRACTICE YOUR SKILLS

● Check Your Understanding
Determining the Principal Parts of a Verb

Make four columns on your paper. Label them *Present, Present Participle, Past,* and *Past Participle.* Then, using all four columns, write the four principal parts of each of the following regular verbs.

1. ask	**6.** climb	**11.** shout	**16.** gaze
2. use	**7.** wrap	**12.** stare	**17.** call
3. hop	**8.** jump	**13.** check	**18.** talk
4. row	**9.** taste	**14.** drop	**19.** shop
5. share	**10.** weigh	**15.** cook	**20.** look

▶ Irregular Verbs

An **irregular verb** does not form its past and past participle by adding −*ed* or −*d* to the present form.

The irregular verbs have been divided into six groups, according to the way they form their past and past participle. Remember, though, that the word *is* is not part of the present participle and the word *have* is not part of the past participle. They have been added to the lists of irregular verbs, however, to remind you that all the present and past participles must have a form of one of these helping verbs when they are used as a verb in a sentence.

CONNECT TO SPEAKING AND WRITING

It is sometimes easier to hear a verb used incorrectly when you are reading aloud than it is to see a mistake when you are reading silently. When you edit your work, you can find errors of many kinds if you simply read the piece aloud.

Group 1 These irregular verbs have the same form for the present, the past, and the past participle.

GROUP 1			
PRESENT	**PRESENT PARTICIPLE**	**PAST**	**PAST PARTICIPLE**
burst	(is) bursting	burst	(have) burst
cost	(is) costing	cost	(have) cost
hit	(is) hitting	hit	(have) hit
hurt	(is) hurting	hurt	(have) hurt
let	(is) letting	let	(have) let
put	(is) putting	put	(have) put
set	(is) setting	set	(have) set

Group 2 These irregular verbs have the same form for the past and past participle.

	GROUP 2		
PRESENT	PRESENT PARTICIPLE	PAST	PAST PARTICIPLE
bring	(is) bringing	brought	(have) brought
buy	(is) buying	bought	(have) bought
catch	(is) catching	caught	(have) caught
feel	(is) feeling	felt	(have) felt
find	(is) finding	found	(have) found
get	(is) getting	got	(have) got or gotten
hold	(is) holding	held	(have) held
keep	(is) keeping	kept	(have) kept
lead	(is) leading	led	(have) led
leave	(is) leaving	left	(have) left
lose	(is) losing	lost	(have) lost
make	(is) making	made	(have) made
say	(is) saying	said	(have) said
sell	(is) selling	sold	(have) sold
send	(is) sending	sent	(have) sent
teach	(is) teaching	taught	(have) taught
tell	(is) telling	told	(have) told
win	(is) winning	won	(have) won

PRACTICE YOUR SKILLS

● Check Your Understanding
Using the Correct Verb Form

Contemporary Life   **Write the past or past participle of each verb in parentheses.**

1. The left fielder has (hit) his second long, high fly ball.
2. Dee (win) the prize for most valuable player.
3. She (put) the trophy on her bookshelf at home.
4. Our coach (tell) us about good sportsmanship.
5. I (find) my lucky bat in the coach's bag.
6. Amanda has (leave) our baseball team.
7. The batter blew a bubble that (burst) all over his face.
8. The concession stand has always (sell) the players bubble gum for half price.
9. Our coach (lead) us to five straight victories.
10. Vince (keep) striking out player after player.
11. My dad has (bring) our team ice and water.
12. Having Dee on our team has not (hurt) our chances to win the championship.
13. Dee has (make) many home runs this season.
14. My mother has (keep) my baseball picture on her desk.
15. The team (hold) their breath when Dee came up to bat.

● Connect to the Writing Process: Editing
Correcting Improperly Used Verbs

Write each sentence, correcting the underlined verb. If the verb in the sentence is correct, write C.

16. Our coach has <u>let</u> us choose our team mascot.
17. We <u>buyed</u> socks to match our uniforms.
18. The players had <u>say</u> the Pledge of Allegiance before the game.
19. Has Val <u>catched</u> a pop fly during this game?
20. Our coach <u>teached</u> us to bunt the ball.

21. I <u>feeled</u> so happy after my home run!

22. The catcher's error <u>costed</u> their team the game.

23. My dad <u>send</u> a letter to the newspaper praising our coach.

24. We all <u>got</u> a trophy.

25. We have <u>losed</u> only two games in two years.

Connect to Speaking: Making an Announcement
Correcting Improperly Used Verbs

Read the following intercom announcement aloud to a classmate or your teacher. As you read, correct any verb errors you find.

Attention all students: We are hold tryouts for next year's baseball teams on Tuesday. If you have ever catch a ball or hitted a home run, you should put your name on the tryout list. Many old players have leave the team, so there are many positions available. All students interested in playing should letted the coaches know by four o'clock today.

Group 3   These irregular verbs form their past participle by adding −*n* to the past form.

	GROUP 3		
PRESENT	**PRESENT PARTICIPLE**	**PAST**	**PAST PARTICIPLE**
break	(is) breaking	broke	(have) broken
choose	(is) choosing	chose	(have) chosen
freeze	(is) freezing	froze	(have) frozen
speak	(is) speaking	spoke	(have) spoken
steal	(is) stealing	stole	(have) stolen

Group 4 These irregular verbs form their past participle by adding –*n* to the present.

GROUP 4			
PRESENT	**PRESENT PARTICIPLE**	**PAST**	**PAST PARTICIPLE**
blow	(is) blowing	blew	(have) blown
draw	(is) drawing	drew	(have) drawn
drive	(is) driving	drove	(have) driven
fly	(is) flying	flew	(have) flown
give	(is) giving	gave	(have) given
grow	(is) growing	grew	(have) grown
know	(is) knowing	knew	(have) known
see	(is) seeing	saw	(have) seen
take	(is) taking	took	(have) taken
throw	(is) throwing	threw	(have) thrown

PRACTICE YOUR SKILLS

● Check Your Understanding
Determining the Correct Verb Form

 Contemporary Life **Write the correct verb form for each sentence.**

1. I have just (chose, chosen) the seeds for our garden.
2. Last year I planted too early, so the seedlings (froze, frozen).
3. Tomatoes have always (grew, grown) well in this soil.
4. By the end of last season, I had (gave, given) many vegetables to our neighbors.
5. The wind (blew, blown) very hard last night!
6. It (broke, broken) some of my small tomato plants.

7. Last summer rabbits (stole, stolen) carrots from my garden.

8. They (took, taken) the carrots before they were mature.

9. I have never (saw, seen) them in the act.

10. I (knew, known) that rabbits were the culprits because of their tracks.

● Check Your Understanding
Using the Correct Verb Form

Contemporary Life **Write the past or past participle of each verb in parentheses.**

11. Mr. Foster has (grow) vegetables for more than fifteen years.

12. He (speak) to me about my rabbit problem.

13. He (drive) rabbits away from his garden by playing a portable radio in the garden at night.

14. Then he (draw) them away from his yard by putting vegetable scraps on the other side of his fence.

15. He said that many farmers have (throw) a party after ridding themselves of rabbits.

● Connect to the Writing Process: Editing
Correcting Improperly Used Verbs

Rewrite the sentences, using the correct verb form. If the verb form is correct, write C.

16. I am glad that Mr. Foster had chose not to hurt the rabbits.

17. Since I have used Mr. Foster's technique, no rabbits have stole carrots this year.

18. I took an organic gardening class last fall.

19. Because of that class, I have chose not to use pesticides this year.

20. I am driving the pests from my garden by natural methods.

Connect to Speaking: Making a Radio Announcement
Correcting Improperly Used Verbs

Read the following radio announcement aloud to a classmate or your teacher, correcting any verb errors you find.

Have you ever drove your car on an icy driveway? Have you ever threw salt on your sidewalk to make ice melt? Well, those days are over. We are introducing new Bye-Ice. Bye-Ice will broke up ice like nothing you've ever saw! Just sprinkle some on icy sidewalks or driveways. It clears any cement or asphalt that has froze over. Don't believe it until you have saw for yourself. Buy Bye-Ice today!

Group 5 These irregular verbs form their past and past participles by changing a vowel.

GROUP 5			
PRESENT	**PRESENT PARTICIPLE**	**PAST**	**PAST PARTICIPLE**
begin	(is) beginning	began	(have) begun
drink	(is) drinking	drank	(have) drunk
fling	(is) flinging	flung	(have) flung
ring	(is) ringing	rang	(have) rung
shrink	(is) shrinking	shrank	(have) shrunk
sing	(is) singing	sang	(have) sung
sink	(is) sinking	sank	(have) sunk
sting	(is) stinging	stung	(have) stung
swim	(is) swimming	swam	(have) swum

Group 6 These irregular verbs form the past and the past participle in other ways.

GROUP 6			
PRESENT	**PRESENT PARTICIPLE**	**PAST**	**PAST PARTICIPLE**
come	(is) coming	came	(have) come
do	(is) doing	did	(have) done
eat	(is) eating	ate	(have) eaten
fall	(is) falling	fell	(have) fallen
go	(is) going	went	(have) gone
ride	(is) riding	rode	(have) ridden
run	(is) running	ran	(have) run
tear	(is) tearing	tore	(have) torn
wear	(is) wearing	wore	(have) worn
write	(is) writing	wrote	(have) written

PRACTICE YOUR SKILLS

● Check Your Understanding
Determining the Correct Verb Form

 Write the correct verb form for each sentence.

1. My friends and I have (went, gone) to the lake every weekend this year.

2. Juan (swam, swum) from the boat to the pier.

3. Mindy has (wrote, written) for a sample of that new sunscreen lotion.

4. I always (wear, worn) a hat to shade my eyes from the sun.

5. My hat has (fell, fallen) in the lake before.

6. Lesli has (sank, sunk) her brother's boat!

7. Cali (rode, ridden) on the inner tube behind the ski boat.

8. Our water polo match has not (began, begun) yet.

9. On the dock my cell phone (rang, rung) so loudly that everyone stared at me.

10. I dropped my phone, and it (sank, sunk) to the bottom of the lake.

● Check Your Understanding
Using the Correct Verb Form

General Interest **Write the past or past participle of each verb in parentheses.**

11. Each spring in Austin, Texas, the Mexican free-tail bats have (come) to the Congress Avenue Bridge to make their homes underneath.

12. Long ago many people feared that bats (drink) human blood.

13. The Austin bats are welcomed by this city, where they have (eat) large numbers of pesky mosquitoes.

14. They have also (do) another helpful thing.

15. Tourists have (begin) to come to see the bats, which constitute the largest urban bat colony in the United States.

16. Many joggers have (run) under the bridge to see the bats.

17. Local musicians have (sing) songs about the flying mammals.

18. For years the bats have (tear) across the darkening sky at sunset.

19. Throughout the summers Austinites have (come) down to watch the spectacle.

20. In the fall disappointed tourists find that the bat population has (shrink) due to the bats' migration to Mexico.

Finding Principal Parts in a Dictionary

Make four columns on your paper. Label them *present, present participle, past,* and *past participle.* Then look up each of the following irregular verbs in a dictionary. Write the principal parts of each one in the appropriate columns.

21. swing

22. strive

23. swear

24. spin

25. shake

26. become

27. arise

28. weave

29. build

30. sleep

31. bend

32. forget

33. lend

34. meet

35. fight

36. pay

37. mean

38. creep

39. hold

40. sweep

Connect to the Writing Process: Drafting
Writing Sentences Using Irregular Verbs

Write sentences using the indicated form of the verb. Use your list from the above exercise to help you.

41. present form of *swing*

42. present participle form of *pay*

43. past form of *shake*

44. past participle form of *become*

45. present form of *build*

46. present participle form of *forget*

47. past form of *meet*

48. past participle form of *arise*

49. past form of *creep*

50. past participle form of *sweep*

APPLY TO WRITING

Announcement: *Verb Forms*

Your teacher has asked you to write a short announcement to be read over the school intercom, inviting students to a meeting of the school's new book club. Remember, a good announcement should give information about the club and the location of the meeting. Use the following forms of the verbs listed as you write your announcement.

- Present participle of *come*
- Past participle of *grow*
- Past participle of *speak*
- Present form of *make*
- Past participle of *put*

QuickCheck Mixed Practice

General Interest **Write the past or past participle of each verb in parentheses.**

1. In first-century Rome, Nero had snow (bring) from the nearby mountains.

2. With the snow he (make) the first frozen dessert.

3. He (experiment) with snow, honey, and fruit.

4. Until the thirteenth century, no one in Europe had (see) a frozen milk dessert.

5. Marco Polo (introduce) a version of ice cream to Europe.

6. Improvements on this dessert (lead) to the creation of ice cream in the sixteenth century.

7. Ice cream, however, (remain) a treat for the rich only.

8. For years the great chefs (keep) the secret of ice cream to themselves.

9. After a French café (begin) serving ice cream, it (become) everyone's favorite.

10. Only a few Americans had (eat) ice cream before 1700.

Six Problem Verbs

In addition to learning the principal parts of irregular verbs, it is sometimes necessary to look closely at the meanings of certain pairs of verbs because they are easily confused with each other. The following six verbs often cause problems in speaking and writing.

lie and *lay*

Lie means "to rest or recline." *Lie* is never followed by a direct object. *Lay* means "to put or set (something) down." *Lay* is usually followed by a direct object.

You can learn about direct objects on pages L149–L151.

PRESENT	PRESENT PARTICIPLE	PAST	PAST PARTICIPLE
lie	(is) lying	lay	(have) lain
lay	(is) laying	laid	(have) laid

LIE   Our puppies always **lie** near the fireplace in the living room.

They **are lying** there now.

They **lay** there all last night.

They **have lain** there in that same spot for an hour.

LAY   **Lay** the puppies' mats on the floor.
(You lay what? *Mats* is the direct object.)

Jon **is laying** the puppies' mats on the floor.

My sister **laid** the mats on the floor last night.

Usually I **have laid** the mats on the floor.

rise and raise

Rise means "to move upward" or "to get up." Rise is never followed by a direct object. Raise means "to lift (something) up," "to increase," or "to grow something." Raise is usually followed by a direct object.

PRESENT	PRESENT PARTICIPLE	PAST	PAST PARTICIPLE
rise	(is) rising	rose	(have) risen
raise	(is) raising	raised	(have) raised

RISE **Rise** out of that bed!

The sick puppy **is rising** off the mat.

He **rose** and went to the kitchen.

He **has risen** early every morning since we took him to the veterinarian.

RAISE **Raise** the litter of puppies carefully.

(You raise what? Litter is the direct object.)

Benjamin **is raising** a litter of puppies at the kennel.

Benjamin **raised** a litter of puppies last year, too.

Benjamin **has raised** litters of puppies for thirteen years now.

sit and set

Sit means "to rest in an upright position." Sit is never followed by a direct object. Set usually means "to put or place (something)." Set is usually followed by a direct object.

PRESENT	PRESENT PARTICIPLE	PAST	PAST PARTICIPLE
sit	(is) sitting	sat	(have) sat
set	(is) setting	set	(have) set

SIT   **Sit** down by the fire and get warm.

My puppy **is sitting** near the fire.

Her puppy **sat** there for almost an hour.

The dogs **have** never **sat** there before.

SET   **Set** the dogs' dishes on the kennel floor.
(You set what? *Dishes* is the direct object.)

He **is setting** the dishes on the kennel floor.

She **set** the dishes on the kennel floor yesterday.

He **has set** the dishes on the kennel floor many times before.

You can learn more about other problem verbs on pages L281–L288.

PRACTICE YOUR SKILLS

 Check Your Understanding
Using the Correct Verb

 Read the following sentences aloud to practice saying the underlined verbs and hearing them used correctly. Be prepared to explain why each verb is correct.

1. My dogs always get excited before I <u>set</u> their food dishes down.

2. One morning Rover actually <u>sat</u> still when I came in with his food.

3. When Rover is sick, he lies on my bed.

4. I had laid Rover's medicine on my nightstand the night before.

5. For a whole day, Rover never raised his head.

6. The next day he felt stronger, but he still lay there.

7. Finally, on the third day, he rose to his feet.

8. He drank the water I had set on the floor for him.

9. I sat and watched as he ate a little food.

10. Then he laid his head on my lap and went to sleep again.

● Check Your Understanding
Using the Correct Verb

Contemporary Life **Write the correct verb for each sentence.**

11. Mom asked me to (sit, set) the dishes on the table for a special dinner.

12. I was (sitting, setting) comfortably in front of the fireplace.

13. I (rose, raised) from my chair and went into the dining room.

14. I (lay, laid) placemats on the table.

15. I decided to use the good china, which had (lain, laid) in the cabinet for months.

16. As I (rose, raised) a china plate to the table, it slipped from my hand.

17. The dish (laid, lay) in shattered pieces all over our tile floor.

18. I (set, sat) down the other plate carefully and started cleaning up the mess.

19. (Raising, Rising) from the floor with the broken dish, I felt bad about the accident.

20. I decided I would (sit, set) aside some of my allowance to buy a new dish.

Correcting Verb Usage

Write each sentence, correcting the underlined verb. If the verb in the sentence is correct, write C.

21. Most hens lay at least one egg each day.

22. They set on the eggs in order to keep them warm enough to hatch.

23. They raise from their nests to eat but return to the eggs as soon as possible.

24. The eggs lay in the nest waiting for the hen's speedy return.

25. If the eggs have been fertilized, the hen will soon be rising baby chicks.

26. Chicks usually are risen on farms.

27. Some farmers also rise cows.

28. Baby calves do not lie in a nest as baby chicks do.

29. Some ranchers will sit hay in a field for their cows to eat.

30. When farmers are not working, you might find them as they set in the shade.

Communicate Your Ideas

APPLY TO WRITING

Informative Paragraph: *Problem Verbs*

Your health teacher has asked you to write about fire safety. Write an informative paragraph that tells your classmates the proper way to react if their clothes catch on fire. Be sure to consult a reliable source for appropriate safety rules. In your paragraph properly use at least one form of the six problem verbs: *lie, lay, sit, set, rise,* and *raise.*

Contemporary
Life
Write the correct form of the verbs in parentheses.

1. The magician (raised, rose) from a deep bow to the audience.

2. He (sat, set) a tall top hat on the table at the front of the stage.

3. His lovely assistant (lay, laid) a feather inside the hat on the table.

4. Then she (set, sat) a blue, silk handkerchief over the hat.

5. The magician (rose, raised) his wand over the hat three times.

6. The hat that was (lying, laying) on the table began to shake violently.

7. The top hat tumbled from the table on which it had (set, sat).

8. As the hat fell, a beautiful dove (rose, raised) from inside it.

9. The audience could not (set, sit) still at the sight of the graceful dove.

10. They (rose, raised) from their seats, applauding the magnificent magician.

Verb Tense

The six tenses of a verb are the present, past, future, present perfect, past perfect, and future perfect.

The time expressed by a verb is called the tense of a verb.

In the following examples, the six tenses of *run* are used to express action at different times.

PRESENT	I **run** a mile every day.
PAST	I **ran** a mile yesterday
FUTURE	I **will run** a mile tomorrow.
PRESENT PERFECT	I **have run** a mile every day since June.
PAST PERFECT	I **had** not **run** that much before.
FUTURE PERFECT	I **will have run** almost two hundred miles before the end of the year.

▶ Uses of Tenses

As the previous examples show, verbs in the English language have six basic tenses: three simple tenses and three perfect tenses. All these tenses can be formed from the four principal parts of a verb and the helping verbs *have, has, had, will,* and *shall.*

Present tense is the first of the three simple tenses. It is used to express an action that is going on now. To form the present tense, use the present form (the first principal part of the verb) or add *–s* or *–es* to the present form.

PRESENT TENSE	I **watch** music videos
	Megan **sings** along with the videos.
	Even her parents **enjoy** some of the videos.

Past tense expresses an action that has already taken place or was completed in the past. To form the past tense of a verb, add *–ed* or *–d* to the present form. To form the past of an irregular verb, check a dictionary for the past form or look for it on pages L281–L288.

> PAST TENSE
>
> I **watched** the music awards program on television.
>
> Megan **sang** beautifully at the concert last night.
>
> Her parents **enjoyed** the concert.

Future tense is used to express an action that will take place in the future. To form the future tense, use the helping verb *shall* or *will* with the present form.

> FUTURE TENSE
>
> I **shall watch** the awards program again this year.
>
> Megan **will sing** at the concert tomorrow night.
>
> Her parents probably **will enjoy** the concert.

In formal English, *shall* is used with *I* and *we,* and *will* is used with *you, he, she, it,* or *they.* In informal speech, however, *shall* and *will* are used interchangeably with *I* and *we* except for questions, which still use *shall.*

You can learn more about shall *and* will *on page L447.*

Present perfect tense is the first of the three perfect tenses. The present perfect tense expresses an action that was completed at some indefinite time in the past. It also expresses an action that started in the past and is still going on. To form the present perfect tense, add *has* or *have* to the past participle.

PRESENT PERFECT TENSE	I **have watched** the award program for several years now.
	Megan **has sung** here before now.
	Her parents **have enjoyed** watching her perform.

Past perfect tense expresses an action that took place before some other action in the past. To form the past perfect tense, add *had* to the past participle.

PAST PERFECT TENSE	I **had watched** my video before I watched yours.
	Megan **had sung** the national anthem before the concert.
	Her parents **had enjoyed** listening to her rehearse.

Future perfect tense expresses an action that will take place before another future action or time. To form the future perfect tense, add *shall have* or *will have* to the past participle.

FUTURE PERFECT TENSE	I **shall have watched** more than ten videos by Friday.
	By Saturday Megan **will have sung** at the concert.
	By Saturday Megan's parents **will have enjoyed** listening to all the music.

Verb Conjugation

One way to see or study all the tenses of a particular verb is to look at a conjugation of that verb. A **conjugation** is a list of all the singular and plural forms of a verb in its various tenses.

Regular verbs are conjugated like irregular verbs. The only variations result from the differences in the principal parts of the verbs themselves. Following is a conjugation of the irregular verb *ride,* whose four principal parts are *ride, riding, rode,* and *ridden.*

SIMPLE TENSES OF THE VERB *RIDE*

Present

SINGULAR	PLURAL
I ride	we ride
you ride	you ride
he, she, it rides	they ride

Past

SINGULAR	PLURAL
I rode	we rode
you rode	you rode
he, she, it rode	they rode

Future

SINGULAR	PLURAL
I shall/will ride	we shall/will ride
you will ride	you will ride
he, she, it will ride	they will ride

PERFECT TENSES OF THE VERB *RIDE*

Present Perfect Tense

SINGULAR	PLURAL
I have ridden	we have ridden
you have ridden	you have ridden
he, she, it has ridden	they have ridden

Past Perfect Tense

SINGULAR	PLURAL
I had ridden	we had ridden
you had ridden	you had ridden
he, she, it had ridden	they had ridden

Future Perfect Tense

SINGULAR	PLURAL
I shall/will have ridden	we shall/will have ridden
you will have ridden	you will have ridden
he, she, it will have ridden	they will have ridden

The present participle is used to conjugate only the progressive forms of a verb. You can learn more about those verbs on pages 307–308.

Since the principal parts of the verb *be* are highly irregular, the conjugation of that verb is different from other irregular verbs. Following is the conjugation of the verb *be,* whose four principal parts are *am, being, was,* and *been.*

SIMPLE TENSES OF THE VERB *BE*

Present

SINGULAR	PLURAL
I am	we are
you are	you are
he, she, it is	they are

Past

SINGULAR	PLURAL
I was	we were
you were	you were
he, she, it was	they were

Future

SINGULAR	PLURAL
I shall/will be	we shall/will be
you will be	you will be
he, she, it will be	they will be

PERFECT TENSES OF THE VERB *BE*

Present Perfect Tense

SINGULAR	PLURAL
I have been	we have been
you have been	you have been
he, she, it has been	they have been

Past Perfect Tense

SINGULAR	PLURAL
I had been	we had been
you had been	you had been
he, she, it had been	they had been

Future Perfect Tense

SINGULAR	PLURAL
I shall/will have been	we shall/will have been
you will have been	you will have been
he, she, it will have been	they will have been

CONNECT TO WRITER'S CRAFT

You have probably noticed that most folk literature is written in the past tense, as is this excerpt from "Hansel and Gretel."

Hard by a great forest dwelt a poor wood-cutter with his wife and his two children. The boy was called Hansel and the girl Gretel. He had little to bite and to break, and once when great dearth fell on the land, he could no longer procure even daily bread.

—Grimm Brothers, "Hansel and Gretel"

When you write about the literature you read, however, it is proper to write about it in the present tense. For example, if you were to write about the passage above, you might say:

The story of "Hansel and Gretel" opens with a description of the sad state of the children's family. Hansel and Gretel live with their father and his wife in a great forest. They barely ever have enough food, and it soon becomes impossible for the wood-cutter to get any food at all to feed his family.

PRACTICE YOUR SKILLS

● Check Your Understanding
Identifying Verb Tense

General Interest   **Write the tense of each underlined verb.**

1. Today popular bands <u>make</u> videos for each of their hit songs.
2. Prior to 1980, filming music videos <u>was</u> rare.
3. Before that year musicians <u>had recorded</u> only audio albums.
4. Even today many bands <u>have</u> never <u>produced</u> any professional recordings of their music.
5. Recording an album in a music studio <u>costs</u> a great deal of money.
6. Writers <u>have composed</u> many songs for other musicians to play.
7. Most people <u>will</u> probably never <u>hear</u> these songs on the radio.
8. Famous singers and bands <u>earn</u> a considerable amount of money.
9. By age eighteen, you <u>will have seen</u> many music videos on television.
10. You <u>will</u> likely <u>watch</u> even more after that.

Using Tenses of the Verb Be

History Topic **For each blank, write the tense of the verb *be* that is indicated in parentheses.**

11. The history of the monarchy in England ▓ (present) truly interesting.

12. Many scholars ▓ (present) experts in this area of British history.

13. Many men and women ▓ (past perfect) rulers of England.

14. King John always ▓ (future) famous as the signer of the Magna Carta.

15. Lady Jane Grey ▓ (past) queen of England for only nine days.

16. Henry VIII's son Edward ▓ (past perfect) ruler before her.

17. Mary ▓ (past) queen of England before her half-sister Elizabeth I.

18. King James I ▓ (present) famous for the English version of the Bible begun during his reign.

19. In the year 2003, Elizabeth I ▓ (future perfect) dead for four hundred years.

20. Who ▓ (future) the next monarch of Britain?

● Connect to the Writing Process: Drafting
Using Verb Tense

Write sentences, using the tense of the verb indicated.

21. Present tense of *share*

22. Past tense of *sell*

23. Future tense of *speak*

24. Present perfect tense of *know*

25. Past perfect tense of *drink*

26. Future perfect tense of *run*

27. Future tense of *wear*

28. Present perfect tense of *lay*

29. Past perfect tense of *rise*

30. Future perfect tense of *set*

Communicate Your Ideas

APPLY TO WRITING
Friendly Letter: *Verb Tenses*

Artist unknown. (Detail) *Queen Tiy, from the Tomb of Userhat,* 18th dynasty. Limestone relief, 16¾ by 15½ inches. Courtesy Musées Royaux d'Art et d'Histoire, Brussels, Belgium.

Imagine that you are the Egyptian queen whose face is carved in the pharaoh's tomb. Write a letter to your sister, who will be coming to visit you soon. Describe for her what a typical day is like at your palace. What do you do to occupy your time? What will you and your sister do when she comes to visit you? Use your imagination to make the letter seem realistic. After you have written your letter, underline seven verbs you have used. Above each verb, label its tense.

Progressive Verb Forms

Each of the six verb tenses has a progressive form. The **progressive form** is used to express continuing or ongoing action. To form the progressive, add a form of the *be* verb to the present participle. Notice in the following examples that all the progressive forms end in *–ing.*

PRESENT PROGRESSIVE	I am riding.
PAST PROGRESSIVE	I was riding.
FUTURE PROGRESSIVE	I will (shall) be riding.
PRESENT PERFECT PROGRESSIVE	I have been riding.
PAST PERFECT PROGRESSIVE	I had been riding.
FUTURE PERFECT PROGRESSIVE	I will (shall) have been riding.

The **present progressive form** shows an ongoing action that is taking place now.

I **am eating** very hot soup.

Occasionally the present progressive can be used to show action in the future when the sentence contains an adverb or a phrase that indicates the future—such as *tomorrow* or *next month.*

I **am eating** at a restaurant tomorrow night.

The **past progressive form** shows an ongoing action that took place in the past.

I **was eating** hot French onion soup when I burned my tongue.

The **future progressive form** shows an ongoing action that will take place in the future.

> By six o'clock tonight, I **will be eating** Grandma's delicious soup.

The **present perfect progressive form** shows an ongoing action that is continuing in the present.

> I **have been eating** Grandma's soup my whole life.

The **past perfect progressive form** shows an ongoing action in the past that was interrupted by another past action.

> I **had been eating** Grandma's soup when the doorbell rang.

The **future perfect progressive form** shows a future ongoing action that will have taken place by a stated future time.

> I **will have been eating** Grandma's soup for at least twenty-one years by the time I graduate from college.

PRACTICE YOUR SKILLS

● Check Your Understanding
Identifying Progressive Verb Forms

Contemporary Life **Write the verbs in the following sentences. Then write which progressive form of the verb is used.**

1. Grandma has been cooking famous dishes for more than forty years.

2. She was serving a variety of great soups and stews before my mother's birth.

3. Until recently, her neighbors had been begging her for the recipes.

4. Now I am helping Grandma with her latest project.

5. We have been writing down all her recipes.

6. Next year a local company will be publishing her recipes in a cookbook.

7. By then Grandma will have been serving her soups for a half century.

8. We are hoping the cookbook will sell well.

9. Grandma has been dreaming of a trip to Paris.

10. My entire family will be joining her on the trip.

● Connect to the Writing Process: Drafting
Writing Sentences

Write sentences, using the indicated progressive form of the verb.

11. Past progressive of *go*

12. Future progressive of *swim*

13. Present perfect progressive of *give*

14. Past perfect progressive of *freeze*

15. Future perfect progressive of *lose*

Communicate Your Ideas

APPLY TO WRITING

Writer's Craft: *Analyzing the Use of the Past Progressive Form*

Writers often use the past progressive form in their writing. In this paragraph from *The Liar's Club*, Mary Karr describes an incident at the beach when her sister Lecia was stung by a jellyfish. Read the paragraph and then follow the directions.

   The guy in the camouflage pants had dragged Lecia out of the water while I was fetching my parents. He was kneeling beside her with his pink grandma gloves on when we came up. Lecia sat on the sand with her legs straight out in front of her like some drugstore doll. She had stopped squealing. In fact, she had a glassy look, as if the leg with the man-of-war fastened to it belonged to some other girl. She wasn't even crying, though every now and then she sucked in air through her teeth like she hurt. The camouflaged guy with the pink gloves was trying to peel the tentacles off her, but it was clumsy work. Mother was looking at Daddy and saying what should they do. She said this over and over, and Daddy didn't appear to be listening.

—*Mary Karr*, The Liar's Club

- Write all the progressive verbs from the passage. Be careful not to confuse gerunds (verb forms used as nouns) with progressive verbs.
- In the first sentence, how does the verb "had dragged" function with "was fetching," which appears later in the sentence?
- How does Karr's use of progressive verb forms work to make the action seem more vivid?

● Shifts in Tense

When you write, it is important to keep your tenses consistent. For example, if you are telling a story that took place in the past, use the past tense of verbs. If you suddenly shift to the present, you will confuse your readers.

Avoid unnecessary shifts in tense within a sentence or with related sentences.

INCORRECT	I **opened** [past] the front door, and something **flies** [present] past me.
CORRECT	I **opened** [past] the front door, and something **flew** [past] past me.
CORRECT	I **open** [present] the front door, and something **flies** [present] past me.

	past
INCORRECT	When the excitement **had passed**, I **looked**

INCORRECT   When the excitement **had passed**, I **looked**
around in the hallway. I **find** a baseball on the
floor.

CORRECT   When the excitement **had passed**, I **looked**
around in the hallway. I **found** a baseball on
the floor.

Notice that there is a change of tense here,
from *had passed* (past perfect) to *looked* and
found (simple past). Sometimes more than one
tense is needed to show a sequence of events.

PRACTICE YOUR SKILLS

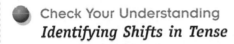

Check Your Understanding
Identifying Shifts in Tense

Sports Topic   **If the sentence contains a shift in tense, change the
second verb to the correct tense. If a sentence is
correct, write C.**

1. Babe Ruth was born in 1895, and his birth name is
George Herman Ruth.

2. Ruth learned to play baseball in school, and a priest
helps him get his first job with the Baltimore Orioles.

3. When Ruth started his professional career, he earned six
hundred dollars for his first season.

4. Babe Ruth began his career as a pitcher, but he is later
shifted to the outfield.

5. Because he was such an amazing hitter, the manager
wants him to play every game.

6. The Orioles sold him to the Boston Red Sox, who later
sell him to the New York Yankees.

7. He had his best year in 1927, when he knocks in a
season record of sixty home runs.

8. Even though he was famous and popular on the field, Babe Ruth has problems off the field.

9. He got in trouble, and in 1925 he is suspended for his behavior off the field.

10. In 1935, he joined the Boston Braves, but before the end of that season, he has quit playing the game.

11. Today baseball is still the popular sport it has been in the past.

12. Each year thousands of fans have flocked to stadiums across the country.

13. Fans always eagerly await the playoffs because the games were so intense.

14. Do you hope the team you watched last year also will have won this year?

15. Whichever team wins the World Series will have had an excellent year.

Connect to the Writing Process: Revising
Correcting Shifts in Tense

History Topic **Rewrite the following paragraph, correcting shifts in tense.**

Modern baseball was once named town ball. It first become popular in the United States in the 1830s. Wooden stakes are the bases, and the playing field is square. A pitcher is called a feeder, and a batter was called a striker. After a batter hits the ball, he ran clockwise. After a fielder catches the ball, he gets a runner out by hitting him with the ball. In the early days of baseball, balls are soft and are made by winding yarn around a piece of rubber.

APPLY TO WRITING

Persuasive Article: *Verb Tenses*

What is your favorite sport? Why do you like it? A sports magazine has asked its readers to write a short article to persuade other people to watch their favorite sport. Write a short article for the magazine, persuading others to enjoy your favorite sport. As you write, be careful to avoid inappropriate shifts in verb tense. Read your article aloud to a classmate, having him or her listen for shifts in tense. Correct any errors and submit a final copy to your teacher.

QuickCheck   Mixed Practice

Music Topic **Rewrite the paragraph below, correcting any incorrect verb forms or shifts in tense.**

Mozart's father play in a string quartet. One day the quartet had planned to practice at his home. When the second violinist did not appear, Mozart takes his place. Even though he had never saw the music before, Mozart plays it perfectly. Mozart was only five years old at the time! Three years later Mozart written his first complete symphony. No one has ever doubted that Mozart is the greatest musical genius of his time.

Active and Passive Voice

In addition to tense, a verb has voice. A verb is used in either the active voice or the passive voice.

The **active voice** indicates that the subject is performing the action.

The **passive voice** indicates that the action of the verb is being performed upon the subject.

In the following examples, the same verb is used in the active voice in one sentence and the passive voice in the other. The verb in the active voice has a direct object. The verb in the passive voice does not have a direct object.

ACTIVE VOICE   Our world history class **studied** the history of Chile.

(*History* is the direct object.)

PASSIVE VOICE   The history of Chile **was studied** by our world history class.

(There is no direct object.)

You can learn more about direct objects on pages L149–L151.

▶ Use of the Active and Passive Voice

Only **transitive verbs**—verbs that take direct objects—can be used in the passive voice. When an active verb is changed to passive, the direct object of the active verb becomes the subject of the passive verb. The subject of the active verb can be used in a prepositional phrase.

		┌── direct object ──┐
ACTIVE VOICE	Pedro de Valdivia founded **Santiago, Chile,** in 1541.	

	┌────── subject ──────┐
PASSIVE VOICE	**Santiago, Chile,** was founded by Pedro de Valdivia in 1541.

A verb in the passive voice consists of a form of the verb *be* plus a past participle.

Early explorers **were startled** by Chile's unfamiliar animals.

Llamas **are** still **used** as beasts of burden in South America.

Use the active voice as much as possible. It adds greater directness and forcefulness to your writing. However, you should use the passive voice when the doer of the action is unknown or unimportant. Also use it when you want to emphasize the receiver of the action.

Notebooks of the early Spanish explorers **will be displayed** at our local museum.
(The doer is unknown.)

Grand descriptions of llamas and other animals **were recorded** by early explorers.
(Emphasis is on the receiver, *descriptions*.)

PRACTICE YOUR SKILLS

Check Your Understanding
Recognizing Active and Passive Voice

Literature Topic **Write the verb in each sentence and label it *A* for active or *P* for passive.**

1. Literature is respected by Chileans.

2. Many poems were written by Chile's most famous poet, Pablo Neruda.

3. He continued his education in Santiago.

4. His life was devoted to writing poetry.

5. Neruda also served the government of Chile as a diplomat.

6. He accepted the Lenin Peace Prize in 1953.

7. His collection *Spain in the Heart* was written during the Spanish Civil War.

8. Neruda is remembered for such poems as "General Song."

9. Many critics consider that poem to be his greatest work.

10. Pablo Neruda was awarded the prestigious Nobel Prize in 1971.

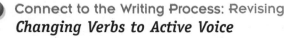

Connect to the Writing Process: Revising

Changing Verbs to Active Voice

History Topic **Rewrite the following paragraph, changing passive-voice verbs to active voice, if appropriate.**

In 1814, the small South American country of Chile was ruled by Spain. However, the freedom of Chile was being fought for by Bernardo O'Higgins and a small band of Chilean patriots. For a while all seemed lost for them. Then an unusual idea came to O'Higgins. A large herd of sheep, mules, goats, and dogs was rounded up by O'Higgins's men. When the Chileans startled the animals, they charged off toward the Spaniards. The Spaniards, of course, got out of their way, and right behind the animals were the patriots. After the battle the Chileans reorganized in the hills. Eventually the Spaniards were defeated by them.

APPLY TO WRITING
Movie Review: *Active and Passive Voice*

Your class is putting together a booklet for ninth graders about the best movies of all time. Write a review of your personal all-time favorite movie. It may be a recent film or something you saw when you were much younger. Use active-voice verbs to make your writing lively. If you use any passive-voice verbs, be prepared to explain why they are appropriate.

QuickCheck Mixed Practice

Science Topic **Rewrite the paragraph below, correcting any incorrect verb forms, shifts in tense, or inappropriate use of the passive voice.**

The seafloor is littered by shipwrecks. Many of these sunken ships will contain treasures made of glass that have been perfectly preserved in the salty water. While the water protects the glass objects, they shrink and become brittle after they are bring to the surface. A way has been discovered by scientists to preserve these artifacts. The objects are submerged in silicone polymers, which invade the pores of the glass. Then the glass is covered in a thin layer of polymers that strengthened the glass and kept it from breaking. This technique has save many artifacts, including glass jars from a sixteenth-century sunken pirate hideout in Jamaica.

Using the Correct Verb Form

Write the past or past participle form of each verb in parentheses.

1. Ten minutes after the downpour, the sun (come) out.
2. How long have you (know) about the party?
3. The sun (rise) at 5:36 yesterday.
4. Lake Erie has never (freeze) over completely.
5. My sister has (sing) twice on television.
6. Have you (write) your history report yet?
7. Who (write) the screenplay for that movie?
8. The telephone hasn't (ring) all day.
9. You should have (go) to the dance last night.
10. Dana has already (take) those books back to the library.
11. Before World War II, the United States had (give) the Philippines a guarantee of independence.
12. I should have (do) my homework earlier.
13. Until 1875, no one had ever successfully (swam) the English Channel.
14. My wallet hadn't been (steal) after all.
15. Who (choose) brown as the color for this room?
16. Tom (fall) off his skateboard yesterday, but fortunately he was wearing a helmet.
17. Have you ever (wear) those hiking boots on a hike of more than two miles?
18. Who (draw) that picture of Mr. Turner's barn?
19. Lately I have (grow) more confident using the laptop computer.
20. Waiting on the windy corner, we nearly (freeze).

Understanding Tenses

Write the tense of each underlined verb.

1. I <u>am going</u> to the library.
2. Lenny <u>has seen</u> Sarah somewhere before.
3. On Monday Mrs. Saunders <u>will announce</u> the names of the new class officers.
4. Tim <u>was</u> enthusiastic about the project.
5. I <u>have been practicing</u> for my recital every night for a month.
6. Next year will be the third year he <u>will have played</u> for the soccer team.
7. Laura <u>discovered</u> that she <u>had left</u> the tickets at home.
8. Pilar <u>knows</u> that we <u>will be working</u> together on the dance committee.
9. Marie <u>has been</u> happy ever since she <u>won</u> the CD player.
10. Susan and Greg <u>were riding</u> the bus when they first met.

Writing Sentences

Write ten sentences that follow the directions below. Write about a pet or a topic of your choice.

Write a sentence that...

1. includes the past tense of *choose*.
2. includes the past perfect tense of *become*.
3. includes the future tense of *take*.
4. includes the present perfect tense of *lie*.
5. includes the past tense of *lay*.
6. includes the present progressive tense of *rise*.
7. includes the future progressive tense of *set*.
8. includes the present tense of *be*.
9. includes any verb in the active voice.
10. includes any verb in the passive voice.

Language and *Self-Expression*

This sculpture shows the tail fins of ten cars buried hood-down in a field in Texas. When its artists visited the field for the first time, they were greeted by an expanse of gently blowing wheat. The rippling waves reminded one artist of an ocean. When he visualized dolphins leaping gracefully from its surface, the idea for the sculpture was born.

A dazzling sight in nature ignited the creativity behind *Cadillac Ranch.* What scenes in nature have inspired your creativity? Think of such a sight—perhaps a vividly colored shell, an imposing mountain, or shadows in a forest. Write a personal narrative that describes what you saw and what it inspired—a poem, a rap song, a photographic collage, or a special conversation, for example. Select verb forms and tenses that will tell your story. Also use the active voice as much as possible. Share your narrative with a small group of classmates.

Prewriting Begin by freewriting about the object or scene that inspired you. Then plan a beginning, middle, and end for your narrative. The beginning will describe what you saw; the middle will describe what it inspired; the end will summarize these details.

Drafting Write your narrative, using ideas from your freewriting and plan. Choose active verbs whenever possible.

Revising Read your narrative aloud, marking places that need work. After you have made changes, ask a classmate to read your story. Ask whether the sequence of your story is easy to follow.

Editing Check your story for errors in spelling and punctuation and check for consistency of tenses.

Publishing Prepare a final copy of your narrative. Read it to a group of classmates.

Another Look

The **principal parts of a verb** are the *present,* the *present participle,* the *past,* and the *past participle.*

Regular and Irregular Verbs
A **regular verb** forms its past and past participle by adding *–ed* or *–d* to the present form. *(pages L279–L280)*

An **irregular verb** does not form its past and past participle by adding *–ed* or *–d* to the present form. *(pages L281–L288)*

Verb Tense
The time expressed by a verb is called the **tense** of a verb. The six tenses of a verb are the *present, past, future, present perfect, past perfect,* and *future perfect. (pages L298–L300)*

Progressive Verb Forms

Each of the six verb tenses has a **progressive form.** The progressive forms are used to express continuing or ongoing action. To form the progressive, add a form of the *be* verb to the present participle. All progressive forms end in *–ing.*

The progressive forms of a verb are the *present progressive, past progressive, future progressive, present perfect progressive, past perfect progressive,* and the *future perfect progressive. (pages L307–L308)*

Active and Passive Voice
The **active voice** indicates that the subject is performing the action. *(pages L314–L315)*

The **passive voice** indicates that the action of the verb is being performed upon the subject. *(pages L314–L315)*

Other Information About Verbs
Using consistent verb tenses *(pages L310–L311)*
Distinguishing among problem verbs *(pages L292–L294)*

Directions

Read the passage and choose the word or group of words that belongs in each underlined space. Write the letter of the correct answer.

EXAMPLE   For the past few summers, action films __(1)__ the list of popular movies.

      1 A top

      B will top

      C are topping

      D have topped

ANSWER   **1 D**

Yesterday my sister and I __(1)__ the movie *A Wild Ride.* The story __(2)__ on an actual event. Joe, the main character, __(3)__ money from his boss for years until he was caught. My sister __(4)__ the movie three times already. She probably __(5)__ to the same movie again! She __(6)__ to one movie a week since last June. My favorite scene __(7)__ at the end of the movie. Three police officers __(8)__ Joe in a dense forest after he had made his break from prison. He __(9)__ to escape through a secret tunnel before they made their move. Since yesterday I __(10)__ to tell everyone I know how the movie ends.

1 **A** see
   B saw
   C will see
   D will be seeing

2 **A** is basing
   B was basing
   C will be based
   D is based

3 **A** steals
   B is stealing
   C had been stealing
   D will steal

4 **A** sees
   B will see
   C has been seeing
   D has seen

5 **A** goes
   B will go
   C will have been going
   D went

6 **A** is going
   B has gone
   C will go
   D will be going

7 **A** has happened
   B will have happened
   C happened
   D is happening

8 **A** will surround
   B will have surrounded
   C surrounded
   D will be surrounding

9 **A** was hoping
   B hopes
   C will hope
   D is hoping

10 **A** will want
   B have been wanting
   C am wanting
   D will have been wanting

CHAPTER 11

Using Pronouns

• •

Directions

Read the passage and choose the pronoun that belongs in each underlined space. Write the letter of the correct answer.

EXAMPLE   Ms. Key, __(1)__ teaches algebra, always gives difficult tests.

      1 A whose

        B whoever

        C who

        D whom

ANSWER   **1 C**

The students in Ms. Key's class knew that __(1)__ would have to study hard for the test. Jan and Marisa asked Jeff, __(2)__ they always called for help, to study with __(3)__. __(4)__ all agreed to meet at Jan's house that afternoon. Both Marisa and Jeff brought __(5)__ review notes. Marisa gave __(6)__ to Jan to look over. Jan, __(7)__ notes were messy, was relieved that her friend took better notes. Jan was also glad to study with Jeff, __(8)__ knew more about solving equations than __(9)__. However, neither Jeff nor Marisa could match __(10)__ skill at graphing.

1	**A**	they	6	**A**	her
	B	it		**B**	his
	C	them		**C**	them
	D	he		**D**	hers
2	**A**	he	7	**A**	whose
	B	whose		**B**	who
	C	whom		**C**	whom
	D	who		**D**	whomever
3	**A**	they	8	**A**	him
	B	them		**B**	he
	C	she		**C**	who
	D	her		**D**	she
4	**A**	He	9	**A**	her
	B	She		**B**	hers
	C	They		**C**	she
	D	Them		**D**	him
5	**A**	them	10	**A**	they
	B	their		**B**	their
	C	her		**C**	her
	D	our		**D**	hers

William H. Johnson.
Jitterbugs I, ca.
1940–1941.
Oil on plywood, 39¾ by 31¼
inches. National Museum of
American Art, Washington, D.C./
Art Resource, New York.

Describe Describe the man and woman in the painting.
What are they wearing? What colors and
patterns does the artist use?

Analyze What kind of music do you imagine is playing
in this room? Why do you think so?

Interpret How do you think a writer of a descriptive
paragraph helps his or her audience "hear"
music?

Judge Do you feel that this painting or a written
description would be more effective in
capturing the mood and sound of lively music?
Why do you think so?

At the end of this chapter, you will use the artwork to stimulate
ideas for writing.

The Cases of Personal Pronouns

In German, words change their form depending upon how they are used in a sentence. You say *kinder* if *children* is the subject, but *kindern* if *children* is the indirect object. This is because all nouns and pronouns have case.

Case is the form of a noun or a pronoun that indicates its use in a sentence.

There are three cases in English: the nominative case, the objective case, and the possessive case. Unlike nouns in German, nouns in English change form only in the possessive case. For example, *Mary* is the nominative form and is used as a subject. *Mary* is also the objective form and is used as an object. *Mary's*, though, is the possessive form and is used to show that Mary has or owns something. Unlike nouns, pronouns usually change form for each of the three cases.

NOMINATIVE CASE
(Used for subjects and predicate nominatives)
SINGULAR I, you, he, she, it
PLURAL we, you, they

OBJECTIVE CASE
(Used for direct objects, indirect objects, and the objects of a preposition)
SINGULAR me, you, him, her, it
PLURAL us, you, them

POSSESSIVE CASE
(Used to show ownership or possession)
SINGULAR my, mine, your, yours, his, her, hers, its
PLURAL our, ours, your, yours, their, theirs

PRACTICE YOUR SKILLS

● Check Your Understanding
Determining Case

Contemporary
Life **Write the pronouns in each sentence. Then identify
the case of each pronoun, using *N* for nominative,
O for objective, and *P* for possessive.**

1. Why wasn't he invited to Anila's party?
2. I hope Anila left me directions to her house.
3. My sister will pick us up after Anila's party.
4. Did my brother go with them to the party?
5. We don't know whether the present they left in the chair is his or hers.
6. They often speak of their respect for Anila.
7. Our friends like to go to your parties rather than ours.
8. You should speak to them about the awful music they play.
9. She knew that the best present was mine.
10. Are the decorations yours or theirs?
11. A professional planned my mother's last party.
12. That party was more successful than our other parties have been.
13. My mother's friends said they were very impressed.
14. When the party ended, we thanked them for coming.
15. The party took a large amount of work, but it was a complete success.
16. Businesses often have their summer parties in June.
17. We went to a summer party last year, and it was fun.
18. I ate watermelon and went swimming.
19. Our friends were there enjoying the fun with us.
20. We would like her to go with us to the next party scheduled.

▶ Nominative Case

The personal pronouns in the nominative case are *I, you, he, she, it, we,* and *they.*

The **nominative case** is used for subjects and predicate nominatives.

Pronouns Used As Subjects

Pronoun subjects are always in the nominative case.

SUBJECTS   If **they** are late, **we** will keep the food warm for at least an hour.

She and I are chopping the vegetables.

Choosing the right case for a single subject does not usually present any problem. Errors occur more often, however, when the subject is compound, but there is a test that will help you check your choice.

Eric and (she, her) are cooking dinner tonight for twenty-seven guests.

To find the correct answer, say each choice separately as if it were a single subject.

She is cooking dinner tonight for twenty-seven guests.
Her is cooking dinner tonight for twenty-seven guests.

Separating the choices makes it easier to see and hear which pronoun is correct. The nominative case *she* is the correct form to use.

Eric and **she** are cooking tonight for twenty-seven guests.

You can learn more about compound subjects on page 18.

You can also use this test when both parts of a compound subject are pronouns.

> (He, Him) and (she, her) planned the menu.
> (She, Her) and (I, me) enjoyed the food.

Try each choice alone as the subject of the sentence.

> **He** planned the menu.
> **Him** planned the menu.
> **She** planned the menu.
> **Her** planned the menu.

> **She** enjoyed the food.
> **Her** enjoyed the food.
> **I** enjoyed the food.
> **Me** enjoyed the food.

You can see that the correct choices are *he* and *she* in the first sentence, and *she* and *I* in the second.

> **He** and **she** planned the menu.
> **She** and **I** enjoyed the food.

A pronoun that is used as a subject can also have a noun appositive. An **appositive** is a word that comes right after the pronoun and identifies or renames it. The appositive in each of the following sentences is underlined.

> **We** siblings worked together to cook dinner.
>
> **I**, the assistant chef, worked hard.

An appositive, however, will never affect the case of a pronoun. In fact, you can check whether you have used the correct pronoun by dropping the appositive.

> **We** worked together to cook dinner.
> **I** worked hard.

You can learn more about appositives on pages L183–L185.

PRACTICE YOUR SKILLS

● Check Your Understanding
Using Nominative Pronouns as Subjects

Contemporary Life | **Write the correct form of the pronoun in parentheses.**

1. My brother Chris and (I, me) love to cook together.
2. (Him, He) can cook great Italian specialties.
3. (They, Them) are his most delicious dishes.
4. When our mom works late, (us, we) prepare the meals.
5. When (he, him) cooks, our neighbor always calls.
6. (Her, She) can smell Chris's lasagna baking.
7. (We, Us) all learned how to cook from our mom.
8. (She, Her) felt that both boys and girls should have this skill.
9. When (we, us) were tall enough to reach the counter, (her, she) put us to work in the kitchen.
10. Before my little brother could walk, (he, him) was tossing salads.
11. Before my dad met my mom, (him, he) had never touched a stove.
12. When Mom married Dad, (her, she) taught him to cook better, too.
13. (She, Her) and (he, him) like to cook spicy dishes.
14. Although (us, we) are all good cooks, Chris is the best.
15. Now (he, him) needs to learn to clean up the kitchen when (he, him) finishes cooking!
16. (I, me) am usually the one who gets to wash the dishes.
17. Sometimes Chris helps, but (he, him) is not very good at it.
18. (We, Us) all joke about Chris's sloppiness.
19. Even (he, him) sees the humor in it.
20. Mom says that (she, her) thinks Chris is a comedian.

Pronouns Used as Predicate Nominatives

A **predicate nominative** is a noun or a pronoun that follows a linking verb and identifies or renames the subject.

> PREDICATE
> NOMINATIVE
>
> The best speller on the team was **he.**
>
> (speller = he)
>
> The finalists were **she** and Greg.
>
> (finalists = she and Greg)

Sometimes using a pronoun as a predicate nominative sounds awkward even though the pronoun is correct. When you write, you can avoid awkwardness if you reword a sentence, making the predicate nominative the subject.

> AWKWARD
>
> The team captain last year was **she.**
>
> The last person to join the team was **he.**
>
> NATURAL
>
> **She** was the team captain last year.
>
> **He** was the last person to join the team.

A pronoun that is used as a predicate nominative can also have a noun appositive. The appositives in the following sentences are underlined.

> The biggest supporters of the team are **we** freshmen.
>
> The most enthusiastic fan of all is **I**, Lisa.

An appositive, however, will never affect the case of a pronoun. In fact, you can check whether you have used the correct pronoun by dropping the appositive and making the predicate nominative the subject.

> **We** are the biggest supporters of the team.
>
> **I** am the most enthusiastic fan of all.

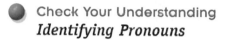

In everyday conversation, people do not always use the nominative case for predicate nominatives. It is common to hear someone say, "It's *me*" instead of "It is *I*," or "That's *him*" instead of "That is *he*." While this usage is common in conversation, you should avoid it when you write.

You can find a list of linking verbs on page L75. You can find out more about predicate nominatives on pages L154–L155.

PRACTICE YOUR SKILLS

● Check Your Understanding
Identifying Pronouns

Oral Expression | **Read the sentence aloud, saying each pronoun separately. Decide which pronoun is correct. Try turning each sentence around, making the predicate nominative the subject.**

1. The coach of the spelling team is (he, him).

2. Our toughest opponents are (them, they).

3. The winners of the championship will be (we, us).

4. Our most enthusiastic supporters are Robert and (she, her).

5. The team's best spellers are (we, us) girls.

● Check Your Understanding
Pronouns as Predicate Nominatives

Contemporary Life | **Write the correct form of the pronoun in parentheses.**

6. Action movies are great, and my favorite films are (they, them).

7. My favorite actor in these movies is (he, him).

8. By far the most exciting films are (they, them).

9. When a new action movie is showing, the first people in line are (us, we).

10. Two other big fans of these movies are Kassidy and (he, him).

11. The best actress to watch is (her, she).

12. I love the parts with special effects; my favorite scenes are (them, they).

13. The finest director of action movies is (he, him).

14. The most realistic movies of the genre are (they, them).

15. The fittest stars in Hollywood are (them, they) who star in these movies.

● Check Your Understanding
Supplying Pronouns in the Nominative Case

Contemporary Life **Complete each sentence by writing an appropriate pronoun in the nominative case.**

16. Do not make a decision about transferring to another school until ▧ have voted.

17. The only people voting will be ▧ students in the ninth grade.

18. The person who ran for class president was ▧.

19. ▧ had to wait in line to vote.

20. The two most popular candidates for vice president were Fallon and ▧.

21. Neither Antoine nor ▧ ran for an office.

22. No one can predict whether ▧ will be elected.

23. If ▧ are patient, we will know the answer soon.

24. The votes have been counted, and the new class president is ▧.

25. ▧ students are all glad that we voted.

26. Now the new president must prove that ▧ is up to the job.

27. Many students think that ▧ should run for office next year.

Rewrite the sentences, correcting any errors in pronoun usage. If the sentence is correct, write C.

28. Us girls decided to start a neighborhood swim team.

29. Our weakest swimmer is either Sammi or she.

30. We will practice hard before our first meet.

31. The best teams in the league are that group of boys and them.

32. The other teams and us will work hard to win the tournament.

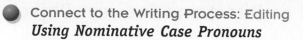

Communicate Your Ideas

APPLY TO WRITING

Friendly Letter: *Nominative Case Pronouns*

Your friend has just suffered a great disappointment. Perhaps he or she lost an election or an important game. Write a letter to your friend, giving him or her advice about dealing with this outcome. Tell your friend about someone you've known or read about who dealt with a similar situation. As you write your letter, include at least four nominative pronouns. Use two of these pronouns as predicate nominatives. After you write, underline all of the nominative pronouns you used.

⏵ Objective Case

The personal pronouns in the objective case are *me, you, him, her, it, us,* and *them.*

The **objective case** is used for direct objects, indirect objects, and objects of a preposition.

Pronouns Used as Direct and Indirect Objects

A **direct object** answers the question *What?* or *Whom?* after an action verb. If a sentence has a direct object, it also can have an indirect object. An **indirect object** answers the questions *To or For Whom?* or *To or For What?*

DIRECT OBJECT	Carlos will join **us** when he returns. (Carlos will join whom? *Us* is the direct object.)
	Mom took **him** to the dentist.
INDIRECT OBJECT	Dr. Garcia showed **him** X-rays of his teeth. (*X-rays* is the direct object. Dr. Garcia showed the X-rays to whom? *Him* is the indirect object.)
	Please give **me** a new toothbrush.

Use the same test you used for compound subjects to find the correct pronoun in a compound direct or indirect object.

Please take Carlos and (he, him) with you.
Please take **he** with you.
Please take **him** with you.

Once more, it is easy to both see and hear that the objective case pronoun *him* is correct. Pronouns in the objective case can also have appositives.

Dr. Garcia's explanations really helped **us** patients.

PRACTICE YOUR SKILLS

● Check Your Understanding
Using Pronouns as Direct and Indirect Objects

Contemporary Life · **Write the correct form of the pronoun in parentheses.**

1. Mom told (us, we) that it was time for our dental appointments.

2. Dr. Garcia, our dentist, always tells (I, me) jokes.

3. It helps (me, I) so that I relax.

4. He gives (we, us) new toothbrushes and dental floss.

5. Dr. Garcia also offers my brother and (I, me) good advice about cavity prevention.

6. My dad knew (him, he) in college.

7. My mother met (they, them) both when she visited their college campus.

8. Mom and Dad always tell (us, we) stories about Dr. Garcia in college.

9. My brother Carlos, who wants to be a dentist, especially admires (he, him).

10. Dr. Garcia lets Carlos watch (him, he) as he works.

Pronouns Used as Objects of Prepositions

An **object of a preposition** is always a part of a prepositional phrase.

OBJECTS OF PREPOSITIONS	That song was written for Pat and **me.**
	(*For Pat and me* is a prepositional phrase. *Pat and me* are the objects of the preposition *for.*)
	Singers like **her** are very rare.

If an object of a preposition is compound, use the same test you used for other compound objects. Say each pronoun separately.

Isn't Marta going with Jeff and (I, me) to the concert?
Isn't Marta going with **I** to the concert?
Isn't Marta going with **me** to the concert?

Again, it is easy to see and hear that the objective form *me* is the correct form to use.

You can find a list of commonly used prepositions on page L125.

CONNECT TO SPEAKING AND WRITING

A common mistake occurs with the preposition *between*. In trying to sound formal or correct, people will often use nominative-case pronouns after *between*. However, all pronouns used as objects of a preposition should be in the objective case. In this case, the more common-sounding expression is correct.

INCORRECT   The agreement is between he and I.

CORRECT   The agreement is between **him** and **me**.

PRACTICE YOUR SKILLS

● Check Your Understanding

Identifying Pronouns

Oral Expression   **Read the sentence aloud, saying each pronoun carefully. Decide which pronoun is correct. If the object is compound, try saying each pronoun separately.**

1. Hand the guitar to (she, her) or (he, him).

2. Between you and (I, me), she is a better guitar player than he is.

3. Brittany gave the microphone to (they, them) when she finished.

4. They sang a ballad for (we, us).

5. The audience offered a round of applause for all of (they, them).

● Check Your Understanding

Using Pronouns as Objects of Prepositions

Contemporary Life   **Write the correct form of the pronoun in parentheses.**

6. For help there is no one like Madison or (he, him).

7. They have been very helpful to my friends and (I, me).

8. Madison and Will are leaders in our class and role models for (we, us).

9. Our class sponsors divide many of the class's duties between (they, them).

10. People like (she, her) are fun to have around.

11. Madison comes to every game and gives her support to Will and (I, me).

12. The rest of the team also looks to (she, her) for support.

13. No other freshman can come close to (she, her) in school spirit.

14. The students in our class should do something to recognize the efforts of (he, him) and (she, her).

15. When we are seniors, I hope that scholarships will be presented to (they, them).

● Check Your Understanding
Supplying Pronouns in the Objective Case

Complete each sentence by writing an appropriate pronoun in the objective case. (Do not use *you* or *it*.) Then indicate how each pronoun is used by writing *D* for direct object, *I* for indirect object, or *O* for object of the preposition.

16. Aunt Laura gave ▓ good advice.

17. Her point of view always comes as a big surprise to ▓.

18. Uncle Fred usually agrees with ▓.

19. After our visit he drove ▓ back home.

20. He took ▓ with us.

21. Did we send ▓ a thank-you note for their hospitality?

22. Aunt Laura always gives ▓ lots of attention.

23. Our family respects ▓ immensely.

24. We wanted to do something special for ▓.

25. He and I are throwing ▓ a big birthday party next month.

Writing Sentences

Write ten sentences that use the expressions correctly.

26. Corey and I   **31.** you and me

27. us students   **32.** we players

28. him and me   **33.** Mom, Dad, and I

29. she and Jan   **34.** she and I

30. Don and he   **35.** Alex or her

Communicate Your Ideas

APPLY TO WRITING

Journal Entry: *Nominative and Objective Case Pronouns*

Miguel Vivancos. *Village Feast*, 1951. Oil on canvas, approximately 22½ by 29¼ inches. Musée National d'Art Moderne, Centre Georges Pompidou, Paris.

Imagine you are a young child from the country, and you have come to the village on the special feast day depicted in this painting. At the day's end, you return home and sit down with your journal to record the exciting events at the feast. Write a vivid account of your day. After writing your journal entry, underline all the nominative and objective case personal pronouns you used. Write *N* above the nominative pronouns and *O* above the objective pronouns.

Mixed Practice

Write each pronoun that is in the wrong case. Then write each pronoun correctly. If a sentence is correct, write C.

1. Without you and I, the trip would have been boring.

2. We told Aaron and she funny stories as we drove.

3. During that trip we friends visited the city's boardwalk.

4. You and me rode the big, wooden roller coaster.

5. We bought saltwater taffy and had some shipped to our cousins and they.

6. Aaron invited we three for a picnic on the beach.

7. Our group ate a picnic lunch packed by Julie and he.

8. We shared a bag of chips among Aaron, you, and me.

9. I divided the leftover melon between Aaron and she.

10. Her and me are planning another trip for next summer.

 Possessive Case

The **possessive case** is used to show ownership or possession.

The personal pronouns in the possessive case are *my, mine, your, yours, his, her, hers, its, our, ours, their,* and *theirs.* Some possessive pronouns can be used to show possession before a noun or a gerund. Others can be used by themselves.

BEFORE A NOUN	Kylie shared **her** latest set of poems with Alyssa.
BEFORE A GERUND	Ryan takes **his** writing seriously.
BY THEMSELVES	This pencil could be **mine.**

Personal possessive pronouns are not written with an apostrophe. Sometimes an apostrophe is incorrectly included because possessive nouns are written with an apostrophe.

| POSSESSIVE NOUN | **Alyssa's** journal is on the table. |
| POSSESSIVE PRONOUN | The notebook is **hers.** (not her's) |

Also, do not confuse a contraction with a possessive pronoun. *Its, your, their,* and *theirs* are possessive pronouns. *It's, you're, they're,* and *there's* are contractions.

| POSSESSIVE PRONOUN | I like the story because of **its** characters. |
| CONTRACTION | **It's** (It is) time to share our ideas. |

CONNECT TO SPEAKING AND WRITING

When you use an apostrophe with a pronoun, you can check whether you have written a contraction or a possessive pronoun. You can do this by removing the apostrophe and adding the letter that it replaced back into the word. Then read the sentence to see if the contraction was used properly or if you really needed to use a possessive pronoun.

CORRECT	You're such a good writer. (You are such a good writer.)
INCORRECT	I am you're writing partner. ("I am you are writing partner" does not make sense.)
CORRECT	It's his turn to walk the dogs. (It is his turn to walk the dogs.)
INCORRECT	We cannot find it's leash. ("We cannot find it is leash" does not make sense.)

PRACTICE YOUR SKILLS

● Check Your Understanding
Possessive Pronoun or Contraction?

Oral Expression **Read the following sentences aloud, saying the word with the apostrophe as two words. Then tell whether the form is correct.**

1. It's a beautiful poem.

2. Are all of you're poems like this one?

3. You're going to keep writing.

4. Is you're story finished?

5. When did you send you're manuscript to them?

● Check Your Understanding
Using Pronouns in the Possessive Case

Contemporary Life **Write the correct word in parentheses.**

6. Are (their, they're) poems well written?

7. (Your, You're) article is due tomorrow.

8. That box of old writings is (hers, her's).

9. Joining the writers' group has improved (me, my) writing.

10. The poem that Ryan wrote doesn't fit (its, it's) title.

● Check Your Understanding
Supplying Pronouns in All Cases

Contemporary Life **Complete the sentence by writing appropriate pronouns. (Do not use _you_ or _it_.)**

11. Read ■ and ■ your poem.

12. ■ listened to ■ and Alyssa read.

13. ■ helped ■ with new ideas for a story.

14. ■ thanked Ryan and ■.

15. Kylie showed ■ and ■ the new literary magazine.

16. ■ was writing with Alyssa and ■.

17. ■ went to the library with ■ for books about poets and playwrights.

Using Possessive Pronouns and Contractions

Write sentences using the following words correctly.

18. your   **22.** their   **25.** we're

19. they're   **23.** it's   **26.** his

20. its   **24.** hers   **27.** theirs

21. ours

Communicate Your Ideas

APPLY TO WRITING

Personal Narrative: *Personal Pronouns*

Imagine that you are one of the people in the picture. You are playing a game of golf with some of your friends; you might even be on vacation. Write a personal narrative about the golf game. Before you begin, think about these questions:

- Who are the people in the picture and where was the picture taken?

- What particularly interesting thing happened while you were playing? Remember that you are more apt to hold a reader's interest with an unusual incident than with a chronological account of the game.

Then write your narrative. When you have finished, check that you have used pronouns correctly.

QuickCheck Mixed Practice

General
Interest **Write the correct word in parentheses.**

1. Both wild and domesticated animals are very protective of (their, they're) young.

2. You should cautiously approach (your, you're) pet if (she, her) is a new parent.

3. (She, Her) is likely to act differently toward you and (your, you're) family.

4. You should give (she, her) a comfortable, secluded place to care for (her, hers) newborns.

5. A wild animal is even more likely to attack humans who come near (its, it's) young.

6. Each spring hikers are mauled by female bears protecting (their, they're) cubs.

7. The bear is just following (she, her) natural instincts.

8. The one to blame for such attacks is not (she, her).

9. (We, Us) hikers endanger ourselves when (we, us) come between a cub and (its, it's) mother.

10. Careful hikers make lots of noise to warn bears of (their, they're) presence when (they, them) walk through the wilderness.

Pronoun Problems

Pronoun choice can be a problem. Should you say, "Who is calling?" or "Whom is calling?" Should you say, "Is Jim taller than I?" or "Is Jim taller than me?" This section will cover these and other common pronoun problems.

Who or *Whom?*

The correct case of *who* is determined by how the pronoun is used in a question or a clause.

Who is a pronoun that changes its form depending on how it is used in a sentence.

WHO OR WHOM?	
NOMINATIVE CASE	who, whoever
OBJECTIVE CASE	whom, whomever
POSSESSIVE CASE	whose

Who and its related pronouns are used in questions and in subordinate clauses.

In Questions

Forms of *who* are often used in questions. The form you choose depends upon how the pronoun is used.

NOMINATIVE CASE	**Who** planned the school dance? (subject)
OBJECTIVE CASE	**Whom** did you call for that information? (direct object)
	To whom is the invitation addressed? (object of the preposition *to*)

When deciding which form to use, turn a question around to its natural order.

QUESTION   **Whom** did you ask?

NATURAL ORDER   You did ask **whom.**

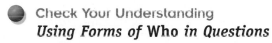

CONNECT TO SPEAKING AND WRITING

While *whom* is not used as much today in everyday speaking and writing, it is important to know its proper use. When you write formal papers and letters or prepare speeches and debates, be sure to use *whom* instead of *who* whenever appropriate.

PRACTICE YOUR SKILLS

● Check Your Understanding
Using Forms of Who *in Questions*

Contemporary Life — **Write the correct form of the pronoun in parentheses. Then indicate how each pronoun is used by writing *S* for subject, *D* for direct object, and *O* for object of the preposition.**

1. (Who, Whom) is on the telephone?
2. (Who, Whom) told you that Ashley was going with me to the dance?
3. With (who, whom) did Paige say she was going?
4. (Who, Whom) will play the music at the dance?
5. From (who, whom) did you get an invitation to the dance?
6. (Who, Whom) sent you that note about the dance?
7. (Who, Whom) will you take to the dance?
8. (Who, Whom) is the best dancer in the ninth grade?
9. (Who, Whom) is designing the decorations?
10. With (who, whom) did you go to the dance last year?

In Clauses

Forms of *who* can be used in both adjective clauses and noun clauses. The form you use depends on how the pronoun is used within the clause—not on any word outside the clause. The following examples show how *who* and *whom* are used in adjective clauses.

NOMINATIVE CASE — Dr. Rush is the woman **who will serve as marshal of the parade.**
(*Who* is the subject of *will serve.*)

OBJECTIVE CASE — She is the woman **whom you met yesterday.**
(You met whom yesterday. *Whom* is the direct object of *met.*)

Have you met Mr. Keats, **from whom we got our idea for the freshman float?**
(We got our idea from whom. *Whom* is the object of the preposition *from.*)

The following examples show how forms of *who* are used in noun clauses.

NOMINATIVE CASE — The prize winners will be **whoever builds the best float.** (The entire noun clause is the predicate nominative of the sentence. *Whoever* is the subject of the noun clause.)

Do you know **who organizes the homecoming parade?** (The entire noun clause is the direct object of the sentence. *Who* is the subject of the noun clause).

OBJECTIVE CASE — I don't know **by whom the parade is organized.** (The entire noun clause is the direct object. *Whom* is the object of the preposition *by.*)

Invite **whomever you want to the homecoming game.** (The entire noun clause is the direct object of the sentence. *Whomever* is the direct object of *want*.)

PRACTICE YOUR SKILLS

● Check Your Understanding
Using Forms of Who *in Clauses*

Contemporary Life

Write the correct form of the pronoun in parentheses. Then, using the following abbreviations, write how each pronoun is used in the clause.

subject = *subj.*   object of the preposition = *o.p.*
direct object = *d.o.*

1. Bailey doesn't know (who, whom) will lead the parade.

2. The organizers of the parade accept (whoever, whomever) they wish.

3. They couldn't tell to (who, whom) the entry form belonged.

4. (Whoever, Whomever) wins the title of homecoming queen will ride on the big float.

5. The person (who, whom) the most students vote for will win the title.

6. Does Shelly know (who, whom) will judge the competition for best float?

7. I spoke with the committee (who, whom) organized the parade.

8. They want all (who, whom) are participating in the parade to be lined up by three o'clock.

9. The people to (who, whom) I spoke informed me that the parade route had changed.

10. The parade will be led by two drum majors (who, whom) will be dressed in gold and white.

Writing Sentences Using Forms of **Who**

Write a sentence using the correct form of *who* or *whom* in the indicated construction.

11. as the object of a preposition

12. as the subject of a sentence

13. as the predicate nominative in a sentence

14. as the direct object of the verb in a noun clause

15. as the subject in an adjective clause

Communicate Your Ideas

APPLY TO WRITING

Explanation: *Forms of* **Who**

Your history teacher has asked you to write a 150-word essay titled "The Greatest Person Who Ever Lived." Choose a person—living or dead, famous or obscure—whom you feel deserves this designation. Write a short essay for your teacher, explaining why you feel that this person is important. As you write, use the following forms of *who* correctly at least once: *who, whom, whoever, whomever.*

QuickCheck   Mixed Practice

General Interest   **Write the correct form of the pronoun in parentheses.**

1. (Who, Whom) was the first president of the United States?

2. There are few Americans (who, whom) could not answer that question.

3. George Washington, (who, whom) is known as "the father of his country," was the first president.

4. He is a person about (who, whom) much history has been written.

5. Even in his own day, Washington did not fail to impress (whoever, whomever) he met.

6. Legend tells us it was George Washington (who, whom) could not lie to his father about chopping down a cherry tree.

7. History tells us that Washington led the Continental Army, against (who, whom) the British and their loyalists fought.

8. (Who, Whom) was the first vice president of the United States?

9. Few Americans know to (who, whom) this distinction belongs.

10. John Adams, (who, whom) was America's second president, was the nation's first vice president.

Pronouns in Comparisons

Over the years writers have introduced shortcuts into the language. One such shortcut, an **elliptical clause,** is a subordinate clause in which words are omitted but are understood to be there. Elliptical clauses begin with *than* or *as.*

Delisa takes more classes **than I.**
Noah takes as many classes **as she.**

In an elliptical clause, use the form of the pronoun you would use if the clause were completed.

In the examples at the top of the following page, both expressions in bold type are elliptical clauses. Both are also correct because they have two different meanings.

Delisa studies with us more **than he.**
Delisa studies with us more **than him.**

He is correct in the first example because it is used as the subject of the elliptical clause.

Delisa studies with us more **than *he* studies with us.**

Him is correct in the second example because it is used as an object of a preposition.

Delisa studies with us more **than she studies with *him*.**

Because the meaning of a sentence with an elliptical clause sometimes depends upon the case of a pronoun, be careful to choose the correct case. One way to do this is to complete the elliptical clause mentally before you say it or write it. Then choose the form of the pronoun that expresses the meaning you want.

Noah helps her as much as (I, me).
Noah helps her as much **as *I* help her.**
Noah helps her as much **as he helps *me*.**

In the previous example, decide which meaning you want. Then choose either *I* or *me*.

PRACTICE YOUR SKILLS

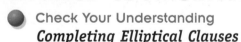 Check Your Understanding
Completing Elliptical Clauses

Oral Expression **Read the sentence aloud, completing the elliptical clause.**

1. Delisa is a better student than he.

2. She spends more time on her homework than I.

3. Jesse knows her better than we.

4. They study together more than we.

5. Jesse and Noah make better grades than we.

6. We work just as hard as they.

7. Noah likes math better than you.

8. Jesse and Delisa have won just as many awards as I.

9. I am just as pleased about my grades as they.

10. Noah will do just as well in school this semester as we.

11. Jessie is as good at science as I.

12. I study more than she.

13. Delisa made better grades this time than we.

14. Noah was not as happy about his grades as she.

15. He still made higher grades than I.

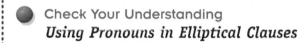

Check Your Understanding

Using Pronouns in Elliptical Clauses

Contemporary Life **Write each sentence, completing the elliptical clause. Then underline the pronoun you chose.**

16. Noah spends more time at the library and in the computer lab than (I, me).

17. Our teacher didn't review the test with us as much as (they, them).

18. I studied longer and harder than (they, them).

19. The topic we covered sounds more exciting to them than (we, us).

20. Did you answer as many questions on the math test as (they, them)?

21. No one was more prepared than (I, me) for the last history quiz.

22. The professor from the university talked to us longer than (them, they).

23. That grade means more to Noah than (she, her).

24. Everyone should be as studious as (he, him).

25. I think Jesse is a better test taker than (I, me).

Write sentences that follow the instructions. Each sentence should contain an elliptical clause.

26. Compare a history class with a math class.

27. Compare two basketball players.

28. Compare two sports.

29. Compare two foods.

30. Compare two television shows.

31. Compare two Hollywood superstars.

32. Compare a summer vacation you had with an ideal winter vacation.

33. Compare your two favorite bands.

34. Compare two kinds of animals as pets.

35. Compare board games with video games.

Communicate Your Ideas

APPLY TO WRITING

Paragraph of Comparison: *Elliptical Clauses*

Your parents cannot understand why you like the music you do. They constantly ask you to turn down the volume on your stereo. Write a paragraph for your parents in which you compare and contrast your music to the music of their generation. Depending on their age and tastes, groups they may have listened to include the Rolling Stones, the Who, the Commodores, or the Bee Gees. Be sure to use elliptical clauses that begin with *than* or *as* to explain the differences and similarities between your music and that of your parents.

Pronouns and Their Antecedents

In Chapter 2 you learned that a pronoun takes the place of a noun. That noun is called the pronoun's antecedent. In the first example below, *Duke Ellington* is the antecedent of *his*. In the second example, *orchestra* is the antecedent of *its*.

Duke Ellington left **his** mark on American music.

Ellington's **orchestra** had **its** own sound.

A pronoun must agree in number and gender with its antecedent.

Number is the term used to indicate whether a noun or pronoun is singular or plural. **Singular** indicates one, and **plural** indicates more than one. **Gender** is the term used to indicate whether a noun or a pronoun is masculine, feminine, or neuter. Remember that the forms of *I, you,* and *they* do not show gender because they can be either masculine or feminine.

	GENDER		
MASCULINE	he	him	his
FEMININE	she	her	hers
NEUTER	it	its	

If the antecedent of a pronoun is one word, there usually is no problem with agreement.

The **man** playing the trumpet lowered **his** horn.

The **listeners** showed **their** appreciation of the music.

If the antecedent of a pronoun is more than one word, there are two rules you should remember.

If two or more singular antecedents are joined by *or, nor, either/or,* or *neither/nor,* use a singular pronoun to refer to them.

These conjunctions indicate a choice. In the following example, Maria will play her long clarinet solo or Lacey will play her long clarinet solo.

> Either **Maria** or **Lacey** will play **her** long clarinet solo next.

If two or more singular antecedents are joined by *and* or *both/and,* use a plural pronoun to refer to them.

These conjunctions always indicate more than one. In the following example, Maria and Lacey—together—volunteered their help with the musical project.

> Both **Maria** and **Lacey** volunteered **their** help with the musical project.

Sometimes you will not know whether an antecedent is masculine or feminine. Standard written English solves this problem by using *his or her* to refer to such vague antecedents.

> Each orchestra **member** will donate two hours of **his or her** time to help with the project.

> Each **violinist** must practice **his or her** solo many times before the opening performance.

You can avoid this problem completely if you rewrite such sentences, using plural forms.

> All orchestra **members** will donate two hours of **their** time to help with the project.

> The **violinists** must practice **their** solos many times before the opening performance.

● Check Your Understanding
Making Pronouns and Antecedents Agree

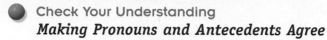

Contemporary
Life

Write the pronoun that correctly completes each sentence. Make sure that the pronoun agrees in both number and gender with its antecedent.

1. Either Felix or Jason left ■ trombone on the stage after practice.

2. All the orchestra members should wear ■ best outfits to the show.

3. Tricia and Max will sing ■ songs while the orchestra accompanies them.

4. Neither Aura nor Tricia remembered to take ■ music stand.

5. Felix took three music stands with ■ on our orchestra's tour.

6. Each player is responsible for ■ own instrument.

7. After the orchestra members left the stage, ■ went to the bus.

8. Jason carried his trombone and put ■ on the bus for the trip home.

9. Either Jane or Tricia will play ■ own song tomorrow night.

10. The trumpet was placed carefully in ■ case after the performance.

▶ Indefinite Pronouns as Antecedents

Sometimes an indefinite pronoun is the antecedent of a personal pronoun. Making the personal pronoun and the indefinite pronoun agree can be confusing because some singular indefinite pronouns suggest a plural meaning. Other indefinite pronouns can be either singular or plural. The following lists break common indefinite pronouns into three groups.

SINGULAR INDEFINITE PRONOUNS			
anybody	either	neither	one
anyone	everybody	nobody	somebody
each	everyone	no one	someone

One of the girls left **her** bike unlocked.

Sometimes the gender of a singular indefinite pronoun is not indicated. You can solve this problem by using *his or her*.

Everyone must keep **his or her** bike locked up.

When you use several instances of *he or she, his or her,* or *him or her* in a short piece of writing, awkwardness may result. You can often eliminate this problem by rewriting the sentences in the plural form.

All students must keep **their** bikes locked up.

PLURAL INDEFINITE PRONOUNS			
both	few	many	several

Many of the younger children have **their** own bikes.

SINGULAR OR PLURAL INDEFINITE PRONOUNS				
all	any	most	none	some

Agreement with one of these indefinite pronouns depends upon the number and gender of the object of the preposition that follows it.

Some of the **chrome** on Stevie's bike has lost **its** shine.

Most of his **friends** keep **their** bikes out of the sun.

PRACTICE YOUR SKILLS

● Check Your Understanding
Making Personal Pronouns Agree with Indefinite Pronouns

Contemporary Life **Write the pronoun that correctly completes each sentence.**

1. All of the little boys in my apartment complex received a bicycle for ▦ birthdays.

2. Each of them had ▦ bike painted a different color.

3. Not one of the boys in the apartment complex painted ▦ bike red.

4. Many of the neighbors near our complex let the boys ride in ▦ driveways.

5. One of our local organizations put up fliers about ▦ bicycle races.

6. All of the boys decided ▦ would enter.

7. Some of us in the complex gave them ▦ encouragement to enter the race.

8. Someone in the boys' group had ▦ bike stolen.

9. One of the winners of the race bought the unfortunate boy a new bike with ▦ prize money.

10. All of the younger boys were glad ▦ friend had a bike again.

● Connect to the Writing Process: Revising
Correcting Pronoun Agreement Errors

Rewrite the following sentences, correcting any problems with pronoun agreement. If a sentence is correct, write C.

11. Each of the girls won their softball letter.

12. No one on the girls' team liked her uniform.

13. Neither of the boys received their trophy for baseball.

14. Both of the Randall sisters practice batting in their backyard.

15. One of the girls lost their baseball glove.

APPLY TO WRITING
Analysis: *Comparing Poems*

Many poets have written poems about parents. In "Taught Me Purple," Evelyn Tooley Hunt writes from a daughter's point of view about her mother. In "Mother to Son," Langston Hughes writes from the mother's point of view in giving advice to her son. Read the two passages below and then follow the directions.

My mother taught me purple
Although she never wore it.
Wash-gray was her circle,
The tenement her orbit.

My mother taught me golden
And held me up to see it,
Above the broken molding,
Beyond the filthy street.

—*Evelyn Tooley Hunt,* "Taught Me Purple"

Well, Son, I'll tell you
Life for me ain't been no crystal stair.
It's had tacks in it,
And splinters,
And boards torn up,
And places with no carpets on the floor,

Bare.
But all the time
I'se been climbin' on
And reachin' landin's
And turnin' corners. . . .

—*Langston Hughes,* "Mother to Son"

- Write a short essay for your English teacher in which you compare these two passages. What do they have in common? How are they different?
- As you write, correctly use the following pairs of words in your essay: *both/their, each/its, several/their.*

QuickCheck Mixed Practice

Write the pronoun that correctly completes each sentence.

1. The high school band prepared for (their, its) first performance.
2. (All, Each) of the band members were a little nervous, but they were ready.
3. Alicia was the only one (who, whom) did not seem prepared.
4. Consuela helped (her, his) friend get ready.
5. Consuela was more prepared than (I, me).
6. Our director, Mrs. Chandler, gave us (their, our) usual pre-game instructions.
7. After her speech, (each, all) in the band gave a cheer and the crowd joined in.
8. Because we had practiced so hard, (we, us) in the band thought we would do our best.
9. As we walked onto the field, the crowd cheered (us, them).
10. That night the band played (its, their) best performance.

Unclear, Missing, or Confusing Antecedents

The object of writing and speaking most often is to communicate with someone else. Sometimes that communication gets cloudy or confused if pronouns have no clear antecedent.

Every personal pronoun should clearly refer to a specific antecedent.

UNCLEAR	We tried to call the employment agency, but **it** was busy. *(The antecedent of it is not clear, but the context of the sentence suggests that the pronoun it refers to the telephone.)*
CLEAR	We tried to call the employment agency, but **its telephone** was busy.
UNCLEAR	I checked the Internet for job listings because **you** can always get good information there. *(You is incorrectly used because it does not refer to the person being spoken to. Instead, it refers to the speaker.)*
CLEAR	I checked the Internet for job listings because **I** can always get good information there.
MISSING	In the newspaper **it** lists the requirements for every job. *(What does it refer to in this sentence? The antecedent in this sentence is missing.)*
CLEAR	The **newspaper** lists the requirements for every job.
MISSING	**It** had many job listings for entry-level computer positions. *(It is unclear. The antecedent is missing.)*
CLEAR	The **employment section of the newspaper** had many job listings for entry-level computer positions.

CONFUSING	My mother drove Liza to the interview, but **she** didn't go into the office.
	(Who didn't go into the office, the mother or Liza?)
CLEAR	My mother drove Liza to the interview, but **my mother** didn't go into the office.
CONFUSING	Liza put the business card into her purse, but now she can't find **it.**
	(Does *it* refer to the business card or the purse?)
CLEAR	Liza put the business card into her purse, but now she can't find **the business card.**

PRACTICE YOUR SKILLS

● Check Your Understanding
Identifying Antecedent Problems

Contemporary Life **Label the antecedent problems in the sentences below as *unclear, missing,* or *confusing* and rewrite the sentences correctly. If the sentence is written correctly, write *C.***

1. Almost all teenagers can find a job if you try hard enough.

2. My dad helped Elizabeth get a job, but she didn't like it very much.

3. So she could choose a date for the interview, Marybeth asked her mother where her calendar was.

4. Almost everyone I know likes to work if it is interesting.

5. I like dog walking because you get lots of outdoor exercise.

6. The employment agent stared at the boy, but he said nothing.

7. To earn a little extra money, Jenni and Michael took the rugs off the floor and cleaned them.

8. Sarah wants to work at a veterinarian's office because you could learn a lot about animals.

9. My sister told Jenni about the job, and then she applied for it.

10. I saw the job listing in the newspaper earlier today, but now I cannot find it.

11. As soon as Elizabeth and Sarah returned home, I asked her to tell me about her job.

12. Sarah said it was a lot of fun.

13. Elizabeth was not as enthusiastic about it.

14. The veterinarian's office was so close that Sarah could walk to it.

15. Our mother had to drive Elizabeth to her job.

● Connect to the Writing Process: Revising
Correcting Pronoun References

Rewrite the following letter, correcting unclear, missing, or confusing pronoun references.

Dear Ms. Gonzalez:

I am writing in response to your classified advertisement in Sunday's newspaper. In the paper it said you wanted someone to work at your day-care center. I have always wanted to work with children because you can help them learn.

Please read the attached résumé and call me if you think I am qualified for it. Although I have never worked with preschool children, I would be good at that.

Sincerely,

Tiffany Washington

APPLY TO WRITING

Response Letter: *Pronoun References*

You have found a job listing in your local newspaper that interests you. Write a response letter to the contact person whose name appears in the advertisement. Remember to indicate what position you are interested in, why you are interested, and what your qualifications are. Be sure to use correct pronoun references.

 **QuickCheck** Mixed Practice

Contemporary Life **Each sentence below contains an error in pronoun usage. Rewrite the sentence, correcting the error.**

1. During the national election, many of the citizens cast his or her votes early.

2. According to the polls, they said the incumbent president will win.

3. Several of the candidates gave his or her speeches.

4. I read the newspaper articles about the candidates, because you can learn a lot.

5. Neither of my parents has cast their vote yet.

6. My parents went to vote, and it was crowded.

7. During the town meeting, all of our neighbors asked the candidates their questions.

8. My mom took Granny to the debate, but she didn't listen to the candidates.

9. All of the candidates were responsible for raising his or her own campaign money.

10. Depending upon who wins the mayoral election, Ms. Sands or Mr. Stone will try their hand at running our city.

Using Pronouns Correctly

Write the correct form of the pronoun in parentheses.

1. Neither Sue nor Rebecca has had (her, their) turn at bat.
2. One of the girls left (her, their) tennis shoes in the gym.
3. Please explain to (we, us) students how to get a pass.
4. To (who, whom) should I send the invitation?
5. Do other students study as hard as (we, us)?
6. (They, Them) made a delicious dinner for us.
7. Sandra went to the movies with David and (I, me).
8. Both Raul and Ted forgot (his, their) skates.
9. Our debaters will be Jorge and (he, him).
10. It was (she, her) who won the local marathon.
11. Jessica and (he, him) went to the game with us.
12. (Whoever, Whomever) draws the best picture will win a prize.
13. That was quick thinking for an inexperienced quarterback like (he, him).
14. No one types as fast as (she, her) on a word processor.
15. Between you and (I, me), we're never going to get there on time.
16. She is the only person (who, whom) arrived early.
17. (We, us) joggers need to pay special attention to the traffic lights.
18. I think that's (she, her) in the blue coat.
19. Yes, I think she dives as well as (I, me).
20. I think Mr. Pentose is someone (who, whom) we met in Florida last year.

Making Personal Pronouns Agree with Their Antecedents

Write the personal pronoun that correctly completes each sentence.

1. Either Mary or Suzanne will bring ■ guitar.
2. One of my brothers just received ■ diploma.
3. Both Heidi and John turned in ■ reports early.
4. The tire has lost most of ■ air.
5. All of the students will be assigned to ■ homerooms.
6. Several of my friends want to add biology to ■ schedules.
7. Both of the girls think that ■ will compete in the race.
8. Sam or Ernesto should drive ■ car to the game.
9. After we painted the posters, we hung ■ in the halls.
10. None of the silver pieces had lost ■ shine.
11. Either of the boys will share ■ lunch.
12. Several of the tourists lost ■ way.
13. That tree is beginning to lose ■ leaves.
14. Neither Mindy nor Sue can finish ■ picture.
15. Either Claire or Erica will have ■ camera at the game.

Writing Sentences

Rewrite these sentences so there is a clear antecedent for each pronoun.

1. Rita tried to call her friend, but she did not feel like talking.
2. Rita drove to Lisa's house and listened to her new CD.
3. Then Rita drove her sister to the library, but she forgot her library card.
4. Rita put her book in a bag, but she left it on the counter at the library.
5. Rita's book fell on the floor, and it was damaged.

Language and *Self-Expression*

In this painting a man and a woman are dancing the jitterbug, a dance form that originated in the African American community and then became popular during the swing era of the 1930s and 1940s. The jitterbug can include slow steps or energetic moves including lifts, swings, and turns.

The artist uses bold colors and patterns of lines and shape to show a dance that is associated with a certain period in history. How could you use words to capture the movements of a dance or sport that is popular today? Choose a dance or sporting event at your school or on television. Watch the event and take notes. Then write a two-minute radio announcement describing it for a listening audience. Be sure to use pronouns with clear antecedents. Record your announcement and play it for your class.

Prewriting List action verbs that describe the movements of the people you watched in the event. Chart sequences of movements you want to describe.

Drafting Write your announcement using ideas from your list and chart. Use pronouns to make your writing concise.

Revising Read your announcement, marking places that need work. After you have made the changes, read the announcement aloud. Do your words help a person "see" the event?

Editing Check your story for errors in spelling and punctuation. Be sure you have used pronouns correctly.

Publishing Prepare a final copy and use an audiocassette recorder to tape it. Play the tape for your classmates.

Another Look

Case is the form of a noun or a pronoun that indicates its use in a sentence.

Kinds of Cases

The **nominative case** is used for subjects and predicate nominatives.
(pages L329–L335)

The **objective case** is used for direct objects, indirect objects, and objects of prepositions. *(pages L335–L341)*

The **possessive case** is used to show ownership or possession.
(pages L341–L345)

Using the Correct Case of *Who*

The correct case of *who* is determined by how the pronoun is used in a question or a clause. *(pages L346–L351)*

NOMINATIVE CASE	who, whoever
OBJECTIVE CASE	whom, whomever
POSSESSIVE CASE	whose

Pronouns in Comparisons

In an elliptical clause, use the form of the pronoun you would use if the clause were completed. *(pages L351–L354)*

Pronouns and Their Antecedents

A pronoun must agree in number and gender with its antecedent.
(page L355)

If two or more singular antecedents are joined by *or, nor, either/or,* or *neither/nor,* use a singular pronoun to refer to them. *(page L356)*

If two or more singular antecedents are joined by *and* or *both/and,* use a plural pronoun to refer to them. *(page L356)*

Every personal pronoun should clearly refer to a specific antecedent.
(page L362)

 **Posttest**

Directions

Read the passage and choose the pronoun that belongs in each underlined space. Write the letter of the correct answer.

EXAMPLE

As Jerome walked onto the stage, __(1)__ knees were shaking.

    1 A his
      B him
      C my
      D mine

ANSWER

    1 A

It was the big night of the talent show. Everybody in school watched as Jerome approached the microphone. __(1)__ singing partner Juan, __(2)__ was already on the stage, handed __(3)__ the guitar. Jerome immediately felt calmer. He began to strum the guitar strings, and __(4)__ began to sing. "__(5)__ have chosen a ballad for __(6)__ first selection," Juan said as Jerome continued to play the guitar. When they finished the song, all of the students clapped and cheered loudly. Mr. Watkins, the principal, went to the microphone. "__(7)__ knew that __(8)__ had such talent right here under __(9)__ noses?" __(10)__ asked.

1   **A**   His
    B   Our
    C   Him
    D   Their

2   **A**   whoever
    B   whom
    C   who
    D   whomever

3   **A**   him
    B   he
    C   who
    D   whom

4   **A**   they
    B   its
    C   his
    D   their

5   **A**   Us
    B   We
    C   Our
    D   Ours

6   **A**   my
    B   we
    C   us
    D   our

7   **A**   Whom
    B   Whose
    C   Who
    D   Whomever

8   **A**   we
    B   us
    C   our
    D   ours

9   **A**   us
    B   our
    C   ours
    D   we

10 **A**   his
    B   him
    C   he
    D   them

CHAPTER 12

Subject and Verb Agreement

Pretest

Directions
Read the passage. Write the letter of the answer that shows the correct way to rewrite each underlined word or group of words. If the underlined part contains no error, write _D_.

EXAMPLE   Scientists who study rocks <u>is called</u>
                geologists.   **(1)**

                1 **A**   has been called
                   B   is calling
                   C   are called
                   D   No error

ANSWER   **1 C**

All geologists <u>categorizes</u> rocks according to origin.
                (1)
Sometimes magma <u>move</u> up through cracks in the earth's crust
                (2)
and <u>cools</u>. This action creates igneous rocks. Sedimentary rocks
    (3)
<u>is made</u> from pieces of rocks, sand, and other material. These
  (4)
sediments <u>is washed</u> into oceans, and they <u>settle</u> to the
          (5)   **(6)**
bottom. Then the layers of sediment <u>is pressed</u> together to
                                      (7)
create rocks. The third group <u>are</u> metamorphic rocks. Heat and
                              (8)
pressure <u>creates</u> these rocks from igneous and sedimentary
          (9)
rocks. Both of these sometimes <u>becomes</u> metamorphic rocks.
                                (10)

1	**A**	is categorizing	6	**A**	settles
	B	categorize		**B**	are settles
	C	has categorized		**C**	is settled
	D	No error		**D**	No error

2	**A**	moves	7	**A**	are pressed
	B	is moving		**B**	is pressing
	C	have moved		**C**	has been pressed
	D	No error		**D**	No error

3	**A**	cool	8	**A**	is
	B	is cooling		**B**	is being
	C	have cooled		**C**	are being
	D	No error		**D**	No error

4	**A**	is being made	9	**A**	has created
	B	was made		**B**	create
	C	are made		**C**	is creating
	D	No error		**D**	No error

5	**A**	is washing	10	**A**	become
	B	are washed		**B**	has become
	C	washes		**C**	is becoming
	D	No error		**D**	No error

Melissa Miller. *Flood,* 1983.
Oil on linen, 59 by 95 inches. Collection, Museum of Fine Arts, Houston. © 1983 Melissa Miller.

Describe   Moving from left to right, describe the subjects in the painting.

Analyze   What statement do you think the artist wanted to make? What elements in the painting support this message?

Interpret   Read the title of the painting. What feelings do you associate with this word? What kind of writing might create the same mood?

Judge   Do you think it is possible for a writer to elicit from an audience feelings that are as intense as those generated by this artist? Explain your ideas.

At the end of this chapter, you will use the artwork as a visual aid for writing.

Agreement of Subjects and Verbs

Language is very much like a jigsaw puzzle. You must put all the pieces of a jigsaw puzzle together correctly to end up with a complete picture. You must also fit all the parts of a sentence together correctly in order to communicate clearly. For example, some subjects and verbs fit together, while others may seem to fit together but actually do not. In the English language, when a subject and a verb fit together, they are said to be in **agreement.**

This chapter will show you how to make subjects and verbs agree so that your speaking and writing will communicate a complete, clear picture to your listener or reader. One basic rule applies to this entire chapter.

A verb must agree in number with its subject.

 Number

In the last chapter, you learned that **number** refers to whether a noun or a pronoun is singular or plural. You know that singular indicates one and that plural indicates more than one. In this chapter you will learn that verbs also have number and that the number of a verb must agree with the number of its subject.

The Number of Nouns and Pronouns

In English the plural of most nouns is formed by adding –*s* or –*es* to the singular form. However, some nouns form their plurals in other ways. You should always check a dictionary to see whether a noun has an irregular plural.

	NUMBER		
Singular	floor	tax	child
Plural	floors	taxes	children

In the last chapter, you also learned that pronouns have singular and plural forms. For example, *I, he, she,* and *it* are singular, and *we* and *they* are plural.

You can find a list of pronoun forms on page L327.

PRACTICE YOUR SKILLS

● Check Your Understanding
Determining the Number of Nouns and Pronouns

Write each word and label it *S* for singular or *P* for plural.

1. Jessica	**6.** hats	**11.** they	**16.** bike
2. everyone	**7.** mice	**12.** both	**17.** he
3. children	**8.** rakes	**13.** women	**18.** Jamison
4. several	**9.** anyone	**14.** cap	**19.** it
5. schools	**10.** lights	**15.** we	**20.** radio

The Number of Verbs

The singular and plural forms of nouns and pronouns are fairly easy to recognize. You can easily see, for example, that *eagle* and *it* refer to only one, while *eagles* and *they* refer to more than one.

The number of verbs, however, is not so easy to recognize. Only the form of the verb indicates its number. Most verbs form their singulars and plurals in exactly the opposite way that nouns form their singulars and plurals. Most verbs in the present tense add *–s* or *–es* to form the singular. Plural forms of verbs in the present tense drop the *–s* or *–es*.

SINGULAR

The eagle }
soars.
swoops.
flies.

PLURAL

The eagles }
soar.
swoop.
fly.

Most verbs have the same form for both singular and plural when the verbs are used in the past tense.

SINGULAR	The eagle **soared.**
PLURAL	The eagles **soared.**

The irregular verb *be* indicates number differently from other verbs. The singular is not formed by adding *–s* or *–es*.

FORMS OF *BE*			
SINGULAR FORMS	am/is	was	has been
PLURAL FORMS	are	were	have been

SINGULAR	The eagle **is** a majestic bird.
PLURAL	Eagles **are** majestic birds.

PRACTICE YOUR SKILLS

● Check Your Understanding
Determining a Verb's Number

Write each verb and label it *S* for singular or *P* for plural.

1. breaks
2. freezes
3. are
4. have been
5. keep
6. works
7. was
8. reads
9. am
10. has
11. is
12. tear
13. look
14. sings
15. walk
16. swim
17. see
18. speak
19. were
20. barks

▶ Singular and Plural Subjects

Because a verb must agree in number with its subject, you need to remember two rules.

A singular subject takes a singular verb.

A plural subject takes a plural verb.

To make a verb agree with its subject, ask yourself two questions: *What is the subject?* and *Is the subject singular or plural?* Then choose the correct verb form.

SINGULAR	A **geologist studies** rocks and minerals.
PLURAL	**Geologists study** rocks and minerals.
SINGULAR	**She examines** layers of the earth.
PLURAL	**They examine** layers of the earth.
SINGULAR	The **emerald is** a beautiful gemstone.
PLURAL	**Emeralds are** beautiful gemstones.

The pronouns *you* and *I* are the only exceptions to these agreement rules. The pronoun *you,* whether singular or plural, always takes a plural verb.

SINGULAR	**You use** a shovel.	**You are** a geologist.
PLURAL	**You** two **use** shovels.	**You are** scientists.

The pronoun *I* also takes a plural verb—except when it is used with a form of *be.*

SINGULAR	**I am** a researcher.	**I was** her assistant.
PLURAL	**I like** minerals and gems.	**I have** some rock samples.

Many errors in subject and verb agreement occur when writers do not edit their work. Never turn in a first draft without reading through your work and correcting errors. Reading a piece aloud to yourself or to a friend can help you find errors more easily than reading your work silently.

PRACTICE YOUR SKILLS

● Check Your Understanding
Making Subjects and Verbs Agree

Science Topic
Write the subject in each sentence. Next to each, write the form of the verb in parentheses that agrees with the subject.

1. Jewelers (place, places) a high value on emeralds of good quality.

2. Emeralds (is, are) a rarer find than diamonds.

3. An emerald (is, are) a special type of the mineral beryl.

4. Geologists (know, knows) the exact minerals that make up all precious stones.

5. Geology also (involve, involves) the study of Earth's landforms and surface features.

6. You (see, sees) these features wherever you look in nature.

7. A volcano (interest, interests) some specialized geologists.

8. Magma (is, are) molten rock contained within the earth.

9. When it comes to the surface, magma (become, becomes) lava.

10. I (study, studies) stones and minerals more than land formations.

Write the verbs that do not agree with their subjects. Then write the verbs correctly. If a sentence is correct, write C.

11. Diamonds is the world's favorite gem.

12. You finds them in most countries of the world.

13. South Africa exports the most diamonds.

14. A diamond's brilliance determine its value.

15. Most diamonds have color.

16. Blue and pink stones is the most valuable.

17. When found, these precious stones resembles glass.

18. It take a diamond to cut a diamond and other hard surfaces.

19. Gem cutters use diamonds to shape other diamonds and gems.

20. Some factories has tools covered with diamonds to cut metal surfaces.

▶ Agreement with Verb Phrases

If a sentence contains a verb phrase, make the first helping verb agree with the subject.

The first helping verb must agree in number with the subject.

In the following sentences, each subject is underlined once and each verb is underlined twice.

Kristy **was** writing a poem.

(*Kristy* is singular, and *was* is singular.)

They **have** been writing all afternoon.

(*They* is plural, and *have* is plural.)

The following chart shows the singular and plural forms of common helping verbs.

COMMON HELPING VERBS	
SINGULAR	am, is, was, has, does
PLURAL	are, were, have, do

In the following sentences, each subject is underlined once and each verb is underlined twice.

SINGULAR	Kristy **is** writing a sonnet.
	The teacher **does** not have a dictionary of rhymes.
PLURAL	The poetry books **are** located in this section of the library.
	Our poems **have** been published in the local newspaper.

PRACTICE YOUR SKILLS

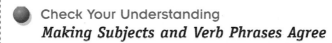

Check Your Understanding
Making Subjects and Verb Phrases Agree

Literature Topic — **Write the subject in each sentence. Next to each, write the form of the verb in parentheses that agrees with the subject.**

1. Sonnets (is, are) written according to certain rules.

2. A new poet (is, are) often intimidated by the sonnet's rigid structure.

3. This particular poetic form (was, were) made popular by Petrarch in the 1300s.

4. His mystery woman Laura (has, have) become immortal through Petrarch's sonnets.

5. Sonnets (was, were) also written by William Shakespeare.

6. Other poets (do, does) attempt this type of verse.

7. They (has, have) tried to write sonnets of Shakespeare's quality.

8. However, Shakespeare's sonnets (is, are) considered to be the finest collection by a single person.

9. I (was, were) awed when I read Shakespeare's sonnets.

10. When you read them aloud, you (do, does) hear the beauty in his words.

● Connect to the Writing Process: Revising
Correcting Errors in Agreement

Rewrite correctly the sentences in which the verb phrases do not agree with their subjects. If a sentence is correct, write C.

11. You was really missed at the poetry reading.

12. They has finished sharing their poems.

13. The poem do sound familiar to me.

14. She have read it to us before.

15. Kevin have submitted three sonnets for publication.

16. His poems is often chosen as our group's best.

17. I were just reading one of his poems.

18. The college coffeehouse does have poetry readings.

19. We has attended several times.

20. I am going next Tuesday.

▶ Agreement and Interrupting Words

If the subject is separated from the verb by a phrase or a clause, it is easy to make a mistake in agreement. The reason is that either the object of a prepositional phrase or some other word is closer to the verb than the subject is. Agreement of the verb may then be incorrectly made with that word—rather than with the subject.

> The agreement of a verb with its subject is not changed by any interrupting words.

In the following examples, notice that the subjects and verbs agree in number—despite the words that come between them. Each subject is underlined once, and each verb is underlined twice.

> A bouquet of roses **was** given to the skater.
>
> (*Was* agrees with the singular subject *bouquet*. The verb does not agree with *roses,* the object of the prepositional phrase, even though *roses* is closer to the verb.)
>
> The skaters who won medals at the competition **were** invited to the White House.
>
> (*Were* agrees with the subject *skaters*—not with *competition,* the object of the prepositional phrase.)

Compound prepositions, such as *in addition to, as well as,* and *along with,* often begin interrupting phrases.

> The gold medal winner, along with her teammates, **was** called back to the ice.
>
> (*Was* agrees with the subject *winner*—not with *teammates,* the object of the compound preposition *along with.*)

PRACTICE YOUR SKILLS

Check Your Understanding
Making Interrupted Subjects and Verbs Agree

Sports Topic **Write the subject in each sentence. Next to each, write the form of the verb in parentheses that agrees with the subject.**

1. The blades on a pair of ice skates (is, are) called runners.
2. The runners on the earliest ice skates (was, were) probably made of bone.
3. The original purpose of ice skates (was, were) for travel.

4. Competition lovers in Scotland (is, are) credited with turning ice skating into a sport.

5. The invention of roller skates (was, were) probably the work of ice skaters who wanted to skate year round.

6. Today skaters from around the world (compete, competes) on the ice before adoring fans.

7. Figure skating at the modern Olympic Games (is, are) one of the most popular attractions.

8. In 1998, Tara Lipinski, together with her teammates, (was, were) a delight to Olympic audiences.

9. Ice dancing in pairs (has, have) been an Olympic sport since 1976.

10. Speed skating by men and women also (draw, draws) a large Olympic audience.

● Connect to the Writing Process: Editing
Correcting Errors in Subject and Verb Agreement

Write the verbs that do not agree with their subjects. Then write the verbs correctly. If a sentence is correct, write C.

11. The best athletes in the world competes at the Olympic Games.

12. A team of athletes is sent to the Games by almost every country.

13. The modern spectacle of competing athletes were named for contests held in ancient Greece.

14. The original Olympic Games in Greece was banned in A.D. 394.

15. The modern international competition of amateur athletes was revived in 1896.

16. Winter sports like figure skating and skiing have been a part of the Olympics since 1924.

17. The summer sports of this worldwide competition includes boxing, gymnastics, soccer, and yachting.

18. In the summer, track and field events including the decathlon attract large crowds.

19. The popularity of the winter games have made figure skaters into celebrities.

20. The countries of the world comes together to honor their best athletes.

Communicate Your Ideas

APPLY TO WRITING

Persuasive Letter: *Subject and Verb Agreement*

Imagine that the Olympic Committee has decided to remove basketball from the list of Olympic sports. Write a letter to the committee either supporting or challenging the committee's decision. Be sure to list at least three strong reasons you feel basketball should or should not be an Olympic sport. After completing your letter to the Olympic Committee, read through your work, correcting any errors in subject and verb agreement.

Write the verbs that do not agree with their subjects. Then write the verbs correctly. If a sentence is correct, write C.

1. My dog Muscles chases squirrels in our backyard.

2. You has to see him!

3. I watches Muscles and laugh at him.

4. Muscles crouches on his haunches and barks at the squirrels.

5. The location of the trees in our backyard are fairly far from the house.

6. The squirrels in that oak tree jumps across to that far elm.

7. Right now, one squirrel on the back steps are chattering at Muscles.

8. The squirrel seem to tease him.

9. Muscles, like most dogs, hate to be teased.

10. Muscles starts toward the squirrel.

11. Squirrels, aware of the danger, always jumps quickly to a nearby tree.

12. Muscles, standing at the bottom of the tree, bark angrily at the intruders.

13. The squirrel, now safe in the branches, resume his chattering.

14. Everyday Muscles wait for his chance to catch a squirrel.

15. The frustrated canine never give up his quest.

Common Agreement Problems

When you edit your written work, look for agreement problems. They are often the result of quickly written first drafts. Compound subjects and subjects in inverted order, for example, can pose problems.

▶ Compound Subjects

Agreement between a verb and a compound subject can sometimes be confusing. The following rules will help you avoid errors of agreement.

When subjects are joined by *or, nor, either/or,* or *neither/nor,* the verb agrees with the subject that is closer to it.

This rule applies even when one subject is singular and the other subject is plural.

Either rain <u>showers</u> or <u>sleet</u> **is** expected tomorrow.

(The helping verb is singular because the subject closer to it is singular.)

<u>Wind</u> or rising <u>temperatures</u> <u><u>dispel</u></u> fog.

(The verb is plural because the subject closer to it is plural.)

Neither my <u>brother</u> nor my <u>parents</u> <u><u>like</u></u> to drive in wet weather.

(The verb is plural because the subject closer to it is plural—even though the other subject, *brother,* is singular.)

When subjects are joined by *and* or *both/and,* the verb is plural.

With *and* or *both/and,* the verb should be plural—whether the subjects are singular, plural, or a combination of singular and plural.

> Both <u>hail</u> and high <u>wind</u> <u>accompany</u> many storms.
>
> (Two things—*hail* and *wind*—accompany storms. The verb must be plural to agree.)
>
> My <u>brother</u> and his <u>roommates</u> **were** not <u>injured</u> in the storm.
>
> (Even though one subject is singular, the verb is still plural because *brother* and *roommates*—together—are more than one.)

There are two exceptions to the second rule. Sometimes two subjects that are joined by *and* refer to only one person or thing. Then a singular verb must be used.

> My family's weather expert and storm lover **is** my sister.
>
> (one person)
>
> Thunder and lightning **is** music to her.
>
> (considered one thing)

The other exception occurs when the word *every* or *each* comes before a compound subject whose parts are joined by *and.* Since each subject is being considered separately in these sentences, a singular verb is called for.

> **Every** thunderclap and lightning bolt **delights** my sister exceedingly.
>
> (*Thunderclap* and *lightning bolt* are considered separately. The verb must be singular to agree.)
>
> **Each** fall and spring **brings** the increased possibility of severe weather.
>
> (*Fall* and *spring* are considered separately. The verb must be singular to agree.)

PRACTICE YOUR SKILLS

● Check Your Understanding

Making Verbs Agree with Compound Subjects

Science Topic **Write the correct form of the verb in parentheses.**

1. Weather and other natural phenomena (is, are) interesting to study.

2. Neither meteorologists nor other scientists (has, have) been able to develop systems for controlling weather.

3. Radar and computer technology (help, helps) them predict and understand the patterns of weather.

4. Climate conditions and soil types (combine, combines) to affect vegetation.

5. Every animal and plant (react, reacts) to the surrounding environment.

6. For instance, moisture and warm air (is, are) needed to make orchids grow.

7. A tropical plant or flower (do, does) not grow in the desert.

8. Due to their white pelts, polar bears and arctic hares (thrive, thrives) in snowy climates.

9. Today great ice caps and glaciers (cover, covers) one tenth of the earth's surface.

10. Dark clouds and high winds (alert, alerts) people to changing weather.

11. The air currents and weather patterns (change, changes) constantly.

12. Neither a lightning strike nor a tornado (is, are) easy to predict.

13. Snow or showers (is, are) easier to forecast.

14. A typhoon or hurricane (has, have) been known to cause mass destruction.

15. Dull sunsets and hot, humid air (signal, signals) the approach of a hurricane.

16. Wind and water (combine, combines) to wear down rocks and create canyons.

17. Both intensive training and a thorough knowledge of climate (is, are) required to be a meteorologist.

18. Every dark cloud and cyclone warning (is, are) taken seriously in tornado-prone areas.

19. Cirrocumulus clouds and humid air (mean, means) rain is certain.

20. Every year, hurricanes and tornadoes (cause, causes) billions of dollars in property damage.

● Connect to the Writing Process: Editing
Correcting Errors in Agreement

Write the verbs that do not agree with their subjects. Then write the verbs correctly. If a sentence is correct, write C.

21. Earthquakes and volcanoes has caused cities to sink beneath the sea.

22. Broken dams or volcanic activity sometimes follows earthquakes.

23. Often fires or flood is caused by earthquakes.

24. Each collapsed building or damaged home presents a danger after a quake.

25. Tsunamis at coastal areas and landslides in mountainous regions is also associated with earthquakes.

26. Both Japan and Indonesia has been the site of disastrous tsunamis.

27. In Alaska in 1958, ice and rock was broken off a glacier by the jolt of an earthquake.

28. The force and fury of the resulting splash cause a tsunami.

29. Buildings and other structures is now being designed to withstand earthquakes.

30. Neither humans nor property are safe from the threat of earthquakes.

Indefinite Pronouns as Subjects

In the last chapter, you learned that not all indefinite pronouns have the same number.

COMMON INDEFINITE PRONOUNS	
SINGULAR	anybody, anyone, each, either, everybody, everyone, neither, nobody, no one, one, somebody, someone
PLURAL	both, few, many, several
SINGULAR/PLURAL	all, any, most, none, some

A verb must agree in number with an indefinite pronoun used as a subject.

SINGULAR	Everyone in the room owns a dog.
PLURAL	Many of the dogs are poodles.

The number of an indefinite pronoun in the last group in the box is determined by the object of the prepositional phrase that follows the pronoun.

SINGULAR OR PLURAL	Most of the training **has** been effective.
	(Since *training*, the object of the prepositional phrase, is singular, *has* is also singular.)
	Most of the dogs **have** learned a lot in obedience school.
	(Since *dogs*, the object of the prepositional phrase, is plural, *have* is also plural.)
	None of the dog owners **were** unhappy with the program.
	(Since *owners*, the object of the prepositional phrase, is plural, *were* is also plural.)

PRACTICE YOUR SKILLS

● Check Your Understanding
Making Verbs Agree with Indefinite Pronouns

Contemporary Life **Write the subject in each sentence. Next to each, write the correct form of the verb in parentheses that agrees with the subject.**

1. Several of her dogs (is, are) collies.
2. Each of you (is, are) needed to train the dogs.
3. Some of the new leashes (is, are) in the closet.
4. One of the dogs in the class (was, were) a beagle.
5. Many of the dogs (has, have) been adopted at the shelter.
6. None of the owners (was, were) disappointed in the class.
7. Nobody (want, wants) a badly behaved dog.
8. Both of her puppies (walk, walks) on a leash together.
9. Most of the dogs (was, were) fast learners.
10. Either of these classes (is, are) a good one to take next.

● Connect to the Writing Process: Drafting
Writing Sentences

Write ten sentences, each using one of the phrases below as a beginning.

11. Both of the dogs
12. Anybody at the shelter
13. Few of the older dogs
14. All of the kittens
15. None of the volunteers
16. Each of the cages
17. No one at the desk
18. Several of the stores
19. Some of the pets
20. Neither of the cats

▶ Subjects in Inverted Order

A verb must agree in number with the subject, regardless of whether the subject comes before or after the verb.

The subject and the verb of an inverted sentence must agree in number.

There are several types of inverted sentences. To find the subject in an inverted sentence, turn the sentence around to its natural order, placing the subject first.

INVERTED ORDER	At the bottom of the trunk were my great uncle's medals.
	(My great uncle's medals were at the bottom of the trunk.)
QUESTIONS	Are the medals from World War II?
	(The medals are from World War II.)
SENTENCES BEGINNING WITH *HERE* OR *THERE*	There were many letters also in the trunk.
	(Many letters were also in the trunk. The word *there* is dropped from the sentence.)

You can learn more about inverted sentences on pages L22–L23.

PRACTICE YOUR SKILLS

● Check Your Understanding
Making Subjects and Verbs in Inverted Order Agree

History Topic **Write the subject in each sentence. Next to each, write the form of the verb in parentheses that agrees with the subject.**

1. There (was, were) many countries involved in World War II.

2. In Europe (was, were) the locations of many of the battles.

3. (Do, Does) any war have only one cause?

4. At the core of the fighting (was, were) many factors.

5. There (was, were) much tension remaining in Europe after World War I.

6. In the numerous battles of the war (was, were) men from all countries.

7. (Was, Were) anyone able to predict that Hitler would gain such power?

8. (Have, Has) the world learned anything from these world wars?

9. At the end of World War II (was, were) a new struggle for political power in Europe.

10. (Is, Are) there any good results that come from such wars?

Connect to the Writing Process: Drafting
Writing Sentences

Write five sentences, each using one of the phrases below as a beginning. Be sure that the verb you choose agrees with the subject.

11. There are

12. In the newspaper was

13. At the top of the page were

14. There is

15. On the front page are

Communicate Your Ideas

APPLY TO WRITING

The Writer's Craft: *Analyzing the Use of Inverted Order*

Writers mix sentences in inverted order with sentences in natural order to vary their sentence structure and make their writing interesting. Read the following passage by Pearl Buck.

But not all the copper pence did Wang Lung spend on food. He kept back all he was able to buy mats to build a shed for them when they reached the south. There were men and women in the firewagon who had been south in other years; some went each year to the rich cities of the south to work and to beg and thus save the price of food.

—*Pearl Buck,* The Good Earth

- List the subject and verb in each sentence. Be sure to list the subject and verb from the last independent clause, which follows the semicolon.
- Arrange the first sentence in natural order.
- Do you prefer Buck's original sentence or your rewritten one? Explain your answer.
- Why do you think Pearl Buck wrote the first and third sentences in inverted order?

 QuickCheck Mixed Practice

General Interest **Find each verb that does not agree with its subject. Then write the correct form of the verb and its subject.**

Everyone have read folktales about cunning wolves. Movies and television has shown wolves attacking people. Is all of these stories about wolves really true? According to Boye Rensberger, they isn't. He says that wolves doesn't like to fight. In fact, wolves often go out of their way to avoid harming humans. Rensberger goes on to say that wolf packs is tightly knit families. Both the mother wolf and the father wolf raises the young. When both of the parents goes out to hunt, another wolf baby-sit the pups.

Other Agreement Problems

A few special situations also may cause agreement problems. Look for the following problems when you edit your written work.

Doesn't or *Don't?*

Doesn't, don't, and other contractions often present agreement problems. When you write a contraction, always say the two words that make up the contraction. Then check for agreement with the subject.

> The verb part of a contraction must agree in number with the subject.

Doesn't, isn't, wasn't, and *hasn't* are singular and agree with singular subjects. *Don't, aren't, weren't,* and *haven't* are plural and agree with plural subjects.

He **does**n't know any musicians.

(He *does* not know)

Don't they know anyone?

(They *do* not know)

Collective Nouns

In Chapter 2 you learned that a collective noun names a group of people or things.

COMMON COLLECTIVE NOUNS			
band	congregation	flock	orchestra
class	crew	gang	swarm
colony	crowd	herd	team
committee	family	league	tribe

How a collective noun is used will determine its agreement with the verb.

Use a singular verb with a collective noun subject that is thought of as a unit. Use a plural verb with a collective noun subject that is thought of as individuals.

The committee **is** planning to hire a band for the big event.

(The committee is working as a single unit. Therefore, the verb is singular.)

The committee **are** unable to agree on the band for the big event.

(The individuals on the committee are acting separately. Therefore, the verb is plural.)

Words Expressing Amounts

Words that express amounts of time or money or that express measurements or weights are usually considered singular.

A subject that expresses an amount, a measurement, a weight, or a time is usually considered singular and takes a singular verb.

Subjects expressing amounts can be confusing because they are sometimes plural in form.

AMOUNTS	Five dollars is the price of admission to the dance.
	(one sum of money)
TIME	Nine tenths of Adriana's spare time **has** been spent planning the dance.
	(one part of time)

Once in a while, an amount is thought of as individual parts. When this happens, a plural verb must be used.

Three quarters **were** left in the cash box.

PRACTICE YOUR SKILLS

● Check Your Understanding
Making Subjects and Verbs Agree

Contemporary
Life

Write the subject in each sentence. Next to each, write the form of the verb in parentheses that agrees with the subject.

1. (Aren't, Isn't) you going to the dance?
2. A group (has, have) been chosen to perform.
3. Those singers (is, are) a big hit now.
4. The swim team (has, have) a meet on the same night as the dance.
5. Invitations to join the dance committee (was, were) extended to them.
6. Three fourths of the refreshment table (was, were) covered with plates of cookies.
7. Thirty dollars (was, were) donated to our class to purchase decorations.
8. Three days (was, were) spent looking for a purple banner for the wall.
9. They (wasn't, weren't) interested in hiring Daria's band for the dance.
10. One result of their choice of bands (is, are) that her feelings were hurt.
11. Eight feet of purple ribbon (was, were) used to make a bow for the stage.
12. Three gallons of lime sherbet (was, were) mixed into ginger ale to make the punch.
13. (Doesn't, Don't) your mother make tropical punch exactly like that?
14. The freshman class (was, were) asked to line up for a picture.
15. Each time they pose, the group (argue, argues) about how to line up for pictures.

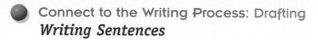

● Connect to the Writing Process: Drafting
Writing Sentences

**Add to the following phrases to make complete sentences.
Be sure that your subjects and verbs agree.**

16. The pack of wolves ■.

17. Seventy-five percent of the forest ■.

18. Three fifty-dollar bills ■.

19. The Sierra Club ■.

20. Three tablespoons of sugar ■.

Singular Nouns That Have Plural Forms

Words like *measles, mathematics, economics,* and *news* each end in
–*s;* but they name single things, such as one disease or one area of
knowledge.

> Use a singular verb with certain subjects that are plural in
> form but singular in meaning.

In middle school, mathematics **was** Felicia's best subject.
The news **is** that she now likes English better.

Subjects with Linking Verbs

Sometimes a sentence will have a subject and a predicate
nominative that do not agree in number.

> A verb agrees with the subject of a sentence, not with the
> predicate nominative.

In the following examples, the number of the predicate nominative
does not affect the number of the verb.

Felicia's topic of discussion **was** the novels of Jane Austen.

The novels of the Victorian period **are** Felicia's passion.

Titles

Titles may have many words, and some of those words may be plural. Nevertheless, a title is the name of only one book or work of art.

A title takes a singular verb.

> _Wuthering Heights_ by Emily Brontë **is** her favorite Victorian novel.
>
> Van Gogh's _Irises_ **hangs** next to the bookshelf in her living room.

Practice Your Skills

● **Check Your Understanding**
Making Subjects and Verbs Agree

General Interest **Write the subject in each sentence. Next to each, write the form of the verb in parentheses that agrees with the subject.**

1. _Sense and Sensibility_ (was, were) much easier to read than I had expected it to be.
2. One challenge in reading the book (is, are) that many words are unfamiliar to us.
3. The news that we would read the book (was, were) not welcomed by the class.
4. Manners in Jane Austen's time (is, are) a fascinating topic.
5. The main focus of our discussion (was, were) the characters in the novel.
6. One result of our discussions (was, were) our reading more of Austen's novels.
7. Picasso's _Three Musicians_ (is, are) our next discussion topic.

8. *The Martian Chronicles* by Ray Bradbury (follow, follows) the work by Picasso.

9. The early blues by B. B. King (is, are) also one of her interests.

10. Topics in Mrs. Smith's class (is, are) one thing you can never predict!

● Connect to the Writing Process: Editing
Correcting Errors in Agreement

Write the verbs that do not agree with their subjects. Then write the verbs correctly. If a sentence is correct, write C.

11. Economics are my hardest class this semester.

12. One problem in the class are lots of homework.

13. The news of a stock market crash were exciting to discuss.

14. Problems in the stock market is a common phenomenon.

15. *Investing Dollars with Sense* are the title of our economics textbook.

16. There is many trading simulation games on the Internet.

17. Blue chip stocks usually has the highest money value.

18. Prices usually rise in a bull market.

19. A bear market generally mean declining prices.

20. A bear market is probably better for a buyer.

21. The economy vary from month to month.

22. Most consumers does not like bear markets.

23. Our professor of economics were a stockbroker.

24. The tests he gives is usually difficult.

25. My grades this semester will be higher than they usually is.

APPLY TO WRITING

Art Review: *Subject and Verb Agreement*

Jacob Lawrence. *Self-Portrait,* 1977.
Gouache, 22⅛ by 30 inches. Collection of the National Academy of Design, New York, NY.

Look carefully at *Self-Portrait* by Jacob Lawrence. You have been asked by the editor of the school newspaper to write a review of this painting, which is currently on display in a local museum. Begin your review by describing the painting. Then tell readers why they should or should not go to see this work at the museum. After you write your review, read it to make sure that your subjects and verbs agree. Correct any errors before you turn it in.

General Interest **Write the verbs that do not agree with their subjects. Then write the verbs correctly. If a sentence is correct, write C.**

1. The groundhog for years have been used to predict the arrival of spring.

2. The fuzz on wooly caterpillars are used to determine how hard a winter will be.

3. Neither a groundhog nor caterpillars is really dependable for forecasting, though.

4. Many of the predictions are wrong.

5. There are reports that some kinds of animals can sense earthquakes.

6. Ten catfish in a research laboratory was observed for two years.

7. During that time twenty earthquakes was experienced in the area.

8. Most of the earthquakes was inaccurately forecast by humans.

9. Seventeen of the quakes, nevertheless, were sensed early by the fish.

10. Catfish does not talk, of course, but they wiggled their whiskers just before the quakes struck.

Making Subjects and Verbs Agree

For each sentence write the subject and the verb that agrees with it.

1. (Isn't, Aren't) these four loaves of bread enough?
2. There (is, are) still horse ranches within the city limits of San Diego.
3. Neither of the loudspeakers (was, were) working by the end of the concert.
4. Two members of the golf team (was, were) able to finish the course at five under par.
5. Off the coast of Maine (is, are) many rocky islands.
6. Ten dollars (was, were) a fair price for the used tennis racket.
7. My height and weight (is, are) average for my age.
8. (Doesn't, Don't) you think we can win?
9. The team (was, were) fighting among themselves over the choice of a new captain.
10. *Incredible Athletic Feats* (is, are) an interesting book by Jim Benagh.
11. Every student and teacher (was, were) at the dedication ceremony.
12. Both Ellen's sister and my sister (is, are) at the University of Wisconsin.
13. One fourth of the world's population (lives, live) on less than two thousand dollars a year.
14. (Wasn't, Weren't) you able to solve the math problem?
15. One of our best pitchers (was, were) unable to play in the county championships.

Subject and Verb Agreement

Find the verbs that do not agree with their subjects and write them correctly. If a sentence is correct, write C.

1. Was you with Les in the crowd after the game?
2. In the picnic basket were sandwiches for everyone.
3. Fifty dollars were contributed by my friends and me.
4. Crackers and cheese are my favorite snack.
5. Either red or green looks good on you.
6. Every actor and dancer were dressed in a colorful costume.
7. Don't that dripping faucet bother you?
8. There are few poisonous snakes in northern regions.
9. Each of the members are assigned to a committee.
10. Is your father and mother at home this evening?

Writing Sentences

Write ten sentences that follow the directions below. The verb in each sentence should be in the present tense.

Write a sentence that...

1. includes *dogs in the park* as the subject.
2. includes *a game of dominoes* as the subject.
3. includes *Mom and Dad* as the subject.
4. includes *neither bats nor balls* as the subject.
5. includes *don't* at the beginning of a sentence.
6. includes *here* at the beginning of a sentence.
7. includes *many* as the subject.
8. includes *team* as the subject.
9. includes *three fourths* as the subject.
10. includes *Romeo and Juliet*, the title of the play, as the subject.

Language and *Self-Expression*

In this painting two tigers are trapped by the tumultuous waters of a flood. Their beautiful markings contrast with the devastation around them. In the painting the artist uses color, line, and shape to depict the physical characteristics of these animals.

How could you use words to describe the characteristics of tigers? Imagine that this pair of tigers is part of a temporary exhibition for a zoo in your area. Write an informative paragraph for a sign that could be placed near the display. Include information that will interest visitors as they view the animals. Use active verbs wherever possible and be sure that your subjects and verbs agree.

Prewriting As you read about tigers, take notes on the information you learn. Highlight the most interesting facts.

Drafting Create an opening sentence that will grab the reader's attention. Then write several sentences that describe the tigers. Your final sentence should summarize the information in the paragraph or leave the reader with an interesting fact.

Revising Invite a classmate to review your paragraph and suggest changes.

Editing Check your story for errors in spelling and punctuation. Do the subjects and verbs in your sentences agree in number?

Publishing Share your paragraph with a group of classmates. You may want to choose a few selections from the class to post on a classroom Website.

Another Look

Agreement of Subjects and Verbs

A verb must agree with its subject in number. *(page L375)*
A singular subject takes a singular verb. *(page L378)*
A plural subject takes a plural verb. *(page L378)*
The first helping verb must agree in number with the subject. *(page L380)*
The agreement of a verb with its subject is not changed by any
   interrupting words. *(pages L382–L383)*
A verb must agree in number with an indefinite pronoun used as a
   subject. *(page L391)*
The subject and the verb of an inverted sentence must agree in number.
   (pages L392–L393)

Common Agreement Problems

When subjects are joined by *or, nor, either/or,* or *neither/nor,* the verb
   agrees with the closer subject. *(page L387)*
When subjects are joined by *and* or *both/and,* the verb is plural.
   (pages L387–L388)
The verb part of a contraction must agree in number with the subject.
   (page L396)
Use a singular verb with a collective noun subject that is thought of as a
   unit. Use a plural verb with a collective noun subject that is thought
   of as individuals. *(page L397)*
A subject that expresses an amount, a measurement, a weight, or a time
   is usually considered singular and takes a singular verb. *(page L397)*
Use a singular verb with certain subjects that are plural in form but
   singular in meaning. *(page L399)*
A verb must agree with the subject of a sentence, not with the predicate
   nominative. *(page L399)*
A title takes a singular verb. *(page L400)*

Directions

Read the passage. Write the letter of the answer that shows the correct way to rewrite each underlined word or group of words. If the underlined part contains no error, write D.

EXAMPLE   What is some signs of an impending earthquake?
(1)

      1 **A** be

           B are

           C is being

           D No error

ANSWER   1 B

According to the United States Geological Survey, there really

is no surefire ways to predict an earthquake. Seismologists,
(1)

nevertheless, is continuing to work on this problem. For example,
(2)

some people have observed unusual animal behavior before a
(3)

quake: a pet dog or rabbit sometimes become strangely agitated; a
(4)

swarm of bees have been seen evacuating its hive in a panic;
(5)

catfish in a lake has leaped out of the water onto dry land. Many
(6)

earthquake researchers throughout the world is seeking a scientific
(7)

explanation for these events. Fluctuations in the earth's magnetic

field, for example, occurs at the epicenter of an earthquake, and
(8)

certain animals is sensitive to electromagnetic changes. Some
(9)

seismologists studying this problem hopes to develop similarly
(10)

sensitive geophysical instruments for detecting earthquakes.

1	A	has been	6	A	have leaped
	B	are		B	is leaping
	C	be		C	leaps
	D	No error		D	No error

2	A	are continuing	7	A	are seeking
	B	continues		B	has been seeking
	C	has continued		C	seeks
	D	No error		D	No error

3	A	observes	8	A	occur
	B	is observing		B	is occurring
	C	has observed		C	has occurred
	D	No error		D	No error

4	A	is becoming	9	A	has been
	B	are becoming		B	are
	C	becomes		C	is being
	D	No error		D	No error

5	A	has been seen	10	A	hope
	B	are seen		B	is hoping
	C	are being seen		C	has hoped
	D	No error		D	No error

CHAPTER 13

Using Adjectives and Adverbs

Pretest

Directions
Read the passage and choose the word or group of words that belongs in each underlined space. Write the letter of the correct answer.

EXAMPLE   The concert was the __(1)__ one in years.

      1 **A** best
          B better
          C good
          D well

ANSWER   **1 A**

The __(1)__ audience in the history of the performance hall filled the auditorium. Robyn and Alison's seats were __(2)__ than the ones they had had the year before. However, the man in front of Alison was __(3)__ than she. Luckily, the girls found empty seats that were __(4)__ to the front.

The six musicians wore hats with the __(5)__ colors Robyn had ever seen. The __(6)__ one was the guitarist with a purple and pink top hat. The __(7)__ hat had sequined antlers and belonged to the drummer.

Robyn said, "I've never been __(8)__ than I am right now!" She pointed out that the drummer seemed __(9)__ than the lead guitarist. The girls decided that, as the leader of the band, the guitarist had to be __(10)__.

1. **A** largest
   B larger
   C most large
   D large

2. **A** good
   B more good
   C better
   D gooder

3. **A** tall
   B taller
   C more tall
   D most tall

4. **A** more close
   B close
   C closest
   D closer

5. **A** brightest
   B most bright
   C more bright
   D bright

6. **A** more interesting
   B interestingest
   C most interesting
   D interestinger

7. **A** most funny
   B funniest
   C funnier
   D more funny

8. **A** most excited
   B excited
   C more excited
   D exciteder

9. **A** most animated
   B more animated
   C animateder
   D animated

10. **A** more serious
    B seriouser
    C most serious
    D seriousest

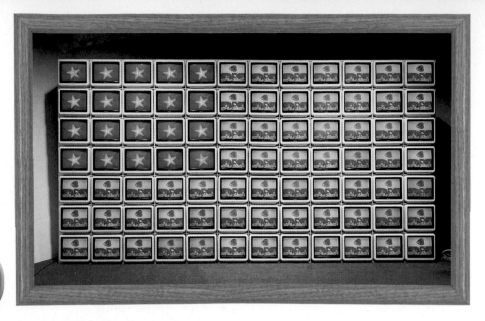

Nam June Paik. *Video Flag Z*, 1985.
Television sets, videocassette players, videotapes, Plexiglas modular cabinet, 74½ by 138¾ by 18 inches.
Los Angeles County Museum of Art.

Describe   Describe the artwork and the materials the artist used to create it.

Analyze   How is this flag like a real flag of the United States? How is it different?

Interpret   Many viewers may compare this artwork to a real flag and attempt to interpret the symbolism of each. How could a writer use words to help an audience interpret an important symbol of the United States?

Judge   Do you think a visual or a verbal medium helps an audience more easily interpret the meaning of a national symbol such as a flag? Explain your answer.

At the end of this chapter, you will use the artwork to stimulate ideas for writing.

Comparison of Adjectives and Adverbs

Before you buy a bicycle, you should do some comparison shopping. You might find out, for example, that one make of bicycle is a *good* buy. A second make, however, is a *better* buy, and a third make is the *best* buy of all. This example shows that different forms of a modifier are used to show comparison.

Most adjectives and adverbs have three forms: the positive, the comparative, and the superlative. These forms are used to show differences in degree or extent.

Most modifiers show degrees of comparison by changing form.

The **positive degree** is the basic form of an adjective or an adverb. It is used when no comparison is being made.

> This is a **hot** summer.
> Carla is **mature.**
> Eric is a **tall** basketball player.

The **comparative degree** is used when two people, things, or actions are being compared.

> This summer is **hotter** than last summer.
> Carla is **more mature** than her sister.
> Eric is **taller** than Josh.

The **superlative degree** is used when more than two people, things, or actions are being compared.

> This is the **hottest** summer of the past three years.
> Carla is the **most mature** of all her sisters.
> Eric is the **tallest** player on the team.

Following are additional examples of the three degrees of comparison.

POSITIVE	Today's game is a **big** one.
	Josh practices **often.**
COMPARATIVE	Today's game is **bigger** than last week's game.
	Josh practices **more often** than Eric.
SUPERLATIVE	Tomorrow's game will be the **biggest** game of the year.
	Josh practices the **most often** of all the team members.

Some adverbs, such as too, somewhere, very, *and* never, *cannot be compared. If you want to review how adjectives and adverbs are used in a sentence, go to pages L91–L113.*

PRACTICE YOUR SKILLS

● Check Your Understanding
Determining Degrees of Comparison

 Write the underlined modifier in each sentence. Then label its degree of comparison *P* for positive, *C* for comparative, or *S* for superlative.

1. Mario ran <u>hurriedly</u> to the locker room with his uniform in hand.
2. The team was dressing for the <u>most important</u> game of the season.
3. This week's game will be <u>more difficult</u> than last week's game.
4. The coach sent in his <u>fastest</u> runners, and Mario led them out.
5. A player on the other team sauntered <u>lazily</u> down the court.
6. Mario, who was <u>quicker</u> than that player, took the ball from him.
7. Eric worked <u>harder</u> than Josh to defend Mario as he dribbled down the court.

8. Josh, however, was the <u>most helpful</u> member of the team.

9. He played a <u>wonderful</u> game.

10. He had <u>fewer</u> chances to score than Mario, but he played great defense.

11. Ming Ho is <u>more serious</u> than the coach is about his game performance.

12. The audience is the <u>loudest</u> one I have ever heard at a school game.

13. John is <u>slower</u> than the other players.

14. The referee jumped <u>clumsily</u> out of the way.

15. In another two months, this team will be <u>better</u> than their opponents.

 ## Regular Comparison

The number of syllables in a modifier determines how it forms its comparative and superlative degrees.

Add _–er_ to form the comparative degree and _–est_ to form the superlative degree of one-syllable modifiers.

POSITIVE	COMPARATIVE	SUPERLATIVE
brave	braver	bravest
kind	kinder	kindest
soon	sooner	soonest

The comparative and superlative degrees of many two-syllable modifiers are formed the same way. However, some two-syllable modifiers sound awkward when _–er_ or _–est_ is added. For these modifiers, _more_ or _most_ should be used to form the comparative and superlative degrees. (_More_ and _most_ are always used with adverbs that end in _–ly_.)

Use *-er* or *more* to form the comparative degree and *-est* or *most* to form the superlative degree of two-syllable modifiers.

POSITIVE	COMPARATIVE	SUPERLATIVE
happy	happier	happiest
helpful	more helpful	most helpful
quickly	more quickly	most quickly

When deciding whether to add *er/est* or to use *more/most* with a two-syllable modifier, let your ear be your guide. If adding *-er* or *-est* makes a word awkward or difficult to pronounce, use *more* or *most* instead. Your ear tells you to avoid awkward comparisons such as "helpfuler" and "faithfuler" or "helpfulest" and "faithfulest."

Use *more* to form the comparative degree and *most* to form the superlative degree of modifiers with three or more syllables.

POSITIVE	COMPARATIVE	SUPERLATIVE
trivial	more trivial	most trivial
serious	more serious	most serious
vigorously	more vigorously	most vigorously

Because *less* and *least* mean the opposite of *more* and *most,* use these words to form negative comparisons.

NEGATIVE COMPARISONS		
trivial	less trivial	least trivial
serious	less serious	least serious
vigorously	less vigorously	least vigorously

Practice Your Skills

● Check Your Understanding
Forming the Comparison of Modifiers

Write each modifier. Then write its comparative and superlative forms.

1. difficult	**11.** safe
2. colorful	**12.** high
3. eagerly	**13.** lively
4. swiftly	**14.** loudly
5. abrupt	**15.** fast
6. quick	**16.** slow
7. sure	**17.** seasick
8. muddy	**18.** dark
9. hastily	**19.** easily
10. heavy	**20.** frisky

● Check Your Understanding
Forming the Negative Comparison of Modifiers

21.–25. Write the first five modifiers in the previous exercise. Then write the negative comparative and superlative forms, using *less* and *least.*

● Connect to the Writing Process: Drafting
Writing Sentences with Comparisons

Write sentences using the indicated form of the words below.

26. positive form of *high*

27. comparative form of *low*

28. superlative form of *eagerly*

29. positive form of *definite*

30. comparative form of *hasty*

31. superlative form of *close*

32. positive form of *serious*

33. comparative form of *sunny*

34. superlative form of *swiftly*

35. positive form of *leisurely*

▶ Irregular Comparison

The following adjectives and adverbs are compared irregularly. The comparative and superlative forms of these modifiers should be memorized.

POSITIVE	COMPARATIVE	SUPERLATIVE
bad	worse	worst
badly	worse	worst
ill	worse	worst
good	better	best
well	better	best
little	less	least
many	more	most
much	more	most

Do not add regular comparison endings to the comparative and superlative degrees of these irregular modifiers. For example, *worse* is the comparative form of *bad*. You should never use "worser."

CONNECT TO SPEAKING AND WRITING

As writers work, they usually have a good dictionary on hand to use as a reference. When you write comparisons, use the dictionary if you are unsure of the comparative or superlative form of an adjective or adverb. The dictionary will list the various forms of adjectives and adverbs if they are irregular. The dictionary also shows if the addition of *–er* or *–est* changes the spelling of the base word in any way. A good collegiate dictionary can be a writer's best friend.

PRACTICE YOUR SKILLS

● Check Your Understanding
Forming the Comparison of Irregular Modifiers

Contemporary
Life

Write the comparative and superlative forms of the underlined modifier.

1. That movie was really <u>bad</u>.
   It was ■ than the movie we saw last week.
   In fact, it was the ■ movie I have ever seen in my entire life.

2. Felipe showed <u>much</u> concern about the poor quality of the movie.
   Belinda showed even ■ concern than Felipe.
   Amazingly, Juana showed the ■ concern of all.

3. <u>Many</u> movies are filmed in Texas.
   ■ movies are filmed in New York.
   The ■ movies are filmed in California.

4. The movie we rented this morning was <u>good</u>.
   The movie we rented yesterday was ■.
   The movie we rented last month was the ■ I had ever seen.

5. I have <u>little</u> interest in watching another movie this week.
   I have ■ interest in watching television.
   I have the ■ interest in listening to music.

● Check Your Understanding
Finding Forms of Comparison in a Dictionary

Write each modifier below. Then write its comparative and superlative forms. (If you are unsure of the form or its spelling, look up the word in a dictionary.)

6. mad
7. lovely
8. timely
9. far
10. hot

11. fun
12. easy
13. homey
14. lonely
15. malevolent

Write each incorrect modifier and then write it correctly. If a sentence is correct, write C.

16. I have the baddest cold I have ever had.

17. One morning I felt a little run down, but by the afternoon I was iller.

18. I wanted to get better in the littlest amount of time possible.

19. My sister called the doctor, who gave me many instructions.

20. In fact, it was the manyest instructions I had ever received from a doctor.

21. He told me to drink mucher water than usual.

22. He also recommended a good night's sleep.

23. The next day I felt gooder than I had the day before.

24. Of all the instructions he gave, I was glad about the recommendation for sleep.

25. I hope I never have a bad cold like that one again.

Communicate Your Ideas

APPLY TO WRITING

Tall Tale: *Comparison with Adjectives and Adverbs*

Tall tales are a part of American legends. Paul Bunyan and Pecos Bill are two heroes of tall tales. Make up a Paul Bunyan–like character and write a tall tale about him or her. Remember that these characters are always strong and powerful, and their actions are often used to explain natural formations like the Grand Canyon or the Great Lakes. After you have finished, underline the adjectives and adverbs you used in your tall tale. Label each modifier *P* if it is the positive form, *C* if it is the comparative form, or *S* if it is the superlative form.

QuickCheck   Mixed Practice

Write each incorrect modifier and then write it correctly. If the modifier in a sentence is correct, write C.

1. Spending the day at an amusement park is the more enjoyable thing to do.
2. Amusement parks are one of the better places on Earth!
3. The more exciting ride of all is the roller coaster.
4. When the car drops down from the tallest hill on the ride, the car almost flies.
5. Roller coasters seem quickest than sports cars.
6. A most crowded place than the roller coaster is the midway.
7. Kids love to try to win the bigger stuffed animals at the ring-toss booth.
8. Of course, children rush most quickly to this booth than their parents do.
9. Their parents know the games are most difficult than they look.
10. Most parents think that the midway is the worse place to spend money in the entire amusement park.
11. Everyone in our family likes the water rides more than the roller coasters.
12. One water ride is scariest than a roller coaster.
13. This summer was lesser enjoyable than last summer.
14. We enjoy the amusement park the mostest of all the parks in town.
15. The worse part about going to the amusement park is having to leave.

The following special problems may arise when you compare people and things.

 Double Comparisons

Use only one method of forming the comparative and superlative degree of a modifier.

Do not use both *-er* and *more* to form the comparative degree, or both *-est* and *most* to form the superlative degree.

DOUBLE COMPARISON	Our city is more larger than most.
CORRECT	Our city is **larger** than most.
DOUBLE COMPARISON	I have the most accuratest map of the city.
CORRECT	I have the **most accurate** map of the city.

Illogical Comparisons

Only similar things should be compared. If you compare different things, you end up with an illogical comparison, a comparison that does not make sense.

Compare only items of a similar kind.

ILLOGICAL COMPARISON	This building's roof is steeper than the bank. (A roof is being compared to a bank.)
LOGICAL COMPARISON	This building's roof is steeper than the bank's. (A roof is being compared with another roof.)

ILLOGICAL COMPARISON	The tour guide's description of the building's history was better than the girls. (The description is being compared to girls.)
LOGICAL COMPARISON	The tour guide's description of the building's history was better than the girls' description. (The description is being compared to a description.)

You can learn about the use of an apostrophe with possessive nouns on pages L575–L577.

Other and *Else* in Comparison

Be sure that you do not make the mistake of comparing one thing with itself when it is part of a group. You can avoid this by adding *other* or *else* to your comparison.

Add *other* and *else* when comparing a member of a group with the rest of the group.

In the first example that follows, the bank building is supposedly being compared with the *other* structures in the city. However, without the word *other,* the building is also being compared with itself. It is a structure in the city.

INCORRECT	The bank building is taller than any structure in the city.
CORRECT	The bank building is taller than any **other** structure in the city.
INCORRECT	The bank president delivers more speeches than anyone in the company. (Since the bank president works in the company, he or she is being compared with himself or herself.)
CORRECT	The bank president delivers more speeches than anyone **else** in the company. (With the addition of the word *else,* the bank president no longer is being compared to himself or herself.)

PRACTICE YOUR SKILLS

● Check Your Understanding
Making Comparisons

Contemporary Life

Write _I_ if the comparison in the sentence is incorrect. Write _C_ if it is correct.

1. Our map of the downtown area made locations more clearer for my visiting uncle.
2. Our city has a more interesting history than any city in the state.
3. Our city is more picturesque than most other cities its size and age.
4. The architecture of the bank is more interesting than the city hall.
5. The sidewalks were constructed of the most beautiful cobblestones.
6. The town hall is more farther south than any building except the old courthouse at the end of Alexandria Street.
7. To make it across town in time for the lecture, we will have to walk more faster than we have been walking so far.
8. Mrs. Little, the mayor of our city, knows more about the city's history than any other citizen has ever known or recorded.
9. I think that was the most interestingest lecture I have ever heard.
10. The mayor's lecture lasted longer than the police officer.

● Connect to the Writing Process: Revising
Correcting Mistakes in Comparisons

11.–18. Rewrite the sentences above that contain errors in comparison.

APPLY TO WRITING

Comparing and Contrasting: *Adjectives and Adverbs*

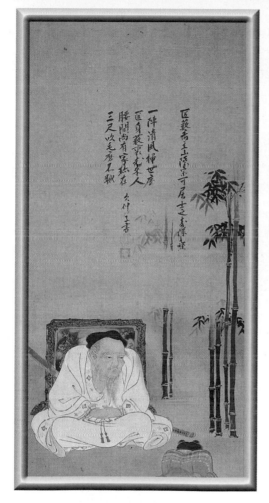

Rembrandt van Rijn.
Self-Portrait, 1659.
Oil on canvas, 33¼ by 26 inches.
National Gallery of Art, Washington,
DC.

Kano Tan'yu. (Detail) *Sakuma Shogen,*
Edo period, ca. 1636.
Ink and color on silk, 25⅛ by
11⅛ inches. ©Shinju-an Temple,
Kyoto, Japan.

Both of these works of art are portraits, artworks that
show likenesses of people. Look carefully at each of the
works. What is similar about them? How do they differ?
Write a short essay for your classmates in which you compare and contrast these two portraits. Be sure to use the
correct form of comparison of adjectives and adverbs.

General Interest **Write each incorrect modifier and then write it correctly. If a sentence is correct, write C.**

1. Norman Rockwell was one of America's best known illustrators.

2. Of these two pictures, I enjoyed this one the most.

3. The painting with the boy and the Santa Claus suit is the most cutest picture I have ever seen.

4. The most versatile artist in our class is Roberta.

5. She is the youngest of the two Compton sisters.

6. In our class the person with the less interest in art is Anthony.

7. His painting is messier than any painting in the class.

8. Sherry's sketch is better than anyone in the show.

9. My class this year is more difficult than last year.

10. I have worked more harder this year than ever before.

11. The museum's exhibit this month is more interestinger than last month.

12. These paintings are more abstracter than other paintings.

13. Charlene likes Picasso's works most than other painters.

14. We enjoyed this exhibit the most of all the exhibits that we visited.

15. Carlos thinks painting with oils is hardest than painting with watercolors.

Problems with Modifiers

Most words that end in *–ly* are adverbs. However, some adjectives such as *friendly* and *lovely* also have this ending. It is important to know whether a word is an adjective or an adverb in order to form the comparisons correctly.

Good or *Well?*

Good is an adjective that follows a linking verb. *Well* is an adverb that often follows an action verb. However, when *well* means "in good health" or "satisfactory," it is used as an adjective.

> That baking bread smells **good.** (adjective)
>
> I like **good,** homemade bread! (adjective)
>
> Jocelyn cooks **well.** (adverb)
>
> I feel quite **well** since I have eaten. (adjective meaning "in good health")

Double Negatives

Words such as *but* (when it means "only"), *hardly, never, no, nobody, not* (and its contraction *n't*), *nothing, only,* and *scarcely* are all negatives. Two negatives should not be used to express one negative meaning.

Avoid using a double negative.

A double negative often cancels itself out, leaving a positive statement. For example, if you say, "There isn't no more time," you are really saying, "There is more time."

DOUBLE NEGATIVE	Don't never cook while Mom is gone.
CORRECT	**Don't** cook while Mom is gone.
CORRECT	**Never** cook while Mom is gone.

PRACTICE YOUR SKILLS

● Check Your Understanding
Comparing with Problem Modifiers

Contemporary Life **Write *I* if the comparison in the sentence is incorrect. Write *C* if it is correct.**

1. I didn't go nowhere near the stove today.

2. We had a well selection of chips and sandwiches, so I ate that instead of cooking.

3. I can hardly wait until Mom returns from her business trip today.

4. I haven't done nothing about preparing our meals since she has been gone.

5. I would have cooked, but I wasn't feeling good.

6. I didn't tell my mom because I didn't never want to worry her.

7. Mom's business trip went good, but she was glad to be home.

8. She cooks very well, and I enjoyed the chicken soup she made me.

9. I'm a good cook, and I don't mind cooking.

10. When I feel well, there is not nothing I'd rather do than cook.

● Connect to the Writing Process: Revising
Using Modifiers Correctly

11.–17. Rewrite correctly the preceding sentences that contain errors in comparison.

APPLY TO WRITING

Persuasive Speech: *Modifiers*

Your school board has proposed ending physical education courses at your high school. At the next meeting of the board, you will have five minutes to explain why you agree or disagree with the proposal. Think about your position on this matter. List reasons and examples that support your position, being as specific as possible. Then arrange your notes in logical order and write the first draft of your speech. Edit your work, paying special attention to comparative and superlative forms of any modifiers. Then write a final draft and practice reading your speech aloud.

QuickCheck Mixed Practice

Sports
Topic
Rewrite the following paragraph, correcting each mistake in the use of comparisons.

The Olympic decathlon is held in greater esteem than any event in sports. The champion of this event is generally considered the most greatest athlete in the world. The performances in the decathlon are watched more than those in any Olympic event. The athletes competing in this event must be well at several different activities. They can't hardly go even one day without running or practicing their sport. A decathlon performer must be able to jump the highest, run the fastest, and throw the javelin the most farthest. The winner must be the bestest.

Using Modifiers Correctly

Write the following sentences, correcting each error. If a sentence is correct, write C.

1. For its size the honeybee is much more stronger than a person.
2. Paul hasn't done nothing yet about the garden.
3. Rainbow Bridge in Utah is larger than any other natural arch.
4. Woodworking is the bestest class I have this year.
5. Sean hasn't never seen *Star Wars*.
6. English contains more words than any language.
7. There isn't no more hamburger for the picnic.
8. The Great Dane is among the most largest of all dogs.
9. I think Molly is smarter than anyone in her class.
10. The copies seem brightest than the originals.
11. Which is hardest, ice-skating or roller-skating?
12. Do people in the United States have a higher standard of living than anyone in the world?
13. Nobody knew nothing about the defective fuse.
14. The flood last week was the worst yet.
15. That was the less expensive gift I could find.
16. Even an expert could hardly tell the difference between the real and the counterfeit bill.
17. Lee plays the drums better than anyone in his band.
18. Of Sarah's parents, her dad is most easygoing.
19. Tulips haven't never done well on that side of the house.
20. Of the two finalists, Carl has the best chance of winning.

Writing with Modifiers

Write the correct form of each modifier below.

1. the comparative of *quickly*
2. the comparative of *wide*
3. the superlative of *good*
4. the superlative of *generous*
5. the comparative of *little*
6. the superlative of *bright*
7. the comparative of *carefully*
8. the superlative of *bad*
9. the comparative of *brave*
10. the comparative of *many*
11. the superlative of *angry*
12. the superlative of *evenly*
13. the comparative of *zany*
14. the negative superlative of *courageous*
15. the comparative of *nervous*
16. the comparative of *easily*
17. the comparative of *swiftly*
18. the superlative of *heavy*
19. the negative comparative of *abrupt*
20. the superlative of *surely*
21. the superlative of *thin*
22. the negative comparative of *seasick*
23. the comparative of *ill*
24. the superlative of *much*
25. the comparative of *fast*

Writing Sentences

Write a paragraph that compares three pets or three desserts. Use modifiers in the positive, comparative, and superlative degrees.

Language and *Self-Expression*

To create this "moving painting," the artist placed a series of televisions and videocassette players side by side. The resulting wall of video represents the flag of the United States. As viewers compare the artwork to a real flag, they often experience a variety of feelings, such as national pride or anxiety about the future effects of technology.

Words can also help people experience a variety of feelings. Write a poem that compares a national symbol with a feeling or a concept. In your poem include at least two modifiers that use the comparative or superlative degree. Post your poem on a classroom bulletin board for your classmates to read. You may also want to share your writing with an American history class.

Prewriting Create a Venn diagram comparing the symbol and the feeling or concept you selected. Your diagram should show how these things are alike and how they are different.

Drafting Write either a rhyming or a free verse poem. Write the first draft quickly, letting your words and ideas flow. Use a variety of adjectives and adverbs to add interest to your writing.

Revising Read your poem aloud to a partner. Ask your partner to listen for the rhythm and flow of the poem. Do transitional words guide him or her from the beginning to the end of the poem?

Editing Read your work again. Check your poem for errors in spelling and punctuation. Be sure that you used the comparative and superlative forms of modifiers correctly.

Publishing Prepare a final copy of your poem and post it in the classroom.

Another Look

The **positive degree** is the basic form of an adjective or an adverb. It is used when no comparison is being made.

The **comparative degree** is used when two people, things, or actions are being compared.

The **superlative degree** is used when more than two people, things, or actions are being compared.

Regular and Irregular Comparison

Add *-er* to form the comparative degree and *-est* to form the superlative degree of one-syllable modifiers. *(page L415)*

Add *-er* or *more* to form the comparative degree and *-est* or *most* to form the superlative degree of two-syllable modifiers. *(page L416)*

Use *more* to form the comparative degree and *most* to form the superlative degree of modifiers with three or more syllables. *(page L416)*

Use *less* and *least* to form negative comparisons of modifiers. *(page L416)*

The comparative and superlative forms of some modifiers must be memorized. These modifiers include: *bad, badly, ill, good, well, little, many, much. (page L418)*

Problems with Comparisons

Do not use both *-er* and *more* to form the comparative degree, or both *-est* and *most* to form the superlative degree. *(page L422)*

Compare only items of a similar kind. *(pages L422–L423)*

Add *other* and *else* when comparing a member of a group with the rest of the group. *(page L423)*

Problems with Modifiers

Good is an adjective that follows a linking verb. *Well* is an adverb that often follows an action word. However, when *well* means "in good health" or "satisfactory," it is used as an adjective. *(page L427)*

Avoid using double negatives. *(pages L427–L428)*

Directions

Read the passage and choose the word or group of words that belongs in each underlined space. Write the letter of the correct answer.

EXAMPLE   Jim saw the __(1)__ car he had ever seen in the showroom window.

            1 A sleekest
               B sleeker
               C most sleek
               D more sleek

ANSWER   **1 A**

The new car was __(1)__ than Jim's old car. With four-wheel drive, it also had __(2)__ brakes for his trips to the mountains. However, it was __(3)__ than what Jim could afford.

Later Jim went to the mall. He saw two jackets. One was __(4)__ than the other. The __(5)__ jacket had __(6)__ buttons. Although they were both blue, the more formal one was a __(7)__ shade. The more formal jacket also had the __(8)__ sleeves. Jim decided to buy the __(9)__ jacket. "Buying a jacket is certainly __(10)__ than buying a car," he thought.

1 A powerful
   B more powerful
   C most powerful
   D powerfulest

2 A better
   B good
   C more good
   D best

3 A expensive
   B more expensive
   C most expensive
   D more expensiver

4 A formaler
   B most formal
   C more formal
   D formal

5 A least formal
   B less formal
   C unformal
   D formal

6 A more fewer
   B fewest
   C fewer
   D most fewer

7 A more deeper
   B most deep
   C deepest
   D deeper

8 A most wide
   B more wide
   C widest
   D wider

9 A lightest
   B lighter
   C more lighter
   D most lightest

10 A affordable
    B affordabler
    C most affordable
    D more affordable

A Writer's Glossary of Usage

In the last four chapters, you covered the fundamental elements of usage. A Writer's Glossary of Usage presents some specific areas that might give you difficulty. Before you use the glossary, though, there are some terms that you should know.

You will notice references in the glossary to various levels of language. Two of these levels of language are standard English and nonstandard English. **Standard English** refers to the rules and the conventions of usage that are accepted and used most widely by English-speaking people throughout the world. **Nonstandard English** has many variations because it is influenced by regional differences and dialects, as well as by current slang. Remember that *nonstandard* does not mean that the language is wrong but that the language may be inappropriate in certain situations. Because nonstandard English lacks uniformity, you should use standard English when you write.

You will also notice references to formal and informal English. **Formal English** is used for written work because it follows the conventional rules of grammar, usage, and mechanics. Examples of the use of formal English can usually be found in business letters, technical reports, and well-written compositions. **Informal English,** on the other hand, follows the conventions of standard English but might include words and phrases that would seem out of place in a formal piece of writing. Informal English is often used in magazine articles, newspaper stories, and fiction writing.

The items in this glossary have been arranged alphabetically so that you can use this section as a reference tool.

a, an Use *a* before words beginning with consonant sounds and *an* before words beginning with vowel sounds.

> Did you buy **a** new CD?
> No, it was given to me as **an** early birthday gift.

accept, except *Accept* is a verb that means "to receive with consent." *Except* is usually a preposition that means "but" or "other than."

> Everyone **except** Bernie **accepted** the news calmly.

advice, advise *Advice* is a noun that means "a recommendation." *Advise* is a verb that means "to recommend."

> I usually follow my doctor's **advice.**
> He **advised** me to exercise more often.

affect, effect *Affect* is a verb that means "to influence" or "to act upon." *Effect* is usually a noun that means "a result" or "an influence." As a verb, *effect* means "to accomplish" or "to produce."

> Does the weather **affect** your mood?
> No, it has no **effect** on me.
> The medicine **effected** a change in my disposition.

CONNECT TO SPEAKING AND WRITING

Professional writers sometimes use *ain't* to enhance a dialect and create a humorous effect. Notice the effectiveness of this device in Mark Twain's writing.

> Tom's most well now, and got his bullet around his neck on a watch-guard for a watch, and is always seeing what time it is, and so there **ain't** nothing more to write about, and I am rotten glad of it, because if I'd 'a' knowed what a trouble it was to make a book I wouldn't 'a' tackled it, and **ain't** a-going to no more.
>
> —*Mark Twain,* The Adventures of Huckleberry Finn

ain't This contraction is nonstandard English. Avoid it in your writing.

> NONSTANDARD   Ken **ain't** here yet.
> STANDARD   Ken **isn't** here yet.

all ready, already *All ready* means "completely ready." *Already* means "previously."

> We were **all ready** to go by seven o'clock.
> I had **already** told my parents that we were going to the movies.

all together, altogether *All together* means "in a group." *Altogether* means "wholly" or "thoroughly."

> Let's try to sing **all together** for a change.
> The traditional song will sound **altogether** different if we do.

a lot People very often write these two words incorrectly as one. There is no such word as "alot." *A lot,* however, even when it is written as two words, should be avoided in formal writing.

> INFORMAL   Famous movie stars receive **a lot** of fan mail.
>
> FORMAL   Famous movie stars usually receive **a large quantity** of fan mail.

among, between These words are both prepositions. *Among* is used when referring to three or more people or things. *Between* is used when referring to two people or things.

> Put your present **among** the others.
> Then come and sit **between** Judith and me.

amount, number *Amount* refers to a singular word. *Number* refers to a plural word.

> Although there were a **number** of rainy days this month, the total **amount** of rain was less than usual.

CONNECT TO SPEAKING AND WRITING

To avoid confusion in usage between *amount* and *number* when speaking and writing, remember that *amount* refers to things in bulk or mass that cannot be counted, whereas *number* refers to things that can be counted.

> I was surprised at the **amount** of coffee he drank.
> (Coffee cannot be counted.)
>
> He put a large **number** of coffee beans into the machine.
> (Coffee beans can be counted.)

anywhere, everywhere, nowhere, somewhere Do not add *–s* to any of these words.

> I looked **everywhere** but could not find my keys.

at Do not use *at* after *where*.

NONSTANDARD	Do you know **where** we're **at?**
STANDARD	Do you know **where** we are?

a while, awhile *A while* is made up of an article and a noun; together, they are mainly used after a preposition. *Awhile* is an adverb that stands alone and means "for a short period of time."

> We can stay on the job for **a while.**
> After we work **awhile,** we can take a break.

PRACTICE YOUR SKILLS

● Check Your Understanding
Finding the Correct Word

Contemporary Life **Write the word in parentheses that correctly completes each sentence.**

1. The junior varsity team has (all ready, already) started football practice.

2. (Accept, Except) for a few players, the team is in excellent condition.

3. This year's team has (a, an) difficult schedule.

4. Their coaches offer the players useful (advice, advise) (everywhere, everywheres) the team plays.

5. In addition, they teach the eager squad a large (amount, number) of plays.

6. Loyalty (among, between) the members of the football team is encouraged.

7. (A lot, A large amount) of time is spent in daily practice.

8. Players arriving late (affect, effect) the practice schedule.

9. The players meet (all together, altogether) before and after practice (a while, awhile) for a pep talk.

10. It (ain't, isn't) long before the first game will be played.

Connect to the Writing Process: Revising
Recognizing Correct Usage

Add interest to this paragraph by replacing the term *a lot* with a more precise word or phrase. As you rewrite the paragraph, use a different word or phrase each time.

A lot of students waited eagerly for the first football game. When the day arrived, a lot of the ninth grade class met for a pep rally. The teachers advised the students not to wander around a lot. After cheering and applauding a lot, they returned to class, a lot satisfied with their class spirit.

bad, badly *Bad* is an adjective and often follows a linking verb. *Badly* is used as an adverb. In the first two examples, *felt* is a linking verb.

NONSTANDARD	Luke felt **badly** all day.
STANDARD	Luke felt **bad** all day.
STANDARD	Luke **badly** needs a haircut.

bring, take *Bring* indicates motion toward the speaker. *Take* indicates motion away from the speaker.

> **Bring** me the stamps.
> Now, please **take** this letter to the post office.

can, may *Can* expresses ability. *May* expresses possibility or permission.

> I **can** baby-sit for you tonight.
> **May** I watch TV after Kenny is asleep?

doesn't, don't *Doesn't* is singular and must agree with a singular subject. *Don't* is plural and must agree with a plural subject, except when used with the singular pronouns *I* and *you*.

> This article **doesn't** make sense to me.
> (singular subject)
>
> These articles **don't** make sense to me.
> (plural subject)

double negative Words such as *barely, but* (when it means "only"), *hardly, never, no, none, no one, barely, nobody, not* (and its contraction *n't*), *nothing, nowhere, only,* and *scarcely* are all negatives. Do not use two negatives to express one negative meaning.

> NONSTANDARD   I **hardly never** see you anymore.
> STANDARD   I **hardly** see you anymore.
> STANDARD   I **never** see you anymore.

etc. *Etc.* is an abbreviation for the Latin phrase *et cetera,* which means "and other things." Never use the word *and* with *etc.* If you do, what you are really saying is "and and other things." You should not use this abbreviation at all in formal writing.

> INFORMAL   Before moving, we had to pack our clothes, books, records, **etc.**
>
> FORMAL   Before moving, we had to pack our clothes, books, records, **and other belongings.**

fewer, less *Fewer* is plural and refers to things that can be counted. *Less* is singular and refers to quantities and qualities that cannot be counted.

> There seem to be **fewer** hours in the day.
> I seem to have **less** time to get my homework done.

good, well *Good* is an adjective and often follows a linking verb. *Well* is an adverb and often follows an action verb. However, when *well* means "in good health" or "satisfactory," it is used as an adjective.

> The biscuits smell **good.** (adjective)
>
> Janice cooks **well.** (adverb)
>
> I feel quite **well** after eating the chicken soup.
> (adjective meaning "in good health")

have, of Never substitute *of* for the verb *have.* When speaking, many people make a contraction of *have.* For example, they might say, "We should've gone." Because *'ve* may sound like *of, of* is often mistakenly substituted for *have* in writing.

> NONSTANDARD We should **of** started earlier.
> STANDARD We should **have** started earlier.

hear, here *Hear* is a verb that means "to perceive by listening." *Here* is an adverb that means "in this place."

> I can't **hear** the music from **here.**

hole, whole A *hole* is an opening. *Whole* means "complete" or "entire."

> Have you noticed the **hole** in your coat?
> Did you leave your coat on for the **whole** movie?

in, into Use *in* when you are referring to a stationary place. Use *into* when you want to express motion from one place to another.

> Is the money **in** your coat pocket?
> Why don't you transfer it **into** your wallet?

its, it's *Its* is a possessive pronoun and means "belonging to it." *It's* is a contraction for *it is*.

> The dog returned home to **its** owner.
> **It's** fun to watch **its** happy expression.

PRACTICE YOUR SKILLS

● Check Your Understanding
Finding the Correct Word

Literature Topic **Write the word in parentheses that correctly completes each sentence.**

1. Who (doesn't, don't) enjoy an interesting detective story?

2. It (can, may) also be referred to as a mystery story or whodunit.

3. Some writers use (fewer, less) clues than others, but all detective stories contain clues designed to solve a crime.

4. The detective story made (its, it's) first appearance in Edgar Allan Poe's writings.

5. Poe also wrote essays, poems, short stories, (etc., and other works).

6. His fictional detective, C. Auguste Dupin, (may have, may of) been based on a real-life detective.

7. Poe wrote a (hole, whole) group of stories that featured Detective Dupin.

8. Detective Dupin first appeared (in, into) Poe's "The Murders in the Rue Morgue."

9. (Its, It's) a known fact that Sir Arthur Conan Doyle, a British writer, later used Dupin as a model for Sherlock Holmes.

10. Would Doyle feel (bad, badly) if he knew that the name Sherlock Holmes is better known today than his?

Rewrite the following paragraph, changing the words that are used incorrectly.

In fiction an author don't often leave readers in suspense. Usually the hole case is carefully tied together into a neat package. Hardly ever is a crime left unsolved in a fictional detective story. In real life, however, its often not what we hear about. On television, for example, news programs sometimes bring us to the scene of a unsolved mystery and try to recreate it. Some shows present the facts good while others present them bad. Regardless of the way the program is presented, the crime don't have a final resolution as fictional detective stories do.

Communicate Your Ideas

APPLY TO WRITING
Explanatory Writing: *Adjectives and Adverbs*

You have been asked to tutor a student who is experiencing difficulty with the following terms: *bad/badly* and *good/well*. In your own words, write an explanation to offer the student for the choice(s) underlined in each of the following sentences.

1. Interest in a detective story often depends on whether the plot is <u>bad</u> or <u>good</u>.

2. Clues that are presented <u>well</u> prevent the reader from solving the crime too quickly.

3. If the description of a possible suspect is presented <u>badly</u>, it detracts from the story.

4. A writer might present a suspect as being in <u>bad</u> health to gain sympathy from the reader for that particular character.

5. Most people feel <u>good</u> at the end of a detective story because justice has been served.

knew, new *Knew,* the past tense of the verb *know,* means "was acquainted with." *New* is an adjective that means "recently made" or "just found."

> Michael's sneakers looked so clean and white that I **knew** they were **new.**

learn, teach *Learn* means "to gain knowledge." *Teach* means "to instruct" or "to show how."

> I just **learned** how to use that computer program that Mom bought for us.
>
> Now I can **teach** you how to use it.

leave, let *Leave* means "to depart" or "to go away from." *Let* means "to allow" or "to permit."

> NONSTANDARD   **Leave** me help you carry those packages into the house.
>
> STANDARD   **Let** me help you carry those packages into the house.
>
> STANDARD   Don't **leave** before you help me carry in my packages.

lie, lay *Lie* means "to rest or recline." *Lie* is never followed by a direct object. Its principal parts are *lie, lying, lay,* and *lain. Lay* means "to put or set (something) down." *Lay* is usually followed by a direct object. Its principal parts are *lay, laying, laid,* and *laid.*

LIE	Our kittens always **lie** on the sofa.
	They are **lying** there now.
	They **lay** there all morning.
	They have **lain** there for a long time.
LAY	**Lay** their food dish on the floor.
	(*Dish* is the direct object.)
	Jill is **laying** the dish on the floor.
	Molly **laid** the dish on the floor yesterday.
	Until recently Gary always has **laid** the dish on the floor.

You can learn more about using the verbs lie *and* lay *on pages L291–L292.*

like, as *Like* is a preposition that introduces a prepositional phrase. *As* is usually a subordinating conjunction that introduces an adverb clause.

STANDARD	Betty should read stories **like** these.
	(prepositional phrase)
NONSTANDARD	Betty usually does **like** she is told.
	(clause)
STANDARD	Betty usually does **as** she is told.

passed, past *Passed* is the past tense of the verb *pass.* As a noun *past* means "a time gone by." As an adjective *past* means "just gone" or "elapsed." As a preposition *past* means "beyond."

In the **past** I have **passed** all math tests.
(*past* as a noun)

I have walked **past** my math class for the **past** few days, hoping to see my final grade posted.
(*past* as a preposition and then as an adjective)

rise, raise *Rise* means "to move upward" or "to get up." *Rise* is never followed by a direct object. Its principal parts are *rise, rising, rose,* and *risen. Raise* means "to lift (something) up," "to increase," or "to grow something." *Raise* is usually followed by a direct object. Its principal parts are *raise, raising, raised,* and *raised.*

> Dad will **rise** at 7:00 A.M.
> At that time, he will **raise** the shades.
> (*Shades* is the direct object.)

You can learn more about using the verbs rise *and* raise *on pages L292–L293.*

shall, will Formal English uses *shall* with first-person pronouns and *will* with second- and third-person pronouns. Today, *shall* and *will* are used interchangeably with *I* and *we,* except that *shall* should be used with *I* and *we* for questions.

> **Shall** I invite her to join the club?
> I **will** ask her tonight.

sit, set *Sit* means "to rest in an upright position." *Sit* is never followed by a direct object. Its principal parts are *sit, sitting, sat,* and *sat. Set* means "to put or place (something)." *Set* is usually followed by a direct object. Its principal parts are *set, setting, set* and *set.*

> After Mom has **set** the timer, we will **sit** and wait thirty minutes for dinner.
> (*Timer* is the direct object of *set.*]

You can learn more about using the verbs sit *and* set *on pages L293–L294.*

than, then *Than* is a subordinating conjunction and is used for comparisons. *Then* is an adverb and means "at that time" or "next."

> NONSTANDARD   Jupiter is much larger **then** Saturn.
>
> STANDARD   After learning that Jupiter is much larger **than** Saturn, we **then** learned some other interesting facts about our solar system.

that, which, who All three words are relative pronouns. *That* refers to people, animals, or things; *which* refers to animals or things; and *who* refers to people.

> The airline tickets **that** I bought for the trip were expensive.
> From the air we saw the cows, **which** looked like little dots.
> The flight attendant **who** was on our plane gave instructions.

PRACTICE YOUR SKILLS

● Check Your Understanding
Finding the Correct Word

Contemporary Life
Write the word in parentheses that correctly completes each sentence.

1. The family (shall, will) go on their annual family picnic tomorrow.

2. Leslie and David (knew, new) they could each invite one friend.

3. They invited the twins (which, who) live in the house down the road.

4. The family members will (raise, rise) early and pack the car.

5. Leslie (lain, laid) out the tablecloth and the paper plates the night before the picnic.

6. Their parents always (leave, let) them help prepare food for the picnic basket and decide on the sporting equipment to use at the picnic.

7. David first wanted to (learn, teach) how to make deviled eggs.

8. His cooking (passed, past) inspection after the family sampled the eggs.

9. Leslie declared that they tasted exactly (like, as) the ones from the deli.

10. (Than, Then) she began baking brownies.
11. Later they took out the sporting equipment, (which, who) was in the garage.
12. Leslie and David (sit, set) a variety of sporting equipment next to the car.
13. David remembered to include his (new, knew) baseball and glove.
14. Leslie and David decided to (teach, learn) the twins how to play volleyball.
15. The whole family agreed they would have a better time (than, then) last year.

Connect to the Writing Process: Drafting
Writing Correct Forms of Verbs

Rewrite the following paragraph, changing the words that are used incorrectly.

On the day of the picnic, Leslie had sat her alarm for 7:00 A.M. After the alarm rang, she set up on the side of the bed. Next, she slowly raised the blinds to see if the sun had raised. Deciding to rest another few minutes, she lied down on the bed again, carefully laying her head on the pillow. When the alarm sounded, she went downstairs to help sit the picnic items inside the basket. Before sitting down to eat, she called David. David came to the table and set down. He watched Leslie rise the blinds so that they could watch the sunrise while they ate. After breakfast, David lay an old blanket on the floor and quickly folded it before the dog could lay down on it.

APPLY TO WRITING

Description: *Verbs*

Pretend you have arrived at the beach or park for a family picnic. Write a well-developed paragraph in which you describe the day's events. Use the scene in the picture to help you get started. In your description, include at least four of the phrases listed below, making sure you use the correct principal parts of the verbs in parentheses.

- on the blanket *(lie, lay)*
- the golden sun *(sit, set)*
- food to the picnic area *(bring, take)*
- the volleyball net *(sit, set)*
- the picnic basket to the car *(bring, take)*
- at the picnic bench *(sit, set)*

their, there, they're *Their* is a possessive pronoun. *There* is usually an adverb, but sometimes it begins an inverted sentence. *They're* is a contraction for *they are.*

> Tell them to take **their** time.
> **There** will be many reporters gathered in the hall.
> **They're** meeting at seven o'clock for the press conference.

theirs, there's *Theirs* is a possessive pronoun. *There's* is a contraction for *there is.*

> These messages are ours; those messages are **theirs.**
> **There's** a message for you in the office.

them, those Never use *them* as a subject or as an adjective.

> NONSTANDARD   **Them** are freshly picked tomatoes.
>   (subject)
>
> STANDARD   **Those** are freshly picked tomatoes.
>
> NONSTANDARD   Did you like **them** tomatoes?
>   (adjective)
>
> STANDARD   Did you like **those** tomatoes?

this here, that there Avoid using *here* or *there* in addition to *this* or *that.*

> NONSTANDARD   **That there** chair is very comfortable.
> STANDARD   **That** chair is very comfortable.
>
> NONSTANDARD   **This here** sofa matches your chair.
> STANDARD   **This sofa** matches your chair.

threw, through *Threw* is the past tense of the verb *throw. Through* is a preposition that means "in one side and out the other."

> Denny **threw** the ball over the fence.
>
> He's lucky that it didn't go **through** the window of the house.

to, too, two *To* is a preposition. *To* also begins an infinitive. *Too* is an adverb that modifies a verb, an adjective, or another adverb. *Two* is a number.

> Keith went **to** the gym **to** practice.
>
> **Two** members of the team arrived **too** late.
>
> Only one was asked **to** play in the game, but the other played **too.**

use to, used to Be sure to add the *d* to *use*.

Nonstandard	I **use to** have three cats, but now I have one.
Standard	I **used to** have three cats, but now I have one.

way, ways Do not substitute *ways* for *way* when referring to a distance.

Nonstandard	We have gone a long **ways** since noon.
Standard	We have gone a long **way** since noon.

when, where Do not use *when* or *where* directly after a linking verb in a definition.

Nonstandard	A *presbyope* is **when** a person is farsighted.
Standard	A *presbyope* is a farsighted person.
Nonstandard	A *domicile* is **where** people live.
Standard	A *domicile* is a place **where** people live.

where Do not substitute *where* for *that*.

Nonstandard	I heard **where** crime rates are going down.
Standard	I heard **that** crime rates are going down.

who, whom *Who,* a pronoun in the nominative case, is used as either a subject or a predicate nominative. *Whom,* a pronoun in the objective case, is used as a direct object, an indirect object, or an object of a preposition.

> **Who** is coming to your party? (subject)
>
> **Whom** did you choose? (direct object)

You can learn more about using who *and* whom *on pages 346–347.*

whose, who's *Whose* is a possessive pronoun. *Who's* is a contraction for *who is.*

> **Whose** is the bicycle that you borrowed?
> **Who's** going to ride with you?

your, you're *Your* is a possessive pronoun. *You're* is a contraction for *you are.*

> Are these **your** campaign posters?
> **You're** the one we want for president of the class.

PRACTICE YOUR SKILLS

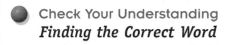

Check Your Understanding
Finding the Correct Word

Social Studies **Write the word in parentheses that correctly completes each sentence.**

1. Edward J. Smith, (who, whom) was called the "Millionaire's Captain" by some, commanded the *Titanic* on its fateful journey.

2. Captain Smith, (whose, who's) reputation for experience and safety were excellent, planned to retire after this voyage.

3. (Their, There) have been many accounts written about the sinking of the *Titanic.*

4. Most people believed the ship (to, too) be unsinkable.

5. Regulations never (use to, used to) require lifeboat space for every person.

6. The *Titanic* had traveled a long (way, ways) from Southampton, England, when it struck an iceberg.

7. Some hours later, passengers were instructed to put on (their, there) life jackets.

8. There were sixteen wooden lifeboats; at first, only women and children were allowed on (them, those) lifeboats.

9. Hundreds of passengers (threw, through) themselves into the freezing water.

10. Today the ship's (too, two) main sections lie on the ocean floor.

Connect to the Writing Process: Revising
Recognizing Correct Usage

Rewrite the following paragraph, changing the words that are used incorrectly.

Imagine the excitement on that day in 1912 when the *Titanic* left port. On shore their would have been many who bid they're farewells by waving, while others through flowers and kisses too their loved ones. Many passengers were used to traveling on large ships. Few, however, could imagine those lavish staterooms that awaited them when they walked threw the corridors. One such passenger, who's name was well known, was John Jacob Astor, a fur trader and American millionaire. This idyllic scene tragically changed on the night of the sinking of the *Titanic*. Astor was among the approximately fifteen hundred passengers to who death came that fateful night.

History Topic **Write the word in parentheses that best completes each sentence.**

1. The *Titanic* tragedy was difficult to (accept, except) because of the ship's "unsinkable" reputation.

2. Everyone (who, whom) had helped design and build the *Titanic* believed it to be unsinkable.

3. In spite of the (advice, advise) of the original designer, however, only sixteen wooden lifeboats were on board.

4. The (amount, number) of other luxury features onboard impressed even those in first class.

5. (There, Their, They're) was even a kennel for the dogs of first-class passengers.

6. First-class passengers could walk (in, into) a gymnasium for a workout or exercise on the tennis court.

7. The ship featured a swimming pool (that, which, who) was filled with seawater.

8. (A lot of, A great many) features on the *Titanic* were inspired by the French.

9. (Among, Between) the ship's many remarkable features was its spectacular Grand Staircase.

10. Even second-class and third-class accommodations were better (than, then) those on other ships.

11. None of the passengers (knew, new) that iceberg alerts had been received on several occasions during the voyage.

12. Even after the *Titanic* had hit an iceberg, passengers throughout the (hole, whole) ship believed themselves to be safe.

13. Many of the passengers boarded the lifeboats (like, as) they were told, but others refused to leave their families.

14. As the water was (raising, rising), the band courageously continued to play.

15. (Fewer, Less) than fifteen people were saved from the freezing water, and only about seven hundred of the more than two thousand aboard the ship survived.

CHAPTER 14

Capital Letters

 **Pretest**

Directions

For each sentence, choose the word or words that should be capitalized. Write the letter of your answer. If the sentence contains no error, write *D*.

EXAMPLE	**1.** i took a poetry class at the community center last summer.

    1 A I, Poetry
       B I
       C I, Community Center
       D No error

ANSWER   **1 B**

1. The class was called poetry I.
2. It was taught by a real poet, winifred smith.
3. She is the author of *down time*.
4. Though she is american, she spoke with a foreign accent.
5. I think she grew up in france.
6. Now she teaches during the year at hampshire college.
7. She read us poems from different eras; I especially liked the ones from the renaissance.
8. I love hearing ms. smith read her poems with her french accent.
9. My favorite poem begins, "did i miss something?/my back was turned for just a moment...."
10. My friend anita and i wrote a lot of poetry for the class.

1	A	Class, Poetry	6	A	Hampshire
	B	Class		B	College
	C	Poetry		C	Hampshire College
	D	No error		D	No error

2	A	Poet, Winifred Smith	7	A	Renaissance
	B	Poet, Smith		B	Eras, Renaissance
	C	Winifred Smith		C	Eras
	D	No error		D	No error

3	A	Author	8	A	Ms. Smith
	B	*Down Time*		B	French
	C	Author, *Down Time*		C	Ms. Smith, French
	D	No error		D	No error

4	A	American, Foreign	9	A	Did
	B	Foreign		B	Did, I, My
	C	American		C	I
	D	No error		D	No error

5	A	France	10	A	Anita
	B	She		B	Poetry
	C	Up		C	Anita, I
	D	No error		D	No error

Architect unknown. *Caerlaverock Castle,* ca. A.D. 1270. Dumfries, Scotland.

Describe   What material is this castle made of? Describe its location.

Analyze   Notice the high walls, small windows, and strong towers of Caerlaverock Castle. Also notice the *crenations,* or curved and scalloped edges, which appear around the top of each tower. What do you think the main function of the castle was?

Interpret   What do you think the main concerns of the people who lived in the castle were? Explain.

Judge   This castle is more than 700 years old. What impression does the castle give? Why does it give you that impression?

At the end of this chapter, you will use the photograph as a visual aid for writing.

Capitalization

Written English is a bit like a detective story. It is filled with many clues that help readers understand the writer's message. Capitalization and punctuation are two such clues. If some of the clues are missing or misused, the message can easily become confused and misleading.

By now you probably know most of the rules for capitalization. This chapter, however, can serve as a review—especially since capital letters provide important clues to the meaning of your writing.

▶ First Words and the Pronoun *I*

A capital letter signals the beginning of a new idea, whether it is in the form of a sentence, a line of poetry, or a formal outline.

Sentences and Poetry

Capitalize the first word of a sentence and of a line of poetry.

SENTENCES	**A** lone rose stood in the vase.
	Crystal vases are beautiful.
	Roses have a special fragrance.
LINES OF POETRY	**S**he went as quiet as the dew
	From a familiar flower.
	Not like the dew did she return
	At the accustomed hour!

–Emily Dickinson

Modern poets often deliberately misuse or eliminate capital letters. Notice the lack of capitalization at the beginning of lines in this excerpt.

> Dead daisies, shriveled lilies, withered bodies
> of dried chrysanthemums. Among these, and waste
>   leaves
> of yellow and brown fronds of palm and fern,
> I came, and found
> a rose
> left for dead, heaped with the hopeless dead,
> its petals still supple.
>
> —*Li-Young Lee, "Always a Rose"*

When you are quoting lines of poetry, copy them exactly as the poet has written them, including any nonstandard capitalization or punctuation.

You can learn about capitalizing quotations on pages L553–L554.

Parts of Letters

Capitalize the first word in the greeting of a letter and the first word in the closing of a letter.

SALUTATIONS AND CLOSINGS		
SALUTATIONS	To whom it may concern:	Dear Ashley,
	Dear Sir or Madam:	Dear boys and girls,
CLOSINGS	Yours truly,	Thank you,
	With love,	Sincerely,

Outlines

Capitalize the first word of each item in an outline and the letters that begin major subsections of the outline.

Wildflowers
 I. **S**tonecrop family
   A. Pigmyweed
   B. Stonecrop
    1. **R**ose-flowered sedum
    2. **Y**ellow stonecrop
   C. Echeveria
    1. **S**avior flower
    2. **B**luff weed
 II. **S**axifrage family
   A. Saxifrage
    1. **M**ountain lettuce
    2. **T**ufted saxifrage
   B. Sullivantia
   C. Boykinia
 III. **F**ireweed family
   A. Purple-leaved willowherb
   B. Pink fireweed
   C. Orange paintbrush

The Pronoun *I*

Capitalize the pronoun *I*, both alone and in contractions.

I hope **I**'ve picked enough greenery for the flower arrangement.

I know **I**'ll enjoy seeing those flowers bloom when spring arrives.

Last spring **I** planted daisies, but this year **I**'m going to plant bluebonnets.

I'd like to grow roses, but they require a great deal of care.

PRACTICE YOUR SKILLS

● Check Your Understanding
Using Capital Letters

Contemporary Life **Rewrite the following items, correcting the errors in capitalization.**

1. dear Mr. Shakespeare,

2. shall i compare thee to a summer's day?
thou art more lovely and more temperate: . . .

—William Shakespeare, Sonnet XVIII

3. i went to the play, and i really enjoyed it.

4. Types of Poems
  I. rhyming
    A. Limerick
    B. Sonnet
      1. petrarchan
      2. shakespearean
    C. Ballad

5. the poems of other Elizabethan writers also interest me.

● Connect to the Writing Process: Editing
Correcting Errors in Capitalization

Rewrite the following letter, correcting the errors in capitalization.

dear Mrs. Wallace,

   i really enjoyed your recent Lecture on the sonnets of Shakespeare. i am interested in finding a copy of one of his sonnets, but i'm not sure what number it is. the first two lines are as follows:

   When in disgrace with fortune and men's eyes,
   i all alone beweep my outcast state. . . .

would you please let me know which of Shakespeare's sonnets this is? you may write me back at the address i've enclosed.

thank You,

Mikayla Simpson

Communicate Your Ideas

APPLY TO WRITING

Writer's Craft: *Analyzing the Use of Capitalization*

When writing poetry, the American poet E. E. Cummings ignored the rules of capitalization and punctuation. He even signed his name using lowercase letters. Read the following excerpt and then follow the directions.

> somewhere i have never travelled, gladly beyond
> any experience, your eyes have their silence:
> in your most frail gesture are things which enclose me,
> or which i cannot touch because they are too near
>
> your slightest look easily will unclose me
> though i have closed myself as fingers. . . .
>
> —*E. E. Cummings,* "somewhere i have never travelled"

- How does the lack of capitalization in this poem affect you as a reader?
- Rewrite the lines of poetry, capitalizing the words that, according to convention, you should capitalize.
- Compare your new version with Cummings's original. How does adding capitalization change the poem?
- Why do you think a poet might choose to leave out capital letters or punctuation?

Proper Nouns

Capitalize proper nouns and their abbreviations.

Names of persons and animals should be capitalized. Also capitalize initials that stand for people's names.

NAMES OF PERSONS AND ANIMALS	
PERSONS	Josh, Tiffany Sheryl Johnson, Susan **B.** Anthony, Grant Lawrence, **T. H.** Murphy, Jr., Chris
ANIMALS	Spot, Muffin, Rover, Scout, Buttercup

You can learn about the capitalization of titles of persons on pages L481–L482.

Geographical names, including particular places and bodies of water, should be capitalized.

GEOGRAPHICAL NAMES	
STREETS, HIGHWAYS	Maple Avenue (**Ave.**), the Pennsylvania Turnpike (**Tpk.**), Route (**Rt.**) 30, Forty-second Street (**St.**) (The second part of a hyphenated numbered street is not capitalized.)
TOWNS, CITIES	San Francisco, Chicago, Minneapolis, Cheyenne, Phoenix, Atlanta, Miami, Austin, Santa Fe
COUNTIES, PARISHES, TOWNSHIPS	Dade County, Iberia Parish, Orange County, Township 531, Hidalgo County
STATES	Texas (**TX**), Maine (**ME**), Wyoming (**WY**), New Mexico (**NM**), Kansas (**KS**), New Hampshire (**NH**)
COUNTRIES	Canada, the United States (**US**), France

SECTIONS OF A COUNTRY	the Midwest, New England, the Sunbelt, the East, the Southwest (Compass directions do not begin with capital letters: *Go east on Route 4.*)
CONTINENTS	Africa, South America, Antarctica, Asia
WORLD REGIONS	Northern Hemisphere, South Pole, Scandinavia, the Middle East
ISLANDS	the Hawaiian Islands, Long Island, the Galapagos Islands
MOUNTAINS	the Himalayas, the Rocky Mountains, Mount Everest, Mount St. Helens, the Andes Mountains
PARKS	Serengeti National Park, Grand Canyon National Park, Yellowstone National Park, Glacier National Park
BODIES OF WATER	the Nile River, the Indian Ocean, the Black Sea, the Great Lakes, Victoria Falls

Words like *street, lake, ocean,* and *mountain* are capitalized only when they are part of a proper noun.

> Which is the smallest lake of the Great Lakes?
> Mount McKinley is the tallest mountain in North America.

PRACTICE YOUR SKILLS

● Check Your Understanding
Capitalizing Geographical Names

Write *a* or *b* to indicate the item that is correctly capitalized in each of the following pairs.

1. **a.** New delhi, india
   b. New Delhi, India

2. **a.** Munroe falls
   b. Munroe Falls

3. **a.** Thirty-third Street
   b. Thirty-Third Street

4. **a.** Great smokey mountains
   b. Great Smokey Mountains

5. **a.** lake Michigan
   b. Lake Michigan

6. **a.** a river in Georgia
   b. a River in Georgia

7. **a.** Ft. Lauderdale
   b. Ft. lauderdale

8. **a.** north Dakota
   b. North Dakota

9. **a.** the South
   b. the south

10. **a.** antarctica
    b. Antarctica

11. **a.** south America
    b. South America

12. **a.** Central Park
    b. Central park

13. **a.** north on Route 20
    b. North on Route 20

14. **a.** el paso, Texas
    b. El Paso, Texas

15. **a.** Dawson County
    b. Dawson county

16. **a.** the Indian Ocean
    b. the indian ocean

17. **a.** Saudi arabia
    b. Saudi Arabia

18. **a.** Catalina island
    b. Catalina Island

19. **a.** Mount Rushmore
    b. mount rushmore

20. **a.** the Memorial highway
    b. the Memorial Highway

Check Your Understanding
Using Capital Letters

Geographic Topic **Identify the words in each sentence that should be capitalized and write them correctly.**

21. here are some facts about the western hemisphere.

22. did you know that quito is the capital of ecuador?

23. lake titicaca in south america is the highest large lake above sea level.

24. on one of his voyages for spain, christopher columbus discovered the virgin islands.

25. brazil, the largest country in south america, is also the most populous country in latin america.

26. la salle, an early explorer, discovered the mouth of the mississippi river.

27. in order to fly to antarctica, a plane usually leaves from chile.

28. charles darwin studied bird species after visiting the galapagos islands.

29. nova scotia lies off the coast of canada.

30. william henry seward purchased alaska for the united states from russia in 1867.

● Connect to the Writing Process: Editing
Correcting Errors in Capitalization

Rewrite the following paragraphs, correcting the errors in capitalization.

high in the lofty, snow-covered andes mountains, the amazon river begins. it runs eastward across the continent of south america, flowing through the jungles of brazil. finally it empties into the atlantic ocean.

the mighty amazon river has more water flowing through it than the mississippi river, the nile river, and the yangtze river—all put together! the reason for this amazing fact is that the drainage basin of this giant river lies in one of the rainiest regions of the world.

Communicate Your Ideas

APPLY TO WRITING

E-mail Message: *Capitalization*

You have invited a new friend to your home. Since he has never been to your house before, you must give him directions. Beginning at your school, write the directions to your house. Remember to be very specific so that your friend does not get lost. Include the names of streets and landmarks. After you have written your directions, check to make sure that you have used capital letters correctly.

Nouns of historical importance, such as historical events, periods, and documents, should be capitalized.

HISTORIC NAMES	
EVENTS	World War II (**WWII**), the Battle of Bull Run
PERIODS	the Renaissance, the Middle Ages, the Shang Dynasty, the Industrial Revolution
DOCUMENTS	the Magna Carta, the Declaration of Independence, the Treaty of Versailles

Prepositions that are part of a proper noun are not usually capitalized.

Names of groups, such as organizations, businesses, institutions, government bodies, teams, and political parties, should be capitalized.

NAMES OF GROUPS	
ORGANIZATIONS	the American Red Cross, the United Nations (**UN**), the Girl Scouts of America (**GSA**)
BUSINESSES	the Dahl Motor Company (**Co.**), the Leed Corporation (**Corp.**), Lexington Lumber
INSTITUTIONS	the University of Chicago (**U** of **C**), Emerson High School, Memorial Hospital
	(Words such as *high school* and *hospital* are not capitalized unless they are a part of a proper noun: *The nearest hospital is Mercy General Hospital.*)
GOVERNMENT BODIES/AGENCIES	Congress, the State Department, the Bureau of Land Management

TEAMS	the Boston Red Sox, the Los Angeles Lakers, the Lake Brandon High School Patriots
POLITICAL PARTIES	the Republican Party, the Labor Party, a Republican, a Democrat

Specific time periods and events, including the days of the week, the months of the year, civil and religious holidays, and special events, should be capitalized.

TIME PERIODS AND EVENTS	
DAYS, MONTHS	Tuesday (Tues.), Friday (Fri.), February (Feb.), October (Oct.)
HOLIDAYS	Valentine's Day, Kwanzaa, the Fourth of July, Veteran's Day
SPECIAL EVENTS	the Rose Bowl Parade, the Boston Marathon, the Junior Prom
TIME ABBREVIATIONS	B.C./A.D., A.M./P.M.

However, do not capitalize a season of the year unless it is part of a proper noun.

I like winter best.
Did you go to the Winter Fair?

PRACTICE YOUR SKILLS

Check Your Understanding
Capitalizing Proper Nouns

Write *a* or *b* to indicate the item that is correctly capitalized in each of the following pairs.

1. **a.** World War I
   b. world war I

2. **a.** Thanksgiving day
   b. Thanksgiving Day

3. a. summer
  b. Summer

4. a. the Orlando Magic
  b. the Orlando magic

5. a. the U.S. senate
  b. the U.S. Senate

6. a. december
  b. December

7. a. the Stone Age
  b. the stone age

8. a. Veterans day
  b. Veterans Day

9. a. monday
  b. Monday

10. a. the united way
  b. the United Way

11. a. a hospital in New Jersey
  b. a Hospital in New Jersey

12. a. a Fourth of July parade
  b. a fourth of july parade

13. a. Acme brick company
  b. Acme Brick Company

14. a. the Rock Island Railroad
  b. the rock island railroad

15. a. a high school in Detroit
  b. a High School in Detroit

16. a. the Monroe doctrine
  b. the Monroe Doctrine

17. a. the Defense Department
  b. the defense department

18. a. the library of Congress
  b. the Library of Congress

19. a. the treaty of paris
  b. the Treaty of Paris

20. a. the Republican party
  b. the Republican Party

Check Your Understanding
Using Capital Letters

History Topic **Identify each word that should begin with a capital letter and then rewrite the words correctly.**

21. Signed in july of 1776, the declaration of independence is an important document in the history of the united states.

22. The treaty of paris ended the american revolution.

23. Written several years after the american revolution, the constitution of the united states is a vital document.

24. The signing of a treaty, such as the treaty of neuilly, is an important event.

25. In the winter of 1918, woodrow wilson, a president representing the democratic party, announced his fourteen points as the basis for the peace settlement of world war I.

26. Wilson was warmly received in paris, where he traveled to sign the treaty of versailles after world war I.

27. Wilson helped establish the league of nations, the precursor of the modern united nations.

28. The republican party controlled congress, and wilson's political enemies refused to allow the united states to enter the league of nations.

29. They even refused to ratify the treaty of versailles.

30. In 1920, whether the united states should join the league of nations became a major issue in the presidential election between candidates from the republican and democratic parties.

● Connect to the Writing Process: Editing
Correcting Errors in Capitalization

Rewrite the following paragraphs, correcting the errors in capitalization.

winning the greatest battle in baseball, the world series, is the goal of every professional baseball player. the first game of the modern world series was played in 1903. in that series the boston pilgrims, who would later become known as the red sox, defeated the pittsburgh pirates.

the first player to be named Most Valuable Player was johnny podres of the brooklyn dodgers in 1955. that was the first world championship for the dodgers, who defeated their rivals from across the city, the new york yankees.

just two years later, the dodgers would disappoint their brooklyn fans by moving the team out of new york to los angeles, california.

APPLY TO WRITING
Business Letter: *Capital Letters*

You are writing a report on a European country, focusing on two of its major cities. You must include information about the history, culture, and major attractions of the cities. Write a letter to a local travel agent, requesting information. After you have written your letter, check that you have capitalized all the proper nouns correctly.

Names of nationalities, races, and languages should be capitalized.

NATIONALITIES, RACES, AND LANGUAGES	
NATIONALITIES	an **A**merican, a **G**erman, **C**anadians
RACES	**C**aucasian, **A**sian, **H**ispanic
LANGUAGES	**S**panish, **E**nglish, **M**andarin, **R**ussian
COMPUTER LANGUAGES	**J**ava, **C**obol, **C**++, **V**isual **B**asic

Religions, religious holidays, and religious references, such as the names referring to the Deity, the Bible, and divisions of the Bible, should be capitalized. Also, capitalize pronouns that refer to the Deity.

RELIGIOUS NAMES	
RELIGIONS	**C**hristianity, **B**uddhism, **J**udaism, **I**slam
RELIGIOUS HOLIDAYS	**H**anukkah, **C**hristmas, **R**amadan, **E**piphany, **P**urim, **P**assover, **P**otlatch, **E**aster
RELIGIOUS REFERENCES	**G**od, the **L**ord, **G**od and **H**is children, the **B**ible, **E**xodus, the **S**criptures, the **K**oran, **A**llah, **B**uddha

Notice that the word god is not capitalized when it refers to gods in polytheistic religions.

Neptune, who was also called Poseidon, was the **g**od of the sea.

Names of stars, planets, and constellations are capitalized.

ASTRONOMICAL NAMES	
STARS	the **D**og Star, **C**anopus, the **N**orth Star

PLANETS	Mars, Saturn, Venus, Pluto, Jupiter
CONSTELLATIONS	the Big Dipper, Orion's Belt, the Milky Way

The words sun *and* moon *are not capitalized.* Earth *is not capitalized if it is preceded by the word* the.

Other proper nouns should also begin with capital letters.

OTHER PROPER NOUNS	
AIRCRAFT, SPACECRAFT	the *Concorde, Titan II, Apollo 13*
AWARDS	the Nobel Prize, the Heisman Trophy
BRAND NAMES	New Foam soap, Silkie shampoo, Crunchies cat food
TECHNOLOGICAL TERMS	E-mail, Internet, Web, World Wide Web, Website, Web Art, Web Page
BRIDGES AND BUILDINGS	the Golden Gate Bridge, the Empire State Building, the Eiffel Tower
MEMORIALS, MUSEUMS, MONUMENTS	the Lincoln Memorial, the Holocaust Museum, the Statue of Liberty
SHIPS, TRAINS, PLANES	the *Mayflower,* the *Wabash Cannonball,* the *Spirit of St. Louis*
NAMES OF COURSES	English I, History IA, Art II, Latin III

Do not capitalize the name of an unnumbered course, such as *history, math,* or *biology,* unless it is the name of a language.

Last year I studied history, art, and Japanese.

CONNECT TO WRITER'S CRAFT

When you are unsure whether to capitalize a word, use a reference source. A good dictionary will include most proper nouns. Many dictionaries contain specific sections with geographical and biographical information where you can find the correct spelling and capitalization of the names of famous people and places. An encyclopedia will also give you such information. A professional writer always has good reference sources available.

PRACTICE YOUR SKILLS

Check Your Understanding
Capitalizing Proper Nouns

Write *a* or *b* to indicate the item that is correctly capitalized in each of the following pairs.

1. **a.** geometry and Spanish
   b. geometry and spanish

2. **a.** Mello cheese
   b. mello cheese

3. **a.** the New Testament
   b. the new testament

4. **a.** satin fur cat food
   b. Satin Fur cat food

5. **a.** god and his kingdom
   b. God and His kingdom

6. **a.** the Vietnam Memorial
   b. the Vietnam memorial

7. **a.** advanced algebra I
   b. Advanced Algebra I

8. **a.** the Pulitzer prize
   b. the Pulitzer Prize

9. **a.** judaism
   b. Judaism

10. **a.** *Spirit of St. Louis*
    b. *spirit of st. louis*

11. **a.** the Sun and Mars
    b. the sun and Mars

12. **a.** Polish and Russian
    b. polish and russian

13. **a.** a presbyterian
    b. a Presbyterian

14. **a.** the *Lusitania*
    b. the *lusitania*

15. **a.** an african
    b. an African

16. **a.** the Statue of Liberty
    b. the statue of liberty

17. **a.** a hindu
    b. a Hindu

18. **a.** the war of 1812
    b. the War of 1812

19. **a.** the world trade center
    b. the World Trade Center

20. **a.** Sirius and other Stars
    b. Sirius and other stars

Using Capital Letters

History Topic **Identify each word that should begin with a capital letter and then rewrite the words correctly.**

21. The middle ages was a historical period in western europe that lasted from about a.d. 400 to a.d. 1400.

22. During the dark ages and middle ages, common people worked only 260 days per year.

23. They did not work on religious holidays such as easter and christmas.

24. On december 6, people would celebrate st. nicholas's day, a children's holiday.

25. On most days between 9 a.m. and noon, people living in a castle would eat dinner, a very large meal.

● Connect to the Writing Process: Editing
Correcting Errors in Capitalization

Rewrite the following paragraph, correcting the errors in capitalization.

every few years a city in a major country like canada, japan, france, or the united states hosts a world's fair. the united states has hosted fairs in major cities like new york, chicago, and st. louis. one of the earliest fairs, however, was held in london, england, in 1851. that was during the early reign of queen victoria. the queen hired joseph paxton, an english architect, to design the exhibition hall in london's hyde park. he created the largest glass building ever made. it contained 3,300 columns to support its three stories. after the exhibition, it was taken down and moved to a different part of london. there it became known as the crystal palace. unfortunately, it was destroyed by a fire in 1936.

APPLY TO WRITING

Advertisement: *Capital Letters*

You are the owner of the first intergalactic travel agency to take people on tours of the planets and outer space. Write an advertisement for an upcoming tour of one of the planets. Inform prospective clients as to the travel accommodations, such as the comfort and safety of your spacecraft, the sites they will see, the cost of space travel, and the activities they might enjoy. In your advertisement, be sure to give your company a name. After you have finished writing your ad, check to make sure that you have used proper capitalization.

General Interest **In each of the following trivia questions, find the words that should be capitalized and write the words correctly. Then see if you can answer the questions!**

1. was william sherman a general in the civil war or the american revolution?

2. who wrote the declaration of independence?

3. who carried the message that the british were coming through massachusetts?

4. is andrew wyeth a painter or a united states senator?

5. who were the two explorers who led an expedition from st. louis, missouri, to the pacific ocean in 1804?

6. was george c. scott a composer or the winner of an oscar?

7. who was the couple that tried to rule the roman empire from egypt?

8. what famous person's address is 1600 pennsylvania avenue, washington, d.c.?

9. is hillary clinton a winner in the olympics or a public figure?

10. did captain james kirk or captain bligh command the starship *enterprise*?

11. who joined the boston bruins at age eighteen and led the team to win the stanley cup?

12. who was the first american to set foot on the moon?

13. who flew across the atlantic ocean in the *spirit of st. louis*?

14. who paid for the statue of liberty in new york by giving donations: the french or the americans?

15. did thomas edison or george eastman invent the first camera?

16. who delivered the gettysburg address during the civil war?

17. who painted the ceiling of the sistine chapel?

18. washington, jefferson, lincoln, and who else are shown on the mount rushmore national memorial?

19. who was the fictitious character who lived on baker street in london, england?

20. who led his troops across the delaware river to attack the british during the american revolution?

21. did tara lipinski win a gold medal for ice skating or for gymnastics?

22. which president's last name is the name of a state in the northwest?

23. in 1848, was gold found in california or in colorado?

24. which is the capital of the state of new york, albany or new york city?

25. which highway goes from maine to florida, interstate 95 or route 66?

▶ Proper Adjectives

Proper adjectives are formed from proper nouns. Like proper nouns, proper adjectives begin with capital letters.

Capitalize most proper adjectives.

PROPER NOUNS	PROPER ADJECTIVES
France	French doors
Rome	Roman numerals
Alaska	Alaskan cruise
Boston	Boston baked beans

Some adjectives that originated from proper nouns are so common that they are no longer capitalized.

> Be careful not to drop the **c**hina plate.

PRACTICE YOUR SKILLS

● Check Your Understanding
Capitalizing Proper Adjectives

Write the following items, adding capital letters where needed.

1. a chinese restaurant
2. a british naval officer
3. a former french colony
4. an ancient egyptian tomb
5. irish stew

6. new england weather
7. a german clock
8. a turkish towel
9. maine lobster
10. a swedish ship

● Connect to the Writing Process: Editing
Correcting Errors in Capitalization

Rewrite the following paragraph, correcting the errors in capitalization.

my sister took a european vacation recently. she brought back more stories and souvenirs than i've ever seen! while visiting madrid, she saw an actual spanish flamenco dance. then she traveled to great britain for a tour of the english countryside. after buying my mother some beautiful irish linen, she flew to france and toured notre dame in paris. she skied in the swiss alps and then toured tuscany. she has promised to take me on her next trip.

 **Titles**

Capital letters indicate the importance of titles of people, written works, and other works of art.

Capitalize certain titles.

Titles Used with Names of Persons

Capitalize a title showing office, rank, or profession when it comes directly before a person's name.

BEFORE A NAME	Have you met **D**r. Anna Richman?
AFTER A NAME	Jennifer Kemp is also a **d**octor.
BEFORE A NAME	Dr. Richman voted for **G**overnor Harper.
AFTER A NAME	Did you think Jennifer Kemp would be elected **g**overnor?

Titles Used Alone

Capitalize a title that is used alone when the title is being substituted for a person's name in direct address.

USED AS A NAME	Please, **G**overnor, may I speak with you?
	I didn't see the sign, **O**fficer.

Titles of high government officials, such as the *President, Vice President, Chief Justice,* and *Queen of England,* are almost always capitalized when they stand alone.

I have come to see the **Q**ueen of England.
The **P**resident visited Governor Harper.

President *and* vice president *are capitalized when they stand alone only if they refer to the current president or vice president.*

Titles Showing Family Relationships

Capitalize a title showing a family relationship when it comes directly before a person's name. When the title is used as a name, or when the title is substituted for a person's name in direct address, it is also capitalized.

BEFORE A NAME	I am going to see **Aunt** **L**ori.
USED AS A NAME	I told **M**om that I would vacuum my room tomorrow.
SUBSTITUTED FOR A PERSON'S NAME IN DIRECT ADDRESS	May I borrow the car for just a few hours, **D**ad?
	Will you come, **G**randpa, to my game on Saturday?

Do not capitalize titles showing family relationships when they are preceded by possessive nouns or pronouns—unless the titles are considered part of someone's name.

Have you met Kristen's **a**unt?
Have you met Kristen's **A**unt Diane?

PRACTICE YOUR SKILLS

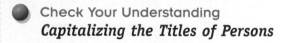

Check Your Understanding
Capitalizing the Titles of Persons

Write *a* or *b* to indicate the correctly capitalized title in each of the following pairs.

1. a. our family doctor
   b. our family Doctor

2. a. Senator Barrientos
   b. senator Barrientos

3. a. aunt Ruthie
   b. Aunt Ruthie

4. a. a Governor
   b. a governor

5. a. Granny Taylor
   b. granny Taylor

6. a. my uncle
   b. my Uncle

7. **a.** a state senator   **9.** **a.** Mayor Wilson
    b. a state Senator   **b.** mayor Wilson

8. **a.** a president of Egypt **10.** **a.** president Nixon
    b. a President of Egypt   **b.** President Nixon

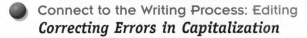

Connect to the Writing Process: Editing
Correcting Errors in Capitalization

Rewrite the following letter, correcting the errors in capitalization.

dear grandma hazel,

    i hope you are doing well. i heard from aunt linda that you had been ill. did you go to the doctor? i enjoyed meeting dr. williams when i visited you last summer. i'm sure she would take good care of you if you would make an appointment.

    well, i'd better close this letter. i promised mom and uncle denny that i would take out the trash before the president's state of the union address on television tonight.

                love always,

                samantha

Titles of Written Works and Other Works of Art

    Capitalize the first word, the last word, and all important words in the titles of books, newspapers, periodicals, stories, poems, movies, plays, musical compositions, and other works of art. However, do not capitalize a preposition, a conjunction, or an article (*a, an,* and *the*) unless it is the first word of a title.

Books and Chapter Titles	I finished reading a chapter called "**The Man on the Tor**" in the book *The Hound of the Baskervilles.*
Short Stories	I enjoyed Truman Capote's story "**Children on Their Birthdays.**"
Poems	My favorite poems are "**From Blossoms**" and "**The Weight of Sweetness**" by Li-Young Lee.
Newspapers and Newspaper Articles	I read an article called "**Local Writer Has Novel Published**" in today's issue of the *New York Times.* (Generally, do not capitalize *the* as the first word of a newspaper or magazine title.)
Magazines and Magazine Articles	I read "**Interview with the New Talent**" about that author in *People* magazine last week.
Television Series	Two popular British television comedy series are *Keeping Up Appearances* and *As Time Goes By.*

You can learn more about the punctuation of titles on pages L544–L548.

PRACTICE YOUR SKILLS

Check Your Understanding
Capitalizing Titles of Written Works and Other Works of Art

Write *a* or *b* to indicate the correctly capitalized title in each of the following pairs.

1. **a.** *the last supper*
   b. *The Last Supper*

2. **a.** "The Raven"
   b. "the Raven"

3. **a.** "amazing grace"
   b. "Amazing Grace"

4. **a.** *seventeen* magazine
   b. *Seventeen* magazine

5. **a.** *American Gothic*
   b. *american gothic*

6. **a.** *The return of the Jedi*
   b. *The Return of the Jedi*

7. **a.** *The Great Gatsby*
   b. *The great gatsby*

8. **a.** "The Lottery"
   b. "the lottery"

9. **a.** *the Dallas Morning News*
   b. *the Dallas morning news*

10. **a.** *Singin' in the Rain*
    b. *Singin' in the rain*

11. **a.** *The Count of Monte Cristo*
    b. *The count of monte Cristo*

12. **a.** *War and peace*
    b. *War and Peace*

13. **a.** "The Listeners"
    b. "the Listeners"

14. **a.** *It Happened One Night*
    b. *It happened one night*

15. **a.** *Life* Magazine
    b. *Life* magazine

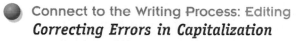

Connect to the Writing Process: Editing
Correcting Errors in Capitalization

Rewrite the following paragraph, correcting the errors in capitalization.

the 1950s was an interesting time in the history of entertainment. In music, rock 'n' roll was born. elvis presley recorded hit songs like "hound dog" and "that's all right." he also made a historic appearance on *the ed sullivan show*. other popular television shows at that time included the comedy *i love lucy* and *the twilight zone*. suspense was popular in the movies and TV shows of alfred hitchcock. two of Hitchcock's most famous movies of the 1950s were *Strangers on a train* and *rear window*. in literature, a new generation of writers was heralded by jack kerouac and allen ginsberg. kerouac's *on the road* tells stories of crossing and recrossing the highways of the united states, far outside the mainstream 1950s culture.

Communicate Your Ideas

APPLY TO WRITING
Friendly Letter: *Capital Letters*

You have a new pen pal who lives across the country from you. Write a letter of introduction to him or her. Tell your pen pal all about yourself, including your school's name, the subjects you're studying, and your favorite book, magazine, song, and television show. After you have written your letter, check to make sure that you have used capital letters correctly.

QuickCheck Mixed Practice

General Interest **In each of the following trivia questions, find the words that should be capitalized and write the words correctly. Then see if you can answer the questions!**

1. what are the names of the stars in the classic comedies *duck soup* and *a night at the opera?*
2. what are the seven roman numerals?
3. what god in greek mythology held the world on his shoulders?
4. an old form of which sport takes place in the story "rip van winkle"?
5. what is the name of a fictional reporter who worked on the *daily planet* in the city of metropolis?

6. what is the name of the movie in which fay wray, the empire state building, and a giant ape are featured?

7. what is the name of the captain of the *nautilus* in the book *20,000 leagues under the sea?*

8. what is the motto of the boy scouts of america?

9. what does the initial stand for in president john f. kennedy's name?

10. is the name of the football team in dallas, texas, the cowboys or the broncos?

11. what was the name of the president of the confederacy during the civil war?

12. what are the chief ingredients in english muffins?

13. what group recorded "i want to hold your hand"?

14. which television series has run longer: *meet the press* or *days of our lives?*

15. who is the author of *the red badge of courage?*

16. in the united states, what is the first monday in september called?

17. which sea separates the scandinavian countries from the rest of europe: the baltic or the mediterranean?

18. in what art museum does the *mona lisa* hang?

19. what is the name of the first united states writer to win a nobel prize?

20. in what book is captain ahab a character: *two years before the mast* or *moby dick?*

Using Capital Letters Correctly

Correctly write each word that should begin with a capital letter.

1. let's turn back the clock to the year 1900 and look at the united states at the turn of that century.

2. the population had reached nearly seventy-six million, and the center of the population was near columbus, indiana.

3. the united states had about ten miles of concrete pavement and fewer than eight thousand automobiles.

4. the first well-organized automobile race was held at springfield, long island, on april 15.

5. in the presidential election, president william mckinley was re-elected for a second term.

6. r. a. fessenden, an american scientist, became the first person to transmit human speech through radio waves.

7. the united states and england inaugurated a tennis competition for the davis cup.

8. casey jones, the famous engineer in song and legend, died on april 30 at the throttle of his locomotive, the *cannonball,* trying to save his passengers' lives.

9. the wright brothers, wilbur and orville, built their first full-scale glider and flew it at kitty hawk, nc.

10. among rising young novelists of the day were such writers as zane grey, edgar rice burroughs, and theodore dreiser.

11. irving bacheller wrote the novel *eben holden*, a best-seller.

12. ray c. ewry won eight olympic gold medals.

13. a notable painter of the time was albert pinkham ryder, whose famous painting, *toilers of the sea,* is a ghostly sea scene.

14. famous archeologist arthur clark discovered artifacts from the minoan culture in his excavations in crete.

15. the largest railroad was the new york central.

Editing for the Correct Use of Capital Letters

Write each sentence using capital letters correctly.

1. the world's largest church is st. peter's in rome.
2. the *voyager* missions studied jupiter and saturn.
3. required courses for juniors are english, math II, biology, and american history.
4. in his novel *the grapes of wrath,* john steinbeck tells about the problems of the poor in oklahoma.
5. the houston oaks hotel is in the southwest.
6. did michigan ever beat nebraska in the cotton bowl?
7. yes, senator parks will speak at logan high school.
8. the west indies form an island arc in the atlantic ocean.
9. the irish potato orginated in south america.
10. the snake river flows from wyoming to washington.

Writing Sentences

At the library, find a fact that pertains to each of the following topics. Each fact should include a proper noun, a proper adjective, or a title.

1. geography
2. political parties
3. the presidency
4. astronomy
5. art
6. literature
7. holidays
8. history
9. space exploration
10. languages

Language and *Self-Expression*

Caerlaverock Castle was built in Scotland in the late 1200s. The castle is surrounded by a moat and built of impregnable rock because, in the Middle Ages, wars often broke out among kings and other wealthy landowners. These nobles built fort-like castles, which served as both home and defense. Windows were small and narrow because rooms were heated only with fireplaces and because knights shot arrows from the windows if the castle was attacked.

Caerlaverock Castle was often attacked. Its moat and thick walls helped keep its inhabitants safe. Imagine what it might be like for those inhabitants during an attack. Write a scene set in Caerlaverock during a battle. Use capitalization for proper nouns and other appropriate words.

Prewriting Create a plot diagram for your scene. Include information about characters and setting in your diagram and describe the rising action, climax, falling action, and resolution of your plot.

Drafting Use your plot diagram as the basis for writing your first draft. Specific details will help capture your readers' interest.

Revising Reread what you have written. Have you created an atmosphere of danger in your story? Does it give readers a sense of life in the Middle Ages? Make any changes you need to help make your action more gripping and realistic.

Editing Correct any errors in grammar, spelling, and punctuation. Be sure the first word of each sentence and all proper nouns and adjectives are capitalized.

Publishing Make a final copy of your scene. Read classmates' scenes and see if you can combine any scenes to make a full story of the battle at Caerlaverock Castle.

Another Look

Capitalizing First Words and the Pronoun *I*

Capitalize the first word of a sentence and of a line of poetry. *(page L459)*

Capitalize the first word in the greeting of a letter and the first word in the closing of a letter. *(page L460)*

Capitalize the first word of each item in an outline and the letters that begin major subsections of the outline. *(page L461)*

Capitalize the pronoun *I*, both alone and in contractions. *(page L461)*

Capitalizing Proper Nouns and Adjectives

Capitalize the following kinds of proper nouns:

Names of persons and animals *(page L464)*

Geographical names *(pages L464–L465)*

Names of historical importance *(page L468)*

Names of groups *(pages L468–L469)*

Specific time periods and events *(page L469)*

Names of nationalities, races, and languages *(page L473)*

Religions, religious holidays, and religious references *(page L473)*

Names of stars, planets, and constellations *(pages L473 L474)*

Aircraft, spacecraft, awards, brand names, bridges, technological terms, buildings, memorials, museums, ships, trains, and names of courses *(page L474)*

Capitalize most proper adjectives. *(pages L479–L480)*

Capitalizing Titles

Capitalize titles showing office, rank, or profession when used directly before a person's name. *(page L481)*

Capitalize titles used alone when substituted for a person's name in direct address. *(page L481)*

Capitalize titles of current high government officials when they stand alone. *(page L481)*

Capitalize titles showing family relationships when directly before a person's name, part of a name, or in place of a name. *(page L482)*

Capitalize the first word, the last word, and all important words in titles of books, newspapers, periodicals, stories, poems, movies, plays, musical compositions, and other works of art. *(pages L483–L484)*

Posttest

Directions

For each sentence, choose the word or words that should be capitalized. Write the letter of your answer. If the sentence contains no error, write *D*.

EXAMPLE

1. I have a pen pal from belgium.

1 **A** Pen Pal

   B Belgium

   C Pal, Belgium

   D No error

ANSWER **1** **B**

1. My friend speaks flemish most of the time at her home near the city of bruges.

2. She also knows the english language well enough to write great letters.

3. Her name is helen.

4. She told me that belgium became a country only in modern times.

5. Long ago during the renaissance, the part of the country where she lives was known as flanders.

6. Some great painters such as hans memling lived there.

7. I've seen one of his paintings, *adoration of the magi*, which now hangs in a museum within a hospital in bruges.

8. almost every month i get a letter from helen.

9. She begins them all, "dear American friend."

10. I write back to her, "Dear belgian friend."

1 **A** Flemish, Bruges
  B Home
  C Flemish, Home
  D No error

2 **A** English
  B Language
  C English Language
  D No error

3 **A** Name
  B Helen
  C Name, Helen
  D No error

4 **A** Modern Times
  B Belgium, Modern
  C Belgium
  D No error

5 **A** Renaissance
  B Renaissance, Flanders
  C Flanders
  D No error

6 **A** Memling
  B Hans Memling
  C Hans
  D No error

7 **A** *Adoration*
  B *Adoration, Of, Magi*
  C *Adoration, Magi,*
     Bruges
  D No error

8 **A** Almost, I
  B Helen
  C Almost, I, Helen
  D No error

9 **A** Dear
  B Dear, Friend
  C Friend
  D No error

10 **A** Belgian, Friend
   B Belgian
   C Friend
   D No error

CHAPTER 15

End Marks and Commas

Pretest

Directions
Write the letter of the term that correctly identifies each type of sentence.

EXAMPLE   **1.** A hurricane hit our town this September.
 1 **A** declarative
    B imperative
    C interrogative
    D exclamatory

ANSWER   **1 A**

1. The winds started rising during the night.

2. They were incredibly strong!

3. The police and other emergency workers patrolled the streets and made loudspeaker announcements.

4. "Prepare to evacuate the island!"

5. Would we suffer a direct hit?

6. The island could be completely submerged under water!

7. By midday most people had packed up and left the island.

8. We were packed and ready to go, but my sister couldn't find her cat.

9. Where was he hiding?

10. My father ordered her to get into the car.

1   A   declarative
    B   imperative
    C   interrogative
    D   exclamatory

2   A   declarative
    B   imperative
    C   interrogative
    D   exclamatory

3   A   declarative
    B   imperative
    C   interrogative
    D   exclamatory

4   A   declarative
    B   imperative
    C   interrogative
    D   exclamatory

5   A   declarative
    B   imperative
    C   interrogative
    D   exclamatory

6   A   declarative
    B   imperative
    C   interrogative
    D   exclamatory

7   A   declarative
    B   imperative
    C   interrogative
    D   exclamatory

8   A   declarative
    B   imperative
    C   interrogative
    D   exclamatory

9   A   declarative
    B   imperative
    C   interrogative
    D   exclamatory

10 A   declarative
    B   imperative
    C   interrogative
    D   exclamatory

Claude Monet. *Arrival of the Normandy Train, Gare Saint-Lazare,* 1877.
Oil on canvas, 23¼ by 31¼ inches. The Art Institute of Chicago.

Describe What does the painting show? What colors does the artist use to create light and shadow?

Analyze Notice the blurry quality of the artist's brushstrokes. What effect do you think the blurred lines of the painting have on its atmosphere? How does Monet convey a real sense of the interior of the train shed?

Interpret Why do you think the artist chose not to show precise details in this painting?

Judge How does this style of painting affect you? Do you have a clear impression of place and time?

At the end of this chapter, you will use the artwork to stimulate ideas for writing.

Kinds of Sentences and End Marks

Imagine New York City without any traffic lights or stop signs. There would be utter confusion. The result of writing without end marks or commas would be very much the same.

In this chapter you will review the three different end marks as well as the four different types of sentences to which those end marks are added. In addition, you will review the use of the period with abbreviations and the uses of the comma.

A sentence may have one of four different purposes or functions. The purpose of a sentence determines the punctuation mark that goes at the end. A sentence may be declarative, imperative, interrogative, or exclamatory.

One purpose of a sentence is to make a statement or to express an opinion.

A **declarative sentence** makes a statement or expresses an opinion and ends with a period.

The following examples are declarative sentences. Notice that the second sentence makes a statement, even though it contains an indirect question.

My brothers were going to the tennis courts.

I asked them what time they were leaving home.

(A direct question would be *What time are they leaving home?*)

A second purpose of a sentence is to give directions, make requests, or give commands. The subject of these kinds of sentences is usually an understood *you*.

An **imperative sentence** gives a direction, makes a request, or gives a command. It ends with either a period or an exclamation point.

Although all of the following examples are imperative, two are followed by a period, and one is followed by an exclamation point.

> Turn left when you see the tennis courts**.**
>
> Please take me with you**.**
>
> Call the police**!**
>
> (This command would be stated with great excitement or emphasis.)

A third purpose of a sentence is to ask a question.

An **interrogative sentence** asks a question and ends with a question mark.

The following examples are interrogative sentences. Notice that the second example is phrased as a statement but is intended as a question.

> Where is my tennis racket**?**
>
> You have played tennis eight times this weekend**?**

Some questions are not expressed completely; nevertheless, they are followed by a question mark.

> You have decided not to play tennis. Why**?**

A fourth purpose of a sentence is to express a feeling—such as excitement, joy, anger, fear, or surprise.

An **exclamatory sentence** expresses strong feeling or emotion and ends with an exclamation point.

The following examples are exclamatory sentences. Notice they express strong feeling.

> I beat my brother at tennis**!**
>
> I feel fabulous**!**

Use exclamatory sentences sparingly when you write. They lose their impact when they are used too often. Remember that an exclamation point also follows an interjection.

> Wow**!** That was my best match ever.

You can learn more about interjections on pages L135–L136.

PRACTICE YOUR SKILLS

● Check Your Understanding
Classifying Sentences

 **Label each sentence *declarative, imperative, interrogative*, or *exclamatory* according to the meaning of the sentence.**

1. I love to play tennis!
2. Please bring me my racket.
3. Are you ready to play?
4. You have never played before?
5. I began playing tennis when I was eight years old.
6. Stand behind the baseline to serve.
7. You have a powerful arm!
8. Drive the ball diagonally across the net.
9. The game is challenging and fun.
10. Would you like to play again?

● Connect to the Writing Process: Editing
Correcting End Punctuation

Write the correct end punctuation for each sentence. Then label each sentence *declarative, imperative, interrogative*, or *exclamatory*.

11. Have you heard of the "Battle of the Sexes"
12. In 1973, Bobby Riggs challenged female tennis player Billie Jean King to a winner-take-all match

13. America watched the amazing match with great excitement

14. Riggs had declared that there was no way a woman could beat a man

15. Wow, King showed him in no uncertain terms how wrong he was

16. King defeated Riggs in each match to handily win the set

17. Look at any magazine of the time

18. You will see how this tennis match captured America's attention

19. Can you imagine how this victory affected the future of women's tennis

20. Find out more about this event by looking at old newspapers

Communicate Your Ideas

APPLY TO WRITING

Instructions: *Sentence Variety*

You have been asked by your coach to explain the rules of your favorite sport to someone who has never played the game before. Write a paragraph in which you explain the basics that everyone beginning the sport should know. Try to give thorough directions while conveying just how much fun the sport is. Use at least one of each type of sentence—declarative, interrogative, exclamatory, and imperative—as you write.

Other Uses of Periods

Periods are also used in places other than at the ends of sentences.

With Abbreviations

ABBREVIATIONS					
TITLES WITH NAMES	Mr. Mrs.	Ms. Dr.	Rev. Gen.	Sgt. Lt.	Jr. Sr.
INITIALS FOR NAMES	R. L. Rosen, Sarah E. Campbell, J. J. Jackson, K. Petra Beck				
TIMES WITH NUMBERS	A.M. (*ante meridiem*—before noon) P.M. (*post meridiem*—after noon) B.C. (before Christ) A.D. (*anno Domini*—in the year of the Lord)				
ADDRESSES	Ave.	St.	Blvd.	Rt.	Dept.
ORGANIZATIONS AND COMPANIES	Co.	Inc.	Corp.	Assn.	

Some organizations and companies are known by abbreviations that stand for their full name. The majority of these abbreviations do not use periods. A few other common abbreviations also do not include periods.

    FAA = Federal Aviation Administration
    UN = United Nations
    CIA = Central Intelligence Agency
    IQ = intelligence quotient
    km = kilometer

If an abbreviation is the last word of a statement, only one period is used. Two marks are needed when a sentence ends with an abbreviation and a question mark or exclamation point.

    I would like to introduce you to Ronald Franklin, Jr.
    Should I meet you at 10:00 P.M.?

Today almost everyone uses the U.S. Postal Service's two-letter state abbreviations. These abbreviations do not include periods.

A list of these abbreviations can be found in the front of most telephone books. The following are a few examples.

AK = Alaska
AL = Alabama
CT = Connecticut
HI = Hawaii
MD = Maryland
ME = Maine
MI = Michigan
NV = Nevada
NY = New York
OH = Ohio
TX = Texas
UT = Utah

CONNECT TO WRITER'S CRAFT

If you are unsure of the spelling or punctuation of an abbreviation, look it up in the dictionary. You can usually find the abbreviation in the entry for the word that you are trying to shorten. Most dictionaries also have a separate section on abbreviations at the back.

With Outlines

Use a period after each number or letter that shows a division in an outline.

I. Guitars
   A. Electric
      1. Hollow body
      2. Solid body
   B. Acoustic

II. Drums
   A. Hand
   B. Zylo

PRACTICE YOUR SKILLS

● Check Your Understanding
Using End Marks

Write the abbreviations that stand for the following items. Be sure to end them with a period whenever appropriate. If you are not sure of the abbreviation, use a dictionary.

1. dozen   **6.** Fahrenheit   **11.** incorporated

2. major   **7.** Rhode Island   **12.** before Christ

3. ounce   **8.** television   **13.** Bachelor of Arts

4. latitude   **9.** association   **14.** miles per hour

5. mountain   **10.** boulevard   **15.** post meridiem

● Connect to the Writing Process: Editing
Correcting End Punctuation

Rewrite the following outline, adding periods where needed.

I   Types of Businesses
     A   Corp
     B   Co
     C   Inc

II   States
     A   Eastern
        1   NY
        2   VT
        3   MA
     B   Western
        1   CA
        2   OR
        3   WA

III   Organizations
     A   FBI
     B   NATO
     C   UN

APPLY TO WRITING

Outline: *Using Periods*

Write an outline of what you ate yesterday. Use a separate Roman numeral for each meal and snack. Be sure to list all the food you had at each meal. As you make your outline, be sure that you place periods appropriately throughout.

QuickCheck Mixed Practice

Contemporary Life **Rewrite the following sentences, adding end punctuation and periods to abbreviations if needed. Then label each sentence *declarative, imperative, interrogative,* or *exclamatory.***

1. Have you called Dr Wilson

2. Dr Barry Wilson, Jr has been our family physician for years

3. Please get the phone book

4. Call him right this minute

5. Mrs Smith, the school nurse, thinks that my right arm is broken

6. Ouch, it hurts

7. I fell off the auditorium stage during Mr Miller's drama class

8. When did it happen

9. It happened just after class started at 2:00 P M

10. What a relief it will be to see Dr Wilson

Commas are used to prevent confusion and to keep items from running into one another. The following are specific rules for commas that are used to separate items.

Items in a Series

Three or more similar items—words, phrases, or clauses—that are placed together form a series.

Use commas to separate items in a series.

WORDS	**Blackberries, raspberries,** and **strawberries** are all members of the rose family. (nouns)
	We **picked, washed,** and **ate** as many fresh berries as we could. (verbs)
	At the end of the day, we were **tired, dirty, and full.** (adjectives)
PHRASES	The buckets for the berries could be **in the garage, in the pantry,** or **on the porch.**
	Are they going **to the picnic, to the park,** or **to the campground?**
CLAUSES	We know **where the berries are, if they are ripe,** and **when they should be picked.**
	She told us **where to go, how to get there,** and **what to wear.**

When a conjunction connects the last two items in a series, some writers omit the last comma. Although this is acceptable, it can be confusing. Therefore, it is better to get into the habit of including the comma before the conjunctions.

| CONFUSING | We fixed sandwiches, glasses of juice and cookies. |
| CLEAR | We fixed sandwiches, glasses of juice, and cookies. |

When conjunctions connect all items in a series, no commas are needed.

We ate **and** rested **and** ate some more.

Some pairs of words, such as *bacon and eggs,* are thought of as a single item. If one of these pairs of words appears in a series, consider it one item.

For dinner you can have a burger and fries, fish and chips, or pork and sauerkraut.

PRACTICE YOUR SKILLS

 Check Your Understanding
Commas in a Series

Contemporary Life

Write *I,* for incorrect, if the sentence is missing one or more commas, and *C* if the sentence is correct. Then, for each incorrect sentence, write the words, phrases, or clauses in a series and add commas.

1. Combine flour shortening pecans and cold water to make a tasty pie crust.

2. Preheat the oven oil the pan and prepare the crust.

3. Shall we bake raisin and nut or apple and cinnamon or butter and oatmeal muffins?

4. Whipped cream ice cream and cheddar cheese make excellent toppings for apple pie.

5. Please mix the batter pour it into a pan, and place it in the oven.

6. Use soap and hot water and a fresh towel to clean your hands before cooking.

7. I enjoy a glass of milk or a small dessert or a piece of fruit after lunch.

8. The best cakes are made with fresh butter and milk powdered sugar and cinnamon and brown eggs.

9. We will bake the dessert cook the steaks, and toss the salad when the guests arrive.

10. Shawna and Jennifer and the twins are all coming to eat with us.

Connect to the Writing Process: Drafting
Writing Sentences

Finish each sentence with a series of three or more appropriate items. Add commas where needed.

11. When I make a hamburger, I like to add ■.

12. This year in school I am studying ■.

13. When we have a holiday dinner, my favorite foods are ■.

14. I ■ to stay in shape.

15. Before leaving for school each morning, I usually like to ■.

16. Three places in the United States I would like to visit are ■.

17. ■ are the friends whom I trust the most to help me in difficult situations.

18. I enjoy watching ■.

19. I enjoy playing ■.

20. After I graduate from high school, I would like to ■.

▶ Adjectives Before a Noun

If a conjunction is missing between two adjectives that come before a noun, a comma is sometimes used to take its place.

> The rabbits disappeared into the tall, thick grass of the Nebraska plain.
>
> That is the oldest, most beautiful tree in the redwood forest.
>
> Several delicate, fragrant flowers blossomed from the desert cactus.

A comma is sometimes needed to separate two adjectives that precede a noun and are not joined by a conjunction.

A useful test can help you decide whether a comma is needed between two adjectives. If the sentence reads sensibly with the word *and* between the adjectives, a comma is needed.

> COMMA NEEDED   Mississippi is a damp, lush place.
>
>   (*A damp and lush place* reads well.)
>
> COMMA NOT   Today was a damp spring day.
> NEEDED
>
>   (*A damp and spring day* does not read well.)

Usually no comma is needed after a number or after an adjective that refers to size, shape, or age. For example, no commas are needed in the following expressions.

ADJECTIVE EXPRESSIONS
six oak trees
a large green meadow
one hundred beautiful butterflies
his old brown guitar
the ancient oral saga

PRACTICE YOUR SKILLS

● Check Your Understanding
Using Commas with Adjectives

Geography Topic | **Read the sentences below. Write *C* if the sentence is punctuated correctly. Write *I* if it is punctuated incorrectly.**

1. America is a land of diverse colorful regions.

2. Prickly cactus produces beautiful delicate flowers in the harsh deserts of Arizona.

3. Some parts of California are famous for sturdy redwood trees.

4. The golden wheat fields of Kansas are a glorious sight to behold.

5. The city of Chicago offers many great vistas of Lake Michigan.

6. The lovely quaint villages of New England attract many tourists.

7. Florida has large sandy beaches along both the Atlantic Ocean and the Gulf of Mexico.

8. Central Texas contains dark rich farmland and a good supply of water.

9. Its numerous active volcanoes make Hawaii like no other state.

10. Minnesota is famous for its ten thousand fresh lakes.

11. Austin, Texas, is well known for its rolling green hills.

12. New Mexico is a mixture of hot dry desert lands and snow-topped mountains.

● Connect to the Writing Process: Editing
Correcting Comma Errors

13.–17. Rewrite the incorrectly punctuated sentences from the exercise above, adding commas where needed.

APPLY TO WRITING
Postcard: *Using Commas*

Henry Moore. (Detail) *Family Group,* 1951. Bronze, 59¼ by 26½ inches.

You are on vacation at a very beautiful place. You have been wandering through a park when you come upon this sculpture. Write a postcard to your best friend and describe this sculpture. In your message use one example of items in a series and another of two adjectives before a noun that require a comma to separate them. Underline these in your writing.

▶ Compound Sentences

A comma is usually used to separate the independent clauses in a compound sentence.

Use a comma to separate the independent clauses of a compound sentence if the clauses are joined by a conjunction.

A coordinating conjunction most often combines the independent clauses in a compound sentence.

COORDINATING CONJUNCTIONS						
and	but	for	nor	or	so	yet

Notice in the following examples that the comma comes before the conjunction.

> I play the flute, and my sister plays the guitar.
> Pick up my guitar, or it might get left behind.

A comma is not needed in a very short compound sentence.

> Lisa played and I sang.

Do not confuse a compound sentence with a sentence that has a compound verb. No comma comes between the parts of a compound verb unless there are three or more verbs.

> COMPOUND SENTENCE   We waited for twenty minutes, but Lisa never appeared on stage.
>
> COMPOUND VERB   We waited for twenty minutes and then left.

A compound sentence can also be joined by a semicolon. You can learn more about compound sentences on pages L242–L243.

PRACTICE YOUR SKILLS

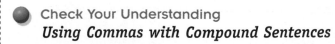

● Check Your Understanding
Using Commas with Compound Sentences

Music Topic **Read the sentences below. Write *C* if the sentence is punctuated correctly. Write *I* if it is punctuated incorrectly.**

1. Musicologists study the history of music and analyze its meaning to society.

2. The history of rap music is interesting and so many musicologists are beginning to examine it.

3. In 1979, Sugar Hill Gang recorded "Rappers' Delight" and this song changed the music world.

4. The song "Rappers' Delight" was a breakthrough and its lyrics provided the term *hip hop.*

5. Hip hop is related to rap music but they are different in some ways.

6. Rap is the spoken words of the song and hip hop refers to the background music.

7. Rappers speak the words of their songs rapidly and accent some phrases more than others.

8. In 1982, the first rap song with a political message was recorded and this song gave a social conscience to rap.

9. Sampling pieces of other songs began in 1986 and opened rap music to many lawsuits.

10. In 1986, rap videos began to appear on TV and attracted a new audience.

● Connect to the Writing Process: Editing
Correcting Comma Errors

11.–16. **Rewrite the incorrectly punctuated sentences from the exercise above. Add or remove commas where needed.**

● Connect to the Writing Process: Drafting
Writing Compound Sentences

Write one compound sentence for each of the following subjects. Make sure the clauses in each compound sentence are related. Add commas where needed.

17. music

18. hobbies

19. friends

20. sports

⏵ Introductory Elements

Some words, phrases, and clauses at the beginning of a sentence need to be separated from the rest of the sentence by a comma.

Use a comma after certain introductory elements.

The following are examples of introductory elements that should be followed by a comma.

WORDS	**No,** I have not heard about the earthquake.
	Yes, it was a bad one.
	(Other words include *now, oh, well,* and *why*—except when they are part of the sentence. *Why didn't you tell me?*)
PREPOSITIONAL PHRASE	**After the earthquake in San Francisco,** neighbors joined together to help one another.
	In just a few seconds, people's lives changed dramatically.
	(A comma comes after two or more prepositional phrases or a single phrase of four or more words.)
PARTICIPIAL PHRASE	**Feeling the ground begin to rumble,** residents ran nervously from their homes and offices into the street.
ADVERB CLAUSE	**As one man exited his home,** the roof caved in.

Notice on the following page that the punctuation of shorter phrases varies. Also, never place a comma after a phrase or phrases followed by a verb.

OTHERS **In Room 37,** 19 students were injured.

(A comma is usually used after an introductory phrase that ends in a number.)

In the road, blocks of wood were a hazard.

(The commas prevent confusion.)

On the floor of a destroyed home lay a child's teddy bear.

(The phrases are followed by the verb.)

PRACTICE YOUR SKILLS

● Check Your Understanding
Using Commas with Introductory Elements

History Topic **Read the sentences below. Write C if the sentence is punctuated correctly. Write I if it is punctuated incorrectly.**

1. Because of its proximity to the San Andreas Fault San Francisco experiences frequent earthquakes.
2. Although not all are violent, several have devastated the city.
3. Yes the 1906 quake was especially destructive.
4. In that earthquake a total of 450 or more people perished.
5. Throughout the city for three long days fires ravaged homes and buildings.
6. Coming together to help one another, the citizens rebuilt their devastated city.
7. From the rubble and ashes of the earthquake and fires, rose a city determined to host the Panama-Pacific International Exhibition in 1915.
8. In 1989 60,000 baseball fans were shaken in Candlestick Park when the city's next severe earthquake occurred.

9. Caving in parts of the Bay Bridge and causing gas mains to rupture the earthquake measured 7.1 on the Richter scale.

10. Because the earthquake occurred at rush hour, many commuters were on the Bay Area's streets and highways.

● Connect to the Writing Process: Editing
Correcting Comma Errors

11.–16. Rewrite the incorrectly punctuated sentences from the exercise above. Add or remove commas where needed.

● Connect to the Writing Process: Drafting
Writing Sentences

Write a sentence using each of the following introductory words or phrases. Add commas where needed.

17. After the long thunderstorm

18. As the sky began to clear

19. Well

20. Hearing the raindrops on our roof

21. In Room 206

22. When the sounds stopped

23. Because the lights went out

24. Hiding under her desk

25. In the heat of the day

● Commonly Used Commas

When you tie your shoelaces, you do not have to think about how to do it as you did when you were little. You do it automatically. There are some comma rules you have been using for so many years that they probably have also become automatic. The following is a brief review of those rules for using commas.

With Dates and Addresses

For clarity, commas are used to separate the various elements in a date or an address from one another.

Use commas to separate the elements in dates and addresses.

Notice in the following examples that a comma is also used to separate a date or an address from the rest of the sentence.

DATE	On Tuesday, February 2, 1941, my grandmother was born.
ADDRESS	Her parents lived at 29 Bank Street, Long Beach, California, at the time.

A comma is not used to separate the state and the ZIP code.

Send your request for information to Genealogy Research, 500 West 52nd Street, New York, NY 10019.

In Letters

Use a comma after the salutation of a friendly letter and after the closing of all letters.

SALUTATIONS AND CLOSINGS	
SALUTATIONS	Dear Uncle Joe,
	Dear Emily,
	Dearest Grandmother,
CLOSINGS	Love,
	Yours truly,
	Sincerely,
	Thank you,
	Regards,

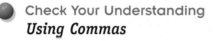
Often the use of too many commas is as confusing as not using enough commas. Use commas only where a rule indicates they are needed. In other words, use commas only where they make the meaning of your writing clearer. If you cannot find a rule that says you need a comma, follow this saying: "When in doubt, leave it out."

PRACTICE YOUR SKILLS

● Check Your Understanding

Using Commas

Write *a* or *b* to indicate which sentence in each pair shows the correct use of commas.

1. **a.** Dear Felipe,
   b. Dear Felipe

2. **a.** Wednesday, June 2, 1999
   b. Wednesday June 2, 1999

3. **a.** Roslyn Donovan, 510 Houghton Street, Marlin, Texas 76661
   b. Roslyn Donovan, 510 Houghton Street, Marlin, Texas, 76661

4. **a.** With love,
   b. With love

5. **a.** Tampa Florida
   b. Tampa, Florida

6. **a.** Thursday, October 3, 1960
   b. Thursday, October 3 1960

7. **a.** Dr. Tonya Jackson 21 Jewel Road Park City Idaho 92714
   b. Dr. Tonya Jackson, 21 Jewel Road, Park City, Idaho 92714

8. **a.** Thank you

   b. Thank you,

9. **a.** Dear Darla,

   b. Dear, Darla

10. **a.** December 7, 1941

    b. December 7 1941

11. **a.** El Paso, Texas

    b. El Paso Texas,

Connect to the Writing Process: Revising
Correcting Comma Errors

Rewrite the following letter, adding commas where needed.

> 27 Duvall Road
>
> Austin, Texas 78702
>
> May 2, 2000
>
> Dear Grandma
>
> I am trying to get some information for a family-tree project that I have to do for social studies. I know that your father was born on March 26 1919. His place of birth was his aunt's home on 26 Lasso Lane Bozeman Montana. What can you tell me about your father's parents?
>
> Please send a response to me at my school address, which is Lake Travis High School 3322 Ranch Road Austin, Texas 78734.
>
> Love
>
> Jake

APPLY TO WRITING

Informative Note: *Commas*

You are applying for a job as a counselor in training for a summer camp. Your prospective employer, Ms. Smythe, has requested that you send her a note that contains all the following information:

- your full name
- your date of birth
- your current address
- your previous work experience
- the date on which you can begin work

Because Ms. Smythe is a prospective employer, you want to make a good impression. Be sure to write in complete sentences and then check your work for the proper use of commas.

QuickCheck Mixed Practice

Science Topic **Read the paragraphs below. Write each word that should be followed by a comma.**

Pinnipeds are fin-footed mammals with limbs that are used as paddles or flippers. The three main kinds of pinnipeds are the walrus the sea lion and the seal. All pinnipeds are meat eaters and they all live in the water. Most pinnipeds live in the cold waters of the Arctic and the Antarctic oceans but several forms live in fresh water. Since pinnipeds spend most of their lives in the water they have become well adapted to this kind of existence. Their tapered streamlined bodies make them excellent swimmers. Their thick layer of blubber gives them added buoyancy and helps keep them warm.

Searching for food pinnipeds can dive two or three hundred feet below the water's surface. When they are underwater their nostrils close. Most pinnipeds have sharp backward-pointing teeth. This feature makes it possible for a pinniped to seize prey and direct it down its throat. Because pinnipeds are sociable animals they live together in large herds.

The walrus is one type of pinniped. Some scientists classify the walrus as a type of large seal. Having tusks to defend itself the walrus can protect itself from the threat of the much larger polar bear. When walruses climb onto ice they can also use their tusks as hooks.

The sea lion lives in the northern Pacific Ocean and parts of the Southern Hemisphere. Using all four flippers sea lions can walk on land. Their thick blubbery layers keep them warm.

The harbor seal and elephant seal are two kinds of earless seals. Without ear flaps but with ears these seals have excellent hearing. They cannot use their rear flippers for walking but they move along on their bellies.

Commas That Enclose

Some expressions interrupt the flow of a sentence. These expressions generally add information that is not needed to understand the main idea of the sentence. If one of these interrupters comes in the middle of a sentence, a comma is placed before and after the expression to set it off.

The movie, **to tell the truth,** was boring.

Sometimes an interrupting expression comes at the beginning or the end of a sentence. When an interrupter appears in one of these places, only one comma is needed to separate it from the rest of the sentence.

To tell the truth, the movie was boring.
The movie was boring, **to tell the truth.**

▶ Direct Address

Names, titles, or words that are used to address someone are set off by commas. These expressions are called nouns of **direct address.**

Use commas to enclose nouns of direct address.

Shelli, what is your opinion?
Your explanation, **Marc,** was excellent.
Did you like the movie, **Maria**?

CONNECT TO WRITER'S CRAFT

Writers often use commas when writing dialogue to indicate pauses in their characters' words. What do the pauses in the following dialogue tell you about what is happening?

"What in the world happened here?" our father asked in disbelief.

"Well, uh, we were just, uh, playing."

PRACTICE YOUR SKILLS

● Check Your Understanding
Using Commas with Direct Address

Contemporary Life **Read the sentences below. Write *C* if the sentence is punctuated correctly. Write *I* if it is punctuated incorrectly.**

1. As our drama teacher, Mrs. Washburn, will you explain that movie to us?

2. Certainly Shelli but the explanation is lengthy.

3. We thought the movie was boring Mrs. Washburn.

4. The plot was complicated, class.

5. Marc, would you like to explain it to the class?

6. The plot, Mrs. Washburn was actually one big story with two smaller subplots.

7. Yes, Marc, that is very true.

8. Mrs. Washburn why did the director make the movie so hard to understand?

9. The movie is not all that difficult to understand if you pay attention, Shelli.

10. Class it is important that you pay attention to all the little details in this film.

● Connect to the Writing Process: Editing
Correcting Comma Errors

11.–15. Rewrite the incorrectly punctuated sentences from the exercise above. Add commas where needed.

● Connect to the Writing Process: Drafting
Writing Sentences

Write sentences using the following nouns in direct address. Add commas where needed.

16. Mr. Green

17. Abby

18. Officer
19. President Smith
20. Sir
21. Dr. Gonzalez
22. Travis
23. Ms. Dalton
24. Mom
25. Erin

▶ Parenthetical Expressions

A parenthetical expression provides additional or related ideas. It is related only loosely to the rest of the sentence. The parenthetical expression could be removed without changing the meaning of the sentence.

Use commas to enclose parenthetical expressions.

COMMON PARENTHETICAL EXPRESSIONS	
after all	in fact
at any rate	in my opinion
by the way	of course
consequently	on the contrary
however	on the other hand
for example	moreover
for instance	nevertheless
generally speaking	to tell the truth
I believe (guess, hope, expect)	

By the way, did you bring your binoculars?

The indigo bunting, **in my opinion,** is a beautiful bird.

We can watch the birds a little longer, **I guess.**

Nicole, **on the other hand,** has to leave.

After all, she has been here for two hours.

We, **however,** just arrived.

Other expressions, as well, can be used as parenthetical expressions.

The roseate spoonbill, **although it looks like a flamingo,** is a different bird.

According to my book, puffins are not found in Florida.

Birds, **it is known,** communicate with one another.

Contrasting expressions, which usually begin with *not,* are also considered parenthetical expressions.

The mockingbird, **not the cardinal,** is the state bird of Texas.

The seagull is found inland, **not just by the ocean.**

My sister, **not I,** is the family bird expert.

PRACTICE YOUR SKILLS

● Check Your Understanding
Using Commas with Parenthetical Expressions

 **Read the sentences below. Write *C* if the sentence is punctuated correctly. Write *I* if it is punctuated incorrectly.**

1. Generally speaking birds are animals that have wings and fly.

2. Not all birds however fit this description.

3. In fact, many birds are unable to fly but have wings.

4. Consequently, scientists classify birds as animals with both wings and feathers.

5. It is not, in fact, the ability to fly that sets them apart.

6. Nevertheless birds are among nature's most interesting creatures.

7. Burrowing owls for example are ingenious birds.

8. After all, they nest in the ground, often in prairie dog towns.

9. Other birds, however, make their homes far off the ground in steep cliff walls.

10. These cliffs of course afford them great safety from predators.

● Connect to the Writing Process: Editing
Correcting Comma Errors

11.–15. **Rewrite the incorrectly punctuated sentences from the preceding exercise, adding commas where needed.**

● Connect to the Writing Process: Drafting
Writing Sentences with Parenthetical Expressions

Write sentences using the parenthetical expression below in the part of the sentence indicated. Add commas where needed.

16. *I know* in the middle of a sentence

17. *by the way* at the beginning of a sentence

18. *to tell the truth* at the end of a sentence

19. *in fact* at the beginning of a sentence

20. *for instance* in the middle of a sentence

▶ Appositives

An appositive with its modifiers identifies or explains a noun or a pronoun in the sentence. Notice in the example at the top of the next page that an appositive is enclosed in commas.

> The Greenville firehouse, **a town landmark,** has finally been restored.

Use commas to enclose most appositives and their modifiers.

Notice in the following examples that an appositive can come in the middle of a sentence or at the end of a sentence. If an appositive comes in the middle of a sentence, two commas are needed to enclose it.

> Greenville, **an old Western town,** is an interesting place to visit.
>
> Hannah bought me a beautiful gift, **some Greenville turquoise.**

Titles and degrees that follow a person's name are a type of appositive. As such, they should also be set off by commas.

> Rose Watts, **Ph.D.,** is a well-known expert on the history of Greenville.
>
> Harry Jackson, **Jr.,** was the first sheriff in Greenville.
>
> Mr. Smith, **CEO,** joined the Greenville Historical Society in 1999.

Commas are not used if an appositive identifies a person or thing by telling which one or ones when there is more than one possibility. Usually these appositives are names and have no modifiers.

> My friend **Greta** will travel to Greenville with us.
>
> The book ***Western History*** devotes two pages to a description of the town.
>
> We **students** studied the Old West last year.

You can learn more about appositives on pages L183–L184.

PRACTICE YOUR SKILLS

● Check Your Understanding
Using Commas with Appositives

History Topic **Read the sentences below. Write *C* if the sentence is punctuated correctly. Write *I* if it is punctuated incorrectly.**

1. Manifest Destiny the belief that it was America's mission to expand westward inspired many explorers and settlers in the 1800s.

2. The explorers Lewis and Clark set out to cross the unmapped continent in 1804.

3. The third president Thomas Jefferson had purchased a large portion of that land from France.

4. Jefferson secured $2,500 a grant from the Congress to support the Lewis and Clark expedition.

5. The Native American guide Sacajawea helped the party cross the unfamiliar terrain.

6. Lewis and Clark also hired Sacajawea's husband, Toussaint Charbonneau to guide them.

7. Sacajawea, a Shoshone, was fluent in many native languages.

8. The explorer Meriwether Lewis was familiar with many Indian tribes.

9. We Americans have mythologized Lewis and Clark's adventures.

10. In 1996, Stephen E. Ambrose Ph.D. published the book *Undaunted Courage* an account of the Lewis and Clark expedition.

● Connect to the Writing Process: Editing
Correcting Sentences with Appositives

11.–15. Rewrite the incorrectly punctuated sentences from the exercise above. Add commas where needed.

Connect to the Writing Process: Drafting
Writing Sentences with Appositives

Write sentences using the phrases below as appositives. Add commas where needed.

16. my favorite animal

17. the best pet

18. a famous dog

19. the most beautiful bird

20. a furry creature

 **QuickCheck** Mixed Practice

General Interest **Rewrite the paragraph below, adding commas where needed.**

A man who lived in California constructed a musical robot. The amazing thing about this achievement however is that the man made it in 1940! The robot by the way looked like a woman. Sitting on a couch the robot would play the zither. The zither a musical instrument has thirty to forty strings. Anyone who was within a twelve-foot radius could ask it to play any of about three thousand tunes. A person's voice not a switch touched off it controls. The machinery inside it included 1,187 wheels and 370 electromagnets. No one has discovered in spite of extensive research whatever happened to Isis the world's first robot musician.

▶ Nonessential and Essential Elements

Sometimes a particular phrase or a clause is not essential to the meaning of a sentence.

> Use commas to set off nonessential participial phrases and nonessential clauses.

A participial phrase or a clause is nonessential if it provides extra information that is not essential to the meaning of the sentence.

NONESSENTIAL	Dallas, **lying in the eastern part of Texas,** receives quite a bit of rain.
	(participial phrase)
NONESSENTIAL	Carol, **wearing a raincoat but no hat,** likes the rain.
	(participial phrase)
NONESSENTIAL	Three inches is the annual rainfall in Yuma, Arizona, **which is in the southwestern part of the state.**
	(clause)

If the nonessential phrase and clause in the preceding examples were dropped, the main idea of the sentences would not be changed in any way.

Dallas receives quite a bit of rain.

Carol likes the rain.

Three inches is the annual rainfall in Yuma, Arizona.

If a participial phrase or a clause is essential to the meaning of a sentence, no commas are used. Essential phrases and clauses usually identify a person or thing and answer the question *Which one?* when there might be confusion otherwise. Adjective clauses that begin with *that* are usually essential whereas those that begin with *which* are often nonessential.

ESSENTIAL	We enjoyed the program **presented by station's meteorologists.**
	(participial phrase)
ESSENTIAL	The speaker **who closed the program** is my father.
	(clause)
ESSENTIAL	His prediction **that the summer would be very dry** proved accurate.
	(clause)

If the essential phrases and clauses in the preceding examples were dropped, necessary information would be missing. The main idea of the sentence would be incomplete.

We enjoyed the program.
(*Which* program?)

The speaker is my father.
(*Which* speaker?)

His prediction proved accurate.
(*Which* prediction?)

Nonessential and essential elements are sometimes called nonrestrictive *and* restrictive *elements.*

Practice Your Skills

 Check Your Understanding
Using Commas with Nonessential Elements

Science Topic **Write *C* if the sentence is punctuated correctly. Write *I* if it is punctuated incorrectly.**

1. Lightning that strikes in dry forests can cause forest fires.

2. Often thunderstorms produce lightning that ignites wet areas.

3. Lightning which occurs all over the world is an amazing phenomenon.

4. Thunder which can be quite loud follows a lightning flash.

5. Lightning which is caused by streams of electricity also strikes humans quite frequently.

6. A bolt of lightning striking a person usually causes very serious injury or death.

7. The phenomenon of lightning bolts traveling between two clouds is quite common.

8. Animals alarmed by the loud noises usually find cover during thunderstorms.

9. Lightning that strikes an airplane can cause severe damage.

10. Lightning which can strike telephone and electrical lines has ruined many televisions and computers not guarded by surge protectors.

● Connect to the Writing Process: Editing
Adding Commas to Sentences

11.–15. Rewrite the incorrectly punctuated sentence from the exercise above. Add commas where needed.

● Connect to the Writing Process: Drafting
Writing Sentences

Write sentences using the following groups of words as nonessential elements. Add commas where needed.

16. which is my favorite desert

17. used as a topping

18. which was a great restaurant

19. who used to visit often

20. located in the mall

21. which is always crowded

22. who prefers to shop closer to home

23. that is on the upper level

24. which has received awards

25. eating at a five-star restaurant

APPLY TO WRITING

Writer's Craft: *Analyzing the Use of Commas*

Professional writers often use commas to make their work easier to read. The following passage is from *Across the Wide Missouri,* a nonfiction book by Bernard DeVoto, who won the Pulitzer Prize in 1947 for his realistic portrayal of Western expansion in America. In the passage below, DeVoto discusses mapmaking of the early 1800s. Read this passage, noticing the author's use of commas. Then follow the directions.

> Tanner's and Burr's bulge at about the Bitterroot Mountains and Tanner's not-so-often imitated Platte were about the only advances over William Clark that had been made by the time we deal with. In fact, apart from Clark's map, they were about the only advances over A. Arrowsmith and L. Lewis, *A New and Elegant General Atlas,* an English work published the year when Lewis and Clark started up the Missouri.
>
> —*Bernard DeVoto,* Across the Wide Missouri

- Reread the sentences that contain commas. Which rules does DeVoto follow in placing those commas?

- Rewrite the second sentence eliminating the commas. Which is easier to read, the new version or DeVoto's original one? Why?

- If you were the editor of DeVoto's book, would you have changed anything he did? Explain your answer.

Science Topic **Rewrite the paragraphs below, adding commas where needed.**

The bald eagle of course is not bald. It was named at a time when *bald* meant "white." Because it has white feathers on its head the adult eagle has its present name. In contrast to its white head and tail the bald eagle's body and wings are brown. Its eyes beak and feet are yellow. An eagle can be over three feet long and its wingspan may be over seven feet. Its toes end in talons which are strong claws.

An eagle is a hunter. It feeds mainly on dead or dying fish but sometimes will eat small animals. It swoops down picks up its prey in its talons and flies off. An eagle that weighs eight to twelve pounds is able to carry an animal weighing as much as seventeen pounds!

Even though the bald eagle is the national emblem it had become an endangered species by the 1960s. After years of federal action and nationwide attention this magnificent bird was declared out of danger in 1999.

Understanding Kinds of Sentences and End Marks

Write each sentence and its appropriate end mark. Then label each one *D* for declarative, *IM* for imperative, *IN* for interrogative, or *E* for exclamatory.

1. Listen to these interesting facts about your body

2. No one else in the whole world has the same fingerprints or voiceprint as you do

3. If it takes fourteen muscles to smile, how many muscles does it take to frown

4. The answer is twenty, which means that it's easier to smile than to frown

5. Wait until you hear this next fact

6. Particles in a sneeze can travel at speeds of over one hundred miles per hour

7. Did you ever cry when you cut an onion

8. A cut onion releases a gas that irritates your eyes

9. Then your tears automatically come to your eyes to wash away the gas—like windshield wipers

10. There are 206 bones in the human body

11. Do you know the name of the longest bone

12. The longest is the femur, or the thigh bone

13. Take care of your bones by drinking plenty of milk

14. What have we learned from these facts

15. Without a doubt, the workings of the human body are extraordinarily amazing

Using Commas Correctly

Write each sentence, adding a comma or commas where needed. If a sentence needs no commas, write C.

1. Pablo is your birthday on Tuesday March 6?
2. Gazelles and prairie dogs seldom drink water.
3. The Marianas Trench in the Pacific the lowest point on Earth is 36,198 feet below sea level.
4. Jennifer is only one day older than her cousin.
5. An old farmhouse owned by Ito stands near a meadow.
6. On Monday my brother will enter the Army at Fort Dix New Jersey.
7. Before locking up the custodian turned off the lights.
8. In Switzerland official notices are printed in French German Italian and Romansch.
9. Generally speaking a worker bee may live for six months but a queen bee may live for six years.
10. No Leslie doesn't live in Louisville Kentucky anymore.

Writing Sentences

Write ten sentences that follow the directions below.

Write a sentence that...

1. includes a series of nouns.
2. includes two adjectives before a noun.
3. has two independent clauses joined by a coordinating conjunction.
4. includes an introductory participial phrase.
5. includes an introductory adverbial clause.
6. includes direct address.
7. includes a parenthetical expression.
8. includes an appositive.
9. includes a nonessential adjective clause.
10. includes a street number and name, city, and state.

Language and *Self-Expression*

Claude Monet was a founder of the Impressionist Movement of the late 1800s. The Impressionists were French painters who painted or drew their impressions of moments of everyday life. Impressionists painted with hundreds of strokes and dabs to reveal the way light changed their subjects.

Arrival of the Normandy Train, Gare Saint-Lazare captures a moment in time as Monet saw it. What other sensory impressions can you imagine from this painting? Write a description of the scene, including the sounds, smells, tastes, sights, and textures of the *gare* (station).

Prewriting Create a sensory details web for your description. Include circles labeled "Sights," "Sounds," "Smells," "Tastes," and "Feels." Use your imagination to think of sense impressions that reflect what you see in the painting.

Drafting Use your details web to write a first draft of your description. Try to create a strong mental image of the train station for your readers.

Revising Read your description to a classmate. Ask if you have successfully captured the feeling of the train station as it is depicted in the painting. Add any details necessary to make your description evocative and complete.

Editing Go over your description, checking for errors in grammar, spelling, and punctuation. Be sure your sentences end with appropriate punctuation and include commas wherever necessary.

Publishing Make a final copy of your description. Read classmates' descriptions, and see who has best captured in writing the sensory impression made by the painting.

Another Look

Recognizing Sentences

A **declarative sentence** makes a statement or expresses an opinion and ends with a period (.).

An **imperative sentence** gives a direction, makes a request, or gives a command. It ends with either a period or an exclamation point (. or !).

An **interrogative sentence** asks a question and ends with a question mark (?).

An **exclamatory sentence** expresses strong feeling or emotion and ends with an exclamation point (!).

Other Uses of Periods

Periods are used in places other than at the ends of sentences. *(page L501)*
  In titles with names (Dr., Ms.)
  With initials for names (R. D. Stein)
  In times with numbers (P.M., A.D.)
  In addresses (St., Dept.)
  In organizations and companies (Co., Inc.)
Use a period after each number or letter in an outline. *(page L502)*

Commas that Separate

Use commas to separate items in a series. *(pages L505–L506)*
Use a comma sometimes to separate two adjectives that precede a noun and are not joined by a conjunction. *(page L508)*
Use a comma to separate the independent clauses of a compound sentence if the clauses are joined by a conjunction. *(pages L510–L511)*
Use a comma after certain introductory elements. *(pages L513–L514)*
Use commas to separate the elements in dates and addresses. *(page L516)*
Use commas in the salutations and closings of letters. *(page L516)*

Commas that Enclose

Use commas to enclose nouns of direct address. *(page L521)*
Use commas to enclose parenthetical expressions. *(pages L523–L524)*
Use commas to enclose nonessential appositives and their modifiers, and to set off nonessential phrases and clauses. *(pages L526–L530)*

Directions

Write the letter of the mark of punctuation that correctly completes each sentence. If the sentence contains no error, write *D*.

EXAMPLE

1 Shopping for school is always a huge production for the Alistair family of Cincinnati Ohio.

   1 A period

      B comma

      C question mark

      D No error

ANSWER

   1 B

1. The Alistairs have ten children, whose ages range from fifteen years to six months.

2. How do they manage a shopping trip

3. They load the kids into two vans and they drive to a large shopping mall.

4. Then the fun begins

5. Each older wiser kid takes charge of a younger one.

6. The Alistairs go to clothing stores shoe stores, and stationery stores.

7. Don't lose anyone

8. By the end of the day everyone is exhausted and ready to go home.

9. They meet in a pizza restaurant inside the mall.

10. With a little bit of luck all of the children and their parents will have accomplished their shopping on time.

1 **A** period
   B comma
   C question mark
   D No error

2 **A** period
   B comma
   C question mark
   D No error

3 **A** period
   B comma
   C exclamation point
   D No error

4 **A** exclamation point
   B comma
   C question mark
   D No error

5 **A** period
   B comma
   C question mark
   D No error

6 **A** period
   B comma
   C question mark
   D No error

7 **A** exclamation point
   B comma
   C question mark
   D No error

8 **A** period
   B comma
   C question mark
   D No error

9 **A** period
   B comma
   C question mark
   D No error

10 **A** period
   B comma
   C question mark
   D No error

CHAPTER 16

Italics and Quotation Marks

Directions

Read the passage and write the letter of the answer that correctly punctuates each underlined part. If the underlined part contains no error, write *D*.

EXAMPLE   Ellie looked forward to reading <u>Beowulf and</u>
                                         (1)
          <u>works by Chaucer</u> in her English class.

    1 **A** Beowulf and works by *Chaucer*

       B *Beowulf* and "works by Chaucer"

       C *Beowulf* and works by Chaucer

       D No error

ANSWER   1 **C**

<u>"Are you taking advanced English, Jay" Ellie asked?</u>
                        (1)
<u>"No," Jay replied, "math is what interests me."</u>
                        (2)
<u>Ellie said, "I hope we do some of Emily Dickinson's</u>

<u>poems, such as 'I Am Nobody.'"</u> I read in a magazine that
                  (3)
our English classes don't feature enough women writers."

   <u>"We have to write five papers"! Anthony exclaimed.</u>
                        (4)
Ellie couldn't believe her ears. Did she just hear him say,

<u>"We have to write five papers"?</u>
              (5)

1 A   "Are you taking advanced English, Jay"? Ellie asked.
   B   "Are you taking advanced English, Jay?" Ellie asked.
   C   "Are you taking advanced English, Jay Ellie asked"?
   D   No error

2 A   "No." Jay replied, "Math is what interests me."
   B   "No." Jay replied. "Math is what interests me."
   C   "No," Jay replied. "Math is what interests me."
   D   No error

3 A   Ellie said, "I hope we do some of Emily Dickinson's poems,
       such as 'I Am Nobody.'
   B   Ellie said, "I hope we do some of Emily Dickinson's
       poems, such as *I Am Nobody.*
   C   Ellie said, "I hope we do some of Emily Dickinson's poems,
       such as '*I Am Nobody.*'
   D   No error

4 A   "We have to write five papers" Anthony exclaimed!
   B   "We have to write five papers." Anthony exclaimed.
   C   "We have to write five papers!" Anthony exclaimed.
   D   No error

5 A   'We have to write five papers'?
   B   'We have to write five papers?'
   C   "We have to write five papers?"
   D   No error

"It's just the architect's model, but I'm very excited."

Leo Cullum. "It's just the architect's model, but I'm very excited." 1997. Ink, 4 by 5 inches.
© *The New Yorker* Collection, 1997. Leo Cullum from http://www.cartoonbank.com. All rights reserved.

Describe What is the setting of this cartoon? What are the characters doing?

Analyze Cartoons are meant to entertain and amuse, and they often mean something different to each person. Think of your favorite cartoon and ask yourself how it expresses humor. How do you think the details and exaggeration of Cullum's cartoon make it funny?

Interpret What does the title of the cartoon mean to you? Why is it funny?

Judge What other things might the dogs say that would be funny?

At the end of this chapter, you will use the artwork to stimulate ideas for writing.

Italics (Underlining)

This chapter will cover the various uses of italics as well as the uses of quotation marks with titles and direct quotations.

As you probably already know, italics are printed letters that slant to the right. If you are using a computer, you need to highlight what should be italicized and then use the command for italics. If you are writing by hand, you need to underline whatever should be italicized.

ITALICS	My mom read *Charlie and the Chocolate Factory* to my little sister.
UNDERLINING	My mom read <u>Charlie and the Chocolate Factory</u> to my little sister.

Certain letters, numbers, and words should be italicized (underlined).

Italicize (underline) letters, numbers, and words when they are used to represent themselves. Also italicize (underline) foreign words that are not generally used in the English language.

When you use the computer, you should italicize. When you write, you should underline. Do not do both.

LETTERS	My little sister has trouble writing *5*s and *B*s.
	or
	My little sister has trouble writing <u>5</u>s and <u>B</u>s.
WORDS, PHRASES	She cannot pronounce the word *teeth*.
	or
	She cannot pronounce the word <u>teeth</u>.

FOREIGN WORDS	We call our German grandmother *Oma*.
	or
	We call our German grandmother <u>Oma</u>.

Notice in the example on the preceding page that only the <u>5</u> and <u>B</u> are italicized (underlined)—not the *s*.

Italicize (underline) the titles of long written or musical works that are published as a single unit. Also italicize (underline) the titles of periodicals, movies, radio and television series, paintings and sculptures, and the names of vehicles.

	TITLES
BOOKS	*Jane Eyre* <u>White Fang</u>
NEWSPAPERS	*Chicago Tribune* <u>Sacramento Bee</u>
PERIODICALS	*Seventeen,* the <u>Reader's Digest</u> (In general, do not underline *the,* which often appears before newspaper or periodical titles.)
PLAYS, MOVIES	*Romeo and Juliet* <u>The Wizard of Oz</u>
BOOK-LENGTH POEMS	*Evangeline* <u>Odyssey</u>
RADIO AND TELEVISION SERIES	*The Shadow* <u>The Wonder Years</u>
LONG MUSICAL WORKS	*Faust* <u>La Traviata</u>
WORKS OF ART	*Mona Lisa* <u>Venus de Milo</u>

SHIPS, PLANES, OTHER CRAFTS	*Titanic* Spirit of St. Louis *Voyager 2* Discovery

You can learn about capitalization of titles on pages L483–L487.

PRACTICE YOUR SKILLS

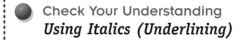 Check Your Understanding
Using Italics (Underlining)

Write *a* or *b* to indicate which item in each pair shows the correct use of underlining.

1. a. the aircraft carrier USS Enterprise
   b. The Aircraft Carrier USS Enterprise

2. a. the novel The Mill on the Floss
   b. the novel The Mill on the Floss

3. a. the opera The Barber of Seville
   b. the opera The Barber of Seville

4. a. the magazine Boy's Life
   b. The Magazine Boy's Life

5. a. the novel The Red Badge of Courage
   b. the novel The Red Badge of Courage

6. a. the book Mathematics for All Ages
   b. the book Mathematics for All Ages

7. a. the play Our Town
   b. the play Our Town

8. a. the Los Angeles Times
   b. the Los Angeles Times

9. **a.** the painting The Last Supper
   b. the painting <u>The Last Supper</u>

10. **a.** <u>The Musical The Phantom of the Opera</u>
    b. the musical <u>The Phantom of the Opera</u>

11. **a.** <u>The Poetry Collection Field: A Haiku Circle</u>
    b. the poetry collection <u>Field: A Haiku Circle</u>

12. **a.** the film <u>Citizen Kane</u>
    b. <u>The Film Citizen Kane</u>

13. **a.** Shakespeare's play <u>Twelfth Night</u>
    b. Shakespeare's play <u>Twelfth Night</u>

14. **a.** the television show <u>The X-Files</u>
    b. the television show The <u>X-Files</u>

15 **a.** <u>The Shuttle Atlantis</u>
   b. the shuttle <u>Atlantis</u>

● Connect to the Writing Process: Editing
Using Underlining

Rewrite the following sentences, underlining the words that should be italicized.

16. I love adventure books like 20,000 Leagues Under the Sea by Jules Verne.

17. I can imagine myself on a submarine like the Nautilus.

18. Of course, this book was written before transportation innovations like the Concorde.

19. In The Wonderful Wizard of Oz, published in 1900, tornadoes, horses, and hot-air balloons are all used for transportation.

20. In 1912, the allegedly unsinkable ship Titanic sank after striking an iceberg.

21. The word titanic actually means "colossal."

22. It is derived from the Greek word titanikos, which relates to the mythological Titans.

23. Other famous vehicles that suffered a tragic end include the zeppelin Hindenburg and the ocean liner Lusitania.

24. The history of steamships, such as the Queen Mary and the Queen Elizabeth, is rich.

25. Magazines like Aviation History and Collectible Automobile regularly feature stories about the history of transportation.

Communicate Your Ideas

APPLY TO WRITING

E-mail: *Titles*

Your English class is exchanging E-mail messages with students from another country. Write a message to another teenager telling him or her about yourself. Recommend two good books and some of your favorite movies. Before you begin writing, look over these questions and jot down some ideas.

- How will you introduce yourself to the other student?
- What is one interesting thing about yourself that you would like to share with the student?
- What do you like to do in your free time?
- What two books will you recommend?
- What two movies will you recommend?
- What reasons will you give for your recommendations?

Then write your message. When you have finished, check to make sure that you have punctuated the titles correctly.

Quotation Marks

When you use quotation marks, always remember that they come in pairs. They are placed at the beginning and at the end of certain titles and uninterrupted quotations.

▶ Quotation Marks with Titles

You have learned that titles of long works are italicized (underlined). Most long works are made up of smaller parts. For example, books are composed of chapters, and magazines contain many articles. The titles of these smaller parts should be enclosed in quotation marks.

> Use quotation marks to enclose the titles of chapters, articles, stories, one-act plays, short poems, and songs.

CHAPTERS	Read "I Am Born," the first chapter in my favorite book, David Copperfield. (The chapter in the book is in quotation marks, but the title of the book is underlined.)
ARTICLES	Have you seen the article "Charles Dickens's England" in Newsweek?
STORIES	I read "Everyday Use" by Alice Walker yesterday.
ONE-ACT PLAYS	Sherry is going to be in the school's performance of "Drama Club."
SHORT POEMS	My favorite poem in the book Famous Twentieth Century Poetry is "Sea Lullaby."
SONGS	When I was younger, I used to love to sing "Puff, the Magic Dragon."

You will learn more about other punctuation, such as commas and periods, with quotation marks later in this chapter.

PRACTICE YOUR SKILLS

● Check Your Understanding
Punctuating Titles

Write *a* or *b* to indicate which title in each pair is correctly punctuated.

1. **a.** The Lottery (short story)
   b. "The Lottery" (short story)
2. **a.** The Elegance of Memory (poem)
   b. "The Elegance of Memory" (poem)
3. **a.** "Somewhere Over the Rainbow" (song)
   b. Somewhere Over the Rainbow (song)
4. **a.** "The Washwoman" (short story)
   b. The "Washwoman" (short story)
5. **a.** The Romantic Poets (chapter)
   b. "The Romantic Poets" (chapter)
6. **a.** Twinkle, Twinkle Little Star (song)
   b. "Twinkle, Twinkle Little Star" (song)
7. **a.** "The Road Not Taken" (poem)
   b. The "Road Not Taken" (poem)
8. **a.** "The Rocking-Horse Winner" (short story)
   b. The Rocking-Horse Winner (short story)
9. **a.** The Art of Georgia O'Keeffe (chapter)
   b. "The Art of Georgia O'Keeffe" (chapter)
10. **a.** "Frozen" (song)
    b. Frozen (song)

● Connect to the Writing Process: Drafting
Writing Titles in Sentences

Write sentences that include a title of each type of work indicated. Add quotation marks where needed.

11. short story
12. chapter of a book
13. article
14. one-act play

APPLY TO WRITING

Persuasive Letter: *Quotation Marks with Titles*

Your music teacher is considering which songs the choir will sing in an upcoming performance. Write a letter to your teacher suggesting two songs that should be included in the choir performance. They can be hymns, recent popular songs, or any songs that you like from opera or musicals. Give her convincing reasons why you think the choir should choose these two songs. After you have finished your letter, check that you have punctuated the titles of the songs appropriately.

 **QuickCheck** Mixed Practice

Contemporary Life **Write each sentence, adding quotation marks or underlining where needed.**

1. The Roots of Old Verse is the lead article in the Atlantic Literary Journal.

2. The familiar lullaby Rock-a-Bye Baby dates from the Elizabethan period.

3. Ring Around the Roses is an old rhyme from the Middle Ages.

4. Did you read the chapter called Early Children's Poetry in the book English Poems and Commentary?

5. No, I read Mending Wall in the book Selected Poems of Robert Frost.

6. I read an article about him called Frost's New England in Newsweek.

7. Two of Robert Frost's most famous poems are Birches and Stopping by Woods on a Snowy Evening.

8. Do you know the song I Can't Choose by John Knight?

9. It is based on The Road Not Taken, which was also written by Frost.

10. There is a great paragraph about his works in the chapter called American Poets in the book Writers to Remember.

Quotation Marks with Direct Quotations

The most important thing to remember when writing direct quotations is that quotation marks enclose only the *exact words* of a speaker. In other words, quotation marks are used only with a **direct quotation.**

Use quotation marks to enclose a person's exact words.

"I just finished my homework," Zoe said.

Will said, "I'll be glad to check it for you."

Sometimes, when you write, you may paraphrase what someone has said—without using his or her exact words. When you paraphrase, you are indirectly quoting a person. Do not use quotation marks with **indirect quotations.**

Zoe said that she had just finished her homework.

Will said he would check it for her.

In the first example above, the word *that* signals the indirect quotation. In the second example, *that* is understood.

A one-sentence direct quotation can be written in several ways. It can be placed before or after a speaker tag, such as *she said* or *Mr. Billings asked.* In both cases quotation marks enclose the person's exact words—from beginning to end.

"Yesterday I left my homework in my locker," Zoe added.

Zoe added, "Yesterday I left my homework in my locker."

For variety or emphasis, a quotation can also be interrupted by a speaker tag. When this interruption occurs, you need two pairs of quotation marks because quotation marks enclose only a person's exact words, not the speaker tag.

"Yesterday," Zoe added, "I left my homework in my locker."

To quote more than one sentence, put quotation marks at the beginning and at the end of the entire quotation. Do not put quotation marks around each sentence within a quotation—unless a speaker tag interrupts.

Zoe added, "Yesterday I left my homework in my locker. Mrs. Cash was very nice about it. She wrote a hall pass so that I could retrieve it."

"Yesterday I left my homework in my locker," Zoe said. "Luckily, Mrs. Cash wrote a hall pass so I could retrieve it."

Notice in the above examples that the comma or period that follows the quotation is placed *inside* the closing quotation marks. Of course, if the sentence ends with the speaker tag, then the period follows the speaker tag.

"I got my homework and returned to class," said Zoe.

CONNECT TO SPEAKING AND WRITING

When you write speaker tags in direct quotations, it is important not to repeat the word *said* too often. Try to convey to your reader the tone or mood of the speaker by using vivid speaker tags. You can do this by using a different word for *said* or by adding an adverb showing how the speaker spoke his or her words.

"You're finally here," **laughed** Jennifer.

"You're finally here," **whined** Jennifer.

"You're finally here," **snapped** Jennifer **impatiently**.

How many other ways can you think of to say *said*?

PRACTICE YOUR SKILLS

● Check Your Understanding
Using Quotation Marks with Direct Quotations

Contemporary Life — **Write *I* If a sentence is punctuated incorrectly.**
Write *C* if a sentence is punctuated correctly.

1. Joey told Mrs. Cash that the dog ate his homework.
2. That's the oldest excuse there is, said Mrs. Cash.
3. Mrs. Cash asked us to get out our math books.
4. "I wonder what our topic is today," said Zoe.
5. Today, Mrs. Cash said, we'll be discussing real-life math.
6. She said that we were going to discuss how to count a customer's change back to him or her.
7. Our teacher continued, We will also talk about how to determine sales tax.
8. "Mrs. Cash, Will said, most cash registers tell a clerk how much change to give a customer."
9. Mrs. Cash reminded the class that it's still important to know how to do some mental math.
10. Joey said, Even my dog can do some mental math."

● Connect to the Writing Process: Editing
Adding Quotation Marks to Direct Quotations

11.–15. Rewrite the incorrect sentences from the preceding exercise, adding quotation marks where needed. When a comma or a period follows a quotation, don't forget to place it *inside* the closing quotation marks.

Capital Letters with Direct Quotations

Begin each sentence of a direct quotation with a capital letter.

"**U**sually, bees swarm in the spring," my teacher said.

My teacher said, "**U**sually, bees swarm in the spring."

If a single-sentence quotation is interrupted by a speaker tag, use only one capital letter—at the beginning of the sentence.

"**U**sually," my teacher said, "bees swarm in the spring."

PRACTICE YOUR SKILLS

● Check Your Understanding
Using Capital Letters with Direct Quotations

Contemporary Life **Read the sentences below. Write *I* if the sentence is capitalized incorrectly. Write *C* if the sentence is capitalized correctly.**

1. "When honey bees swarm," said Mr. Johnson, "They are usually engorged with honey."

2. Maya asked, "Will they sting people then?"

3. "Yes, they might," replied the teacher, "But they are less likely to sting than at other times."

4. "Bees are not native to America," Mr. Johnson said.

5. Greg said, "in a magazine I read an article that said they were brought here from Europe."

6. "Mr. Johnson, what's the difference between a regular bee and a killer bee?" asked Maya.

7. The teacher answered, "well, they're not actually killers."

8. "The African honey bee is a more aggressive bee suited to tropical climates," He explained.

9. Greg asked, "How did they get to the United States?"

10. "They escaped," said Mr. Johnson, "From an apiary in Brazil in 1957."

● Connect to the Writing Process: Editing
Capitalizing Direct Quotations

11.–16. Rewrite each incorrect sentence from the preceding exercise, adding capital letters where needed.

Commas with Direct Quotations

When you are reading quoted material aloud, your voice naturally pauses between the speaker tag and the direct quotation. In written material these pauses are indicated by commas.

Use a comma to separate a direct quotation from a speaker tag. Place the comma inside the closing quotation marks.

"The ice cream isn't frozen yet," Jordan cautioned.

Jordan cautioned, "The ice cream isn't frozen yet."

"The ice cream," Jordan cautioned, "isn't frozen yet."

In the second and third examples above, note that the comma before the opening quotation marks is placed after the speaker tag, outside the opening quotation marks.

PRACTICE YOUR SKILLS

Check Your Understanding
Using Commas with Direct Quotations

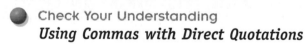 Contemporary Life **If the use of commas in the sentence is incorrect, write I. If the use of commas is correct, write C.**

1. "I love making homemade ice cream", said Jordan.
2. Lori admitted, "I've never done that before."
3. "It's not hard," said Jordan "as long as you have an ice cream maker."
4. "My grandfather has one of the old ones," said Lori, "with a crank."
5. "Ours is electric", said Jordan "but either one will do."
6. "Let's use my grandfather's ice cream maker with the crank", suggested Lori.
7. "It'll give us a good workout," said Jordan.
8. "Mix the ingredients listed on page twenty-four of that cookbook," said Jordan.

9. "Add ice and rock salt to the outside area" said Jordan, "and then turn the crank for about thirty minutes."

10. "This is the best ice cream", said Lori.

● Connect to the Writing Process: Editing
Using Commas in Direct Quotations

11.–16. Rewrite each incorrect sentence from the preceeding exercise, adding commas where needed.

End Marks with Direct Quotations

End marks come at the end of a quoted sentence, just as they do in a sentence that is not a quotation.

Place a period inside the closing quotation marks when the end of the quotation comes at the end of the sentence.

Carlos said, "This afternoon we'll hike in Grand Canyon."

"This afternoon," Carlos said, "we'll hike in Grand Canyon."

If a quotation comes at the beginning of a sentence, the period follows the speaker tag.

"This afternoon we'll hike in Grand Canyon," Carlos said.

A period comes at the end of each sentence within a quotation that has more than one sentence.

"This afternoon we'll hike in Grand Canyon," Carlos said. "Tomorrow we'll visit an archaeological dig. The next day we'll go home."

Sometimes you may want to quote a question someone has asked or a sentence someone has said with strong feeling.

Place a question mark or an exclamation point inside the closing quotation marks when it is part of the quotation.

Madison asked, "Is the canyon close or will we drive there**?**"

"Is the canyon close," Madison asked, "or will we drive there**?**"

"Is the canyon close or will we drive there**?**" Madison asked.

Dani screamed, "Watch out for that snake**!**"

"Watch out for that snake**!**" Dani screamed.

A question mark or an exclamation point is placed inside the closing quotation marks when it is part of the quotation. When either of these punctuation marks is part of the whole sentence, however, it is place *outside* the closing quotation marks.

Did I hear the guide say, "That snake is not harmful"**?**

(The whole sentence—not the quotation—is the question.)

It was the happiest moment of my life when Carlos said, "It's time for a break"**!**

(The whole sentence is exclamatory, not the quotation.)

Notice that in the preceding examples, the end marks for the quotations themselves are omitted.

Practice Your Skills

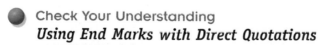

Check Your Understanding
Using End Marks with Direct Quotations

Contemporary Life
**Write *I* if the end mark in the sentence is incorrect.
Write *C* if the sentence is correct.**

1. "Hiking the Grand Canyon can be fun," said Carlos. "However, you have to be careful."

2. "Going down is much easier than coming up," exclaimed Madison!

3. Carlos said, "It's also much hotter down by the river than at the canyon rim".

4. "Bring plenty of water," warned the guide. "It's also important to wear proper shoes or hiking boots."

5. Did you hear that ranger say, "Some trails are closed?"

6. "Maybe we should stop every fifteen minutes" suggested Tim. "We could go back to the top if one of us is too tired."

7. The guide shouted, "Don't get too close to the edge!"

8. From a few feet down the path, our friends shouted, "Wait until you see this!".

9. I was very excited when the guide said, "There is an Indian Reservation in the canyon"!

10. "Can we make it all the way to the river today," asked Madison?

● Connect to the Writing Process: Editing
Punctuating Direct Quotations

11.–16. Rewrite each incorrect sentence from the preceding exercise, placing the end punctuation properly.

Communicate Your Ideas

APPLY TO WRITING

Editorial: *Quotations*

What is love? Why do people fall in love? Nikki Giovanni once said, "We love because it's the only true adventure." Also on the subject of love, Frances Ellen Watkins Harper said, "Intense love is often akin to suffering."

Collect two quotations about love from two people you know. Then using all four quotations, the preceding two and the two you collect, write an editorial about the meaning of love. Your local paper wants to run a special Valentine's section with your article featured in it. After you write your article, read it to correct any errors. Don't forget to punctuate the quotations properly.

 QuickCheck Mixed Practice

General Interest **Write each sentence, adding capital letters, quotation marks, and other punctuation marks where needed.**

1. a cat has absolute honesty Ernest Hemingway noted

2. someone once said it's nice for children to have pets— until the pets start having children

3. if things went by merit Mark Twain announced you would stay out and your dog would go in

4. young gorillas are friendly Will Cuppy said

5. Samuel Butler said the hen is an egg's way of producing another egg

6. if ants ever take over the world he mused I hope they remember that I invited them to all my picnics

7. all animals are equal said George Orwell but some are more equal than others

8. money will buy a pretty good dog commented Josh Billings but it won't buy the wag of its tail

9. what modest claim do kittens make David Irvine asked they claim the ownership of humans

10. animals are such agreeable friends George Eliot stated they ask no questions and pass no criticisms

11. it amuses me to talk to animals George Bernard Shaw said

12. He added the intellectual content of our conversations may to some extent escape them

13. can one love animals or children too much Jean-Paul Sartre once asked

14. a cat can be trusted to purr when she is pleased said William Inge which is more than can be said for humans

15. it is odd Frederick Goodyear once said that few animals are more unsteady on their feet than centipedes

16. William Lyon Phelps asked what is a dog's ideal in a life That's easy. it is a life of active uselessness.

17. of this I am sure someone once said that nothing is sure

18. Emily Dickinson said my ideal cat always has a huge rat in its mouth

19. The caribou seem to have no idea whatever of personal comfort William Parker Greenough noted

20. to me someone once said the noblest of dogs is the hot dog it feeds that hand that bites it

⊙ Other Uses of Quotation Marks

Once you know how to punctuate a direct quotation correctly, you will be able to apply what you know to the following situations.

Dialogue

Dialogue means "a conversation between two or more persons." In writing, dialogue is treated in a special way so that a reader always knows who is speaking, even if there are no speaker tags such as "he said" or "she asked."

When writing dialogue, begin a new paragraph each time the speaker changes.

In the following excerpt from *Oliver Twist* by Charles Dickens, each sentence follows the rules that you have just studied for direct quotations. Notice, however, that a new paragraph begins each time the housekeeper or Oliver speaks. They are discussing a painting of a beautiful woman that has been taken from the wall.

> "Ah!" said the housekeeper, watching the direction of Oliver's eyes. "It is gone, you see."
>
> "I see it is, ma'am," replied Oliver. "Why have they taken it away?"
>
> "It has been taken down, child, because Mr. Brownlow said, that as it seemed to worry you, perhaps it might prevent your getting well, you know," rejoined the old lady.
>
> "Oh, no, indeed. It didn't worry me, ma'am," said Oliver. "I liked to see it. I quite loved it."
>
> —*Charles Dickens,* Oliver Twist

CONNECT TO WRITER'S CRAFT

One writer who chooses not to add the conventional punctuation to his dialogue is Cormac McCarthy. While he does begin a new paragraph when the speaker changes, McCarthy provides readers with no quotation marks, so dialogue blends with the speaker tags and the narrative uninterrupted. McCarthy eliminates some apostrophes, as well. The following excerpt is a conversation between two characters.

> She pushed the tray forward between them. Please, she said. Help yourself.
>
> I better not. I'll have crazy dreams eatin this late.
>
> She smiled. She unfolded a small linen napkin from off the tray.
>
> I've always had strange dreams. But I'm afraid they are quite independent of my dining habits.
>
> Yes mam.
>
> —*Cormac McCarthy,* All the Pretty Horses

Long Passages

When you write a report and want to support a point, you may want to quote more than one paragraph from a book. If this is the case, you use quotation marks in a slightly different manner.

> When quoting a passage of more than one paragraph, place quotation marks at the beginning of each paragraph—but at the end of only the last paragraph.

Closing quotation marks are omitted at the end of each paragraph, except the last one, to indicate to a reader that the quotation is continuing.

"Charles Dickens wrote some of the most popular books of the nineteenth century. He was one artist who enjoyed as much fame during his lifetime as after his death.

(no closing quotation marks)

"The characters created by Dickens still resonate with modern readers of all ages. From the rags-to-riches-to-rags Pip of *Great Expectations* to the tragic Sydney Carton of *A Tale of Two Cities,* Dickens wrote remarkable accounts of the human condition.

(no closing quotation marks)

"Known after his first novel *The Pickwick Papers* as a writer of humor, Dickens turned to the darker side of orphanages and the Victorian workhouse in *Oliver Twist,* his second book. Through Oliver's eyes, readers experience the ugliness of poverty and the cruelty of adults to children."

(closing quotation marks)

Another way to quote a long passage is to set it off from the rest of the text by indenting both left and right margins. If you are using a computer, you also could set the passage in a smaller type size. When you use this method of quoting a long passage, no quotation marks are needed.

Italics and Quotation Marks

Quotations Within Quotations

A quotation within a quotation follows all the rules covered previously in this chapter. However, to avoid confusion, use single quotation marks to make a distinction between the two quotations.

> To distinguish a quotation within a quotation, use single quotation marks to enclose the inside quotation.

> "Is the song 'Food, Glorious Food' from the musical *Oliver!* by Lionel Bart?" Li asked.
>
> Mr. Sanders said, "The most famous of Oliver Twist's lines in Dickens's book and Bart's musical is 'Please, Sir, I want some more.'"

Notice in the second example above that the closing single quotation mark and the closing double quotation marks come together.

PRACTICE YOUR SKILLS

Check Your Understanding
Using Quotation Marks Correctly

Literature Topic

Write *I* if the quotation marks in a sentence are used incorrectly. Write *C* if the quotation marks in a sentence are used correctly.

1. Mr. Sanders explained, "Charles Dickens's works have now become a part of our everyday language."

2. He continued, "Few educated people do not recognize these opening lines from *A Tale of Two Cities*. It was the best of times; it was the worst of times."

3. "Mr. Sanders," Li interrupted, "who is your favorite character from *Great Expectations?*"

4. "That's hard to say," answered Mr. Sanders, "but I do love the blacksmith Joe."

5. "I like it when he calls Miss Haversham Miss A," laughed Steve.

6. Cindi said, "I love it when Sydney Carton says, It is a far, far better thing I do than I have ever done."

7. "Yes, that's the beginning of the last sentence in *A Tale of Two Cities*," said Mr. Sanders.

8. "Why does Mr. Grimwig keep saying I'll eat my head in *Oliver Twist*?" asked Cindi.

9. Li said, "I think that's his way of saying, I'll do anything to prove I'm right."

10. Mr. Sanders finished the discussion by saying, "Yes, Dickens liked his eccentric characters!"

● Connect to the Writing Process: Editing
Using Quotation Marks

11.–15. Rewrite each incorrect sentence from the preceding exercise, correcting the use of single and double quotation marks.

Communicate Your Ideas

APPLY TO WRITING

Short Story: *Dialogue*

Think about the word *trunk*. Then write freely for several minutes, jotting down anything your mind associates with that word. When you are finished, choose one of the ideas as the basis for a short story. (Limit your characters to two or three.)

Write the first draft of your short story in which a trunk has some part. Be sure to include dialogue between the main characters of your story. As you edit, correct any punctuation errors in the dialogue. Make a final copy and read your story to a classmate.

Contemporary Life

Rewrite each sentence, adding quotation marks, end punctuation, capital letters, commas, and underlining where needed.

1. Where asked Leesha did you find that book of short stories

2. I got it at the library said Sarah I don't own a copy of it

3. The cover says true stories for dog lovers said Leesha

4. Yes, but the title said Sarah is James Herriot's Dog Stories

5. Who said dogs are a man's best friend

6. My favorite chapter in the book is Shep's Hobby said Leesha

7. What other books do you like asked Grant I'm looking for some good poetry

8. I don't know about Sarah said Leesha I like the book Modern and Contemporary Afro-American Poetry

9. There are many poems by Langston Hughes in that book stated Sarah

10. My two favorite poems said Leesha are Mother to Son and The Weary Blues

11. Did you see asked Grant the article about Langston Hughes in Newsweek?

12. No said Sarah was it interesting

13. Yes, it was answered Grant the writer discussed Hughes's book of verse called Shakespeare in Harlem

14. When was that published inquired Leesha

15. In 1942 said Grant five years before his book Fields of Wonder

Punctuating Quotations Correctly

Write each sentence, adding capital letters, quotations marks, and other punctuation marks where needed.

1. Abigail Adams once wrote to her husband we have many high sounding words, and too few actions that correspond to them

2. trees are swayed by winds, but men are swayed by words wrote the author Joan Aiken

3. she went on to say words are like spices too many is worse than too few

4. in the book Little Women, the character Jo said I like good strong words that mean something

5. look was Pa's favorite word it meant admire, wonder, goggle at the beauty and excitement all around us said Lucy in the book The Ballad of Lucy Whipple

6. Scrooge said bah! humbug! in Charles Dickens's A Christmas Carol

7. words can destroy said Jeane Kirkpatrick what we call each other ultimately becomes what we think of each other, and it matters

8. the ballpoint pen said Noah in the book The View from Saturday has been the biggest single factor in the decline of Western Civilization it makes the written word cheap, fast, and totally without character

9. the famous artist Georgia O'Keeffe once said I found I could say with color and shapes what I couldn't say in any other way

10. polite words open iron gates says a Serbo-Croatian proverb

Punctuating Quotations Correctly

Write each sentence, adding underlining, capital letters, quotation marks, and other punctuation marks where needed.

1. where asked Ina did you find those incredible, fluorescent earrings?
2. A hairstylist's sign on Bradbury St. read we curl up and dye for you.
3. I just read Oliver Twist, Jan said it was better than any movie version I have ever seen.
4. News Ben Bradlee once said is the first rough draft of history.
5. Have you ever read the Christian Science Monitor Dan asked.
6. Cathleen asked is the ocean rough today
7. Ken declared I'm going to be the new class president
8. Please don't break us apart the sign over the bananas read
9. Arlene remarked we grew up together
10. That was an incredible pass exclaimed Dave
11. Work is the best escape from boredom Eleanor Dean once said
12. Who said little things affect little minds
13. Defeat is not the worst of failures said G. E. Woodberry not to have tried is the true failure
14. We saw a production of the Shakespearean play As You Like It at the Lyric State Cheryl announced
15. Life shrinks or expands in proportion to one's courage Anaïs Nin commented

Writing Sentences

Follow the directions below.

1. Write a dialogue between you and a fictional person: a superhero, a character in a book, a cartoon character, or someone created in your imagination. Punctuate the dialogue correctly.
2. After an introductory paragraph, quote a long passage.

Language and *Self-Expression*

"It's just the architect's model, but I'm very excited."

Leo Cullum creates cartoons for periodicals such as the *New Yorker* and the *Harvard Business Review.* When he is not drawing, he works as a pilot for a commercial airline.

This cartoon is particularly funny because the cartoonist places dogs in a human situation. Many people think of their pets as nearly human and have conversations with them, making them a part of the family. Imagine what dogs think of their owners, though. Create a dialogue that two dogs might have if they could talk. What do they think of a particular aspect of their owners' behavior?

Prewriting Freewrite a description of the dogs, their humans, and the behavior that the dogs are commenting on. Include as many details as you can imagine.

Drafting Use your freewriting details to write a first draft of your dialogue. Try to picture the humans' behavior from the dogs' point of view. Include details the dogs might find bewildering or comical.

Revising Read your dialogue aloud with a partner. Ask your partner to comment on your interpretation of the dogs' eye view of life with humans. Make any changes necessary to sharpen your dialogue and make it more amusing.

Editing Check your dialogue to be sure you have used quotation marks, punctuation, and capitalization correctly. Ensure that when each new speaker talks, you begin a new paragraph.

Publishing With your partner, read your dialogue aloud to the class. Encourage listeners to comment on your version of the dogs' dialogue.

Another Look

Italics (Underlining)

Italicize (underline) letters, numbers, and words when they are used to represent themselves. Also italicize (underline) foreign words that are not generally used in English. *(pages L543–L544)*

Italicize (underline) the titles of long written or musical works that are published as a single unit. Also italicize (underline) titles of paintings and sculptures and the names of vehicles. *(pages L544–L545)*

Quotation Marks

Use quotation marks to enclose the titles of chapters, articles, stories, one-act plays, short poems, and songs. *(page L548)*

Use quotation marks to enclose a person's exact words. *(pages L551–L552)*

Begin each sentence of a direct quotation with a capital letter. *(pages L553–L554)*

Use a comma to separate a direct quotation from a speaker tag. Place the comma inside the closing quotation marks. *(page L555)*

Place a period inside the closing quotation marks when the end of the quotation comes at the end of the sentence. If a quotation comes at the beginning of a sentence, the period follows the speaker tag. A period comes at the end of each sentence within a quotation that has more than one sentence. *(page L556)*

Place a question mark or exclamation point inside the closing quotation marks when it is part of the quotation. *(pages L556–L557)*

Other Uses of Quotation Marks

When writing dialogue, begin a new paragraph each time the speaker changes. *(pages L560–L561)*

When quoting a passage of more than one paragraph, place quotation marks at the beginning of each paragraph—but at the end of only the last paragraph. *(page L562)*

To distinguish a quotation within a quotation, use single quotation marks to enclose the inside quotation. *(page L563)*

Directions

Read the passage and write the letter of the answer that correctly punctuates each underlined part. If the underlined part contains no error, mark *D*.

EXAMPLE   Kayla got a part in the television series

<u>A Day in the Life</u>
(1)

   1 A "A Day in the Life"

      B *A Day in the Life.*

      C "A Day in the Life."

      D No error

ANSWER   **1 B**

The show got a favorable review in our <u>newspaper, the Enquirer.</u>
(1)

In the first show, Kayla's only line was, <u>"Coming, Mother"!</u>
(2)

Kayla was also interviewed in our newspaper.

<u>"How," the reporter asked, "did you get this part"?</u>
(3)

Kayla answered, <u>"In my tryout, I read from the poem The Lake</u>
(4)

<u>Isle of Innisfree.</u> The director told me that his favorite poet is

Yeats!"

"Really, it was just luck, then," the reporter said.

"Oh, no," Kayla protested, <u>"he really liked my work."</u>
(5)

1
  A newspaper, the "Enquirer."
  B newspaper, the *Enquirer.*
  C newspaper, the "Enquirer."
  D No error

2
  A "Coming, Mother!"
  B "Coming, *Mother*"!
  C *"Coming, Mother"*
  D No error

3
  A "How," the reporter asked, "did you get this part?"
  B "How?" the reporter asked, "did you get this part?"
  C "How," the reporter asked? "did you get this part?"
  D No error

4
  A "In my tryout, I read from the poem "The Lake Isle of Innisfree."
  B "In my tryout, I read from the poem *The Lake Isle of Innisfree.*
  C "In my tryout, I read from the poem 'The Lake Isle of Innisfree.'
  D No error

5
  A "He really liked my work."
  B he really liked my work."
  C He really liked my work."
  D No error

CHAPTER 17

Other Punctuation

• •

Directions
Write the letter of the answer that correctly punctuates the underlined part in each sentence. If the underlined part contains no error, write *D*.

EXAMPLE   **1**   I was in charge of a group of <u>third grade kids</u> at a summer camp.

        1 **A** third grade kids'
            B third-grade kids
            C third-grade kids'
            D No error

ANSWER   **1**   **B**

1. This summer was the <u>camps first year</u>.
2. The counselors were all <u>nervous many of us</u> had never worked with kids before.
3. Our day began at <u>930 A.M.</u>
4. The <u>kids at least most of them</u> were eager to play.
5. In my group one girl was incredibly <u>self assured</u>.
6. She organized groups for <u>games helped me</u> hand out lunches, snacks, and drinks; and soothed nervous kids.
7. She was the <u>camp directors niece</u>, so I shouldn't have been surprised at her maturity.
8. <u>I couldnt have</u> done my job without Anna's help.
9. I like to think that it was <u>Annas and my work</u> that made the third-grade group do so well.
10. The <u>Matthews family</u> were new to the area and had seven children in the camp.

1. **A** camp's first year
   B camps' first year
   C camp's first-year
   D No error

2. **A** nervous; many of us
   B nervous: many of us
   C nervous (many of us)
   D No error

3. **A** 9:30 (AM).
   B 93:0 A.M.
   C 9:30 A.M.
   D No error

4. **A** kids—at least most of them—
   B kids—at least most of them
   C kids: at least most of them
   D No error

5. **A** self; assured
   B self-assured
   C selfassured
   D No error

6. **A** games; helped me
   B games: helped me
   C games—helped me
   D No error

7. **A** camp directors—niece
   B camp directors-niece
   C camp director's niece
   D No error

8. **A** I couldn't have
   B I could'nt have
   C I couldnt' have
   D No error

9. **A** Annas, and my work
   B Annas' and my work
   C Anna's and my work
   D No error

10. **A** Matthews family,
    B Matthew's family
    C Matthews' family
    D No error

Honoré Daumier. *The Third-Class Carriage,* ca. 1863.
Oil on canvas, 25¾ by 35½ inches. The Metropolitan Museum of Art.

Describe   In this painting the artist Honoré Daumier gives us a glimpse into a railway compartment of the 1860s. What does this scene show? What are the people in the carriage doing? Describe their facial expressions.

Analyze   What do you think the title of the painting means?

Interpret   What message do you think the artist is trying to convey in the painting? How might a writer convey the same message?

Judge   How would you feel if you were a passenger on this train? Explain.

At the end of this chapter, you will use the artwork to stimulate ideas for writing.

Apostrophes

The most costly punctuation error of all time occurred in 1962. A hyphen was omitted from a set of directions sent to the rocket powering the *Venus* space probe. As a result of the omission, the rocket self-destructed. Most errors that are made in punctuation do not have such disastrous results. Nevertheless, correct punctuation is necessary for clear communication—right here on Earth.

Omitting a tiny apostrophe, for example, can make a big difference in a sentence. In fact, including apostrophes in certain words is as important as spelling those words correctly. Without an apostrophe, the first sentence in the following examples does not make any sense. With an apostrophe, however, the meaning of the sentence instantly becomes clear.

Well go with you to the game tonight.

We'll go with you to the game tonight.

In addition to being used in contractions, apostrophes are commonly used with nouns and some pronouns to show ownership or relationship.

Apostrophes to Show Possession

One of the most common uses of an apostrophe is to show that someone or something owns something else.

Lani's softball = the softball of Lani

a woman's house = the house of a woman

the Spensers' garage = the garage of the Spensers

As you can see from these examples, nouns have a special form to show possession. An apostrophe or an apostrophe and an *s* are added to the noun.

Possessive Forms of Singular Nouns

To form the possessive of a noun, first decide whether the noun is singular or plural.

Add 's to form the possessive of a singular noun.

Remember that you do not need to add or omit a letter. Just write the word and put 's at the end.

baby + 's = baby's   Give me the baby**'s** blanket.
Joey + 's = Joey's   That is Joey**'s** little sister.
boss + 's = boss's   Joey is my boss**'s** best worker.

The 's is added to the last word of compound words and the names of most businesses and organizations.

The passerby**'s** gaze fell on the cute child.
The baby broke the jack-in-the box**'s** spring.
The YMCA**'s** advertisements appeal to young families.

CONNECT TO SPEAKING AND WRITING

Occasionally a singular noun will end in *s*. When the noun—especially a name—is two or three syllables long, it may be awkward to pronounce with *'s*. In such cases, add only an apostrophe.

The **Prentiss's** house is on the corner.

The **Prentiss'** house is on the corner.

PRACTICE YOUR SKILLS

● Check Your Understanding
Forming Possessive Singular Nouns

Write the possessive form of each noun.

1. apple   **3.** starfish   **5.** cat

2. Pep Club   **4.** Georgia   **6.** mother-in-law

7.	brother	10.	Bess	13.	Hope College
8.	Mike	11.	girl	14.	maid-of-honor
9.	sailor	12.	Reese Company	15.	Mr. Rogers

● Connect to the Writing Process: Drafting
Writing Sentences

16.–20. Use five of the singular possessive nouns from the preceding exercise in sentences of your own.

Possessive Forms of Plural Nouns

There are two rules to follow to form the possessive of plural nouns.

Add only an apostrophe to form the possessive of a plural noun that ends in *s.*

Add *'s* to form the possessive of a plural noun that does not end in *s.*

Deciding which rule to follow is simple if you take two steps. First, write the plural of the noun. Second, look at the ending of the word. If the word ends in *s,* add only an apostrophe. If it does not end in *s,* add an apostrophe and an *s.*

POSSESSIVE FORMS OF PLURAL NOUNS			
PLURAL	**ENDING**	**ADD**	**POSSESSIVE**
babies	s	' =	babies'
foxes	s	' =	foxes'
mice	no *s*	's =	mice's
children	no *s*	's =	children's
sheep	no *s*	's =	sheep's

PRACTICE YOUR SKILLS

● Check Your Understanding
Forming Possessive Plural Nouns

Write the plural form of each noun. Then make it possessive.

1. friend	**6.** wolf	**11.** book	**16.** man
2. box	**7.** tomato	**12.** goose	**17.** Smith
3. house	**8.** girl	**13.** store	**18.** woman
4. deer	**9.** Lutz	**14.** cloud	**19.** paper
5. boy	**10.** city	**15.** album	**20.** Ryan

● Check Your Understanding
Forming Possessive Nouns

Contemporary Life **Write the possessive form, singular or plural, of each underlined word.**

21. We went to the hospital to see my <u>sister-in-law</u> new baby.

22. My <u>brother</u> first child is a girl.

23. My <u>parents</u> excitement was obvious as they gazed at their first grandchild.

24. The <u>hospital</u> policy allowed the newborn to sleep in her <u>mother</u> room.

25. The <u>infant</u> cries were certainly loud for such a small baby.

26. I helped my sister-in-law write comments in the baby <u>book</u> pages.

27. Several <u>nurses</u> comments were complimentary.

28. My new <u>niece</u> name is Sabrina.

29. <u>Sabrina</u> crib was surrounded by flowers.

30. My brother had balanced a teddy bear on the <u>crib</u> edge.

● Connect to the Writing Process: Editing
Using Possessive Nouns

If the underlined possessive form is incorrect, write it correctly. If the possessive form is correct as is, write C.

31. Many people were astonished by <u>scientists'</u> discoveries in the twentieth century.

32. In 1903, the Wright brother's accomplishment led to an explosion of transportation possibilities.

33. Alternative energy sources had to be developed to satisfy peoples' need for electrical power.

34. In 1900, most Americans' homes did not have electricity.

35. By the year 2000, very few places in the United States were without electricitys' effects.

36. Marconi's invention of the radio revolutionized mass communication.

37. The telephone's development throughout the century was truly remarkable.

38. The Soviet Union's achievement in launching the first manned satellite into space challenged the U.S. space program.

39. America's success in sending the first humans to the moon sparked the nation's imagination.

40. The future promises more evidence of sciences' advancements.

Possessive Forms of Pronouns

Unlike nouns, personal pronouns do not use an apostrophe to show possession. Instead, they change form: *my, mine, your, yours, his, her, hers, its, our, ours, their,* and *theirs.*

Do not add an apostrophe to form the possessive of a personal pronoun.

The camera is **hers.**

The dog wagged **its** tail for the photographer.

Indefinite pronouns, however, form the possessive the same way singular nouns do—by adding *'s.*

Add 's to form the possessive of an indefinite pronoun.

> This seems to be everyone's favorite photo.
> Someone's film cartridge was left under the seat.

You can find a list of common indefinite pronouns on page L54.

PRACTICE YOUR SKILLS

● Check Your Understanding
Using the Possessive of Pronouns

Contemporary Life **Write the correct form of the pronoun in parentheses.**

1. Are these photographs (yours, your's)?

2. (Anyone's, Anyones') photos may be entered in the contest.

3. The album is beautiful with (its, it's) photos of the Rocky Mountains.

4. They looked at my portfolio, but Heather hasn't submitted (hers, her's) yet.

5. (No one's, No ones') photographs were chosen for the prize.

6. I hope (everybody's, everybodys') photos are published.

7. Those cameras are (ours, our's).

8. Has (everyones, everyone's) film been developed?

9. It was (nobody's, nobodys') fault that the film was ruined.

10. The best photographs are (their's, theirs).

● Connect to the Writing Process: Revising
Using Possessive Pronouns

Rewrite the following sentences, using possessive personal or indefinite pronouns.

11. Does that photograph album belong to him?

12. The cover of it has gold lettering.

13. The snapshots of everyone are in that box.

14. The puppy belongs to her.

15. Did the entry of anyone make it to the finals?

Apostrophes to Show Joint and Separate Ownership

Sometimes it is necessary to show that something belongs to more than one person.

> **To show joint ownership, make only the last word possessive in form.**
>
> > These are Nan and Faron**'s** compact discs.
> >
> > (The compact discs belong to both Nan and Faron.)

The only exception to this rule occurs when one word showing joint ownership is a possessive pronoun. In such cases the noun must also show possession.

> > This is Hannah**'s** and **my** stereo.

Separate ownership is shown in a different way from joint ownership.

> **To show separate ownership, make each word possessive in form.**
>
> > These are Nan**'s** and Faron**'s** compact discs.
> >
> > (Each girl has her own compact discs.)

Apostrophes with Nouns Expressing Time or Amount

When you use a noun that expresses time or amount as an adjective, write it in the possessive form.

> **Use an apostrophe with the possessive form of a noun that expresses time or amount.**

That compact disc player cost Nan two week**s'** salary.
Nan really got her money**'s** worth.

Other words that express time include such words as *minute, hour,*
day, month, and *year.* Other words that express amount include
such words as *dollar, quarter, dime, nickel,* and *penny.*

PRACTICE YOUR SKILLS

 Check Your Understanding
Using Apostrophes Correctly

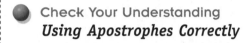 **Add an apostrophe and *s,* if needed, to each**
underlined word to make it possessive. If the word
is correct as is, write C.

1. The <u>woman</u> and man's voices on that compact disc
   sound great together.

2. The woman on the recording was <u>Nan</u> and my music
   teacher.

3. I picked up two more compact discs for <u>Jason</u> and Dad's
   birthdays.

4. <u>Dawn</u> and Tiffany's song was recorded by a professional
   group.

5. My family spent a <u>week</u> vacation watching them
   record in the studio.

6. The band we watched earns a <u>month</u> rent in one night
   at a concert.

7. The crew brought in the <u>guitarist</u> and the drummer's
   instruments.

8. <u>Nan</u> and my excitement was very high!

9. My <u>father</u> and brother's opinions of the band were very
   different.

10. Watching the recording session increased <u>Faron</u> and my
    interest in becoming singers.

Write the possessive forms that are used incorrectly in the following sentences. Then write the correct possessive forms. If a sentence does not contain any errors in the use of possessives, write C.

11. My uncles ranch is a days drive from the town of Rock Springs.

12. On almost all ranches, there are many workers.

13. During our visit my brothers and I stayed in the workers bunkhouse.

14. Everyone's is coming to my uncles' ranch for a big dance tonight.

15. Dad's and Mom's suggestions for party decorations were immediately accepted.

16. Have you seen Uncle Ryan's new hat?

17. My efforts at learning to square dance were finally rewarded.

18. Her's were not.

19. I spent a months allowance on a new pair of beautiful red boots.

20. The times we have at Uncle Ryan's ranch are always the best.

● **Connect to the Writing Process: Drafting**
Writing Sentences

Write sentences using the following possessives correctly.

21. any possessive personal pronoun

22. any possessive indefinite pronoun

23. two proper nouns showing joint ownership

24. two proper nouns showing separate ownership

25. a proper noun and a personal pronoun showing joint ownership

APPLY TO WRITING

Dialogue: *Possessive Nouns and Pronouns*

Horace Pippin. *Domino Players,* 1943.
Oil on composition board, 12¾ by 22 inches. ©The Phillips Collection, Washington, D.C.

Imagine that you are listening to the conversation taking place around this domino table. What is the topic? What are they saying? Write a brief dialogue using the subjects in this painting as the speakers. In your dialogue use at least three possessive nouns and three possessive pronouns. Underline the nouns and pronouns you used.

 QuickCheck Mixed Practice

General Interest **Write the following paragraph, correcting any errors in the use of possessives.**

One of the most popular childrens books of all times is L. Frank Baum *The Wonderful Wizard of Oz,* published in 1900.

While many people have read the book, most are more familiar with Metro-Goldwyn Mayer 1939 movie version, *The Wizard of Oz*.

Both the book and the movie feature Dorothy Gayle and friends of her—the Scarecrow, the Tin Woodsman, and the Cowardly Lion. Everybody favorite little dog Toto is also in both versions. The makers of the movie were true to Baum book in many other ways.

One major change in the movie version is the color of Dorothy shoes. In the movie they are ruby red. In the book they are silver. Technicolor was new to Hollywoods studios in 1939. While silver didn't show up well on the big screen, red looked dazzling. The filmmakers decision changed forever how many people would remember Baum work.

Other Uses of Apostrophes

Apostrophes have other uses besides showing the possessive of nouns and some pronouns.

Apostrophes with Contractions

A contraction is a shortcut. It usually combines two words into one. An apostrophe is added to take the place of one or more missing letters.

Use an apostrophe in a contraction to show where one or more letters have been omitted.

These examples show how some contractions are formed.

CONTRACTIONS	
do n̶o̶t̶ = don't	there i̶s̶ = there's
we a̶r̶e̶ = we're	who i̶s̶ = who's
of t̶h̶e̶ clock = o'clock	let u̶s̶ = let's

In most contractions, no letters are added or changed around. There is one common exception: *will + not = won't.*

Do not confuse the contractions *it's, you're, they're, there's,* and *who's* with the possessive pronouns *its, your, their, theirs,* and *whose.*

PRACTICE YOUR SKILLS

Check Your Understanding
Using Apostrophes with Contractions

Write the contraction for each pair of words.

1. are not	**6.** do not	**11.** we will	**16.** were not
2. will not	**7.** is not	**12.** that is	**17.** they are
3. did not	**8.** let us	**13.** I would	**18.** there is
4. has not	**9.** I have	**14.** does not	**19.** I am
5. you are	**10.** we have	**15.** have not	**20.** who is

Check Your Understanding
Distinguishing Between Contractions and Possessive Pronouns

Contemporary Life **Write the correct word in parentheses to complete each sentence.**

21. If (were, we're) going to breakfast, (its, it's) now or never.

22. Please tell the server how you would like (your, you're) eggs.

23. I don't know if (their, they're) joining us or not.

24. If (theirs, there's) anything you need, let the server know.

25. (Whose, Who's) going to pay for this meal?

26. Do you know if (your, you're) going to order pancakes?

27. This bill must be (theirs, there's).

28. (Whose, Who's) orange juice is this?

29. (Its, It's) mine.

30. Did you speak to (their, they're) server?

Apostrophes with Certain Plurals

To prevent confusion, certain items form their plurals by adding 's.

Add 's to form the plural of lowercase letters, some capital letters, and some words that are used as words.

> Sue's *i*'**s** and *e*'**s** look similar.
> Jon's report card has two *A*'**s**.

The plurals of most other letters, symbols, numerals, and other words used as words can be formed by adding *s*.

> My little sister writes *3***s** for *E***s**.
> Why did you put two *!***s** after that sentence?
> This composition has too many *and***s**.

Notice the number *3*, the letter *E*, the exclamation point, and the word *and* are italicized. However, the *s* or the apostrophe and *s* with them are *not* italicized.

Some writers prefer to add 's, instead of just s, to form the plural of all letters, symbols, numerals, and words used as words.

Apostrophes with Certain Dates

An apostrophe is also used when numbers are dropped from a date.

Use an apostrophe to show that numbers were omitted in a date.

We moved here in '01. (2001)
My grandfather joined the army in '41. (1941)

PRACTICE YOUR SKILLS

● Check Your Understanding
Using Apostrophes

Contemporary Life | **If a sentence is missing one or more apostrophes, write *I* for incorrect. If a sentence is correct, write *C*.**

1. Have you ever tried to read documents from early America?

2. Many times the *ss* look like *f*s.

3. The numbers can also be hard to read.

4. The *1*s, *9*s, and *6*s all look different than ours today.

5. When the years are written without the first digits, such as *04* or *76,* it's hard to know in what year the document was produced.

6. Take a look at an original draft of the Declaration of Independence.

7. Some of Jefferson's letters look very strange to our modern eyes.

8. His cursive *t*s and *r*s are formed differently than ours.

9. If you look at an earlier document like the Magna Carta, which was written in 1215, you can recognize some letters, such as *a*s, *n*s, and *c*s.

10. However, it's difficult for modern Americans to read the original Magna Carta because it's written in Latin!

● Connect to the Writing Process: Editing
Correcting Possessive Forms

11.–14. Rewrite the incorrect sentences from the preceding exercise, adding apostrophes where needed.

APPLY TO WRITING

Friendly Letter: *Apostrophes*

A young child you know is having difficulty learning to write his or her letters and numbers. Can you remember the challenges you faced when you learned to write? Write a short letter to this child encouraging him or her to keep trying. Share your experiences learning to write. What letters and numbers did you have difficulty with? As you write, use as least two plural letters, two plural numbers, and two contractions. Be sure to punctuate them properly.

QuickCheck Mixed Practice

Science Topic **Write correctly the words that need an apostrophe.**

Has a moth ever turned one of your favorite sweaters into a tasty meal for itself? If so, you might be able to prevent future feasts by knowing the difference between a moth and a butterfly. Listen carefully. Recognizing the difference wont be easy. First, look at the insects feelers. If theyre thin, they belong to a butterfly. A moths feelers are usually broad and feathery. Next, observe the insect in question when its resting. Butterflies wings are folded in an upright position, with the wings undersides facing toward you. A moth sits holding its wings horizontally, with only the upper sides of the wings showing. If this information doesnt help, youd better buy a summers supply of mothballs!

Semicolons

Independent clauses in a compound sentence can be joined by a conjunction and a comma.

> Josh's favorite animal is the tiger, **but** mine is the bear.

The clauses in a compound sentence can also be joined by a semicolon.

> Josh's favorite animal is the tiger; mine is the bear.

Use a semicolon between the clauses of a compound sentence that are not joined by a conjunction.

Use a semicolon only if the clauses are closely related.

INCORRECT	Eagles usually nest in pairs; wolves hunt for prey.
CORRECT	Eagles usually nest in pairs; wolves travel in packs.

You can find out more about independent clauses on pages L221–L222.

Semicolons with Conjunctive Adverbs and Transitional Words and Phrases

The following list contains conjunctive adverbs and transitional words and phrases that, with a semicolon, can be used to combine the clauses of a compound sentence.

COMMON CONJUNCTIVE ADVERBS		
accordingly	besides	finally
also	consequently	furthermore

hence	nevertheless	still
however	otherwise	therefore
instead	similarly	thus

COMMON TRANSITIONAL WORDS		
as a result	in addition	in other words
for example	in fact	on the other hand

Use a semicolon between clauses in a compound sentence that are joined by certain conjunctive adverbs or transitional words.

Notice in the following examples that the conjunctive adverb *nevertheless* and the transitional words *as a result* are preceded by a semicolon and followed by a comma.

Giraffes are not hunters**; nevertheless,** they manage to get plenty of food.

Giraffes can close their nostrils**; thus,** they can keep out sand and dust.

Their necks are very long**; as a result,** they can reach the leaves of very tall trees.

Some of the conjunctive adverbs and transitional words listed in the preceding boxes can also be used as parenthetical expressions within a single clause.

JOINING CLAUSES — The hippopotamus is related to the hog**; however,** it looks very different.

WITHIN A CLAUSE — The hippopotamus, **however,** has a huge mouth.

You can learn more about parenthetical expressions on pages L523–L524.

PRACTICE YOUR SKILLS

● Check Your Understanding
Using Semicolons with Compound Sentences

General Interest | **Write *a* or *b* to indicate the letter of the correctly punctuated sentence in each of the following pairs.**

1. **a.** An ailurophile loves cats, an ailurophobe dislikes cats.
   b. An ailurophile loves cats; an ailurophobe dislikes cats.

2. **a.** Elephants are found in both Africa and Asia, however, the two species differ in some ways.
   b. Elephants are found in both Africa and Asia; however, the two species differ in some ways.

3. **a.** African bull elephants, for example, may weigh six to eight tons.
   b. African bull elephants; for example, may weigh six to eight tons.

4. **a.** A male kangaroo is called a boomer, a female kangaroo is called a flyer.
   b. A male kangaroo is called a boomer; a female kangaroo is called a flyer.

5. **a.** The emu is an unusual species of bird; for example, it is the male that cares for the young.
   b. The emu is an unusual species of bird, for example, it is the male that cares for the young.

6. **a.** Parrots are a large family of birds; and different species of parrots include the parakeet and the cockatiel.
   b. Parrots are a large family of birds, and different species of parrots include the parakeet and the cockatiel.

7. **a.** A polecat is not a cat at all; the term actually designates a skunk.
   b. A polecat is not a cat at all, the term actually designates a skunk.

8. **a.** The ostrich is unable to fly, therefore, it runs at great speeds to escape predators.
   b. The ostrich is unable to fly; therefore, it runs at great speeds to escape predators.

9. **a.** A crocodile cannot move its tongue; it is rooted to the base of its mouth.

   b. A crocodile cannot move its tongue, it is rooted to the base of its mouth.

10. **a.** The giant panda of western China resembles a bear; however, it is more closely related to the raccoon.

   b. The giant panda of western China resembles a bear, however, it is more closely related to the raccoon.

● Check Your Understanding
Using Semicolons and Commas with Compound Sentences

Science Topic **Write _C_ if a sentence is punctuated correctly. Write _I_ if a sentence is punctuated incorrectly.**

11. Many plants are good for humans and animals, and some have no effect at all.

12. Plants are necessary to life on earth, however, many of these plants are harmful to us.

13. Some plants will simply make a person sick, others can kill humans and animals.

14. The precatory pea has a beautiful red berry, but just a single seed of this plant can kill an adult human.

15. A plant known as fiddleneck is fatal to horses, it can also kill cows and pigs.

16. In small doses St. John's wort is safe for humans, however, it can kill rabbits and cause sheep to lose their wool.

17. Wisteria is a beautiful flowering plant, still it can cause abdominal pain and nausea if ingested by humans.

18. You should always know therefore about a plant before you eat it.

● Connect to the Writing Process: Editing
Correcting Punctuation Errors

19.–24. Rewrite the incorrect sentences from the previous exercise, adding commas or semicolons where needed.

Semicolons to Avoid Confusion

Sometimes a semicolon is used to take the place of a comma between the clauses of a compound sentence.

Use a semicolon, instead of a comma, between the clauses of a compound sentence connected with a coordinating conjunction if there are commas within a clause.

> To get to Maine from New York, we travel through Connecticut, Massachusetts, and New Hampshire; but the trip takes us only four hours.

A semicolon takes the place of a comma in another situation as well.

Use a semicolon instead of a comma between the items in a series if the items themselves contain commas.

> I have relatives in Hartford, Connecticut; in Boston, Massachusetts; and in Portsmouth, New Hampshire.

You can find out more about using commas on pages L505–L533.

PRACTICE YOUR SKILLS

 Check Your Understanding
Using Semicolons to Avoid Confusion

Geography Topic | **Write C if a sentence is punctuated correctly. Write I if a sentence is punctuated incorrectly.**

1. Popular tourist attractions around the world include Parliament in London, England, the Eiffel Tower in Paris, France, and the Coliseum in Rome, Italy.

2. The white marble exterior of the Taj Mahal in Agra, India, is inlaid with semiprecious stones, floral designs, and arabesques.

3. Three sites in the United States that many Europeans like to visit are the Grand Canyon in Arizona, Las Vegas, Nevada, and San Francisco, California.

4. Most travelers make the choice of flying, driving, or taking a train, but some people still choose to travel by ship.

5. Other favorite world sites are the Great Wall of China and Red Square in Moscow, Russia.

6. Copenhagen is a major port, cultural center, and the capital of Denmark, and so it is a popular place to visit.

7. During World War II, Copenhagen was occupied by the German army, and this occupation lasted for almost five years.

8. Many tours of Scandinavia include stops in Copenhagen, Rotterdam, and Stockholm.

9. A popular tourist destination in New York, New York, is the United Nations headquarters.

10. Former Secretaries General of the United Nations include Dag Hammarskjold of Sweden, Kurt Waldheim of Austria; and Boutros Boutros-Ghali of Egypt.

● Connect to the Writing Process: Editing
Correcting Errors in Punctuation

11.–16. Rewrite the incorrect sentences from the preceding exercise, using the correct punctuation.

Communicate Your Ideas

APPLY TO WRITING

Persuasion: *Semicolons*

Your family has won a two-week vacation. All of you must decide where you will go. Your mom has asked you to choose three places, anywhere in the world, that you would like to visit.

Write a paragraph about each of the destinations you have chosen, emphasizing why your family should visit there. Order your paragraphs so that you write about your least favorite choice first and your most favorite choice last. Use semicolons at least three times in your writing.

QuickCheck Mixed Practice

Contemporary Life **Write the following sentences, adding commas and semicolons where needed.**

1. I love spending summers at my Aunt Betty's farm she is so much fun.

2. For breakfast she cooks bacon eggs and sausage squeezes fresh orange juice and serves strawberries fresh from the garden.

3. Aunt Betty grew up on a ranch therefore she loves having lots of animals around.

4. She keeps three horses in her stable moreover I'm allowed to ride them whenever I want.

5. She taught me how to tie a lasso mend a saddle and brush a horse and so she expects me to help out when I visit.

6. It is hard work nevertheless I enjoy doing it.

7. I could spend all day brushing the horses for example.

8. My sister and I feed the hogs they even seem to recognize us.

9. Aunt Betty says pigs are smarter than dogs furthermore they are easier to train.

10. She has in fact trained one pig to fetch a ball!

Colons

A colon (:) is used most often to introduce a list of items. Commas should separate the items in the list.

Use a colon before most lists of items, especially when the list comes after the expression *the following*.

All students will need the following: a pen, a sheet of paper, and a dictionary.

There are five stages in the writing process: prewriting, drafting, revising, editing, and publishing.

Three common prewriting strategies are these: lists, outlines, and graphic organizers.

Never use a colon directly after a verb or a preposition.

INCORRECT	My three favorite authors are: Charles Dickens, Jane Austen, and Thomas Hardy.
CORRECT	My three favorite authors are Charles Dickens, Jane Austen, and Thomas Hardy.
CORRECT	These are my three favorite authors: Charles Dickens, Jane Austen, and Thomas Hardy.

Colons are also used in a few other situations.

Use a colon to introduce a long, formal quotation.

Catherine Drinker Bowen once had this to say about writing: "Writing, I think, is not apart from living. Writing is a kind of double living. The writer experiences everything twice. Once in reality and once in that mirror which waits always before or behind."

You can learn more about writing long quotations on page L562.

Use a colon in certain special situations.

COLON USAGE	
HOURS AND MINUTES	5:30 a.m.
BIBLICAL CHAPTERS AND VERSES	John 3:16
SALUTATIONS IN BUSINESS LETTERS	Dear Sir or Madam:

PRACTICE YOUR SKILLS

● Check Your Understanding
Using Colons

Literature
Topic
Write *I* for incorrect if the sentence contains an error in the use of a colon. Write *C* if the sentence is correct.

1. My three favorite books by Dickens are: *A Christmas Carol, Great Expectations,* and *A Tale of Two Cities.*

2. In *A Christmas Carol,* the spirit of Jacob Marly warns Scrooge that a ghost will visit him at 1;00 A.M.

3. Through the ghosts' visits, Scrooge learns the kind of love Paul wrote about in I Corinthians 13:13.

4. In *Oliver Twist* the two most evil characters are: Fagin and Bill Sikes.

5. Thomas Hardy wrote many controversial novels, including his masterpieces *Jude the Obscure* and *Tess of the d'Urbervilles.*

6. He also wrote *The Dynasts:* an epic historical drama in verse.

7. Three of Hardy's most memorable characters are the following Bathsheba Everdene, Gabriel Oak, and Michael Henchard.

8. My favorite books of this period are: *Northanger Abbey, The Mayor of Castorbridge,* and *Nicholas Nickleby.*

9. The four novels of Jane Austen published before her death did not have her name on the title page.

10. These novels included: *Sense and Sensibility, Pride and Prejudice, Mansfield Park,* and *Emma.*

● Connect to the Writing Process: Editing
Using Colons Correctly

11.–17. **Rewrite the incorrect sentences from the preceding exercise, adding or deleting colons or other punctuation where needed.**

Communicate Your Ideas

APPLY TO WRITING
Informative Article: *Colons*

You have been asked to write an article about the local animal shelter for your town's newspaper. What kind of animals does the shelter house? How many animals does it get in a day? What kinds of donations does it need? As you write your article, use three colons in your work. Be sure that you can explain the reason for each one.

QuickCheck Mixed Practice

Science Topic **Write the following paragraph, adding apostrophes, semicolons, and colons where needed.**

Whos the worlds champion jumper? If youre thinking of a person, youre wrong. The kangaroo lays claim to this title. This curious-looking Australian mammal cannot walk however, it certainly can jump. It can easily hop over a parked car it can also travel over thirty-nine miles per hour.

The kangaroo has some quite unusual physical characteristics a small head, large pointed ears, very short front limbs, and hindquarters the size of a mules. Its feet sometimes measure ten inches from the heel to the longest toe. The kangaroos thick tail is so strong that it can use the tail as a stool. The kangaroo is strictly a vegetarian it will not eat another animal.

There are five groups of large kangaroos the eastern grey kangaroo, the western grey kangaroo, the red kangaroo, the wallaroo, and the antilopine wallaroo. You would have to travel far to see one of these kangaroos in its native home in fact, you would have to travel to Australia.

Hyphens

The principal use of a hyphen (-) is to divide a word at the end of a line. Whenever possible, avoid dividing words in your writing. Sometimes, however, it is necessary to divide words in order to keep the right-hand margin of a composition or story fairly even.

Use a hyphen to divide a word at the end of a line.

GUIDELINES FOR DIVIDING WORDS

Using the following six guidelines will help you divide words correctly.

1. Divide words only between syllables.

gym-nastics or gymnas-tics

2. Never divide a one-syllable word.

myth   rhyme   strength

3. Never separate a one-letter syllable from the rest of the word.

DO NOT BREAK   e-vent, sleep-y, o-boe, i-tem.

4. A two-letter word ending should not be carried over to the next line.

DO NOT BREAK   cred-it, hang-er, part-ly.

5. Divide hyphenated words only after the hyphens.

mother-in-law   maid-of-honor   attorney-at-law

6. Do not divide a proper noun or a proper adjective.

Beckerman   Memphis   Atlantic   Indian

If you are unsure how to divide a word, you can always check a dictionary.

PRACTICE YOUR SKILLS

● Check Your Understanding
Using Hyphens to Divide Words

Write each word, adding a hyphen or hyphens to show where the word can be correctly divided. If a word should not be divided, write *no*.

1. event
2. hamster
3. growth
4. invoice
5. son-in-law

6. amazement
7. action
8. jury
9. syllable
10. Cairo

11. gathering
12. Timothy
13. forgery
14. flip-flop
15. avoid

● Connect to the Writing Process: Drafting
Writing Sentences

Write sentences using the words below. Place a hyphen where the word could break if it needed to be divided.

16. science
17. mathematics
18. history

19. economics
20. athletic

▶ Other Uses of Hyphens

In addition to dividing words, hyphens have other important uses.

Hyphens with Numbers   Hyphens are needed with certain numbers.

Use a hyphen when writing out the numbers *twenty-one* through *ninety-nine.*

> There are thirty-one students in this class.
> Our teacher asked us to find twenty-five soil samples for the experiment.

Hyphens with Compound Nouns   Some compound nouns need one or more hyphens.

Use one or more hyphens to separate the parts of some compound nouns.

> Our teacher is my great-uncle.
> His son-in-law is my favorite relative.

Hyphens with Certain Adjectives   Hyphens are needed with fractions used as adjectives and with some compound adjectives.

Use a hyphen when writing out a fraction used as an adjective. Also use one or more hyphens between words that make up a compound adjective in front of a noun.

COMPOUND ADJECTIVE	I found some **dark-brown** soil in our backyard.
	It was **foul-smelling** dirt.

A hyphen is used only when a fraction is used as an adjective, not when it is used as a noun.

FRACTION USED AS AN ADJECTIVE	Our teacher said our soil samples should measure at least **one-quarter** cup.
FRACTION USED AS A NOUN	We put **one half** of the soil sample in the beaker.

A hyphen is used only when a compound adjective comes before a noun, not when it follows a linking verb and comes after the noun it describes.

ADJECTIVE BEFORE A NOUN	Our science teacher insists on **well-written** lab reports.
ADJECTIVE AFTER A NOUN	I always try to make sure that my lab reports are **well written**.

Hyphens with Prefixes

Use a hyphen after certain prefixes and before the suffix -*elect.*

HYPHENS USED WITH PREFIXES AND SUFFIXES

Use hyphens in the following situations:

1. between a prefix and a proper noun or proper adjective.

all-American   mid-Atlantic   pre-Columbian

2. after the prefix *self-*

self-righteous   self-satisfied

3. after the prefix *ex-* when it means "former" or "formerly"

ex-mayor   ex-governor   ex-senator

4. after a person's title when it is followed by the suffix -*elect*

president-elect   mayor-elect

PRACTICE YOUR SKILLS

Check Your Understanding
Using Hyphens

Write *a* or *b* to indicate the letter of the correctly written words in each of the following pairs.

1. a. seventy seven
   b. seventy-seven

2. a. self-assured
   b. self assured

3. a. governor elect
   b. governor-elect

4. a. four-teen
   b. fourteen

5. **a.** ex-husband
   b. exhusband

6. **a.** mid-Pacific
   b. mid Pacific

7. **a.** one-quarter teaspoon
   b. one quarter teaspoon

8. **a.** mother in law
   b. mother-in-law

9. **a.** jack in the box
   b. jack-in-the-box

10. **a.** one quarter of the pie
    b. one-quarter of the pie

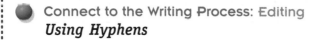 **Connect to the Writing Process:** Editing
Using Hyphens

Correctly write each word that should be hyphenated. If none of the words in a sentence needs a hyphen, write C for correct.

11. I will enjoy having a new sister in law when my brother finally marries.

12. My brother is going to marry my friend's step sister in June.

13. She is twentyseven years old.

14. Her mother, May Meriwether, is the mayor elect of our city.

15. She beat the ex mayor by the narrow margin of only ninety two votes.

16. My brother and his fiancée have invited seventyfive people to the wedding.

17. One half of the guests are our relatives.

18. I will serve as the bride's maid of honor.

19. The bride, who is very self reliant, will bake her own wedding cake.

20. I believe that the new mayor will like having my brother as her son in law.

APPLY TO WRITING

The Writer's Craft: *Analyzing the Use of Hyphens*

Writers of poetry and prose often use hyphenated adjectives before nouns. Read the following excerpt from Li-Young Lee's poem "Furious Versions" and answer the questions that follow.

It was a tropical night.

It was a half a year of sweat and fatal memory.

It was one year of fire

out of the world's diary of fires,

flesh-laced, mid-century fire,

teeth and hair infested,

napalm-dressed and skull-hung fire,

and imminent fire, an elected

fire come to rob me

of my own death, my damp bed

in the noisy earth,

my rocking toward a hymn-like night.

–*Li-Young Lee*, "Furious Versions"

- List all the hyphenated words in the excerpt.
- Why are these words hyphenated?
- How does Lee's use of these hyphenated words affect the rhythm of the poem?
- Would the poem have the same effect without the hyphenated words? Explain your answer.

A dash (—) and parentheses ( ) are used like commas in some situations because they separate certain words or groups of words from the rest of the sentence. There are, of course, some distinctions among the uses of these three marks of punctuation.

 ## Dashes

Dashes indicate a greater pause between words than commas do. They can be used in the following situations.

Use dashes to set off an abrupt change in thought.

> Mr. Becker—at least I think that's his name—is the drivers' education teacher.
>
> "Where's the —?" Dana began and then hesitated when she saw the car.
>
> The Drivers' Ed car—it's old and dented—is parked in the next lot.

Use dashes to set off an appositive that is introduced by words such as *that is, for example,* or *for instance.*

> Certain traffic laws—for instance, making a right turn on a red light—vary from state to state.

Use dashes to set off a parenthetical expression or an appositive that includes commas.

> Driving a car—like taking a test, performing in a play, or singing a song—requires concentration.

If you do not know how to make a dash on the computer, you can use two hyphens together. Do not leave a space before or after a dash.

You can find out more about appositives on pages L183–L184.

You can find out more about parenthetical expressions on pages L523–L524.

▶ Parentheses

Always remember that parentheses come in pairs.

Use parentheses to enclose information that is not related closely to the meaning of the sentence.

To decide whether or not you should use parentheses, read the sentence without the parenthetical material. If the meaning and structure of the sentence are not changed, then add parentheses. Just keep in mind that parenthetical additions to sentences slow readers down and interrupt their train of thought. As a result, you should always limit the amount of parenthetical material that you add to any one piece of writing.

> During the late teen years **(**16–19**)**, many drivers pay higher rates for car insurance.

When the closing parenthesis comes at the end of a sentence, the end mark usually goes outside the parenthesis. However, occasionally the end mark goes inside the parenthesis if the end mark actually belongs with the parenthetical material.

> END MARK WITHIN PARENTHESES — Take your written driver's exam in pencil. **(**Be sure to use a number 2 pencil.**)**
>
> END MARK OUTSIDE PARENTHESES — To earn your driver's license, you must pass both tests **(**with a score of 70 or better**)**.

PRACTICE YOUR SKILLS

● Check Your Understanding
Using Dashes and Parentheses

General
Interest **Write *I* for incorrect if the commas in a sentence should be dashes or parentheses. If a sentence is correct as is, write *C*.**

1. Three rules of the road, courtesy to others, respect of pedestrians' right of way, and careful driving should always be followed.

2. Motor vehicles, such as cars and trucks, can be difficult to control on icy streets.

3. Certain privileges, like driving at night, should not be granted to novice drivers.

4. Use your blinker, located on the steering column by your right hand, to signal a turn.

5. Certain states, like Texas, will take away a teenager's license if he or she commits a crime.

6. During the first days of automobiles, the early twentieth century, drivers weren't required to be licensed.

7. In cities like New York and Boston, many people use public transportation rather than drive a car.

8. Certain innovations, like automatic transmission and power steering, have made cars easier to drive.

9. Driving while intoxicated, a very serious offense, is severely punished in most states.

10. Georgia has three stages of graduated licensing, supervised learner, intermediate, and full-privilege, for beginning drivers.

● Connect to the Writing Process: Editing
Using Dashes and Parentheses

11.–16. Rewrite the incorrect sentences from the preceding exercises, adding dashes or parentheses where needed.

APPLY TO WRITING

The Writer's Craft: *Analyzing the Use of Dashes*

Emily Dickinson is one poet who made liberal use of dashes in her poetry. Read the following poem by Emily Dickinson and then follow the directions.

He ate and drank the precious Words—

His spirit grew robust—

He knew no more that he was poor,

Nor that his frame was Dust—

He danced along the dingy Days

And this Bequest of Wings

Was but a Book—What Liberty

A loosened spirit brings—

–Emily Dickinson

- Read the poem aloud, ignoring all the punctuation marks.
- Next, read the poem aloud, making long pauses only where the dashes are. You should pause briefly at the comma.
- How did your readings of the poem differ?
- Would any other punctuation marks have served the purpose of these dashes? If so, which ones? Explain your answer.
- Why do you think Dickinson chose to use dashes?

General Interest **Rewrite the following paragraph, adding hyphens, dashes, and parentheses where needed.**

Humphrey Bogart 1899–1957 was voted the greatest screen legend male screen legend, that is, by the American Film Institute AFI in 1999. Bogart who is my favorite movie star was a stage actor at the beginning of his career. His movie credits include *The Maltese Falcon* 1941 and *Casablanca* 1942. In 1951, he won an Oscar for his role in *The African Queen.* In this award winning role, he played opposite Katherine Hepburn who, by the way, was the AFI pick for the greatest female screen legend.

 **QuickCheck** Mixed Practice

History Topic **Rewrite the following paragraphs, adding apostrophes, semicolons, colons, and hyphens where needed.**

The Mayas occupied much North American land in pre Spanish times. There was quite a variety of land mountains, rain forests, plains, and coastal areas. Today, this area covers many of the Mexican states the current countries of Guatemala, Belize, El Salvador, and parts of Honduras also were homes to the Mayas.

The Mayas religion was perhaps the most important part of their lives. Some of their gods included *Chaac,* god of rain and lightning *Ik,* god of the wind and *Ah Puch,* god of death.

Using Punctuation Correctly

Write each sentence, adding punctuation where needed. If a sentence is punctuated correctly write C.

1. Rattlesnakes don't lay eggs they bear live young.

2. The worlds largest gem is a 596 pound topaz.

3. The soybean is a versatile vegetable for example, forty different products can be made from it.

4. Greg wont be satisfied until hes totally self sufficient.

5. The following famous people had red hair George Washington, Thomas Jefferson, and Mark Twain.

6. Lenny Burns received a two thirds majority vote in this years mayoral election.

7. When Snuffys leash broke, he jumped the neighbors fence and dove into their pool.

8. The official name of India is not *India* it is *Bharat*.

9. My brother in law is president elect of the club.

10. Salt is found in the earth in three basic forms salt water, brine deposits, and rock salt crystal.

11. The rarely seen Indian sea snake is the most poisonous snake in the world.

12. The poet H.D.s real name is Hilda Doolittle.

13. The people on the panel included Terry Hayden, an editorial writer Thelma Casey, a fashion consultant and Judith Howe, a high school teacher.

14. Today, there are more than seven thousand varieties of apples nevertheless only twenty varieties are widely grown.

15. Twenty two people how could we have invited so many! are supposed to arrive for dinner at 630 P.M.

Editing for Correct Punctuation

Write the paragraph, adding apostrophes, semicolons, colons, and hyphens where needed.

Everyone has heard of the Nobel Prizes but most people havent heard about Alfred Nobel, the man who established the prizes. He was born in Sweden in 1833. Thirty three years later, he invented dynamite. This invention made him very rich it also made him feel very guilty later on. As a result, his will set up a trust fund that annually awards prizes to people throughout the world who excel in the following categories literature, physics, chemistry, medicine, and peace. Now, every December 10, the anniversary of Nobels death, each winner receives up to $959,070.

Writing Sentences

Write ten sentences that follow the directions below.

Write a sentence that . . .

1. includes the possessive form of the nouns *uncle* and *dollars*.
2. includes the possessive form of the pronouns *it* and *no one*.
3. includes the joint ownership of something.
4. includes the plural of *no*.
5. includes the word *nevertheless* between two independent clauses in a compound sentence.
6. includes a series of dates.
7. includes a specific time.
8. includes *three fourths* as an adjective.
9. includes a dash.
10. includes parentheses.

Language and *Self-Expression*

Honoré Daumier was a nineteenth-century French artist who focused on social and political problems in his art. Much of his work depicted poor people in anonymous surroundings. In *The Third-Class Carriage*, Daumier shows a group of travelers who are unable to afford first-class tickets on a train.

In 1861, the time the painting was done, France was gripped by high unemployment and great poverty. The clothing, body language, and facial expressions of the travelers reveal much about them. Imagine how the travelers might have lived, and write a brief biography of one of the figures in the third-class carriage. Explain in detail his or her experiences and expectations. Include various kinds of punctuation in the sentences you write.

Prewriting Make a time line for the figure you have chosen to write about. Note the subject's date of birth and other events important in his or her life. Include details about births and deaths of family members.

Drafting Use your time line to help you write a first draft of your biography. Include any events you imagine had an impact on your subject's life.

Revising Reread your biography. Be sure you have included information about your subject's home, work, and family. Also include details that reveal how your subject views his or her life.

Editing Check your biography for errors in grammar, spelling, and punctuation. Be sure you have used apostrophes, semicolons, colons, hyphens, dashes, and parentheses correctly.

Publishing Read your biography aloud to the class. Ask classmates to guess which figure in the painting you have chosen as a subject.

Another Look

Using Apostrophes

To show joint ownership, make only the last word possessive in form. *(page L581)*

To show separate ownership, make each word possessive in form. *(page L581)*

Use an apostrophe with the possessive form of a noun that expresses time or amount. *(pages L581–L582)*

Use an apostrophe in a contraction to show where one or more letters in a word or numbers in a date have been omitted. *(pages L585–L588)*

Using Semicolons and Colons

Use a semicolon between the clauses of a compound sentence that are not joined by a conjunction. *(page L590)*

Use a semicolon, instead of a comma, between the clauses of a compound sentence if there are commas within a clause. *(page L594)*

Use a semicolon, instead of a comma, between the items in a series if the items themselves contain commas. *(page L594)*

Use a colon before most lists of items, especially when the list comes after the expression *the following. (page L597)*

Use a colon to introduce a long, formal quotation. *(page L597)*

Use a colon in certain special situations:

  Between hours and minutes

  Between Biblical chapters and verses

  After salutations in business letters *(page L598)*

Using Hyphens

Use a hyphen to divide a word at the end of a line. *(page L601)*

Use a hyphen when writing out the numbers *twenty-one* through *ninety-nine. (page L602)*

Use one or more hyphens to separate the parts of some compound nouns or to separate words of a compound adjective in front of a noun. *(page L603)*

Use a hyphen when writing out a fraction that is used as an adjective. *(page L603)*

Use a hyphen after certain prefixes and before the suffix *-elect. (page L604)*

Using Dashes and Parentheses

Use dashes to set off an abrupt change in thought. *(page L607)*

Use dashes to set off a parenthetical expression or an appositive that includes commas. *(page L607)*

Use parentheses to enclose information. *(page L608)*

Posttest

Directions
Write the letter of the answer that correctly punctuates the underlined part in each sentence. If the underlined part contains no error, write D.

EXAMPLE   **1.** According to a study by <u>American Sports Data, Inc.</u>, the treadmill is the most popular kind of exercise equipment.

　　　　　1 A　American Sports Data—Inc.
　　　　　　B　American Sports Data Inc.
　　　　　　C　American Sports' Data, Inc.
　　　　　　D　No error

ANSWER   **1 C**

1. There has been a huge increase in the number of treadmill <u>users in fact,</u> while only 4.4 million used treadmills in 1987, 37.1 million used them in 1998.

2. The second most popular machine is <u>the stair climber</u>.

3. There are several reasons for the treadmill's <u>popularity it keeps</u> you fit, it is easy to use, and it is safe and reliable.

4. The treadmill is a <u>home exercisers dream</u>.

5. When it rains outside, you can <u>still exercise there</u> is no excuse for slacking off.

6. For some people <u>those who love exercise</u> that is reason enough to own a treadmill.

7. Some people <u>dont like the treadmill</u> because they find it boring.

8. For them, <u>its difficult</u> to stay motivated.

9. Even the <u>self motivated</u> can get bored doing the same exercise day after day.

10. One <u>answer (though it's not</u> for everyone) is to place the treadmill in front of a television.

1 A users—in fact
   B users; in fact,
   C users: in fact
   D No error

2 A the stair, climber
   B (the stair climber)
   C the stair-climber
   D No error

3 A popularity: it keeps
   B popularity; it keeps
   C popularity—it keeps
   D No error

4 A home-exerciser's dream
   B home-exercisers' dream
   C home exercisers' dream
   D No error

5 A still exercise: there
   B still exercise—there
   C still exercise; there
   D No error

6 A (those who love
         exercise)
   B those who love
         exercise;
   C those who love
         exercise:
   D No error

7 A dont' like the treadmill
   B don't like the treadmill
   C do'nt like the treadmill
   D No error

8 A it's difficult
   B its' difficult
   C its: difficult
   D No error

9 A (self motivated)
   B self; motivated
   C self-motivated
   D No error

10 A answer, though, it's not
   B answer: though it's not
   C answer; though it's not
   D No error

A Writer's Guide to Citing Sources

When you use someone else's words or ideas in your own report—even if you only paraphrase—you must give that person proper credit. One way to do this is to follow the guidelines of the Modern Language Association (MLA), which credits the source in parentheses.

Parenthetical citations give readers just enough information to identify the source of the material you have borrowed. The complete source information will appear on the works-cited page at the end of your report. The following examples will help you use parenthetical citations.

BOOK BY ONE AUTHOR	Give author's last name and page number(s): (McKluskie 68–72).
BOOK BY MORE THAN ONE AUTHOR	Give both authors' names and page number(s): (Geller and Eaton 79).
ARTICLE WITH AUTHOR NAMED	Give author's last name and page number(s): (Natale 4).
ARTICLE WITH AUTHOR UNNAMED	Give a shortened form of the title (unless full title is already short) and page number(s): ("Gimme That Sinking Feeling" 11).
ARTICLE IN A REFERENCE WORK; AUTHOR UNNAMED	Give title (full or shortened) and page number(s); if the article is a single page from an encyclopedia, no page number is needed: ("Titanic").

Parenthetical citations should be close to the words or ideas being credited. Therefore, place them at the end of a phrase, clause, or sentence. If a parenthetical citation falls at the end of a sentence, place it before the period. With a quotation, place it after the closing quotation mark and before the period.

You may prefer to use **footnotes** or **endnotes** to identify sources. For either type of note, place a small number halfway above the line immediately after the borrowed material. This number matches that of the complete citation at the bottom of the page—the footnote—or at the end of the report—the endnote.

¹Tom McKluskie, Anatomy of the Titanic. (San Diego: Thunder Bay, 1998) 120.

A **works-cited page** is the alphabetical list, by author, of sources in a research paper. If an author is unknown, the source is alphabetized by title. In the following examples, note the order of the sources, the indentation, and the punctuation.

GENERAL REFERENCE WORKS	Marcus, Geoffrey J. "Titanic." Encyclopedia Americana. 1999 ed.
BOOKS BY ONE AUTHOR	McKluskie, Tom. Anatomy of the Titanic. San Diego: Thunder Bay Press, 1998.
BOOKS BY TWO OR MORE AUTHORS	Geller, Judith B. and John P. Eaton. Titanic: Women and Children First. New York: W. W. Norton & Co., 1998.
ARTICLES IN MAGAZINES; AUTHOR NAMED	Koretz, Gene. "How the Titanic Hit Wall Street." Business Week 7 Dec. 1998:22.
ARTICLES IN MAGAZINES; AUTHOR UNNAMED	"Gimme That Sinking Feeling." People Weekly 18 Jan. 1999: 11.
ARTICLES IN NEWSPAPERS	Natale, Richard. "Box-Office Showing Good, If Not 'Titanic.'" Los Angeles Times 7 May 1999, sec. C: 4.
REVIEWS	Biel, Steven. Rev. of Titanic, dir. James Cameron. Journal of American History Dec. 1998: 1177-1179.
ARTICLE FROM A CD-ROM	"Titanic Disaster." Encarta 1998. CD-ROM. Redmond: Microsoft, 1998.
ARTICLE FROM AN ONLINE DATABASE WITH A PRINT VERSION	Maslin, Janet. Rev. of Titanic, dir. James Cameron. The New York Times on the Web. 19 Dec. 1997. 7 Sept. 1999 <http://www.nytimes.com/library/film/archive main-t.html>.
ARTICLE FROM AN ONLINE DATABASE WITHOUT A PRINT VERSION	Gilbert, John. MSN Online Tonight with James Cameron. 21 Jan. 1999. 7 Sept. 1999 <http://onlinetonight.msn.co.uk/titanic/transcript.htm>.

CHAPTER 18

Spelling Correctly

 **Pretest**

Directions

Read the passage. Write the letter of the choice that correctly spells each underlined word. If the word contains no error, write *D*.

EXAMPLE   The <u>preperation</u> for their cross-country
                          (1)
                   trip was long and painstaking.

> 1 **A**   preperration
>   **B**   preparation
>   **C**   prepareation
>   **D**   No error

ANSWER   1 **B**

In history class we read some <u>correspondance</u> between
                                                (1)
pioneers and their <u>familys</u> back home. As they <u>proceded</u> on
                            (2)   (3)
their <u>journies</u>, these pioneers often stopped at trading posts.
          (4)
There they were <u>ocasionally</u> able to post letters to relatives.
                          (5)
These tales of <u>inconceivable</u> hardship and <u>couragous</u> actions
                        (6)   (7)
teach us today. Reading the actual words of our ancestors

helps us relate to the <u>lonelyness</u>, terrors, and everyday joys
                                  (8)
of pioneer life. We delight in their innocent <u>beleif</u> in a better
                                                            (9)
life, and we recall that <u>heros</u> start out as ordinary people.
                                (10)

1
  A corespondance
  B correspondence
  C correspondants
  D No error

2
  A familyes
  B familes
  C families
  D No error

3
  A proceeded
  B proseded
  C preceeded
  D No error

4
  A journys
  B journeys
  C journeyses
  D No error

5
  A ocasionaly
  B occasionally
  C occassionally
  D No error

6
  A inconcievable
  B inconceiveable
  C inconcevable
  D No error

7
  A courageous
  B couragious
  C couraggous
  D No error

8
  A lonlyness
  B lonelynes
  C loneliness
  D No error

9
  A belief
  B beleef
  C beleiv
  D No error

10
  A heroses
  B hero
  C heroes
  D No error

Strategies for Learning to Spell

Learning to spell involves a variety of senses. You use your senses of hearing, sight, and touch to spell a word correctly. Here is a five-step strategy that many people have used successfully as they learned to spell unfamiliar words.

1   Auditory
Say the word aloud. Answer these questions.
- Where have I heard or read this word before?
- What was the context in which I heard or read the word?

2   Visual
Look at the word. Answer these questions.
- Does this word divide into parts? Is it a compound word? Does it have a prefix or a suffix?
- Does this word look like any other word I know? Could it be part of a word family I would recognize?

3   Auditory
Spell the word to yourself. Answer these questions.
- How is each sound spelled?
- Are there any surprises? Does the word follow spelling rules I know, or does it break the rules?

4   Visual/Kinesthetic
Write the word as you look at it. Answer these questions.
- Have I written the word clearly?
- Are my letters formed correctly?

5   Visual/Kinesthetic
Cover up the word. Visualize it. Write it. Answer this question.
- Did I write the word correctly?
- If the answer is no, return to step 1.

Spelling Strategies

Spelling is easier for some people than it is for others, but everyone needs to make an effort to spell correctly. Misspellings are distracting for the reader, and they make writing hard to read. Here are some strategies you can use to improve your spelling.

STRATEGY **Use a dictionary.** If you are not sure how to spell a word, or if a word you have written doesn't "look right," check the word in a dictionary.

STRATEGY **Proofread your writing carefully.** Be on the lookout for misspellings and for words you are not sure you spelled correctly. One way to proofread your writing for misspellings is to start at the end of your paper and read backward. That way misspellings should pop out at you.

PRACTICE YOUR SKILLS

● Check Your Understanding
Recognizing Misspelled Words

Write the letter of the misspelled word in each line. Then write the word correctly.

1. (a) abbreviation (b) boulevard (c) extream
2. (a) burea (b) confer (c) forgery
3. (a) fasinating (b) guarantee (c) illustrate
4. (a) irritate (b) luxury (c) mischeif
5. (a) authentic (b) brillance (c) disguise
6. (a) mysterious (b) ocasionally (c) prestige
7. (a) legislasure (b) merchandise (c) notch
8. (a) punctual (b) resign (c) resterant

9. (a) ridicilous   (b) sizable   (c) thesaurus

10. (a) coupon   (b) chrystal   (c) dissatisfied

STRATEGY **Be sure you are pronouncing words correctly.**
"Swallowing" syllables or adding extra syllables can cause
you to misspell a word.

PRACTICE YOUR SKILLS

Check Your Understanding
Pronouncing Words

Oral Expression **Practice saying each syllable in the following words to help you spell the words correctly.**

1. mis•chie•vous   **5.** light•ning   **9.** sim•i•lar

2. lit•er•a•ture   **6.** ath•lete   **10.** prob•a•bly

3. pros•per•ous   **7.** li•brar•y   **11.** fi•er•y

4. tem•per•a•ture   **8.** es•cape   **12.** qui•et

STRATEGY **Make up mnemonic devices.** A phrase like "My niece is nice" can help you remember to put *i* before *e* in *niece*. A device like "2 *m's*, 2 *t's*, 2 *e's*" can help you remember how to spell *committee*.

STRATEGY **Keep a spelling journal.** Use it to record the words that you have had trouble spelling. Here are some suggestions for organizing your spelling journal.

- Write the word correctly.
- Write the word again, underlining or circling the part of the word that gave you trouble.
- Write a tip to help you remember how to spell the word.

weird   we*ir*d   *Weird* is weird. It doesn't follow the *i* before *e* rule.

Spelling Generalizations

Knowing common spelling generalizations can help you to spell hundreds of words. Some of these generalizations are based on spelling patterns, such as the choice between *ie* and *ei*. Other generalizations deal with forming plurals, writing numbers as numerals or as words, and adding prefixes and suffixes to words.

Spelling Patterns

Understanding certain common word patterns can help take the guesswork out of spelling many new words.

Words with *ie* and *ei*

When you spell words with *ie* or *ei*, *i* comes before *e* except when the letters follow *c* or when they stand for the long *a* sound.

	IE AND *EI*		
EXAMPLES	**ie**	bel**ie**ve	f**ie**ld
	ei after **c**	c**ei**ling	rec**ei**ve
	sounds like **a**	n**ei**ghbor	w**ei**gh
EXCEPTIONS	anc**ie**nt	effic**ie**nt	n**ei**ther	s**ei**ze
	consc**ie**nce	spec**ie**s	h**ei**ght	w**ei**rd
	suffic**ie**nt	**ei**ther	l**ei**sure	for**ei**gn

The generalization about *ie* and *ei* applies only when the letters occur in the same syllable and spell just one vowel sound. It does not apply when *i* and *e* appear in different syllables.

IE AND *EI* IN DIFFERENT SYLLABLES			
be ing	re imburse	sci ence	soci ety

The words *siege* and *seize* are sometimes confused. Be sure you use the word that suits your meaning.

siege—[noun] the surrounding of an area by military forces trying to stage a takeover; a steady try to get something

> The rebel forces planned a *siege* of the capital.

seize—[verb] to snatch or grab suddenly; to capture

> The security guard *seized* the photographer's camera.

Words ending in *–sede, –ceed,* and *–cede*

Words ending with a syllable that sounds like "seed" are usually spelled with *–cede.* Only one word in English is spelled with *–sede,* and only three words are spelled with *–ceed.*

	–SEDE, –CEED, AND –CEDE			
EXAMPLES	con**cede**	pre**cede**	re**cede**	se**cede**
EXCEPTIONS	super**sede**	ex**ceed**	pro**ceed**	suc**ceed**

PRACTICE YOUR SKILLS

● Check Your Understanding
Using Spelling Patterns

Write each word correctly, adding *ie* or *ei*.

1. th ▨ f   **8.** rec ▨ pt   **15.** rel ▨ ve

2. n ▨ ce   **9.** gr ▨ ve   **16.** br ▨ f

3. y ▨ ld   **10.** ▨ ght   **17.** rec ▨ ve

4. w ▨ gh   **11.** p ▨ ce   **18.** retr ▨ ve

5. h ▨ ght   **12.** r ▨ ns   **19.** n ▨ ghbor

6. bel ▨ f   **13.** n ▨ ther   **20.** l ▨ sure

7. c ▨ ling   **14.** dec ▨ ve

Write each word correctly, adding _-sede, -ceed,_ or _-cede._

21. re ■   **25.** suc ■   **29.** super ■

22. ex ■   **26.** con ■   **30.** inter ■

23. ac ■   **27.** pre ■

24. se ■   **28.** pro ■

● Connect to the Writing Process: Editing
Using Spelling Patterns

History
Topic **Rewrite this paragraph, correcting any spelling errors.**

For the state of Kentucky, the War Between the States was truly a civil war. Kentucky did not sesede from the Union, as did the nieghboring states of Tennessee and Virginia. Officially Kentucky supported niether the Union nor the Confederacy. Kentucky proceded to declare neutrality on May 16, 1851, but Kentuckians did not succeed in staying out of the conflict. The number of Kentuckians who fought for the Confederacy exceded 30,000, and twice that number joined the Union Army. Neighbors, freinds, and families were greivously divided in thier loyalties. President Lincoln concedeed that Kentucky was one of the country's "troubling stepchildren" because its location bordered Union states, but many residents supported the Confederacy.

▶ Plurals

You know that many nouns form their plural form by adding _s_ or _es_ to the singular form. Some nouns form their plurals in other ways, though. Forming the plural of a noun becomes easier when you remember to use the following generalizations.

Regular Nouns

To form the plural of most nouns, simply add *s.*

	MOST NOUNS			
SINGULAR	artist	symbol	maze	sardine
PLURAL	artist**s**	symbol**s**	maze**s**	sardine**s**

If a noun ends with *s, ch, sh, x,* or *z,* add *es* to form the plural.

	S, CH, SH, X, AND Z			
SINGULAR	loss	chur**ch**	di**sh**	fox
PLURAL	loss**es**	chur**ches**	di**shes**	fox**es**

Nouns Ending in *y*

Add *s* to form the plural of a noun ending with a vowel and *y.*

	VOWELS AND Y			
SINGULAR	d**ay**	displ**ay**	journ**ey**	t**oy**
PLURAL	d**ays**	displ**ays**	journ**eys**	t**oys**

Change the *y* to *i* and add *es* to a noun ending in a consonant and *y.*

	CONSONANTS AND Y			
SINGULAR	memo**ry**	trop**hy**	la**dy**	socie**ty**
PLURAL	memo**ries**	trop**hies**	la**dies**	socie**ties**

PRACTICE YOUR SKILLS

● Check Your Understanding
Forming Plurals

Write the plural form of each noun.

1. theme	**6.** reflex	**11.** ability	**16.** galaxy
2. valley	**7.** theory	**12.** stitch	**17.** effect
3. crash	**8.** tomboy	**13.** holiday	**18.** trolley
4. comedy	**9.** waltz	**14.** apology	**19.** issue
5. virus	**10.** image	**15.** trapeze	**20.** vacancy

● Connect to the Writing Process: Editing
Spelling Plural Nouns

General Interest **Rewrite these sentences, changing singular nouns to plural nouns as needed.**

21. Television set as we know them today were invented in the 1930s.

22. World War II interrupted the development and manufacturing of all consumer product.

23. In 1947, when the war was over, factory started making product for consumer again.

24. The period from 1947 to 1957 is regarded as the "Golden Year" of television.

25. During this time popular radio program became television show, and radio listener became TV watcher.

26. "I Love Lucy," which premiered in 1951, was one of the few early situation comedy that did not start out as a radio program.

27. It began the practice of filming show in front of live audience using three camera.

28. In those day all performance were live.

29. If actor and actress forgot their lines, they had to make up something.

30. When you watch those early show, you can sometimes notice the blunder and glitch.

Nouns Ending with *o*

Add *s* to form the plural of a noun ending with a vowel and *o*.

		VOWELS AND *O*		
SINGULAR	rat**io**	stud**io**	rod**eo**	ig**loo**
PLURAL	rat**ios**	stud**ios**	rod**eos**	ig**loos**

Add *s* to form the plural of musical terms ending in *o*.

		MUSICAL TERMS WITH *O*		
SINGULAR	alt**o**	du**o**	pian**o**	cell**o**
PLURAL	alt**os**	du**os**	pian**os**	cell**os**

The plurals of nouns ending in a consonant and *o* do not follow a regular pattern.

		CONSONANTS AND *O*		
SINGULAR	ec**ho**	ve**to**	si**lo**	e**go**
PLURAL	ec**hoes**	ve**toes**	si**los**	e**gos**

When you are not sure how to form the plural of a word that ends in *o,* consult a dictionary. If the dictionary does not give a plural form, the plural is usually formed by adding *s.*

Nouns Ending in *f* or *fe*

To form the plural of some nouns ending in *f* or *fe*, just add *s.*

		F AND FE		
SINGULAR	belie**f**	gul**f**	che**f**	fi**fe**
PLURAL	belie**fs**	gul**fs**	che**fs**	fi**fes**

For some nouns ending in *f* or *fe,* change the *f* to *v* and add *es* or *s.*

F AND FE TO V				
SINGULAR	half	shelf	leaf	knife
PLURAL	hal**ves**	shel**ves**	lea**ves**	kni**ves**

Consult a dictionary to check the plural form of a word that ends with *f* or *fe.*

PRACTICE YOUR SKILLS

● Check Your Understanding
Forming Plurals

Write the plural form of each noun. Check a dictionary to be sure you have formed the plural correctly.

1. radio   **5.** potato   **9.** tariff

2. stereo   **6.** taco   **10.** elf

3. shampoo   **7.** yo-yo   **11.** calf

4. solo   **8.** roof   **12.** self

● Connect to the Writing Process: Editing
Spelling Plural Nouns

Music Topic **Rewrite this paragraph, correcting any spelling errors.**

Most high schools do not have room or funds for music studioes. However, music teachers themselfs continue to teach the fundamentals of reading music to interested students. The notes for music are positioned on a set of lines and spaces called a staff. Two stafves always appear together, one above the other. Each one is marked with a clef. The clefs tell what notes the lines and spaces stand for. The high notes played by piccoloes or sung by sopranos are on the top staff. The low notes played by celloes and sung by basses are on the bottom staff.

Compound Nouns

Most compound nouns are made plural in the same way as other nouns. The letter *s* or *es* is added to the end of the word. But when the main word in a compound noun appears first, that word becomes plural.

COMPOUND NOUNS			
EXAMPLES	snowflake snowflakes	lunchbox lunchboxes	hallway hallways
EXCEPTIONS	passerby passersby	editor-in-chief editors-in-chief	mother-in-law mothers-in-law

Numerals, Letters, Symbols, and Words as Words

To form the plurals of numerals, letters, symbols, and words used as words, add an *s*. To prevent confusion, it is best to use an apostrophe and *s* with lowercase letters, some capital letters, and some words used as words.

EXAMPLES   Those *G*s look like *6*s.
                     Swing dancing from the 1940s is back.
                     Use **s* to mark footnotes.
                     Don't give me any *ifs*, *ands*, or *buts*.

EXCEPTIONS   There are four *i*'s and four *s*'s in *Mississippi*.
                     Name five foods that are shaped like *O*'s.
                     We need an equal number of *he*'s and *she*'s.

PRACTICE YOUR SKILLS

● Check Your Understanding
Forming Plurals

Write the plural form of each item.

1. attorney-at-law   **8.** *z*   **15.** 1900

2. bystander   **9.** *&*   **16.** maid of honor

3. '90   **10.** mousetrap   **17.** *in* and *out*

4. sergeant-at-arms   **11.** toothache   **18.** classroom

5. hummingbird   **12.** runner-up   **19.** *X* and *O*

6. *?*   **13.** *S*   **20.** *ABC*

7. sister-in-law   **14.** pen pal

● Connect to the Writing Process: Editing
Spelling Plural Nouns

Science Topic   **Write each sentence, changing the underlined items from singular to plural.**

21. In the 1960, the alligator was classified as an endangered species.

22. Before the end of the '70, however, alligators made a comeback, and they were reclassified as threatened.

23. There are two *l* in the word *alligator.*

24. Write about the animals in your observation log, and put *?* beside spellings you are unsure of.

25. Hummingbird are always seen in flight because their weak feet cannot support them on flat surfaces.

26. Man-o'-war bird can soar motionless for hours, but they are awkward on land and their feathers get waterlogged in the water.

27. People used to use lily of the valley as a heart medicine.

28. The dried roots of the butterfly bush have been used as a medicine to prevent spasms.

29. The fuzzy brown spikes are actually the fruits of cattail.

30. Some kinds of firefly lay eggs that glow just as the adult insects do.

Other Plural Forms

Irregular plurals are not formed by adding *s* or *es*.

IRREGULAR PLURALS					
SINGULAR	tooth	foot	mouse	child	woman
	goose	ox	man	die	
PLURAL	tee**th**	fee**t**	m**ice**	child**ren**	wom**en**
	ge**e**se	ox**en**	men	d**ice**	

Some nouns have the same form for singular and plural.

SAME SINGULAR AND PLURAL			
Vietnamese	Sioux	salmon	headquarters
Japanese	deer	species	measles
Swiss	moose	scissors	politics

Words from Latin and Greek

Some nouns from Latin and Greek have plurals that are formed as they are in the original language. For a few Latin and Greek words, there are two ways to form the plural.

FOREIGN WORDS				
EXAMPLES	alumnus	memorandum	crisis	thesis
	alumn**i**	memorand**a**	cris**es**	thes**es**
EXCEPTIONS	hippopotamus			
	hippopotam**uses** or hippopot**ami**			
	formula			
	formula**s** or formula**e**			

Check a dictionary when forming the plural of words from Latin and Greek. When two forms are given, the first one is preferred.

PRACTICE YOUR SKILLS

● Check Your Understanding
Forming Plurals

Write the plural form of each noun. Check a dictionary if you are not sure of the preferred form.

1. mouse	**6.** woman	**11.** hypothesis	**16.** deer
2. child	**7.** synopsis	**12.** appendix	**17.** Swiss
3. tooth	**8.** octopus	**13.** spectrum	**18.** pliers
4. foot	**9.** stylus	**14.** analysis	**19.** corps
5. louse	**10.** vacuum	**15.** salmon	**20.** trout

● Connect to the Writing Process: Editing
Forming Plurals

General Interest **Decide if the underlined plurals are formed correctly. If any are incorrect, write the correct form.**

Deer and Canadian gooses have become a serious nuisance in many communities, according to the news mediums. Various hypothesises have been put forth, but apparently a major cause of the problem is demographicses. According to the latest analyses, people are living in areas that used to be wilderness. Places that in the 1940s were home to many specieses of wild animals are suburban neighborhoods now. Deers, with no other place to forage, devour gardens and shrubbery and ruin lawns with their sharp, pointed feet. Geese foul lawns and parks and can turn aggressive toward men, womans, and childs who try to shoo them away.

APPLY TO WRITING
Opinion Paragraph: *Plurals*

Some people look at land like this and see something that should be kept exactly as it is. Other people look at land like this and see endless possibilities for developing it and turning it into something different. What do you see? Answer that question by writing a paragraph to share with your classmates. Use at least ten plural nouns in your paragraph. Before writing, brainstorm answers to the following questions.

- What are the beautiful characteristics of this land?
- Where is the nearest city or town?
- What would happen to the water and trees if the land were developed?
- How would the people of the area benefit from leaving the land as it is?
- Should the land remain as it is? Explain why or why not.

Write the plural form of each word. Use a dictionary whenever necessary.

1. antenna	**6.** hero	**11.** belief	**16.** lamb
2. synopsis	**7.** hoof	**12.** 100	**17.** appendix
3. scissors	**8.** echo	**13.** opus	**18.** stadium
4. ox	**9.** 1980	**14.** *X*	**19.** lexicon
5. cello	**10.** buffalo	**15.** valley	**20.** *why*

Spelling Numbers

When you are writing something that includes numbers, you may be unsure whether you should write the number in words or use a numeral or numerals. Use the following generalizations to help guide you.

Numerals or Number Words

Spell out numbers that can be written in one or two words. Use numerals for other numbers. Always spell out a number that begins a sentence.

> The election was held **ten** days ago.
> The final vote was **563** for and **1,067** against.
> **Six hundred thirty** people came out to vote.

When you have a series of numbers, and some are just one or two words while others are more, use numerals for them all.

> In the "Favorite Ice Cream Flavor Poll," **347** young people said chocolate was their favorite flavor; **158** liked brownie fudge; **121** liked chocolate chip; and **40** liked vanilla best.

Ordinal Numbers

Always spell out numbers used to tell the order.

He promised to be here **first** thing in the morning.
Andrea wanted to finish **first,** but she came in **third.**

Numbers in Dates

Use a numeral for a date when you include the name of the month. Always use numerals for the year.

EXAMPLES
Dr. Seuss's birthday is March 2.
He was born in 1904.

EXCEPTION
Do you know anyone whose birthday is the twenty-ninth of February?
(Always spell out ordinal numbers.)

PRACTICE YOUR SKILLS

● Check Your Understanding
Spelling Numbers

Write the correct form of the number given in parentheses to complete each sentence.

1. (9)   This year's marathon was scheduled for October 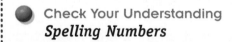.

2. (2)   The deadline for entering the race was ▤ weeks before, on September 17.

3. (15th)   On the ▤ of September, organizers were disappointed by the lack of interest.

4. (58)   Only ▤ people had signed up for the race.

5. (1996)   That was very different from the first marathon the town had in ▤.

6. (590)   ▤ people had signed up for that race just days after it had been announced.

7. (3)   Now, just ■ days before the deadline, very few people seemed interested.

8. (48)   But in ■ hours, everything changed.

9. (768)   By the deadline, a total of ■ runners had entered.

10. (2,000)   That was amazing, considering that the entire population of the town was only ■.

11. (18)   The marathon was open to runners ■ and older.

12. (50)   Among the entrants, there were 410 college-age runners, 308 adults, and ■ seniors.

13. (12)   Runners ran the length of the town and then ran to the next town, which was ■ miles away, and back again.

14. (1st)   No one knew who would finish ■.

15. (26)   Very few runners actually ran the entire ■ miles.

● Connect to the Writing Process: Editing
Writing Numbers Correctly

History Topic **Rewrite this paragraph, correcting any mistakes in writing numbers.**

The marathon race was first included in the Olympic games in Athens in 1896. Just 1 year later, in 1897, the very first Boston Marathon was run. Originally called the American Marathon Race, the Boston Marathon has been held every year, except 1918, for more than 100 years. The very first winner of the race was John J. McDermott of New York City, who finished the race in two hours, 55 minutes, and ten seconds. For finishing 1st, McDermott received a laurel wreath and a pot of beef stew.

⏵ Prefixes and Suffixes

A **prefix** is one or more syllables placed in front of a base word to form a new word. When you add a prefix, the spelling of the base word does not change.

PREFIXES	
in + accurate = **in**accurate	**re** + tell = **re**tell
pre + arrange = **pre**arrange	**over** + do = **over**do
dis + satisfied = **dis**satisfied	**mis** + use = **mis**use
re + evaluate = **re**evaluate	**un** + able = **un**able
ir + regular = **ir**regular	**il** + legal = **il**legal

A **suffix** is one or more syllables placed after a base word to change its part of speech and possibly also its meaning.

Suffixes –*ness* and –*ly*

The suffixes –*ness* and –*ly* are added to most base words without any spelling changes.

–*NESS* AND –*LY*	
open + **ness** = open**ness**	cruel + **ly** = cruel**ly**
plain + **ness** = plain**ness**	real + **ly** = real**ly**

Words Ending in *e*

Drop the final *e* in the base word when adding a suffix that begins with a vowel.

SUFFIXES WITH VOWELS	
EXAMPLES	drive + **ing** = driv**ing**
	isolate + **ion** = isolat**ion**
	sane + **ity** = san**ity**
EXCEPTIONS	courage + **ous** = courage**ous**
	pronounce + **able** = pronounce**able**

Keep the final *e* when adding a suffix that begins with a consonant.

SUFFIXES WITH CONSONANTS	
EXAMPLES	care + **ful** = care**ful** price + **less** = price**less** like + **ness** = like**ness** state + **ment** = state**ment**
EXCEPTIONS	argue + **ment** = arg**ument** true + **ly** = tru**ly**

If you are adding *–ly* to a word to make the word an adverb, be sure you add the suffix to the correct word. Two adverbs that are often confused are *respectively* and *respectfully*.

respectively—[respective + ly] in the order given

The postal abbreviations for Nebraska and Nevada are *respectively* NE and NV.

respectfully—[respectful + ly] in a polite or courteous manner

He answered his grandmother's curious questions *respectfully*.

PRACTICE YOUR SKILLS

 Check Your Understanding
Adding Suffixes

Combine the base words and suffixes. Remember to make any necessary spelling changes.

1. lone + some	**6.** guide + ance	**11.** one + ness
2. move + ment	**7.** peace + ful	**12.** outrage + ous
3. like + ness	**8.** pure + ity	**13.** love + ly
4. note + able	**9.** create + ion	**14.** close + est
5. notice + able	**10.** sure + ly	**15.** hope + ful

Spelling Words with Prefixes and Suffixes

Science Topic · **Find the words in this paragraph that have prefixes or suffixes, and correct those that are spelled incorrectly.**

The continueous movment of air in the troposphere is the cause of all our weather. This air is not only restless, but it is full of water vapor. If all the water in the air were suddenly released, it would actualy cover the earth completly with three feet of water. The air moves constantly because the sun warms the earth unnevenly. In warmer places, the air rises, causing updrafts and the createion of clouds. In colder places, the air sinks. When masses of warm air and cold air meet, unpleaseant weather is the predictable effect.

Words Ending with *y*

To add a suffix to most words ending with a vowel and *y*, keep the *y*.

	SUFFIXES WITH VOWELS AND Y	
EXAMPLES	enjoy + **able** = enjoy**able**	joy + **ful** = joy**ful**
EXCEPTIONS	day + **ly** = dai**ly**	gay + **ly** = gai**ly**

To add a suffix to most words ending in a consonant and *y*, change the *y* to *i* before adding the suffix.

	SUFFIXES WITH CONSONANTS AND Y	
EXAMPLES	easy + **ly** = eas**ily**	worry + **ed** = worr**ied**
EXCEPTIONS	shy + **ness** = shy**ness**	study + **ing** = study**ing**

Doubling the Final Consonant

Sometimes the final consonant in a word is doubled before a suffix is added. This happens when the suffix begins with a vowel and the base word satisfies both these conditions: (1) It has only one syllable or is stressed on the final syllable, and (2) it ends in one consonant preceded by one vowel.

DOUBLE CONSONANTS	
ONE-SYLLABLE WORDS	hop + ing = ho**pp**ing grin + ed = gri**nn**ed red + est = re**dd**est
FINAL SYLLABLE STRESSED	refer + al = refe**rr**al begin + er = begi**nn**er refer + ing = refe**rr**ing remit + ed = remi**tt**ed

PRACTICE YOUR SKILLS

 Check Your Understanding
Adding Suffixes

Combine the base words and suffixes. Remember to make any necessary spelling changes.

1. regret + able
2. play + ful
3. repel + ent
4. rely + able

5. mercy + less
6. slug + ish
7. grumpy + ly
8. deter + ent

9. sly + ness
10. defy + ant
11. coy + ly
12. pig + ish

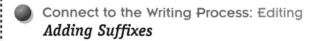 Connect to the Writing Process: Editing
Adding Suffixes

Contemporary Life **Rewrite this dialogue, correcting the words with suffixes that are spelled incorrectly.**

"Mine is not an envyable duty," Inspector Fields began, struggling to overcome his shyness, "but I must ask you,

Lady Penelope, where you were when this regretable crime was commited?"

"It was midnight," Lady Penelope said huffyly. "I was where I ordinarily am at that hour—asleep in bed."

"What would you say if I told you that a relyable witness has testified that he saw you in the garden?"

"I would be compeled to question your witness's vision," Lady Penelope replyed with icy haughtyness.

APPLY TO WRITING
Dialogue: *Suffixes*

Continue the dialogue between Inspector Fields and Lady Penelope to share with your classmates. You can decide what the regrettable crime was and what, if anything, Lady Penelope had to do with it. Use five words with suffixes in your dialogue.

✓ QuickCheck Mixed Practice

Add the prefix or suffix to each base word, and write the new word.

1. pre + determine
2. move + able
3. prepare + ation
4. gay + ly
5. open + ness
6. true + ly
7. timid + ity
8. il + logical

9. create + ive
10. like + ly
11. play + ful
12. full + ly
13. believe + able
14. shake + ly
15. worry + ed
16. lonely + ness
17. pre + occupied
18. likely + hood
19. outrage + ous
20. begin + er
21. rebel + ed
22. spin + ing

WORDS TO MASTER

Make it your goal to learn to spell these fifty words this year. Use them in your writing and practice writing them until spelling them correctly comes automatically.

achievement
acknowledgment
actually
argument
beginning
believe
chief
conceivable
continuous
correspondence
courageous
curiosity
eighth
exceedingly
excellent
excitable
glorious

gracious
happiness
ignorance
indispensable
insurance
interesting
judgment
leisure
loneliness
marriage
mileage
naturally
niece
noticeable
occasionally
occurrence
precede

preferred
preparation
proceed
readily
reasonably
removal
requirement
resistance
ridiculous
separate
succeed
successful
truly
unfortunately
unnecessary
weird

Applying Spelling Rules

Write the letter of the misspelled word in each group. Then write the word, spelling it correctly.

1. (a) niece   (b) ratios   (c) happyness
2. (a) intercede   (b) foriegn   (c) innumerable
3. (a) embarass   (b) seize   (c) engagement
4. (a) offered   (b) criticize   (c) atheletics
5. (a) conceit   (b) branches   (c) niether
6. (a) accidentally   (b) thinness   (c) payed
7. (a) peaceful   (b) immediatly   (c) misstep
8. (a) twentieth   (b) rideing   (c) argument
9. (a) journies   (b) rained   (c) proceed
10. (a) trapped   (b) knives   (c) permited
11. (a) mispell   (b) relieve   (c) patios
12. (a) immobile   (b) occuring   (c) betrayal
13. (a) forcible   (b) spying   (c) mathmatics
14. (a) surprised   (b) reign   (c) ridiculeous
15. (a) realy   (b) stepping   (c) valleys
16. (a) passersby   (b) leafs   (c) holidays
17. (a) caring   (b) decieve   (c) studying
18. (a) receipt   (b) beliefs   (c) easyly
19. (a) echos   (b) misguided   (c) geese
20. (a) joyful   (b) seperate   (c) interfere
21. (a) biggest   (b) delaying   (c) liesure
22. (a) generaly   (b) boxes   (c) roofs
23. (a) pettiness   (b) disatisfied   (c) writer
24. (a) anonymous   (b) likeness   (c) dayly
25. (a) editors-in-chief   (b) grammer   (c) eighth

Another Look

Spelling Patterns *(pages L625–L626)*

When you spell words with *ie* or *ei*, *i* comes before *e* except when the
letters follow *c* or when they stand for the long *a* sound.

Words that end in a syllable that sounds like "seed" are usually spelled
with *–cede*. Only one word in English is spelled with *–sede*, and only
three words are spelled with *–ceed*.

Plurals *(pages L627–L634)*

If a noun ends with *s*, *ch*, *sh*, *x*, or *z*, add *es* to form the plural.

Add *s* to form the plural of a noun ending with a vowel and *y*.

Change the *y* to *i* and add *es* to a noun ending in a consonant and *y*.

Add *s* to form the plural of a noun ending with a vowel and *o*.

The plurals of nouns ending in a consonant and *o* do not follow a regular
pattern.

To form the plural of some nouns ending in *f* or *fe*, just add *s*.

For some nouns ending in *f* or *fe*, change the *f* to *v* and add *es* or *s*.

Most compound nouns are made plural in the same way as other nouns.
The letters *s* or *es* are added to the end of the word. However, when the
main word in a compound word appears first, that word becomes plural.

Spelling Numbers *(pages L637–L638)*

Spell out numbers that can be written in one or two words. Always spell
out a number that begins a sentence.

Always spell out numbers used to tell order, or ordinal numbers.

Use a numeral for a date when you include the name of the month.
Always use numerals for the year.

Prefixes and Suffixes *(pages L640–L643)*

The suffixes *–ness* and *–ly* are added to most base words without any
spelling changes.

Drop the final *e* in a base word when adding a suffix that begins with a
vowel.

Keep the final *e* when adding a suffix that begins with a consonant.

To add a suffix to most words ending with a vowel and *y*, keep the *y*.

To add a suffix to most words ending in a consonant and *y*, change the *y*
to *i* before adding the suffix.

To add *–ing* or *–ed* to most words ending in a consonant, double the final
consonant.

 **Posttest**

Directions

Read the passage. Write the letter of the choice that correctly spells each underlined word. If the word contains no error, write D.

EXAMPLE   Whatever else you might say about P. T.

Barnum, he was an <u>exellent</u> salesman.
                  (1)

     1 A excellent
        B excellant
        C excelent
        D No error

ANSWER   **1 A**

P. T. Barnum began his life of odd <u>acheivements</u> with the
                                      (1)
opening of his American Museum in 1842. When <u>passersby</u> were
                                                (2)
treated to advertisements promising "The <u>Eigth</u> Wonder of the
                                          (3)
World" and the like, it is little wonder that <u>curiousity</u> brought the
                                              (4)
public in by the <u>1000s</u>. Barnum went on to manage the <u>outragously</u>
                  (5)   (6)
<u>successfull</u> tour of Swedish singer Jenny Lind. In 1871, he opened
 (7)
"The Greatest Show on Earth," designed to put all other <u>circusses</u> to
                                                          (8)
shame. <u>Featureing</u> everything from men swallowing <u>knifes</u> to the
        (9)   (10)
best of European acrobats, the circus merged with its major

competitor in 1881 and was subsequently known as "Barnum &

Bailey."

1 **A** achevements
   B achievements
   C achiefments
   D No error

2 **A** passerbys
   B passerbyes
   C passers by
   D No error

3 **A** 8th
   B Eight
   C Eighth
   D No error

4 **A** curiosity
   B curiusity
   C curiousty
   D No error

5 **A** 1000's
   B 1000
   C thousands
   D No error

6 **A** outrageously
   B outragousally
   C outragely
   D No error

7 **A** successful
   B sucesfull
   C succesful
   D No error

8 **A** circusies
   B circi
   C circuses
   D No error

9 **A** Featurring
   B Featuring
   C Featureng
   D No error

10 **A** kniffes
   B knives
   C knife
   D No error

A Study Guide for Academic Success

To succeed academically, you should be not only familiar with the material but also aware that there are various test-taking strategies. In some ways, preparing for a test is like learning to play chess. You can't simply sit across from an opponent and announce, "Checkmate." You must first learn the rules of the game, the ways the pieces can move, and the strategies for attacking and defending. If you learn the strategies and apply helpful tips and pointers, for example, you can become both a better chess player and a better test taker. Also, the more practice you have, the better prepared you will be to play a difficult match or take an important test.

In the following chapter, you will become familiar with the various questions used in standardized tests. Pay close attention to the "rules" for each kind of question and the strategies used to master them. These lessons and practice exercises will help you develop your test-taking strengths.

Keep in mind that many of the abilities you acquire in this chapter will carry over into homework and daily classroom assignments and beyond. Learning how to read different kinds of information and developing strategies for approaching different types of questions will help you sharpen the critical thinking skills you use when you do homework, play sports, and make important decisions.

Learning Study Skills

Applying good study habits helps you in taking tests as well as in completing daily classroom assignments. Begin to improve your study habits by using the following strategies.

> **Strategies for Effective Studying**

- Choose an area that is well lighted and quiet.
- Equip your study area with everything you need for reading and writing, including a dictionary and a thesaurus.
- Keep an assignment book for recording due dates.
- Allow plenty of time. Begin your assignments early.
- Adjust your reading rate to suit your purpose.

Adjusting Reading Rate to Purpose

Your reading rate is the speed at which you read. Depending on your purpose in reading certain material, you may decide to read quickly or slowly. If your purpose is to get a general impression of the material, you may quickly read only parts of a page. If your purpose is to find the main point of a selection, you read more thoroughly. When you are reading to learn specific information, you slow your reading rate considerably to allow for close attention to facts and details.

Scanning

Read the title, headings, subheadings, picture captions, words and phrases in boldface or italics, and any focus questions. You can quickly determine what the material is about and what questions to keep in mind. **Scanning** is reading to get a general impression and to prepare for learning about a subject.

Skimming

After scanning a chapter, section, or article, quickly read the introduction, the topic sentence and summary sentence of each paragraph, and the conclusion. **Skimming** is reading quickly to identify the purpose, thesis, main ideas, and supporting ideas of a selection. Skimming is useful for reading supplementary material and for reviewing material previously read.

Close Reading

After scanning a selection, read it more slowly, word for word. **Close reading** is for locating specific information, following the logic of an argument, or comprehending the meaning or significance of information. Most of your assignments for school will require close reading.

▶ Taking Notes

Taking notes helps you to identify and remember the essential information in a textbook or lecture. Three methods of taking notes are the informal outline, the graphic organizer, and the summary.

In an **informal outline,** you use words and phrases to record main ideas and important details. This method is especially useful when you are studying for a multiple-choice test because it allows you to see the most important facts.

In a **graphic organizer,** words and phrases are arranged in a visual pattern to indicate the relationships between main ideas and supporting details. This is an excellent tool for studying information for an objective test, for an open-ended assessment, or for writing an essay. The visual organizer allows you, instantly, to see important information and its relationship to other ideas.

In a **summary** you use sentences to express important ideas in your own words. A good summary should do more than restate the information. It should express relationships among the ideas and draw conclusions. For this reason, summarizing is a good way to prepare for an essay test.

Whether you are taking notes in modified outline form or in summary form, include only the main ideas and important details. In the following passage from a science textbook, the essential information is underlined.

Characteristics of Fish

All fish have certain characteristics in common. For example, all fish have backbones and are cold-blooded. In addition, most fish breathe through gills. The gills, which are found on either side of a fish's head, take up oxygen that is dissolved in water. As a fish opens its mouth, water enters and passes over the gills, where oxygen molecules diffuse from the water into the fish's blood. At the same time, carbon dioxide passes out of its blood into the water.

Other characteristics of most fish include scales, which cover and protect their bodies, and fins, which aid fish in swimming. Certain fins act as steering guides, while others help a fish keep its balance in the water. Another aid in swimming that most fish have is a streamlined body, one in which the head and tail are smaller and more pointed than the middle part of the body. This streamlined shape helps fish swim by making it easier for them to push water aside as they propel themselves through the water.

Characteristics of Fish

INFORMAL
OUTLINE:

1. Have backbones and are cold-blooded (all)

2. Breathe through gills (most)

3. Have scales, fins, and streamlined bodies (most)

Characteristics of Fish

GRAPHIC
ORGANIZER:

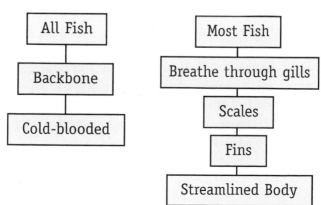

All Fish — Backbone — Cold-blooded

Most Fish — Breathe through gills — Scales — Fins — Streamlined Body

Characteristics of Fish

SUMMARY: All fish share two common characteristics: backbones and cold-bloodedness. Most fish breathe through gills and have scales for protection. Most fish also have fins and streamlined bodies for efficient swimming.

No matter which note-taking method you use, the following strategies will help make your notes clear and useful.

 Strategies for Taking Notes

- Label your notes with the title and page numbers of the chapter or the topic and date of the lecture.

- Record only the main ideas and important details, using key words and phrases.

- Use the titles, subtitles, and words in special type to help you select the most important information.

- Use your own words; do not copy word for word.

- Use as few words as possible.

Preparing Subject-Area Assignments

The strategies you have learned in this chapter for reading textbooks and taking notes can be applied to assignments in any subject area.

Mathematics and science textbooks often list rules, formulas, equations, or models. In these subjects, you should focus on applying the rules or models to solve problems or show the truth of scientific principles.

History, government, and economics courses, on the other hand, emphasize reading and interpreting maps, charts, graphs, time lines, documents, and statistical data. In preparing for these assignments or tests, you should pay special attention to information provided in those formats.

Taking Standardized Tests

Standardized tests measure your skills, progress, and achievement in such a way that the results can be compared with those of other students in the same grade. Standardized tests that measure your verbal or language skills are divided into two broad categories: analogy tests and tests of reading and writing ability.

Strategies for Taking Standardized Tests

- Read the test directions carefully. Answer sample questions to be sure you are following the instructions.

- Try to relax. You can expect to be a little nervous, but concentrate on doing your best.

- Skim the entire section to get an overview of the kinds of questions you will be asked.

- Plan your time carefully. Be aware of how much time you are allotted for each part of the test.

- Answer first the questions you find easiest. Skip questions you find too difficult, but come back to them later.

- Read all the choices before selecting the best answer. If you are not sure of an answer, eliminate choices that are obviously incorrect. Educated guessing often helps.

- If you have time, check your answers. Be sure you have correctly marked your answer sheet.

Analogies

Analogy questions test your skill at figuring out relationships between words. The first step is to determine how the two words are related. The second step is to decide which other pair has the same relationship as the words in capital letters.

The punctuation in an analogy question stands for the words *is to* and *as*.

CLOCK : TIME :: thermometer : temperature

The example reads, "A *clock* is to *time* as a *thermometer* is to *temperature*." That is, a clock has the same relationship to time as a thermometer has to temperature. A clock measures time as a thermometer measures temperature.

Try to explain to yourself in one sentence the relationship between the two words in capital letters. In the following example, you might say, "Handlebars are part of a bicycle."

HANDLEBARS : BICYCLE ::
(A) moose : antlers   (B) tire : fender
(C) carpenter : hammer   (D) steering wheel : automobile
(E) golf : sport

(The answer is *(D) steering wheel : automobile* because the relationship between these two words is that of part to whole; a steering wheel is part of an automobile.

Remember that the words in the answer must be in the same order as the words in the given analogy. If the given pair of words in the analogy expresses a cause-to-effect relationship, the words in the correct answer should also be in order of cause to effect.

Rain is to *flood* as *virus* is to ▇.
(A) computer   (B) drought   (C) illness   (D) energy
(E) nurse

(The first two italicized words are a cause and an effect: rain causes flood. Therefore, the correct answer is *(C) illness,* an effect of a virus.)

Knowing some of the common types of analogies, like those in the following chart, will help you figure out word relationships.

COMMON TYPES OF ANALOGIES	
Analogy	**Example**
word : synonym	plain : simple
part : whole	lens : camera
cause : effect	burn : pain
worker : tool	gardener : shovel
item : purpose	pencil : write

PRACTICE YOUR SKILLS

● Check Your Understanding
Recognizing Analogies

Write the letter of the word pair that has the same relationship as the word pair in capital letters.

1. DENTIST : DRILL ::
   - (A) calendar : date
   - (B) sculptor : chisel
   - (C) lumberjack : forest
   - (D) eyeglasses : sight
   - (E) hammer : carpenter

2. HASTEN : HURRY ::
   - (A) laugh : talk
   - (B) trust : doubt
   - (C) stammer : whisper
   - (D) attempt : try
   - (E) explain : understand

● Check Your Understanding
Completing Analogies

Complete the analogy by writing the letter of the word that best completes the sentence.

3. *Carelessness* is to *error* as *exploration* is to ■.
   - (A) invention
   - (B) bravery
   - (C) sailing
   - (D) artifacts
   - (E) discovery

4. *Page* is to *book* as *card* is to ■.
   - (A) king
   - (B) clubs
   - (C) deck
   - (D) suit
   - (E) joker

● Sentence-Completion Tests

Sentence-completion tests measure your ability to comprehend what you read and to use context correctly. Each item consists of a sentence with one or more words missing. First read the entire sentence. Then read the answer choices and select the one that completes the sentence in a way that makes sense.

The town of Odessa, Delaware, now has a population of only five hundred, but it was once a ■ seaport.
- (A) fascinating
- (B) tiny
- (C) Pacific
- (D) bustling
- (E) sleepy

(The answer is *(D) bustling*. The sentence contrasts the small size of the town today with its previous size.)

Some sentence-completion questions have two blanks in the same sentence, with each answer choice including two words.

Even today, the ■ of the soldiers who bravely fought in World War II is remembered with ■.
(A) fear . . . scorn   (B) courage . . . horror
(C) honor . . . indifference   (D) story . . . anger
(E) heroism . . . pride

(The answer is *(E) heroism . . . pride.* None of the other choices fit the idea of remembering brave soldiers.)

PRACTICE YOUR SKILLS

● Check Your Understanding
Completing Sentences

Write the letter of the word that best completes each of the following sentences.

1. Sharks do not have good eyesight, but their sense of smell is ■.
   (A) poor   (B) keen   (C) decisive
   (D) huge   (E) inferior

2. After ten to fourteen days in its chrysalis, the monarch caterpillar ■ as a beautiful monarch butterfly.
   (A) transforms   (B) becomes   (C) emerges
   (D) looms   (E) struggles

● Check Your Understanding
Completing Sentences with Two Blanks

Write the letter of the words that best complete each of the following sentences.

3. The ■ empire fell shortly after a series of ■ battles with an invading army.
   (A) new . . . successful   (B) Roman . . . victorious
   (C) mighty . . . easy   (D) crumbling . . . ruinous
   (E) old . . . jubilant

4. The abandoned warehouse was an eyesore with its windows ■, its paint ■, and its roof sagging.
   (A) gleaming . . . shining   (B) sparking . . . fading
   (C) open . . . bright   (D) cracked . . . peeling
   (E) broken . . . vivid

▶ Reading Comprehension Tests

Reading comprehension tests assess your ability to understand and analyze written passages. The information you need to answer the test questions may be either directly stated or implied in the passage. You must study, analyze, and interpret a passage in order to answer the questions that follow it. The following strategies will help you answer questions on reading tests.

> ### ▷ Strategies for Answering Reading Questions
>
> - Begin by skimming the questions that follow the passage.
> - Read the passage carefully and closely. Notice the main ideas, organization, style, and key words.
> - Study all possible answers. Avoid choosing one answer the moment you think it is a reasonable choice.
> - Use only the information in the passage when you answer the questions. Do not rely on your own knowledge or ideas on this kind of test.

Most reading questions will focus on one or more of the following characteristics of a written passage.

- **Main idea** At least one question will usually focus on the central idea of the passage. Remember that the main idea of a passage covers all sections of the passage—not just one section or paragraph.

- **Supporting details** Questions about supporting details test your ability to identify the statements in the passage that back up the main idea.

- **Implied meanings** In some passages not all information is directly stated. Some questions ask you to interpret information that the author has merely implied.

- **Purpose and Tone** Questions on purpose and tone require that you interpret or analyze the author's attitude toward his or her subject and purpose for writing.

Read the following passage and write the letter of each correct answer.

KIDNAPPED BY UFO ALIENS. You have seen countless newspaper headlines or television stories like this. Although such tales are common today, hoaxes and rumors about space creatures go back many years. One famous example, the *"Sun* moon story," dates to 1835. In August of that year, the *New York Sun* announced that a distinguished British astronomer had made some wondrous discoveries while using a new telescope. The newspaper printed a series of articles describing the plants, animals, and winged men that lived on the moon. The stories helped make the *Sun* the best-selling daily newspaper in the world. Eventually reporter Richard Adams Locke admitted making up the articles. After the truth was discovered, Edgar Allan Poe abandoned a story he had begun about a man who flies to the moon in a balloon. He claimed to have been "outdone" by the newspaper's tales.

While readers of the *Sun* enjoyed the fantastic descriptions of life on the moon, listeners of another great hoax were terrified. Orson Welles's 1938 broadcast of "War of the Worlds" caused alarm all across the United States. In 1898, when the story was actually written, Mars was in close proximity to Earth. People could easily observe it and speculate about possible life on the planet. The writer, H. G. Wells, created a tale of Martian invaders with powerful new weapons resembling the atomic, nuclear, and biological weapons known to us today. When the story was broadcast over the radio in 1938, World War I was a recent event and World War II was fast approaching. Most listeners were panic-stricken; few recognized the program as fiction. Today, we are less afraid of an alien invasion, but we are just as fascinated by the idea of meeting life from outer space.

1. The "*Sun* moon story" met with
   (A) contempt from the scientific community.
   (B) enthusiasm from readers worldwide.
   (C) skepticism from the public.
   (D) fear about an alien invasion.
   (E) jealousy from other American writers.

2. The passage indicates that space creature hoaxes
   (A) are always believed.
   (B) are usually treated as harmless practical jokes.
   (C) often involve little green men.
   (D) have existed for over a hundred years.
   (E) began in the 1930s.

3. This passage would most likely appear in
   (A) a science fiction novel.
   (B) a textbook on the solar system.
   (C) a history of American newspapers.
   (D) an article on the rise of NASA.
   (E) a book on public fascination with life in outer space.

The Double Passage

You may also be asked to read a pair of passages and answer questions about each passage individually and about the way the two passages relate to each other. The two passages may present similar or opposing views or may complement each other in other ways. A brief introduction preceding the passages may help you anticipate the relationship between them.

PRACTICE YOUR SKILLS

● Check Your Understanding
Reading for Double-Passage Comprehension

These passages present two descriptions of tropical islands. The first passage is from an article called "An Aloha State of Mind" by William Ecenbarger. The second is from *In the South Seas* by Robert Louis Stevenson. Read each passage and answer the questions that follow.

Passage 1

Hot golden sunshine covers everything along Maui's southern coast, as though someone has spilled it. On the beaches, children, sugared in sand, whittle away at their parents' patience, while honeymooners stroll by, hand in hand, through the white lace left by the retreating surf. Coppery sunbathers stretch out like cookies on a baking sheet. . . .

Not far inland, Haleakala volcano begins its steep, 10,000-foot ascent, and about halfway up, there are thin layers of drifting clouds. It's twenty degrees cooler here, and the air is redolent with eucalyptus, woodsmoke, and the odors of earth and cattle. Looking down the slope you can see the beach five miles away. The sea appears as an immense blue fabric, rumpled and creased, and ends with the scrawling signature of the shore.

Passage 2

I have watched the morning break in many quarters of the world; it has been certainly one of the chief joys of my existence, and the dawn that I saw with the most emotion shone upon the Bay of Anaho. The mountains abruptly overhang the port with every variety of surface and of inclination, lawn, and cliff, and forest. Not one of these but wore its proper tint of saffron, of sulphur, of the clove, and of the rose. The lustre was like that of satin; on the lighter hues there seemed to float an efflorescence; a solemn bloom appeared on the more dark. The light itself was the ordinary light of morning, colourless and clean; and on this ground of jewels, pencilled out the least detail of drawing. Meanwhile, around the hamlet, under the palms, where the blue shadow lingered, the red coals of cocoa husk and the light trails of smoke betrayed the awakening business of the day . . . .

1. The tone of Passage 1 is
   (A) humorous
   (B) poetic
   (C) sarcastic
   (D) objective
   (E) ironic

2. The author of Passage 1 probably wrote the passage to
   (A) encourage people to visit Maui.
   (B) warn people about the dangers of sunbathing.
   (C) inform people about the volcanoes of Hawaii.
   (D) describe the tourists who visit the islands.
   (E) persuade people to write for travel magazines.

3. Which of the following best describes the author's purpose in Passage 2?
   (A) to argue for conservation of tropical islands
   (B) to persuade other travelers to visit the Bay of Anaho
   (C) to describe a beautiful morning scene
   (D) to show off his writing skills
   (E) to inform people what life is like for the people of the South Seas.

4. Both authors would probably agree with which of the following statements?
   (A) The Bay of Anaho is a beautiful site.
   (B) Maui is a popular destination for tourists.
   (C) The richest colors on earth exist in the sunrise.
   (D) Too much sun is bad for your skin.
   (E) Tropical islands are wonderful to visit.

Tests of Standard Written English

Objective tests of standard written English assess your knowledge of the language skills used for writing. They contain sentences with underlined words, phrases, and punctuation. The underlined parts will contain errors in grammar, usage, mechanics, vocabulary, and spelling. You are asked to find the error in each sentence, or, on some tests, to identify the best way to revise a sentence or passage.

Error Recognition

The most familiar way to test grammar, usage, capitalization, punctuation, word choice, and spelling is through an error-recognition sentence. A typical test item of this kind is a sentence with five underlined choices. Four of the choices suggest possible errors. The fifth choice, *E*, states that there is no error.

> Some scientists <u>believe</u> that the first <u>dog's</u> <u>were</u> tamed <u>over</u>
>   A   B   C   D
> 10,000 years ago.
>
> (The answer is *B*. The word *dogs* should not have an apostrophe because it is plural, not possessive.)

Some sentences have no errors. Before you choose *E (No error)*, however, be sure that you have carefully studied every part of the sentence. The errors are often hard to notice.

Remember that the parts of a sentence not underlined are presumed to be correct. You can use clues in the correct parts of the sentence to help you search for errors in the underlined parts.

PRACTICE YOUR SKILLS

● Check Your Understanding
Recognizing Errors in Writing

Write the letter that is below the underlined word or punctuation mark that is incorrect. If the sentence contains no error, write *E*.

(1) Temperatures on summer nights <u>are</u> often <u>cooler</u> in
                                   A   B
the suburbs <u>then</u> <u>in</u> the city. (2) One reason for the
           C   D
difference <u>is</u> <u>that</u> suburbs have <u>less</u> buildings <u>than</u> the city
          A   B   C   D
has. (3) <u>During</u> the day city streets, sidewalks, and
                                A
<u>buildings</u> <u>absorb</u> the <u>Summer</u> heat. (4) At night the suburbs
  B   C   D
cool down, <u>but,</u> the city <u>does</u> not. (5) Buildings and streets
 A   B   C   D
<u>release</u> the heat absorbed during the <u>day,</u> this heat <u>keeps</u>
  A   B   C

the city warmer throughout the night. **(6)** The suburbs have
$$\overline{\text{D}}\qquad\qquad\qquad\qquad\qquad\overline{\text{A}}$$
more trees and grass that hold rainwater near the surface.
$$\overline{\text{B}}\qquad\qquad\quad\overline{\text{C}}\qquad\qquad\quad\overline{\text{D}}$$
(7) The water evaporates in the heat, and cools down the
$$\qquad\qquad\overline{\text{A}}\qquad\qquad\qquad\qquad\overline{\text{B}}\qquad\overline{\text{C}}$$
temperature. **(8)** Furthermore, the trees, like a fan, keeps a
$$\overline{\text{D}}\qquad\qquad\qquad\qquad\qquad\overline{\text{A}}\ \overline{\text{B}}\qquad\overline{\text{C}}\ \overline{\text{D}}$$
breeze blowing. **(9)** Tall and unbending, the buildings in
$$\qquad\qquad\qquad\qquad\qquad\qquad\qquad\qquad\overline{\text{A}}$$
the city retain the warm air as an oven does. **(10)** Its easy
$$\qquad\ \overline{\text{B}}\qquad\qquad\quad\overline{\text{C}}\qquad\quad\overline{\text{D}}\qquad\qquad\overline{\text{A}}$$
to understand why people often try to leave the city to visit
$$\qquad\qquad\qquad\overline{\text{B}}\qquad\quad\overline{\text{C}}$$
the countryside on a hot July weekend.
$$\qquad\qquad\qquad\qquad\qquad\overline{\text{D}}$$

Sentence-Correction Questions

Sentence-correction questions assess your ability to recognize appropriate phrasing. Instead of locating an error in a sentence, you must select the most appropriate way to write the sentence.

In this kind of question, a part of the sentence is underlined. The sentence is then followed by five different ways of writing the underlined part. The first way shown, (A), simply repeats the original underlined portion. The other four give alternative ways of writing the underlined part. The choices may involve grammar, usage, capitalization, punctuation, or word choice. Be sure that the answer you choose does not change the meaning of the original sentence.

Many colleges and universities in the United States, such as The College of William and Mary in Virginia, <u>is named after historical figures.</u>
(A) Virginia, is named after historical figures.
(B) Virginia. Is named after historical figures.
(C) Virginia is named after historical figures.
(D) Virginia, are named after historical figures.
(E) Virginia are named after historical figures.

(The answer is *(D)*. The verb *is* must be changed to agree with the subject *colleges and universities*. Choices *(A)*, *(B)*, and *(C)* do not correct the subject-verb agreement problem. Choice *(E)* adds an error by removing the comma.)

PRACTICE YOUR SKILLS

● Check Your Understanding
Correcting Sentences

Write the letter of the correct way, or the best way, of phrasing the underlined part of each sentence.

1. Is it true that Betsy Ross probably <u>didn't never sew the first American flag?</u>
   (A) didn't never sew the first American flag?
   (B) didn't ever sew the first american flag?
   (C) didn't never sewed the first American flag?
   (D) didn't sew the first American flag?
   (E) did not never sew the first american flag?

2. <u>There is shiny white and gold fish</u> in the pool in my grandmother's garden.
   (A) There is shiny white and gold fish
   (B) There is shiny white, and gold fish
   (C) There are shiny white and gold fish
   (D) There are shiny white, and gold fish
   (E) Here is shiny white and gold fish

Revision-in-Context

Another type of multiple-choice question that appears on some standardized tests is called revision-in-context. The questions following the reading ask you to choose the best revision of a sentence, a group of sentences, or the essay as a whole or to clearly identify the writer's intention.

PRACTICE YOUR SKILLS

● Check Your Understanding
Correcting Sentences

Carefully read the passage, which is the beginning of an essay about *The Jungle Book*. Answer the questions that follow.

(1) Rudyard Kipling's collection of stories known as *The Jungle Book* features tales about animals and people living in India. **(2)** One story is about a mongoose named Rikki-Tikki-Tavi. **(3)** It is his job to protect his adopted family from two cobras. **(4)** The cobras are called Nag and Nagaina. **(5)** Threatening the other animals in the garden and the family in the house are the large and powerful cobras. **(6)** Despite the odds against him, the little mongoose must find a way to defeat the deadly cobras.

1. In relation to the rest of the passage, which of the following best describes the writer's intention in sentence 6?
   (A) to restate the opening sentence
   (B) to propose an analysis of the story
   (C) to explain a metaphor
   (D) to interest the reader in the outcome of the story
   (E) to summarize the paragraph

2. Which best combines sentences 2, 3, and 4?
   (A) One story is about Rikki-Tikki-Tavi, a mongoose who must protect his adopted family from the cobras Nag and Nagaina.
   (B) One story is about Rikki-Tikki-Tavi, who must protect his adopted family from two cobras.
   (C) One story is about a mongoose who must protect his adopted family from Nag and Nagaina.
   (D) One story is about Rikki-Tikki-Tavi, who must protect his adopted family from Nag and Nagaina.
   (E) Protecting his adopted family from the cobras Nag and Nagaina is the mongoose Rikki-Tikki-Tavi.

Taking Essay Tests

Essay tests are designed to assess both your understanding of important ideas and your ability to see connections, or relationships, between these ideas. You must be able to organize your thoughts quickly and express them logically and clearly.

 Kinds of Essay Questions

Always begin an essay test by reading the instructions for all the questions. Then, as you reread the instructions for your first question, look for key words, such as those in the box.

KINDS OF ESSAY QUESTIONS	
ANALYZE	Separate into parts and examine each part.
COMPARE	Point out similarities.
CONTRAST	Point out differences.
DEFINE	Clarify meaning.
DISCUSS	Examine in detail.
EVALUATE	Give your opinion
EXPLAIN	Tell how, what, or why.
ILLUSTRATE	Give examples.
SUMMARIZE	Briefly review main points.
TRACE	Show development or progress.

As you read the instructions, jot down what is required in your answer or circle key words and underline key phrases.

> (Evaluate) the contributions of Louis Pasteur to the world of science in a short essay of three paragraphs. Use (specific examples). Be sure to include his "germ theory of disease," which states that most infectious diseases are caused by germs.

Writing an Effective Essay Answer

Writing an essay for a test is basically the same as writing any essay. Therefore, you should recall and apply all you have learned about using the writing process to write an essay. The major difference is that you will have a very strict time limit.

Because of the limited time in a test situation, you must carefully plan your essay. You should first brainstorm for ideas and organize your answer by writing a simple informal outline or constructing a graphic organizer. This plan will give structure to your essay and help you avoid omitting important points.

OUTLINE: **Louis Pasteur's Contributions to Science**
(thesis statement)
1. Contribution 1: "germ theory of disease"
2. Contribution 2: immunization
3. Contribution 3: pasteurization
(conclusion)

Your next step is to write a thesis statement. It is often possible to reword the test question into a thesis statement.

ESSAY QUESTION: Evaluate the contributions of Louis Pasteur to the world of science in a short essay. Use specific examples. Be sure to include his "germ theory of disease," which states that most infectious diseases are caused by germs.

THESIS STATEMENT: Louis Pasteur was a great scientist whose contributions, including the "germ theory of disease," revolutionized the world of science.

As you write your essay, keep the following strategies in mind.

▷ **Strategies for Writing an Essay Answer**
- Write an introduction that includes the thesis statement.
- Follow the order of your outline, writing one paragraph for each main point.

- Provide adequate support for each main point—using specific facts, examples, and/or other supporting details.
- Use transitions to connect your ideas and/or examples.
- End with a strong concluding statement that summarizes the main idea of the essay.
- Write clearly and legibly.

Model: Essay Test Answer

THESIS STATEMENT:

Louis Pasteur was a great scientist whose contributions, including the "germ theory of disease," revolutionized the world of science. Before Pasteur proposed the "germ theory of disease," the causes of infectious diseases were unknown. After Pasteur discovered that tiny microbes passed from person to person, infecting each with disease, he argued for cleaner hospital practices. The germs of one patient were no longer passed to another through nonsterile instruments, dirty bed linens, and shared air.

Pasteur's research also led him to immunization. Although another scientist first created the vaccine for smallpox, Pasteur took the idea and applied it to other diseases, including rabies. He discovered that by using a weaker form of the virus that causes rabies, he could protect dogs from contracting the stronger form of the virus. Also, he was able to develop a cure for humans who had been bitten by rabid animals.

Pasteur's reputation as a great scientist led the Emperor Napoleon III to request his help with another problem. The French economy was suffering because French wine was diseased and unsellable. After some investigation, Pasteur discovered that the wine could be heated so that the germs were killed, but the wine remained

Conclusion: unaffected. This process is now called pasteurization and is applied to many perishable foods, including beer and milk. Pasteur's research and discoveries have led to healthier lives all over the world.

Revising — Writing Process

Always leave a few minutes to revise and edit your essay answer. As you revise, think of the following questions.

- Did you thoroughly follow the instructions?
- Did you begin with a thesis statement?
- Did you include facts, examples, and other details?
- Did you use transitions to connect ideas and examples?
- Did you end with a strong concluding statement that summarizes your essay?
- Did you stick to the topic?

Editing — Writing Process

Once you have made revisions, quickly read your essay for mistakes in spelling, usage, or punctuation. Use proofreading symbols to make changes. As you edit, check for the following:

- agreement between subjects and verbs *(chapter 12)*
- agreement of antecedents and pronouns *(pages L355–L358)*
- avoidance of tense shift *(pages L310–L311)*
- correct capitalization of proper nouns and proper adjectives *(pages L464–L480)*
- correct use of apostrophes *(pages L575–L588)*

Timed Writing

Throughout your school years, you will be tested on your ability to organize your thoughts quickly and to express them in a limited time. Time limits can vary from twenty to sixty to ninety minutes, depending upon the task. For a twenty-minute essay, you might consider organizing your time in the following way:

5 minutes: Brainstorm and organize ideas.

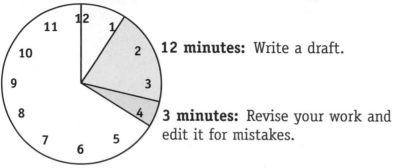

12 minutes: Write a draft.

3 minutes: Revise your work and edit it for mistakes.

The more you practice writing under time constraints, the better prepared you will be for tests.

Communicate Your Ideas

APPLY TO WRITING

Prewriting, Drafting, Revising, Editing: *Timed Writing*

You will have twenty minutes to write a complete essay on the following topic.

- Discuss an important issue facing people of your age today. Explain why this issue is important and how you think people should respond to it.

Plan time for each stage of the writing process, set a timer, and begin your response.

A **Abbreviation** shortened form of a word.

Abstract summary of points of writing, presented in skeletal form.

Action verb word that tells what action a subject is performing.

Active voice the voice a verb is in when it expresses that the subject is performing the action.

Adequate development quality of good writing in which sufficient supporting details develop the main idea.

Adjective word that modifies a noun or a pronoun.

Adjective clause subordinate clause that is used like an adjective to modify a noun or a pronoun.

Adjective phrase prepositional phrase that is used to modify a noun or a pronoun.

Adverb word that modifies a verb, an adjective, or another adverb.

Adverb clause subordinate clause that is used like an adverb to modify a verb, an adjective, or an adverb.

Adverb phrase prepositional phrase that is used like an adverb to modify a verb, an adjective, or an adverb.

Alliteration repetition of a consonant sound at the beginning of a series of words.

Analogies logical relationships between pairs of words.

Antecedent word or group of words that a pronoun replaces or refers to.

Antonym word that means the opposite of another word.

Appositive noun or a pronoun that identifies or explains another noun or pronoun in a sentence.

Article the special adjectives *a*, *an*, *the*.

Audience person or persons who will read your work or hear your speech.

B **Body** one or more paragraphs comprised of details, facts, and examples that support the main idea.

Brainstorming prewriting technique of writing down everything that comes to mind about a subject.

Business letter writing form that uses formal language and contains six parts: heading, inside address, salutation, body, closing, and signature.

C **Case** form of a noun or a pronoun that indicates its use in a sentence. In English there are three cases: the nominative case, the objective case, and the possessive case.

Cause and effect method of development in which details are grouped according to what happens and why it happens.

Characterization variety of techniques used by writers to show the personality of a character.

Chronological order the order in which events occur.

Clarity the quality of being clear.

Classics literary works that withstand the test of time and appeal to readers from generation to generation and from century to century.

Classification method of development in which details are grouped into categories.

Clause group of words that has a subject and verb and is used as part of a sentence.

Clause fragment subordinate clause standing alone.

Cliché overused expression that is no longer fresh or interesting to the reader.

Clustering a visual form of brainstorming that is a technique used for developing supporting details.

Coherence logical and smooth flow of ideas connected with clear transitions.

Colloquialism informal phrase or colorful expression appropriate for conversation but not for formal writing.

Comparison and contrast method of development in which details are grouped according to similarities and differences.

Complement word that completes the meaning of an action verb.

Complete predicate all the words that tell what the subject is doing or that tell something about the subject.

Complete subject all the words used to identify the person, place, thing, or idea that the sentence is about.

Complex sentence one independent clause and one or more subordinate clauses.

Composition writing form that presents and develops one main idea in three or more paragraphs.

Compound-complex sentence two or more independent clauses and one or more subordinate clauses.

Compound noun word made up of two smaller words that can be separated, hyphenated, or combined.

Compound sentence two or more independent clauses in one sentence.

Compound subject two or more subjects in one sentence that have the same verb and are joined by a conjunction.

Compound verb two or more verbs that have the same subject and are joined by a conjunction.

Concluding sentence a strong ending added to a paragraph that summarizes the major points, refers to the main idea, or adds an insight.

Conclusion paragraph that completes an essay and reinforces its main idea.

Conflict struggle between opposing forces around which the action of a work of literature revolves.

Conjunction word that joins together sentences, clauses, phrases, or other words.

Connotation the meaning that comes from attitudes attached to a word.

Context clue clue to a word's meaning provided by the sentence, the surrounding words, or the situation in which the word occurs.

Contraction word that combines two words into one. It uses an apostrophe to replace one or more missing letters.

Cooperative learning strategy in which a group works together to achieve a common goal or accomplish a single task.

Coordinating conjunction single connecting word used to join words or groups of words.

Correlative conjunction pairs of conjunctions used to connect compound subjects, compound verbs, and compound sentences.

Creative writing writing style in which the writer creates characters, events, and images within stories, plays, or poems to express feelings, perceptions, and points of view.

D **Dangling modifier** phrase that has nothing to describe in a sentence.

Declarative sentence a statement or expression of an opinion. It ends with a period.

Definition method of development in which the nature and characteristics of a word, object, concept, or phenomenon are explained.

Demonstrative pronoun word that substitutes for a noun and points out a person or a thing.

Denotation the literal meaning of a word.

Descriptive writing writing that creates a vivid picture of a person, an object, or a scene by stimulating the reader's senses.

Dewey decimal system system by which nonfiction books are arranged on shelves in numerical order according to ten general subject categories.

Dialect regional variation of a language distinguished by distinctive pronunciation and some differences in word meanings.

Dialogue a conversation between two or more persons.

Direct object noun or pronoun that receives the action of a verb.

Direct quotation passage, sentence, or words written or spoken exactly as a person wrote or said them.

Double negative use of two negative words to express an idea when only one is needed.

Drafting stage of the writer's process in which he or she draws together ideas on paper.

E **Editing** stage of the writing process in which the writer polishes his or her work by correcting errors in grammar, usage, mechanics, and spelling.

Elaboration addition of explanatory or descriptive information, such as supporting details, facts, and examples, to an essay.

Electronic publishing various ways to present information through the use of technology. It includes desktop publishing (creating printed documents on a computer), audio and video recordings, and online publishing (creating a Website).

Elliptical clause subordinate clause in which words are omitted but understood to be there.

E-mail electronic mail that can be sent all over the world from one computer to another.

Emoticons symbols used by E-mail users to convey emotions.

Encyclopedia reference that contains general information about a variety of subjects.

Endnote complete citation of the source of borrowed material at the end of a research report.

Essay composition that presents and develops one main idea in three or more paragraphs.

Essential phrase or clause group of words essential to the meaning of a sentence; therefore, not set off with commas.

Etymology history of a word, from its earliest recorded use to its present use.

Exclamatory sentence expression of strong feeling. It ends with an exclamation point.

F **Fact** statement that can be proved.

Fiction prose works of literature, such as short stories and novels, which are partly or totally imaginary.

Figurative language imaginative, nonliteral use of language.

Footnote complete citation of the source of borrowed material at the bottom of a page in a research report.

Free verse poetry without meter or a regular, patterned beat.

Freewriting prewriting technique of writing freely about ideas as they come to mind.

Friendly letter writing form that may use informal language and contains a heading, salutation, body, closing, and signature.

G **Gerund** a verb form ending in *–ing* that is used as a noun.

Glittering generality word or phrase that most people associate with virtue and goodness that is used to trick people into feeling positively about a subject.

H **Helping verb** auxiliary verb that helps to make up a verb phrase.

I **Idiom** phrase or expression that has a meaning different from what the words suggest in their usual meanings.

Imperative sentence a direction, a request, or a command. It ends with either a period or an exclamation point.

Indefinite pronoun word that substitutes for a noun and refers to an unnamed person or thing.

Independent clause group of words that stands alone as a sentence because it expresses a complete thought.

Indirect object noun or a pronoun that answers the question *to* or *from whom?* or *to* or *for what?* after an action verb.

Infinitive verb form that usually begins with *to* and is used as a noun, an adjective, or an adverb.

Informative writing writing that provides information or explains a process.

Inquiring prewriting technique in which the writer asks questions such as *Who? What? Where? Why?* and *When?*

Interjection a word that expresses strong feeling.

Internet a worldwide network of computers (see also *Basic Internet Terminology* in *a Writer's Guide to Using the Internet*).

Interrogative pronoun used to ask a question.

Interrogative sentence a question. It ends with a question mark.

Intransitive verb action verb that does not pass the action from a doer to a receiver.

Introduction paragraph in an essay that introduces a subject, states or implies a purpose, and presents a main idea.

Irregular verb verb that does not form its past and past participle by adding *–ed* to the present form.

J **Jargon** specialized vocabulary used in particular professions.

Journal a daily notebook in which a writer records personal thoughts and feelings.

L **Linking verb** verb that links the subject with another word in the sentence. This other word either renames or describes the subject.

Listening the process of comprehending, evaluating, organizing, and remembering information presented orally.

Literary analysis interpretation of a work of literature supported by appropriate responses, details, and quotations.

Loaded words subjective words that are interjected into a seemingly objective context to emotionally sway the audience without the audience knowing it.

M **Metaphor** figure of speech that compares by implying one thing is another.

Meter rhythm of a specific beat of stressed and unstressed syllables found in many poems.

Misplaced modifier phrase or clause that is placed too far away from the word it modifies, thus creating an unclear sentence.

Mood overall atmosphere or feeling created by a work of literature.

N **Narrative writing** writing that tells a real or an imaginary story.

Nonessential phrase or clause group of words that is not essential to the meaning of a sentence and is therefore set off with commas.

Nonfiction prose writing that contains facts about real people and real events.

Noun word that names a person, a place, a thing, or an idea. A common noun gives a general name. A proper noun names a specific person, place, or thing and always begins with a capital letter. A collective noun names a group of people or things.

Noun clause subordinate clause that is used like a noun.

Novel long work of narrative fiction.

O **Observing** prewriting technique that helps a writer use the powers of observation to gather details.

Occasion motivation for composing; the factor that prompts communication.

Onomatopoeia use of words whose sounds suggest their meaning.

Opinion belief or judgment that cannot be proved.

Oral interpretation performance or expressive reading of a literary work.

Order of importance order in which supporting evidence is arranged from least to most (or most to least) important.

Outline information about a subject organized into main topics and subtopics.

P **Paragraph** group of related sentences that present and develop one main idea.

Parallelism one or more ideas linked with coordinate or correlative conjunctions and expressed in the same grammatical form.

Parenthetical citation credit for a source of information within or at the end of a sentence; cites source and page number.

Participial phrase participle with its modifiers and complements—all working together as an adjective.

Participle verb form that is used as an adjective.

Passive voice the voice a verb is in when it expresses that the action is being performed upon its subject.

Peer conference meeting with one's peers, such as other students, to share ideas and offer suggestions for revision.

Personal pronoun type of pronoun that can be categorized into one of three groups, dependent on the speaker position: first person (*I*), second person (*you*), and third person (*she/he*).

Personal writing writing that expresses the writer's personal point of view on a subject drawn from the writer's own experience.

Personification comparison in which human qualities are given to an animal, an object, or an idea.

Persuasive writing writing that expresses an opinion on a subject and uses facts, examples, and reasons to convince readers.

Phrase group of related words that functions as a single part of speech and does not have a subject and a verb.

Plagiarism act of using another person's words, pictures, or ideas without giving proper credit.

Play composition written for dramatic performance on the stage.

Plot sequence of events leading to the outcome or point of the story.

Poem highly structured composition that expresses powerful feeling with condensed, vivid language, figures of speech, and often the use of meter and rhyme.

Point of view vantage point from which a writer tells a story or describes a subject.

Portfolio collection of work representing various types of writing and the progress made on them.

Possessive pronoun pronoun used to show ownership or possession.

Predicate part of a sentence that gives information about the subject.

Predicate adjective adjective that follows a linking verb and modifies the subject.

Predicate nominative noun or pronoun that follows a linking verb and identifies, renames, or explains the subject.

Prefix one or more syllables placed in front of a root or base word to modify the meaning of the root or base word or to form a new word.

Preposition word that shows the relationship between a noun or a pronoun and another word in the sentence.

Prepositional phrase group of words that has no subject or verb and that modifies, or describes, other words in a sentence.

Prewriting invention stage in the writing process in which the writer plans for drafting based on the subject, occasion, audience, and purpose for writing.

Principal parts of a verb the *present*, the *past*, and the *past participle*. The principal parts help form the tenses of verbs.

Progressive verb form verbs used to express continuing or ongoing action. Each of the six verb tenses has a progressive form.

Pronoun word that takes the place of one or more nouns.

Proofreading carefully rereading and making corrections in grammar, usage, spelling, and mechanics in a piece of writing.

Proofreading symbols kind of shorthand that writers use to correct their mistakes while editing.

Propaganda effort to persuade by distorting and misrepresenting information or by disguising opinions as facts.

Proper adjective adjective formed from a proper noun.

Publishing stage of a writer's process in which the writer may choose to share the work with an audience or make the work "public."

Purpose reason for writing or speaking.

Q **Quatrain** four-line stanza in a poem.

R **Readers' Guide to Periodical Literature** print or online index of magazine and journal articles.

Reflecting act of thinking quietly and calmly about an experience.

Reflexive pronoun pronoun that is formed by adding –*self* or –*selves* to a personal pronoun. It is used to reflect back to the subject of the sentence.

Regular verb verb that forms its past and past participle by adding *–ed* to the present.

Relative pronoun pronoun that relates an adjective clause to the modified noun or pronoun.

Research paper a composition of three or more paragraphs that uses information drawn from books, periodicals, media sources, and interviews with experts.

Revising stage of a writer's process in which the writer rethinks what is written and reworks it to increase its clarity, smoothness, and power.

Rhyme scheme regular pattern of rhyming in a poem.

Rhythm sense of flow produced by the rise and fall of accented and unaccented syllables.

Root part of a word that carries the basic meaning.

Run-on sentence two or more sentences that are written together and are separated by a comma or have no mark of punctuation at all.

S **Sensory details** details that appeal to one of the five senses: seeing, hearing, touching, tasting, and smelling.

Sentence group of words that expresses a complete thought.

Sentence base a subject, a verb, and a complement.

Sentence combining method of combining short sentences into longer, more fluent sentences by using phrases and clauses.

Sentence fragment group of words that does not express a complete thought.

Sequential order the order in which details are arranged according to when they take place or where they are done.

Setting environment (location and time) in which the action takes place.

Short story short work of narrative fiction.

Simile figure of speech comparing two objects using the words *like* or *as*.

Simple predicate main word or phrase in the complete predicate.

Simple sentence one independent clause.

Simple subject main word in a complete subject.

Slang nonstandard expressions developed and used by particular groups.

Sound devices ways to use sounds in poetry to achieve certain effects.

Spatial order order in which details are arranged according to their location.

Speech oral composition presented by a speaker to an audience.

Stanza group of lines in a poem that the poet decides to set together.

Style visual or verbal expression that is distinctive to an artist or writer.

Subject word or group of words that names the person, place, thing, or idea that the sentence is about; topic of a composition.

Subject complement renames or describes the subject and follows a linking verb. The two kinds are predicate nominatives and predicate adjectives.

Subordinate clause group of words that cannot stand alone as a sentence because they do not express a complete thought.

Subordinating conjunction single connecting word used in a complex sentence to introduce an adverb clause.

Suffix one or more syllables placed after a root or base word to change the word's part of speech and possibly also its meaning.

Summary information written in a condensed, concise form, touching only on the main ideas.

Supporting sentences specific details, facts, examples, or reasons that explain or prove a topic sentence.

Symbol object, event, or character that stands for a universal idea or quality.

Synonym word that has nearly the same meaning as another word.

T **Tense** form a verb takes to show time. The six tenses are the *present*, *past*, *future*, *present perfect*, *past perfect*, and *future perfect*.

Theme underlying idea, message, or meaning of a work of literature.

Thesaurus specialized print or online dictionary of synonyms.

Thesis statement statement of the main idea that makes the writing purpose clear.

Tired word word that has been so overused that it has been drained of meaning.

Tone writer's attitude toward the subject and audience of a composition (closely related to the writer's *voice*).

Topic sentence statement of the main idea of the paragraph.

Transitions words and phrases that show how ideas are related.

Transitive verb action verb that passes the action from a doer to a receiver.

U **Understood subject** unstated subject that is understood.

Unity combination or ordering of parts in a composition so that all the sentences or paragraphs work together as a whole to support one main idea.

V **Verb** word that expresses action or a state of being.

Verbal verb form used as some other part of speech.

Verb phrase main verb plus any helping, or auxiliary, verbs.

Voice particular sound and rhythm of language that the writer uses (closely related to *tone*).

W **World Wide Web** network of computers within the Internet, capable of delivering multimedia content and text over communication lines into personal computers all over the globe.

Wordiness use of words and expressions that add nothing to the meaning of a sentence.

Working thesis statement that expresses the possible main idea of a composition or research report.

Works cited page an alphabetical listing of sources cited in a research paper.

Writing process recursive stages that a writer proceeds through in his or her own way when developing ideas and discovering the best way to express them.

Note: Italic page numbers indicate skill sets.

Note: Italic page numbers indicate skill sets.

Note: Italic page numbers indicate skill sets.

Note: Italic page numbers indicate skill sets.

used as predicate
nominatives, L332
used as subjects, L329–31
who, whom, L346–51, *L347*
Phrase fragments, L260, L261
Phrases
adjective, L174–*76*
adverb, L176–*79*
appositive, L183–*85*
diagraming, L208–*9,* L208–*11*
distinguishing from clauses,
L221
fragments of, L260–*63*
gerund, *L193–98,* L195–*98*
infinitive, *L199,* L201–*4*
participial, L189–*93*
prepositional, L173–*74*
Poetry
capitalization, L459–*60, L463*
Positive degree, L413
Possessive pronouns
confused with contractions,
L342, L443, L451, L453
possessive case, L341
Predicate adjectives, L156–*59*
Predicate nominatives, L154–*56*
pronoun, nominative case,
L327, L332
subject-verb agreement,
L399–*401*
Predicates, L7, L11–*13*
Prefixes
hyphens, L604–*6*
spelling, L640–*42*
Prepositional phrases
adjective phrases, L174–*76*
adverb phrases, L176–*79*
definition, L127–*29,* L173–*74*
distinguishing from
infinitives, L199
misplaced modifiers, L180–*82*
Prepositions, L39, L125–*27*
compound, L125–*27*
distinguishing from adverbs,
L130–31
examples, L173
objects, L127, L337
Present perfect verb tense, L300
Present progressive verb form,
L307–*8*
Present tense verbs, L298
Principal parts of a verb
in compositions, C144
definition, L279
irregular verbs, L281–*91*
problem verbs, L292–*97*
regular verbs, L279–80
Progressive verb tenses, L307–8
Pronoun antecedents, L47–*49*
Pronouns. *See also* Personal
pronouns

as appositives, L183–*85*
definition, L39, L47
demonstrative, L56–*58*
distinguishing from
adjectives, L100–*102*
indefinite, L54–*56,* L391–*92*
interrogative, L57–*58*
number, L375–*76*
personal, L50–*51*
reflexive and intensive,
L52–*54*
relative, L229–30, *L230–31,*
L233–34, L448
who or *whom,* L346–*51*
Proper adjectives
capitalization, L479–*80*
definition and use, L96–*98*
Proper nouns
capitalization, L464–*79*
definition, L42
Punctuation
adjective clauses, L232–33
adjectives, L94
adverb clauses, L225–26
adverb phrases, L178–*79*
apostrophes, L342, L575–*89*
colons, L597–*600*
commas, L504–*20,* L521–*35*
compound sentences, L243
dashes, L607–*12*
dialogue, L560–*61*
direct quotation, L551–*59*
hyphens, L601–*6*
interjections, L135
parentheses, L607–*12*
participial phrases, L190
periods, L497–*504*
run-on sentences, L267
semicolons, L590–*96*
sentence fragments, L257–58
titles, L544–*51*
Purpose in reading, L651–52

Q | Question marks, L498–*500*
Questions
inverted order, L23
use of *who* or *whom,* L346–*51*
Quotation marks
dialogue, C358
direct quotation, L551–*53,*
L553–*54*
long passages, L562
within quotations, L562–*64*
titles, L548–*51*

R | *Raise, rise,* L293, L447
Reading
close, L652
with purpose, L651–*54*
tests, L659–*62*

Reflexive pronouns, L52
Regular comparison
-er or *-est,* L415–*17*
more, most, L416
negative, L416
Regular verbs, L279–80, L301
Relative pronouns
definition, L229
functions of, L232
that, which, who, L448
Research reports
citing sources, L618–19
Revising
checklist, L671
Revision in context questions,
L668–67
Ride, conjugation, L301–2
Run-on sentences, L267–*69*

S | Salutations
capitalization, L460
punctuation, L516–*19*
Scanning (reading), L651
Second person pronouns, L50
Self-expressive writing,
-selves or *-self,* L52
Semicolons
for clarity, L594–*96*
between clauses, L590–*94*
Sentence base, L162
Sentence beginnings, C76–77
Sentence completion tests,
L657–*58*
Sentence correction tests,
L665–66
Sentence fragments
clause fragments, L263–*66*
correcting, L257–58
definition, L5, L257
phrase fragments, L260–*63*
Sentence patterns, L160–*61*
Sentences
beginning with *here* or *there,*
L23
capitalization, L459, *L462*
complete, L5–*6*
complex, compound-complex,
L243–45
compound, L510–*12*
conversational, L5
diagraming, L28–*29*
fragments, L257–*59,* L263–65
patterns, L160–*61*
predicates, L11–*13*
run-on, L267–*69*
simple, compound, L242–*43*
subject order, L22–*25*
subjects, L7–10, *L19*
types of, L497–*500*
Sentence skeletons, L141

Note: Italic page numbers indicate skill sets.

Note: Italic page numbers indicate skill sets.

ACKNOWLEDGMENTS

Every effort has been made to trace the ownership of all copyrighted selections in this book and to make full acknowledgment of their use. Grateful acknowledgment is made to the following authors, publishers, agents, and individuals for their permission to reprint copyrighted material.

L10: Excerpt from "The Washwoman" from *A Day of Pleasure* by Isaac Bashevis Singer. Copyright © 1969 by Isaac Bashevis Singer. Copyright renewed © 1997 by the Estate of Isaac Bashevis Singer. Reprinted by permission of Farrar, Straus and Giroux, LLC. **L22:** Copyright 1975 Lilian Moore. Used by permission of Marian Reiner for the author. **L41:** Excerpt from *In the Heart of the Country* by William Gass. Copyright © 1968 by William Gass. Reprinted by permission of the author. **L360:** "Taught Me Purple" courtesy of *Negro Digest* magazine. **L360:** From *The Collected Poems* by Langston Hughes. Copyright © 1994 by the Estate of Langston Hughes. Reprinted by permission of Alfred A. Knopf, Inc. **L459:** Reprinted by permission of the publishers and the Trustees of Amherst College from *The Poems of Emily Dickinson*, Ralph W. Franklin ed., Cambridge, Mass. The Belknap Press of Harvard University Press, copyright © 1998 by the President and Fellows of Harvard College. Copyright 1951, 1955, 1979 by the President and Fellows of Harvard College. **L460:** Excerpt from "Always a Rose," copyright © 1986 by Li-Young Lee. Reprinted from *Rose* by Li-Young Lee with the permission of BOA Editions, Ltd. **L463:** The lines from "somewhere i have never travelled, gladly beyond." Copyright 1931, © 1959, 1991 by the Trustees for the E.E. Cummings Trust. Copyright © 1979 by George James Firmage, from *Complete Poems: 1904–1962* by E.E. Cummings, edited by George J. Firmage. Used by permission of Liveright Publishing Corporation. **L606:** Excerpt from "Furious Versions" copyright © 1990 by Li-Young Lee. Reprinted from *The City in Which I Love You,* by Li-Young Lee, with permission of BOA Editions, Ltd. **L610:** Reprinted by permission of the publishers and the Trustees of Amherst College from *The Poems of Emily Dickinson,* Ralph W. Franklin ed., Cambridge, Mass. The Belknap Press of Harvard University Press, copyright © 1998 by the President and Fellows of Harvard College. Copyright 1951, 1955, 1979 by the President and Fellows of Harvard College.

PHOTO CREDITS

Key: (t) top, (c) center, (b) bottom, (l) left, (r) right.

Title page: (cl) *Patiently Waiting* by Michael Mortimer Robinson. Michael Mortimer Robinson/SuperStock

L4, L22: © Jaune Quick-to-See Smith. Courtesy of Bernice Steinbaum Gallery, Miami, FL. **L25:** National Gallery, Oslo, Norway/Bridgeman Art Library. **L265:** © 1996 Board of Trustees, National Gallery of Art, Washington, D.C. Chester Dale Collection. © 2000 Estate of Pablo Picasso/Artists Rights Society (ARS), New York. **L38, L62:** The Museum of Modern Art, New York, Mrs. Simon R. Guggenheim Fund. Photograph © 2001, The Museum of Modern Art, New York. © 2001 Artists Rights Society (ARS), New York/ADAGP, Paris. **L49:** © 1999, Sotheby's, Inc. **L68, L84:** Albright-Knox Art Gallery, Buffalo, New York. Gift of Seymour H. Knox, 1958. © Estate of Joan Mitchell. **L80:** © VCG/FPG International. **L90, L118:** © 2001 Artists Rights Society (ARS), New York/VG Bild-Kunst, Bonn. Photograph by Wolfgang von Contzen. **L112:** Photograph by Wolfgang Dietze, courtesy of Carmen Lomas Garza. **L124, L142:** © FPG International. **L148, L166:** The Roland P. Murdock Collection, Wichita Art Museum, Wichita, Kansas. **L172, L214:** The Metropolitan Museum of Art. Anonymous gift, 1983 (1983.251). Photograph © 1983 The Metropolitan Museum of Art. © Fernando Botero, *Dancing in Colombia,* 1980. Courtesy Marborough Gallery, NY. **L179:** The Art Institute of Chicago. Gift of Elizabeth R. Vaughan. Photograph © 1996, The Art Institute of Chicago. 1950.1846. All rights reserved. **L180:** Billy R. Allen Folk Art Collection. African American Museum, Dallas, Texas. Gift of Mr. and Mrs. Robert Decherd. **L220, L250:** Gift of the Container Corporation of America, National Museum of American Art, Smithsonian Institution, Washington, D.C./Art Resource, New York. Courtesy of the artist and Francine Seders Gallery, Seattle, Washington. **L235:** Copyright the Dorothea Lange Collection, The Oakland Museum of California, The City of Oakland. Gift of Paul S. Taylor. **L256, L272:** Courtesy of the Pennsylvania Academy of the Fine Arts, Philadelphia. Gift of Mrs. Sarah Harrison (The Joseph Harrison, Jr., Collection). **L278, L320:** Photograph by C. Lord. **L326, L368:** National Museum of American Art, Washington, D.C./Art Resource, New York. **L344:** © Bob Daemmrich. **L380, L412:** Photograph by Bill Kennedy. **L385:** LPI/M. Yada/FPG International. **L418, L438:** Copyright © 1996 Museum Associates, Los Angeles County Museum of Art. Gift of the Art Museum Council. **L425: (l)** Photograph courtesy Kyoto National Museum; **(r)** Andrew W. Mellon Collection. © 1996 Board of Trustees, National Gallery of Art, Washington, D.C. Photograph by Richard Carafelli. **L444:** Corbis. **L450:** © Charles Schneider/FPG International. **L458, L461:** Manley/SuperStock. **L477:** Barry Blackman/SuperStock. **L502, L542:** The Art Institute of Chicago, Mr. and Mrs. Martin A. Ryerson Collection, 1933.1158. Photograph © 1998 The Art Institute of Chicago. All rights reserved. **L510:** © Boltin Picture Library, Croton-on-Hudson, New York. **L574, L614:** The Metropolitan Museum of Art, H.O. Havemeyer Collection, bequest of Mrs. H.O. Havemeyer, 1929 (29.100.129). Photograph by Schecter Lee, © 1986 The Metropolitan Museum of Art. **L532, L569:** © The New Yorker Collection 1997 Leo Cullum from cartoonbank.com. All rights reserved. **L584:** © The Phillips Collection, Washington, D.C. **L599:** Zigy Kaluzny/Tony Stone Images. **L636:** Roine Magnusson/Tony Stone Images.